The Zohar

TRANSLATED BY HARRY SPERLING
AND MAURICE SIMON

FIVE VOLUMES

II

Published by Parker Publishing Company

www.parkerpub.co

Contact us: **info@parkerpub.co**

CONTENTS

TRANSLATORS' NOTE

This volume carries the translation of the *Zohar* down to the end of Genesis. As in the previous volume, notes have been added sparingly, and an attempt has been made to supply the needed assistance by means of a Glossary and an Appendix. The Glossary is complete for this volume, material having been incorporated from the first volume where necessary. The Appendix is in a sense a continuation of that of Vol. I, but it deals with a side of the esoteric doctrine which comes much more to the fore in this volume, and may serve as a sort of *vade mecum* to the reader in perusing it.

HAYE SARAH

Gen. XXIII, 1–XXV, 18

AND THE LIFE OF SARAH WAS A HUNDRED AND SEVEN AND TWENTY YEARS. R. Jose discoursed on the verse: *And they took up Jonah, and cast him forth into the sea ; and the sea ceased from its raging* (Jonah I, 15). 'The question may here be asked,' he said, 'why it was the sea and not the earth that raged against him, seeing that he fled to prevent the Shekinah from resting upon him. In fact, however, it was appropriate that it should be so. Our teachers say that the sea resembles the sky and the sky resembles the Throne of Glory; hence the sea seized him and held him fast. For as he, in effect, fled from the sea, the sea was the proper agent to fill him with fear and trembling. "And they took up Jonah and cast him into the sea." Tradition says that as they took him up and plunged him into the water up to his thighs, the sea was assuaged, and when they lifted him up again the sea resumed its violence. This happened repeatedly, until finally Jonah said: "Take me up, and cast me forth into the sea" (*Ibid.* I, 12). Forthwith they did so. No sooner was he cast forth into the sea than his soul took flight from him and ascended to the Throne of the King, before whom she was brought to judgement. She was then restored to Jonah, and then the fish swallowed him. The fish died, but afterwards came to life again. This is the accepted explanation. [121*b*] In the same way, every night when a man retires to his bed his soul leaves him and ascends to be judged before the King's tribunal. If she is found deserving to continue in her present state, she is allowed to return to this world. In the judgement, good and evil actions are not weighed in the same way. No account is taken of evil deeds which a man is likely to perpetrate in the future, for so it is written, "for God hath heard the voice of the lad *where he is*" (Gen. XXI, 17). But in regard to good actions, not only those already performed in the past are taken into consideration, but also those which a man is going to perform in the future; so that even if the present account would prove a man guilty, the Holy One in His bounty towards His creatures puts to his credit all his future good deeds, and the man is thus saved. Observe that when Jonah was cast forth into the sea, "the sea"—as we read—"stood still from raging". This means the supernal sea, which is said to "stand still" when its wrath is assuaged. For the heavenly tribunal, at a time when the world is under judgement, is like a pregnant woman who is convulsed with the pangs of childbirth, which cease, however, as soon as she is delivered of the child. Similarly the heavenly tribunal in time of judgement is agitated and convulsed, but once judgement is executed it becomes pacified and resumes with gladness its wonted calm, as it is written, "And when the wicked perish there is joy" (Prov. XI, 10). There is, indeed, a passage to the contrary, saying, "Have I any pleasure at all that the wicked should die ?" (Ezek. XVIII, 23). This passage, however, speaks of those sinners who have not yet gone to the limit of provocation, whereas the previous passage speaks of those sinners whose measure is full.'

AND THE LIFE OF SARAH WAS, ETC. How is it that the death of Sarah alone, among all women mentioned in the Bible, is recorded ? R. Hiya said: 'Is that so ? Do we not find it written, "And Rachel died, and was buried in the way to Ephrah" (Gen. XXXV, 19), and again, "and Miriam died there, etc." (Num. XX, 1), also, "and Deborah [122*a*] Rebekah's nurse died" (Gen. XXXV, 8), and finally, "and Shuah's daughter the wife of Judah died" (*Ibid.* XXXVIII, 12)?' Said R. Jose: 'The problem is, why is the record of Sarah's years given with so much particularity, such as we find in the case of no other woman ? Why, moreover, to Sarah alone of all the women of Scripture was a whole section of the Torah devoted ? There is an esoteric reason, namely, that Sarah reached that grade on which depend all the years and the days of a son of man.' R. Jose discoursed on the verse: *And the abundance of the earth is in all (ba-kol), and a king to a laboured field* (Eccl. V, 8). 'The abundance of the earth,' he said, 'is certainly in *kol* (the Whole), as that is the source from whence issue spirits and souls, and from which beneficence is vouchsafed to the world. By "king" we have to understand the Holy One, blessed be He, the most high King, who, if the field be tilled and cultivated properly, attaches himself to it. What is this field ? It is the field mentioned in the words, "as the smell of a field which the Lord hath blessed" (Gen. XXVII, 27).' R. Eleazar said: 'Herein are contained various deep esoteric ideas. The term "king" here is an allusion to the Shekinah, who does not dwell in a house unless the master of the house is married and is united to his wife for the purpose of bearing offspring; the Shekinah then brings forth souls to plant in that house. Hence the King, or Shekinah, is only attached to a cultivated field, but to no other. According to another explanation we translate, "a king is subjected to a field". "King" in this case is an allusion to the God-fearing woman of whom it is written, "but a woman that feareth the Lord, she shall be praised" (Prov. XXXI, 30), while "field" alludes to the strange woman of whom it says, "that they may keep thee from the strange woman" (*Ibid.* VII, 5). For there are fields and fields. There is the field in which abide all blessings and sanctities, and of which it is said, "as the smell of a field which the Lord hath blessed" (Gen. XXVII, 27); and there is another kind of field which is the abode of desolation, impurity, war and slaughter. And that king is sometimes enslaved to such a field, as it says, "For three things the earth doth quake . . . for a servant when he reigneth [122*b*] . . . and a handmaid that is heir to her mistress" (Prov. XXX, 21–2–3). Such a king is plunged in darkness until he purifies himself and regains the supernal sphere. It is for that reason that a he-goat is offered up on New-Moon days, namely, because that field has been estranged from the Divine King, so that no blessings from that King could rest upon it; so when the other king is enslaved to the field, we may apply the words, "for in the field he found her, etc." (Deut. XXII, 27). Thus when Eve came into the world she attached herself to the serpent, who injected his impurity into her, so that she brought death into the world and to her husband. Then came Sarah, who, though she went down, came up again, and never attached herself to the serpent, as we read, "And Abram

went up out of Egypt, he, and his wife, and all that he had"
(Gen. XIII, 1). Of Noah, too, it is written, "And he drank of
the wine, and was drunken; and he was uncovered within his
tent" (Gen. IX, 21). And because Abraham and Sarah kept
afar from the serpent, Sarah obtained life eternal for herself,
her husband and all her descendants after her, who were
bidden to "look unto the rock whence ye were hewn, and to
the hole of the pit whence ye were digged" (Is. LI, 1). Hence
the Scripture says, "and the life of Sarah was, etc.", a formula
not used in the case of Eve or any other woman. For Sarah
attached herself throughout to life, and thus life was made
her own.

AND THE LIFE OF SARAH WAS A HUNDRED YEARS AND
TWENTY YEARS AND SEVEN YEARS. Each of these periods
was marked by its own peculiar degree of virtue. R. Simeon
said: [123*a*] 'There is an inner significance in the fact that
with the other numbers the word for "years" (*shanah*) is in
the singular, whereas with the number seven it is in the
plural (*shanim*). The hundred forms a unit because the Holy
One is united with the highest and most mysterious by the
secret of the hundred benedictions pronounced each day.
Similarly the number twenty symbolises the unity of the
Thought with the Jubilee. Hence the singular *shanah* (year).
Whereas the seven years correspond to the seven lower realms
that issue separately from the mysterious supernal essence,
and which, though they also form, in a sense, a unity,
diverge in respect of the categories of justice and mercy into
diverse sides and paths. This is not so in the supernal region.
Hence, there we have "year", but here we have "years".
But they are all called "life". Thus "the life of Sarah was"
means "*really* was", having been created and established in
the supernal regions.' R. Hiya said: 'It has been established
that when Isaac was bound on the altar he was thirty-seven
years old, and immediately after Sarah died, as it is written,
"And Abraham came to mourn for Sarah, and to weep for
her." Whence did he come ? He came from Mount Moriah,
after his binding of Isaac. These thirty-seven years from
Isaac's birth to the time of his being bound were thus the

real life of Sarah, as indicated in the expression "and the life of Sarah was (*vayihyu*)", the word *VYHYV* having the numerical value of thirty-seven.'

R. Jose discoursed on the verse: *A Psalm. O sing unto the Lord a new song, for he hath done marvellous things; his right hand and his holy arm hath wrought salvation for him* (Ps. xcviii, 1). 'According to the companions, this verse was uttered by the cows, of whom it is said, "and the kine sang (*vayisharnah*) on the way" (1 Sam. vi, 12). What they sang was this Psalm, commencing: "O sing unto the Lord a new song, for he hath done marvellous things." It should here be observed that while everything that the Holy One has created sings songs and praises before Him, both on high and here below, the chanting of these cows was not of the kind that falls within this mystical category, but was due to the fact that they were bearing the sacred ark; for as soon as the ark was removed from them they reverted to their brutishness and began lowing after the manner of other kine. Hence it was assuredly the feeling of the ark on their backs [123*b*] that worked within them and made them utter song. The difference between "Psalm of David" and "To David a psalm" has been expounded elsewhere. Here, however, we have "Psalm" simply. The reason is that this Psalm is one destined to be sung by the Holy Spirit at the time when the Almighty will raise Israel from the dust. Hence the epithet "new song", since such a song will never have been chanted since the creation of the world.' Said R. Hiya: 'It is written, "there is nothing new under the sun" (Eccl. 1, 9), whereas this song is going to be something new, and is going to happen under the sun. How can this be ? The truth is that this is the moon, and is thus both "new" and "under the sun". Why will there be a new song ? Because "He hath done marvellous things; his right hand and his holy arm hath wrought salvation for him." For whom ? [124*a*] For that grade that intones the chant, for on that grade He supports Himself, as it were, by His right hand and by His left hand. When will that Psalm be chanted ? When the dead will come to life and rise from the dust; then there will be something new that had never yet been in the world.' Said R. Jose: 'When the Holy

One will avenge Israel on the nations, then will this Psalm be chanted. For after the resurrection of the dead the world will be perfectly renewed, and will not be as before, when death prevailed in the world through the influence of the serpent, through whom the world was defiled and disgraced. Observe this. It is written, "And I will put enmity between thee and the woman" (Gen. III, 15). The term *ebah* (enmity) is akin to a similar word in the verse, "they are passed away as the ships of *ebeh*" (Job IX, 26), for on the great ocean there float numerous ships and boats of many kinds, and those in which the serpent sails are called "ships of *ebeh*" (enmity). The "woman" referred to here is the God-fearing woman; "thy seed" refers to the idolatrous nations; "her seed" to Israel; "he shall bruise thy head", to wit, the Holy One, who will one day destroy him, as it is written: "He will swallow up death for ever" (Is. xxv, 8), and also, "and I will cause the unclean spirit to pass out of the land" (Zech. XIII, 2). "In the head" means in the time to come when the dead will come to life; for then the world will be the "head", since it will be established by the "head", that is, the supernal world. "In the heel" means now in this world, which is merely "heel" and not endowed with permanence, and so the serpent bites and mankind is in disgrace. See, now, a man's days were created and are located in the supernal grades, but when they draw to the end of their term, when they reach the Scriptural limit of threescore and ten (Ps. xc, 10), there remains then no grade any more for them to abide in, and so "their pride is but travail and vanity" (*Ibid.*), and they are as nought. Not so the days of the righteous. [124*b*] They have a permanent abiding. Thus we read "And the life of Sarah was" (*vayihyu*, lit. "and they were" or "remained"); similarly, "And these are the days of the years of Abraham's life" (Gen. xxv, 7). You may object that similarly in the case of Ishmael it is written, "And these are the years of the life of Ishmael" (*Ibid.* 17). Ishmael, however, had in fact repented of his evil ways, and the days of his life thus attained permanency.'

AND SARAH DIED IN KIRYATH-ARBA, ETC. R. Abba

said: 'Of Sarah alone among all women do we find recorded the number of her days and years and the length of her life and the place where she was buried. All this was to show that the like of Sarah was not to be found among all the women of the world. You may object that we find a somewhat similar record in connection with Miriam, of whom it is written, "And Miriam died there, and was buried there" (Num. xx. 1). But the object there was to show the unworthiness of Israel, for whom water was made to flow forth only through the virtue of Miriam. Hence Miriam's death was not recorded with such full details as that of Sarah.'

R. Judah discoursed on the verse: *Happy art thou, O land, when thy king is a free man* (Eccl. x, 17). 'This verse,' he said, 'the companions have already explained, but further lessons may be derived from it. Happy are Israel, to whom the Holy One, blessed be He, gave the Torah, by the study of which all hidden paths should be made known to them and sublime mysteries should be revealed to them. The "land" here is "the land of life", and it is "happy" because its King showers upon it all the blessings pronounced upon it by the patriarchs. This is through the mystic influence of the *Vau*, who is always in readiness to pour on it blessing, and who is the "son of freedom" and "son of Jubilee", who obtains for slaves their freedom. He is a scion of the supernal world, and the author of all life, of all illuminations, and all exalted states. All this does the first-born son draw towards that land. Hence, "Happy art thou, O land." On the other hand, the words "Woe to thee, O land, when thy King is a boy" (*Ibid.*) refer to the nether earth and the nether world which draw their sustenance only from the dominion of the uncircumcised, and from that king called "boy".[1] Woe to the land that has to draw its sustenance in this manner ! For this "boy" [125*a*] possesses nothing of himself, but only such blessings as he receives at certain periods. But when these blessings are withheld from him, when the moon is impaired and darkness prevails, then woe to the world that needs to draw sustenance at that time ! And how much the world has to endure before it obtains sustenance from him !

[1] Metatron.

'Observe, now, that in the words "And Sarah died in Kiryath-arba" there is an inner meaning, to wit, that Sarah's death was not brought about by the tortuous serpent, which possessed no power over her as over the rest of mankind. For through him the people of the world have died since the sin of Adam, with the exception of Moses, Aaron, and Miriam, who died, as it is written, "by the mouth of the Lord" (although this expression is not used in connection with Miriam, out of respect for the Shekinah). The Scripture, however, here indicates that Sarah died not merely *in*, but *by the hands of* Kiryath-arba (lit. city of four), so called because it is the same as Hebron, where David joined the patriarchs. Her death thus was brought about by the hands of no one save Kiryath-arba.

'Observe that when the days of a man are firmly established in the supernal grades, that man has a permanent abiding in the world; but if not, those days gradually descend until they approach the grade wherein death resides. The angel of death then receives authority to take away the soul, traverses the world with one sweep, takes away the man's soul, and pollutes his body, which remains permanently unclean. Happy are the righteous who have not polluted themselves and in whom no pollution has remained. In the centre of the heaven there is an illumined path, which is the celestial dragon, and in it are fixed multitudes of little stars which are charged to keep watch over the secret deeds of human beings. In the same way myriads of emissaries go forth from the primeval celestial serpent, by whom Adam was seduced, to spy out the secret deeds [125b] of mankind. Whoever, therefore, strives to live a life of purity is assisted from on high, and is encircled by the protecting hand of his Master, and is called saintly. On the other hand, when a man seeks to pollute himself, hosts of demons, who lie in wait for him, hover over him and surround and pollute him, so that he is called unclean. They all walk in front of him and cry, "unclean, unclean", as the Scripture says, "and he shall cry, Unclean, unclean" (Lev. XIII, 45).'

R. Isaac and R. Jose were walking from Tiberias to Lud. Said R. Isaac: 'I marvel at the wicked Balaam, how all his actions proceeded from the side of impurity. We here learn the mystical lesson that all species of witchcraft are linked up with, and proceed from, the primeval serpent who is the foul and unclean spirit. Hence all sorceries are called *n'hashim* (lit. serpents). And whoever becomes addicted to them pollutes himself, nay more, he has first to become polluted in order to attract to himself the side of the unclean spirit. For it is a dictum of our teachers that corresponding to the impulses of a man here are the influences which he attracts to himself from above. Should his impulse be towards holiness, he attracts to himself holiness from on high and so he becomes holy; but if his tendency is towards the side of impurity, he draws down towards himself the unclean spirit and so becomes polluted. For this reason, in order to draw towards himself the unclean spirit from that supernal serpent, the wicked Balaam besmirched himself nightly by bestial intercourse with his ass, and he would then proceed to his divinations and sorceries. To begin with he would take one of the familiar serpents, tie it up, break [126*a*] its head, and extract its tongue. Then he would take certain herbs, and burn them as incense. He would then take the head of the serpent, split it into four sections, and offer it up as a second offering. Finally, he traced a circle round himself, mumbled some words, and made some gestures, until he became possessed of the unclean spirits, who told him all that they knew from the side of the heavenly dragon; and he thus continued his magical practices until he became possessed of the spirit of the primeval serpent. It is thus that we understand the passage, "he went not, as at the other times, to meet with *n'hashim*" (enchantments, lit. serpents) (Num. xxiv, 1).' Said R. Jose: 'Why is it that many kinds of magic and divination are only found in women ?' R. Isaac replied: 'Thus I have learnt, that when the serpent had intercourse with Eve he injected defilement into her but not into her husband.' R. Jose then went up to R. Isaac and kissed him, saying, 'Many a time have I asked this question, but not until now have I received a real answer.' R. Jose further asked him: 'In which place and from whom did Balaam derive all his magical practices and knowledge ?' R. Isaac replied: 'He learned it first from his father, but it was in the "mountains of the East", which are in an eastern country, that he obtained a mastery of all the arts of magic and divination. For those mountains are the abode of the angels Uzza and Azael whom the Holy One cast down from heaven, and who were chained there in iron fetters. It is they who impart to the sons of men a knowledge of magic. Hence the Scripture says: "From Aram Balak bringeth me, the King of Moab, from the mountains of the East" (Num. XXIII, 7).' 'But,' said R. Jose, 'is it not written, "and he went not as at the other times to meet with enchantments, but he set his face toward the wilderness" (*Ibid.* XXIV, 1) ?' Said R. Isaac to him: 'The lower side, which comes from the unclean spirit above, was the unclean spirit prevailing in the wilderness when Israel made the calf in order to defile themselves therewith; and Balaam tried every device of magic [126b] to uproot Israel, but without success.' Said R. Jose: 'You rightly said that when the serpent had carnal intercourse with Eve he injected into her defilement. We have, however, been taught that when Israel stood at Mount Sinai that defilement left them. But only Israel, who have received the Torah, were freed from it; whereas all the other nations, the idolaters, remained infected with it.' R. Isaac said: 'What you say is right. But observe that the Torah was only given to males, as it is written, "And this is the law which Moses set before the sons of Israel" (Deut. IV, 44), so that women are exempt from the precepts of the Torah. Furthermore, after they sinned they reverted to their former state of infection, of which it is more difficult for a woman to rid herself than for a man. Hence greater numbers of women are found to be addicted to magic and lasciviousness than men, as they come from the left side, and so are under the ægis of the divine rigour, and this side cleaves to them more than to men. Here is a proof of what I have just said, namely, that Balaam polluted himself first in order to draw unto himself the unclean spirit. During the period of a woman's menstruation a man must keep away from her, as then she is in close touch with the unclean spirit, and therefore at such a period she will be more successful in the use of magical arts than at any other time. Whatever thing she touches becomes unclean, and all the more so any man coming too near her. Happy are Israel, to whom the Holy One gave the Torah containing the precept, "and thou shalt not approach unto a woman to uncover her nakedness, as long as she is impure by her uncleanness" (Lev. XVIII, 19).' R. Jose asked: 'Why is one who attempts to interpret the chirping of birds called *naḥash* (magician, also "serpent") ?' R. Isaac replied: 'Because such a one certainly comes from the left side, as the unclean spirit hovers over such a bird and imparts to it [127*a*] a knowledge of future events; and all unclean spirits are attached to the serpent (*naḥash*), from whom none can escape, since he is with everyone and will remain so until the time when the Holy One will remove him from the world, as already said, and as it is written, "He will swallow up death for ever, and the Lord God will wipe away tears from all faces, etc." (Is. xxv, 8), and also, "and the unclean spirit I will cause to pass out of the land" (Zech. XIII, 2).'

R. Judah said: 'Abraham recognised the cave of Machpelah by a certain mark, and he had long set his mind and heart on it. For he had once entered that cave and seen Adam and Eve buried there. He knew that they were Adam and Eve because he saw the form of a man, and whilst he was gazing a door opened into the Garden of Eden, and he perceived the same form standing near it. Now, whoever looks at the form of Adam cannot escape death. For when a man is about to pass out of the world he catches sight of Adam and at that moment he dies. Abraham, however, did look at him, and saw his form and yet survived. He saw, moreover, a shining light that illumined the cave, and a lamp burning. Abraham then coveted that cave for his burial place, and his mind and heart were set upon it. Observe now with what tact Abraham made his request for a burial place for Sarah. He did not ask at first for the cave, neither did he indicate any desire to separate himself from the people of the land, but simply said: GIVE ME A POSSESSION OF A BURYING PLACE WITH YOU, THAT I MAY BURY MY DEAD OUT OF SIGHT. Although he addressed himself to the sons of Heth, we cannot suppose that Ephron was not present then, since it says: NOW EPHRON WAS SITTING IN THE MIDST OF THE CHILDREN OF HETH. Abraham, however, did not at first say anything to him, but spoke only to them, as it says: AND HE SPOKE TO THE CHILDREN OF HETH, ETC. Now it cannot be imagined that Abraham wished to be buried among them, among the impure, or that he desired to mix with them. But Abraham acted tactfully, giving a lesson to the [127*b*] world. Though his whole desire was centred on that cave, he did not ask for it forthwith, but asked for something else of which he had no need, and he addressed his request to the others, not to Ephron himself. It was only after they said to him in the presence of Ephron: "Hear us, my lord; thou art a mighty prince among us, etc." that he said, "hear me, and entreat for me to Ephron the son of Zohar, that he may give me the cave of Machpelah, which he hath, etc." Abraham as much as said: Do not think that I wish to separate from you as being superior to you. No, in the midst of you I desire to be buried, for as I am fond of you I do not wish to keep aloof from you.'

R. Eleazar said: 'Abraham came to enter the cave in this way. He was running after that calf of which we read, "and Abraham ran unto the herd, and fetched a calf" (Gen. XVIII, 7), and the calf ran until it entered a cave, and then Abraham entered after it and saw what we have described. Further, Abraham used to offer up his prayer daily, and in so doing used to proceed as far as that field, which emitted heavenly odours. Whilst there he saw a light issuing from the cave, so that he prayed on that spot, and on that spot the Holy One communed with him. On that account Abraham now asked for it, having always longed for it since then. Why did not he ask for it before that time? Because the people would not have listened to him, as he had no obvious need for it. Now that he needed it, he thought it was time to demand it. Observe that had Ephron seen inside the cave what Abraham saw, he would never have sold it to him. But he never saw there anything, since such things are never revealed except to their rightful owner. It was thus revealed to Abraham and not to Ephron: to Abraham, who was its rightful owner, but not to Ephron, [128*a*] who had no part or portion in it, and who therefore only saw darkness in it; and for that reason he sold it. Nay, he even sold him more than he had mentioned in his original request. For Abraham only said, "that he may give me the cave of Machpelah which he hath . . . for the full price let him give it to me", whereas Ephron said, "the field give I thee, and the cave that is therein", as he felt indifferent to the whole thing, not realising what it was.

'Observe that when Abraham entered the cave for the first time he saw there a bright light, and as he advanced, the ground lifted, revealing to him two graves. Adam then arose in his true form, saw Abraham and smiled at him. (Abraham thereby knew that there he was destined to be buried.) Abraham then said to him: "Could you tell me, is there not a tent for me close to you ?" Adam replied: "The Holy One buried me here, and from that time until now I have been lying hid like a corn seed in the ground, until thou camest into the world. But from now there is salvation for me and for the world for thy sake." Hence it is written, AND THE FIELD AND THE CAVE THAT IS THEREIN AROSE, that is, there was literally an arising before the presence of Abraham, as up to that time nothing there had been visible, but now what had been hidden rose up, and thus the whole spot was devoted to its lawful purpose.' R. Simeon said: 'When Abraham brought Sarah in there for burial, Adam and Eve arose and refused to receive her. They said: "Is not our shame already great enough before the Holy One in the other world on account of our sin, which brought death into the world, that ye should come to shame us further with your good deeds ?" Abraham made answer: "I am already destined to make atonement before the Almighty for thee, so that thou mayest nevermore be shamed before Him." Forthwith Abraham after this buried Sarah [128*b*] his wife, to wit, after Abraham had taken upon himself this obligation. Adam then returned to his place, but not Eve, until Abraham came and placed her beside Adam, who received her for his sake. Hence the text says, AND AFTER THIS, ABRAHAM BURIED (*eth*) SARAH HIS WIFE: the augmenting particle *eth* indicates that the burial included, as it were, Eve. Thus they were all settled in their proper places. Hence the Scripture says,

"These are the generations of heaven and earth when they were created (*b'hibar'am*)" (Gen. II, 4), which according to tradition, means "on account of Abraham" (*b'Abraham*). Now "the generations of the heaven and the earth" can only be Adam and Eve, they having been the direct issue of the heaven and earth and not of human parents, and it was they who became established through Abraham: before Abraham, Adam and Eve were not established in their places in the other world.'

R. Eleazar asked his father, R. Simeon, for an explanation of the term Machpelah (lit. "twofold", or "folded"). 'How is it,' he said, 'that first it is written "the cave of Machpelah", and subsequently "the cave of the field of Machpelah", implying that the field and not the cave was "Machpelah" (doubled)?' R. Simeon replied: 'The term *Machpelah* belongs properly neither to the cave nor to the field, but to something else with which both were connected. The cave belongs to the field, and the field to something else. For the whole of the Land of Israel and of Jerusalem is folded up beneath it, since it exists both above and below, in the same way as there is a Jerusalem both above and below, both of the same pattern. The Jerusalem above has a twofold attachment, above and below; similarly the Jerusalem below is linked to two sides, higher and lower. Hence it is folded in two; and that field partakes of the same character, seeing that it is therein situated. The same reference is contained in the passage, "as the smell of a field which the Lord hath blessed" (Gen. XXVII, 27), to wit, both above [129*a*] and below. Hence its name, "field of folding", but not "folded field". Further, the esoteric implication of the term *Machpelah* relates it to the Divine Name, in which the letter *Hé* is doubled, though both are as one. It is, indeed, true that the cave was a twofold one, a cave within a cave, yet the name "cave of the field of Machpelah" has a different connotation, as already explained. Abraham, on his part, who knew its true character, in speaking to the children of Heth called it simply "cave of Machpelah", as if to imply merely "double cave", which it also was in fact. Scripture, however, describes it as "the cave of the field of Machpelah", this being its true description. For the Holy

One has disposed all things in such a way that everything in this world should be a replica of something in the world above, and that the two should be united so that His glory should be spread above and below. Happy the portion of the righteous in whom the Holy One finds pleasure both in this world and in the world to come !'

AND ABRAHAM WAS OLD, HE HAD COME INTO DAYS; AND THE LORD BLESSED ABRAHAM IN ALL THINGS. R. Judah discoursed on the verse: *Happy is the man whom thou choosest and bringest near, that he may dwell in thy courts* (Ps. LXV, 5). 'This verse', he said, 'may be explained as follows. Happy is the man whose ways are found right before the Holy One and in whom He finds pleasure so as to bring him near to Himself. Observe how Abraham strove to come nearer and nearer to Him, making Him the object of his longing the whole of his days. Not just one day, or just every now and then, but by his works advancing day by day from grade to grade, until he rose, when he was old, to the higher grades proper to him. Hence we read that when Abraham was old he "came into days", i.e. he entered into those supernal days, the days familiar in the doctrine of true faith. Further, "the Lord blessed Abraham in all things (*ba-kol*)", the region called *kol* (all) being the source whence issue all boons and blessings. Happy are the penitent who in the space of one day, one hour, nay, one second, can draw near to [129*b*] the Holy One, as near as even the truly righteous in the space of many years. Abraham did not reach that high grade until he was old, as already said. So, too, David, of whom it is written, "and King David was old, he came into days" (1 Kings I, 1). But the penitent immediately finds entrance, and is brought close to the Holy One, blessed be He.' R. Jose said: 'We have been taught that the place assigned to the penitent in the next world is one where even the wholly righteous are not permitted to enter, as the former are the nearest of all to the King; they are more devoted and strive more intently to draw near to the King. For there are many abodes prepared by the Holy One, blessed be He, for the righteous in the next world, each one according to his grade.

It is written: "Happy is the man whom thou choosest, and bringest near, that he may dwell in thy courts", that is, those whom the Holy One brings near unto Him, those souls who mount from below on high so as to possess themselves of the heritage prepared for them; "that he may dwell in thy courts", to wit, the outer halls and grades, referred to in the words, "then I will give thee free access among these that stand by" (Zech. III, 7), i.e. a grade among the supernal holy angels. Those who attain that grade are messengers of the Lord, on an equality with the angels, and are constantly being used in the service of their Master, because in life they always strove to remain holy and keep afar from impurity. Contrariwise, whoever pollutes himself in this world draws to himself the spirit of uncleanness, and when his soul leaves him the unclean spirits pollute it, and its habitation is among them. For according to a man's strivings in this world is his habitation in the next world; hence such a man is polluted by the spirits of uncleanness and cast into Gehinnom. Thus whoever sanctifies himself and is on his guard against defilement in this world finds his habitation in the next world among the supernal holy [130*a*] angels, where they carry out God's messages. These are they who abide in the court—"the court of the Tabernacle" (Ex. XXVII, 9). But there are others who penetrate further, of whom David said, "we will be satisfied with the goodness of thy house" (Ps. LXV, 5). (The use of the term "we" here instead of "he", as we should have expected, is explained by the dictum that in the Temple Court no seats are permitted save to the kings of the Davidic dynasty.) Still further within is a compartment reserved for the pious of a higher grade, referred to in the verse, "and those that were to pitch before the tabernacle eastward, before the tent of meeting toward the sunrising, were Moses and Aaron and his sons, etc." (Num. III, 38). Thus there is in the next world a gradation of glorious abodes and resplendent lights, each outshining the other.

'As the works of the righteous differ in this world, so do their places and lights differ in the next world. Further, it has been laid down that even in this world, when men sleep at night and their souls leave them and flit about through the world, not every one alike rises to behold the glory of the Ancient of Days, but each one in proportion to a man's constancy of attachment to God and to his good deeds. The soul of the man who is besmirched, when it leaves the body asleep, meets with throngs of unclean spirits of the infernal orders traversing the universe, who take her up and to whom she clings. They disclose to her events about to come to pass in the world ; occasionally they delude her with false information. This has been already stated elsewhere. But the soul of the worthy man, when it leaves him in sleep, ascends and cleaves its way through the unclean spirits, which cry aloud, "Make way, make way ! Here is one not belonging to our side !" The soul then ascends among the holy angels, who communicate to it some true information. When the soul is on its descent again, all those malignant bands are eager to meet it in order to obtain from it that information, in exchange for which they impart to it many other things. But the one thing it learnt from the holy angels is to those [130b] other things as grain to chaff. This is a rare privilege for one whose soul is still in this world. Similar adventures await the souls when they altogether leave the body to depart from this world. In their attempt to soar upwards they have to pass through many gates at which bands of demons are stationed. These seize the souls that are of their side and deliver them into the hands of Duma in order that he may take them into Gehinnom. They then seize them again and ascend, and make proclamation concerning them, saying, "These are they who transgressed the commands of their Lord." They then sweep through the universe and bring the souls back to Gehinnom. This procedure goes on for the whole of the first twelve months. After that they are assigned each to its appropriate place. On the other hand, the worthy souls soar upwards, as already explained, and are assigned the places corresponding to their merits. Happy, therefore, are the righteous, for whom many boons are reserved in the next world. But for none is a more interior abode reserved than for those who penetrate into the divine mystical doctrines and enter each day into close union with their Divine Master. Of such it is written, "What no eye hath seen, O God, beside thee, that will he do for those who wait for him" (Is. LXIV, 3). The word "wait" here has a parallel in the verse, "now Elihu had waited to speak unto Job" (Job XXXII, 4), and refers to those who are importunate for any word of esoteric wisdom, who study it minutely and patiently to discover its true significance and so to gain knowledge of their Lord. These are those in whom their Master glorifies Himself each day, who enter the company of the supernal holy angels, and pass through all the celestial gates without let or hindrance. Happy their portion in this world and the next!

'In this way Abraham penetrated into the Divine Wisdom and united himself with his Divine Master after he had duly prepared himself by a life of pious deeds. He thus merited those supernal days, and received blessings from the region whence all blessings flow, as it is written, "And the Lord blessed Abraham *ba-kol*" (in all things), where the term *kol* is the designation of the river the waters of which never fail.' R. Hiya said: 'Observe that Abraham abstained from intermarrying with other nations and from attaching himself to idolatrous peoples. For the women of idolatrous nations pollute their husbands and those who come into close contact with them. But Abraham, having penetrated into the mystic doctrines of Wisdom, knew the source whence the unclean spirits emerge to traverse the universe, and it was for this reason that he adjured his servant not to take a wife for his son from other nations.'

R. Isaac discoursed on the verse: *And the dust returneth to the earth as it was, and the spirit returneth unto God who gave it* (Eccl. XII, 7). He said: 'When the Holy One, blessed be He, created Adam, He took his dust from the site of the Temple and built his body out of the four corners of the world, all of which contributed to his formation. After that He poured over him the spirit of life, as it says, "and he breathed into his nostrils the breath of life" (Gen. II, 7). Adam then arose and realised that he was both of heaven and of earth, and so he united himself to the Divine and was endowed with mystic Wisdom. Each son of man is, after the same model, a composite of the heavenly and the earthly; and all those who know how to sanctify themselves in the right manner in this world, when they beget a son cause the holy spirit to be drawn upon him from the region whence all sanctities emerge. Such are called the children of the Holy One; and as their bodies were formed in sanctity, so are they given a spirit from the supernal holy region. Observe that the day on which a man is about to depart from this world is a day of reckoning when the body and the soul in combination have to give an account of their works. The soul afterwards leaves him, and the body returns to the earth, both thus returning to their original source, where they will remain until the time when the Holy One will bring the dead to life again. Then God will cause the identical body and the identical soul to return to the world in their former state, as it is written, "Thy dead shall live, my dead bodies shall arise" (Is. XXVI, 19). The same soul is meanwhile stored up by the Holy One, thus returning to its original place, as it is written, "And the spirit returns to God who gave it" (Eccl. XII, 7). And at the time when the Holy One will raise the dead to life He will cause dew to descend upon them from His head. By means of that dew all will rise from the dust, as it says, "for thy dew is as the dew of lights" (Is. XXVI, 19), these being the supernal lights through which the Almighty will in future pour forth life upon the world. For [131*a*] the tree of life exudes life unceasingly into the universe. Life in the present dispensation is cut short through the influence of the evil serpent, whose dominion is symbolised by the darkened moon. Under the same influence the celestial waters, as it were, fail, and life is not dispensed in the world in proper measure. At that time, however, the evil tempter, who is none other than the evil serpent, will be removed from the world by the Almighty and disappear, as it is written, "and I will cause the unclean spirit to pass out of the earth" (Zech. XIII, 2). After he disappears the moon will no more be obscured, and the waters of the celestial river will flow on perennially. Then will be fulfilled the prophecy, "Moreover the light of the moon shall be as the light of the sun, and the light of the sun shall be sevenfold, as the light of the seven days, etc." (Is. XXX, 26).'

Said R. Hizkiah: 'If it be so that all the dead bodies will

rise up from the dust, what will happen to a number of bodies which shared in succession the same soul ?' R. Jose answered: 'Those bodies which were unworthy and did not achieve their purpose will be regarded as though they had not been: as they were a withered tree in this world, so will they be regarded at the time of the resurrection. Only the last that had been firmly planted and took root and prospered will come to life, as it says, "For he shall be as a tree planted by the waters . . . but its foliage shall be luxuriant, etc." (Jer. XVII, 8). This alludes to the body that struck deep root, produced fruit and prospered. But of the former body which remained fruitless, which did not take root, which was unworthy and did not achieve its end, it is written, "For he shall be like a tamarisk in the desert, and shall not see when good cometh, etc." (*Ibid.* 6), i.e. he will not be included in the resurrection, and will not see the light stored up at the Creation for the delectation of the righteous, regarding which it says, "And God saw the light that it was good" (Gen. I, 4), and also, "But unto you that fear my name shall the sun of righteousness arise, etc." (Mal. III, 20). The Holy One will thus in the future raise the dead to life again, and the good principle will prevail in the world and the Evil One will vanish from the world, as already said, and the previous bodies will be as though they never had been.' Said R. Isaac: 'For such bodies the Holy One will provide other spirits, and if found worthy they will obtain an abiding in the world, but if not, they will be ashes under the feet of the righteous, as it is written, "and many of them that sleep in the dust of the earth shall awake, etc." (Dan. XII, 2). All then will rise up and will be ranged before the Holy One, who will enumerate them, as it were, as it says, "He that bringeth out their host by number" (Is. XL, 26). Observe that it has been laid down that the dead of the Land of Israel will be the first to rise, and of them it is written, "Thy dead shall live" (*Ibid.* XXVI, 19). On the other hand, the words "my dead bodies shall arise" (*Ibid.*) allude to the dead of other lands, since instead of "shall live" it says "shall arise". The living spirit, in fact, will only infuse the bodies in the Land of Israel. "*Thy* dead", then, "shall live". But the other dead bodies will rise without

the spirit of life, and only after they shall have rolled themselves underground and reached the Land of Israel will they
receive souls—only there, but not in other realms—so that
they may be really resurrected.' R. Eleazar and R. Jose were
one night studying the Torah. Said R. Eleazar: 'Observe
that at the time when the Holy One will bring the dead back
to life, all the souls mustered before Him will bear each a
form identical with the one it bore in this world. The Holy
One will bring them down, and will call them by their names,
as it says, "He calleth them all by name" (*Ibid.* XL, 26). Every
soul will then enter into its own place, and the dead will be
fully resurrected, and the world will thus reach its consummation. Of that time it is written, "And the reproach of his
people will he take away from off all the earth" (*Ibid.* XXV, 8),
which is a reference to the evil tempter, who darkens the faces
of men and leads them astray.'

R. Jose, interposing, said: 'How is it that a man whilst the
spirit of life is in him is not a source of defilement, whereas
after his soul leaves him he becomes a source of defilement?'
R. Isaac replied: 'Assuredly this is the law, and the explanation given is that the evil tempter, in the act of taking away
the spirit of a man, defiles it, and thus the body is left in a
state of defilement. This, however, is not the case with
idolatrous nations. For since they carry defilement during
life, as their souls are derived from the side of defilement, when
this defilement is removed the body remains without any
defilement whatever. For this reason [131*b*] whoever forms
an attachment with a woman of any of the idolatrous nations
becomes defiled, and the offspring born from such an attachment receives a defiled spirit. It may be asked why, seeing
that the father is an Israelite, the offspring should receive a
defiled spirit. The reason is that as soon as the father attached
himself to that woman, defilement entered into him. Now if
the father became defiled through the unclean woman, how
much more must the offspring born of her be defiled to its
very spirit. Such a man, moreover, transgresses the precept
of the Torah, contained in the words, "For thou shalt bow
down to no other god; for the Lord whose name is Jealous,

is a jealous God" (Ex. XXXIV, 14), i.e. He is jealous for the sanctity of the holy covenant.'

R. Eleazar said: 'Observe that, as has been stated elsewhere, our father Abraham, after he acquired Wisdom, determined to keep separate from all other nations and not to enter into matrimonial alliance with them. Hence we read: AND I WILL MAKE THEE SWEAR BY THE LORD, THE GOD OF HEAVEN AND THE GOD OF EARTH, THAT THOU SHALT NOT TAKE A WIFE FOR MY SON OF THE DAUGHTERS OF THE CANAANITES, ETC. The words "daughters of the Canaanites" are parallel to the expression "daughters of a strange god" (Mal. II, 11). So, too, the word "I" (*Anokhi*) which follows is a reference to the Deity, as in the verse, "I (*Anokhi*) made the earth." The purpose of this injunction was to save Isaac from being defiled by them. For whoever impairs the sanctity of the holy covenant by contact with a woman of an idolatrous nation causes the defilement of a certain other place, alluded to in the passage, "For three things the earth doth quake, etc." (Prov. XXX, 21). And although Abraham adjured his servant by the holy covenant, he did not feel satisfied until he had made supplication on his behalf to the Holy One, blessed be He, saying: THE LORD, THE GOD OF HEAVEN . . . MAY HE SEND HIS ANGEL BEFORE THEE, ETC., to wit, "the angel of the covenant", so that the covenant might be preserved in its sanctity, and not be defiled among the nations. He continued: BEWARE THOU THAT THOU BRING NOT MY SON BACK THITHER. Why so? Because Abraham knew that none among those nations had knowledge of the true God like himself, and so he desired that Isaac should not settle among them, but should continue to dwell with him, so that he might constantly learn the ways of the Holy One, and turn neither to the right nor to the left.' R. Jose said: 'Of a certainty the merits of Abraham stood his servant in good stead, for on the very day on which he set out he reached the fountain, as it says, AND I CAME THIS DAY UNTO THE FOUNTAIN.'

R. Eleazar discoursed on the verse: *Open thou mine eyes, that I may behold wondrous things out of thy law* (Ps. CXIX, 18). 'How devoid of discernment,' he said, 'are those sons of men who abide in ignorance of the Torah and pay no regard to its study. For it is the Torah that spells life and freedom and felicity in this world and in the world to come. It is life in this world, earning for its devotees fulness of days, as it says, "the number of thy days I will fulfil" (Ex. XXIII, 26), as well as length of days in the world to come; for the Torah is the very fulness of life, life of bliss without any gloom; it is freedom in this world, complete freedom; for when a man applies himself to the study of the Torah all the nations of the world cannot prevail against him. Such a one also obtains deliverance from the angel of death, who has no power over him. (You may object, What of the martyrs who suffered in times of persecution, such as R. Akibah and his colleagues ? These suffered, however, under a special decree from on high in accordance with a special purpose.) Assuredly, had Adam held fast to the tree of life, which is nothing else but the Torah, he would not have brought death upon himself and upon the rest of the world. Hence, in connection with the giving of the Law it is written, "*Heruth* (freedom) on the tables" (Ex. XXXII, 16), as explained elsewhere. And had Israel not sinned and forsaken the tree of life they would not have brought death anew into the world. Hence God could say to them, in the words of the Psalmist, "I said, Ye are godlike beings, and all of you sons of the Most High" (Ps. LXXXII, 6), but ye have done hurt to yourselves, and so: "verily like Adam shall ye die, etc." (*Ibid.*). Thus whoever applies himself to the study of the Torah is not subject to the power of the evil serpent, the darkener of the world.' R. Yesa put the question: 'If that is so, why did Moses die, he having committed no sin ?' R. Eleazar replied: 'Moses assuredly died, but not by the power of the evil serpent, and so he was not defiled by his hands. Besides, from another aspect, he did not die, [132*a*] but was only drawn up by the Shekinah and departed to eternal life, as has already been explained in connection with the passage, "And Benaiah the son of Jehoiada, the son of a living man, etc." (II Sam. XXIII, 20).[1] Thus whoever applies himself to the study of the Torah attains perfect freedom: freedom in this world from the

---

[1] v.p. 6*b*.

bondage of the idolatrous nations, and freedom in the next world, as no accusation will be brought against him there. For the Torah contains sublime and recondite truths, as it says, "she is more precious than rubies" (Prov. III, 15). Treasures innumerable are indeed concealed therein, so that David, when he considered the Torah in the spirit of wisdom, and realised how many wondrous truths unfold themselves therefrom, was moved to exclaim, "Open thou mine eyes, that I may behold wondrous things out of thy Law" (Ps. CXIX, 18).'

AND IT CAME TO PASS, THAT BEFORE HE HAD DONE SPEAKING, BEHOLD, REBEKAH WENT OUT. Instead of "went out" (*yozeth*) we should have expected "came" (*baah*). The implication is that God brought her away from the people of the town, and made her an exception to them. AND SHE WENT DOWN TO THE FOUNTAIN. This fountain was none other than the well of Miriam; hence the word "to" here is expressed by the letter *hé* (*ha-'aynah*). According to another explanation, the term "went out", like the similar term in the passage, "young maidens going out to draw water" (I Sam. IX, 11), implies modesty, that is, that they kept at home and only went out at a certain hour to draw water. This was the sign by which Abraham's servant recognised her. For when he reached Haran and met Rebekah "at the time of evening" it was the time of the afternoon prayer (*minhah*). Thus the moment when Isaac began the afternoon prayer coincided with the moment when the servant encountered Rebekah. So, too, it was at the very moment of his afternoon prayer that Rebekah came to Isaac himself. Thus all was fitly disposed through the working of the Divine Wisdom. It was as part of the same scheme that the servant came to the well of water, the inner significance of which is to be found in the passage, "Thou art a fountain of gardens, a well of living waters, and flowing streams from Lebanon" (S.S. IV, 15).

R. Simeon was once on his way to Tiberias in company with R. Abba. Said R. Simeon to him, 'Let us proceed, for I foresee that a man will come up to us who has something new to say, some new expositions of the Torah.' Said R. Abba:

'Verily I know that wherever you go the Holy One sends you winged angels to entertain you.' When they had gone a little further, R. Simeon raised his eyes and saw a man running along. R. Simeon and R. Abba then sat down. When the man came up to them R. Simeon asked him, 'Whence art thou ?' He said, 'I am a Judean and am coming from Cappadocia, and I am on my way to the abode of the son of Yohai, to whom the companions sent me in order to communicate certain decisions to which they have come.' R. Simeon said to him, 'Speak, my son.' The man asked, 'Art thou the son of Yohai ?' 'I am,' was the reply. The man then said: 'It is an established rule that a man whilst praying should not let anything interpose between himself and the wall, as it is written, "then Hezekiah turned his face to the wall" (Is. XXXVIII, 2); and it is further forbidden to pass within four cubits of the man who stands in prayer, and they have now laid down that this means on any side save directly in front of him. Further, that a man may not pray standing behind his teacher, etc. These are the decisions of the companions.' The man then discoursed on the verse: *Hear my prayer, O Lord, and give ear unto my cry ; keep not silence at my tears* (Ps. XXXIX, 13). 'Why', he asked, 'is the word for "hear" in this place written *shim'ah* instead of the usual *sh'ma'* ? The truth is that the form *sh'ma'* is always addressed to the male aspect of the Deity, whereas the form *shim'ah* is addressed to the female aspect. Hence the term *shim'ah* is used because it is addressed to that grade which receives all the prayers of mankind, and, according to our tradition, weaves them into a crown which it puts on the head of the *Zaddik*, the life of the universe, referred to in the words, "Blessings upon the head of the Just One" (Prov. x, 6). Further, the words "Hear, O Lord, my prayer" allude to silent prayer, whereas the succeeding words "and give ear unto my cry" refer to prayer which a man cries aloud in his anguish, as we read, "and their cry came up to God" (Ex. II, 23). (The term *shav'atham* (their cry) indicates the raising of the voice and the raising of the eyes towards heaven; it is akin to the term *sho'a* (turning) in the passage "and turning (*v'sho'a*) to the mount" (Is. XXII, 5).) Such a prayer [132b] breaks through all gates and ascends to heaven. "Keep not silence at my tears": prayerful tears ascend before the King, no gate can withstand them, and they are never turned away empty. Further, there are in this passage three grades of supplication: prayer, cry, and tears, corresponding to the three grades mentioned in the verse, "For I am a stranger with thee, a sojourner, as all my fathers were" (Ps. xxxix, 13). First "a stranger", then "a sojourner", and last "as all my fathers", who were the basis of the world. Observe that there are two categories of prayer, one to be said standing and the other sitting, although they form but one whole. There are also two phylacteries, one for the arm and one for the head, corresponding to day and night, the two again making one whole. The sitting prayer corresponds to the arm phylactery, which prepares and adorns it like a bride before entering under the bridal canopy. So the prayer is surrounded and escorted, mystically speaking, by the chariots and legions mentioned in the prayer, "Creator of ministering spirits. . . . And the Ophanim and holy Hayoth . . ." This prayer, therefore, is recited sitting, but when the prayer approaches the Supreme King and He is about to receive it, then we are to stand up before the most high King, for then the male is united with the female. Hence there must be no interruption between the redemption benediction at the end of the sitting prayer and the beginning of the standing prayer. Also, since one is standing before the Supreme King, he must on concluding step backwards four cubits, which has been explained to be a divine measure. Thus, whatever part of the prayer is symbolic of the male principle has to be recited standing. Similarly the supplicant bends his knee at the utterance of *barukh* (blessed be), and erects himself to his full height at the utterance of the Divine Name, to symbolise the superiority of the male over the female. Observe, further, that we have laid down that one should not while praying stand immediately behind his teacher. The reason is this. It is written: "Thou shalt fear the (*eth*) Lord thy God" (Deut. vi, 13). The particle *eth* here indicates that the teacher is associated with God as the object of fear. Hence during prayer a man should not be faced with that object of fear, so that he may be filled exclusively with the fear of the Holy One alone without any adjunct. Isaac instituted afternoon prayer in the same way as Abraham instituted morning prayer. Each of them instituted the prayer corresponding with the grade to which he was attached. Hence the time for the afternoon prayer begins with the sun's decline towards the west, inasmuch as the period preceding that time, from the dawn onward, is termed day, as in the passage, "the mercy of God endureth the whole day" (Ps. LII, 3). Nor can it be said that "the whole day" lasts until darkness sets in, since it is written, "Woe unto us, for the day hath departed, for the shadows of the evening are stretched out" (Jer. VI, 4). This shows that the term "day" is limited to the time for receiving the morning prayer, of which it is written, "the mercy of God endureth the whole day", for at that time the sun is still on the east side. As soon as the sun declines in its passage towards the west, the time of the afternoon prayer sets in, as the day has already departed, and has given place to the shadows of the evening, when the quality of rigour asserts itself. "The day has departed", that is, the period when the grade of mercy (*ḥesed*) prevails, and "the shadows of the evening are stretched out", at what time there rages the grade of rigour, that very hour when the Sanctuary was destroyed and the Temple burnt down. For this reason tradition teaches us that a man should be careful not to miss the afternoon prayer, as then is the time when the world is under the ægis of rigour. Jacob instituted evening prayer ('*arbith*), thereby causing the letter *Vau* (symbolic of Jacob) to supplement the letter *Hé* (symbolic of Isaac), which is nourished by the *Vau*, having no light of its own. For that reason the evening prayer is optional, inasmuch as it is a continuation of the day prayer, having for its aim to illumine the obscurity of the night. That obscurity prevails until midnight, at which hour the Holy One disports Himself with the righteous in the Garden of Eden. Hence it is an opportune time for a man to busy himself in the study of the Torah, as already explained elsewhere. Observe that David in his psalms made allusion to the three periods of prayer, in the words, "Evening, and morning, and at noon-day, do I meditate, and moan" (Ps. LV, 18). Here we have allusion to three periods, although David himself observed only two prayers, one alluded to in "do I meditate" and the second in "and moan". The first is the prayer of the morning, the period of mercy; hence "meditating" suffices. The second is the prayer of the afternoon, the period of rigour; hence, "and I do moan". At midnight David arose to chant songs and hymns, [133*a*] as it is written, "and in the night his song is with me" (Ps. XLII, 9).'

R. Simeon then rose up and they proceeded on their way, the stranger accompanying them as far as Tiberias. On the way R. Simeon said: 'Observe that the members of the Great Synod[1] instituted the prayers in correspondence to the fixed daily offerings, of which there were two, as it is written, "the one lamb shalt thou offer in the morning, and the other lamb shalt thou offer between the two evenings" (Num. XXVIII, 4), that is, at the two periods which coincide with the periods of prayer.' Said the stranger: 'Since originally it was the patriarchs who instituted the prayers, why should those instituted by Abraham and Isaac be of primary importance, while the one instituted by Jacob, who was the cream of the patriarchs, be only voluntary?' R. Simeon replied: 'The reason, as has been affirmed, is as follows: The two periods of the two earlier prayers have for their object only to unite Jacob to his heritage, but once this has been effected we need nothing further: as soon as the Woman is placed between the two arms and is joined to the Body, nothing more is needed. The two prayers are thus the two arms between which Jacob is united to the body, that is, to heaven, in accordance with the verse, "but thou, O Lord, art on high for evermore" (Ps. XCII, 9). All this contains deep mysteries known only to the initiated.' R. Abba and the Judean then approached R. Simeon and kissed his hand, after which R. Abba remarked: 'Until this day I always found here a difficulty, but now happy is my portion that I have been privileged to solve it!'

[1] A body which, according to Rabbinic tradition, regulated the affairs of the Jewish community during the lifetime of Ezra and for some time afterwards.

AND ISAAC BROUGHT HER INTO THE TENT (OF) SARAH HIS MOTHER. R. Jose remarked: 'The letter *hé* at the end of the word *haohelah* (into the tent) is a reference to the Shekinah, which now returned to the tent. For during the whole of Sarah's life the Shekinah did not depart from it, and a light used to burn there from one Sabbath eve to the other; once lit, it lasted all the days of the week. After her death the light was extinguished, but when Rebekah came the Shekinah returned and the light was rekindled. Thus the verse reads literally: "And he brought her into the tent—Sarah his mother", the last phrase implying that Rebekah was in all her works a replica of Sarah his mother.' R. Judah said: 'Just as Isaac was the very image of Abraham, so that whoever looked at Isaac said, "there is Abraham", and knew at once that "Abraham begat Isaac", so was Rebekah the very image of Sarah. She was thus, so to say, in the phrase of our text, "Sarah his mother".' R. Eleazar said: 'All this is truly said. But observe a deeper mystery here. For, verily, although Sarah died, her image did not depart from the house. It was not, however, visible for a time, but as soon as Rebekah came it became visible again, as it is written, "and he brought her into the tent—Sarah his mother", as much as to say, "and forthwith Sarah his mother made her appearance". No one, however, saw her save Isaac, and thus we understand the words, "and Isaac was comforted after his mother", that is, after his mother became visible and was installed in the house again.'

R. Simeon said: 'Why does the Scripture tell us with so much detail that Isaac TOOK REBEKAH, AND SHE BECAME HIS WIFE, AND HE LOVED HER ? The last statement seems to be unnecessary, for naturally if she became his wife he loved her, as is the way of all men to love their wives. The explanation is that the attraction of the male to the female is derived from the left, as we read, "Let his left hand be under my head" (S. S. II, 6), the left being symbolic of night and darkness; hence although Abraham loved Sarah, the statement "and he loved her" is only mentioned in the case of Isaac (he being of the left). Of Jacob also it is written that he "loved Rachel" (Gen. XXIX, 18); but here the explanation

is that this was due to the side of Isaac which was contained
in him. Observe that Abraham, on seeing Sarah, only embraced her, and nothing more, whereas Isaac seized Rebekah
and put his arm under her head, as it is written, "Let his left
hand be under my head, and his right hand embrace me"
(S. S. II, 6). Jacob afterwards had intercourse with his wives
and begat twelve tribes. Observe, too, that all the patriarchs
followed the same course, [133*b*] in that each one of them
espoused four women. Abraham had four spouses, besides
Sarah and Hagar, two concubines, as is seen from the passage,
"but unto the sons of the concubines that Abraham had"
(Gen. xxv, 6). Isaac had four spouses, in that Rebekah,
mystically speaking, combined in herself the virtues of four
women. This is indicated in Scripture in the following
manner: "And he took Rebekah" alludes to one; "and she
became his wife" indicates a second; "and he loved her"
indicates a third; "and Isaac was comforted for his mother"
makes four. Correspondingly, Jacob had four spouses; and
one mystic purpose guided them all.' R. Hiya said: 'Abraham and Isaac had each one wife for a union of holiness, the
one Sarah, the other Rebekah, and Jacob had as many as both
together twice over, namely four.' R. Simeon said: 'It practically comes to the same thing, since all was arranged by a
divine dispensation to one and the same mystical purpose.'

AND ABRAHAM TOOK ANOTHER WIFE, AND HER NAME
WAS KETURAH. Keturah was none other than Hagar. For
we know by tradition that though Hagar when she left
Abraham went astray after the idols of her ancestors, yet in
time she again attached herself to a life of virtue. Hence her
name Keturah (lit. attached). Abraham then sent for her
and took her to wife. From here we learn that a change of
name acts as an atonement for sin, since that was the reason
why her name was changed. The term *vayoseph* (lit. and
he added) here indicates not that Abraham took another
wife, but that he took again his former spouse whom he had
driven out on account of Ishmael, and who had now abandoned
her evil practices, and had made a change in her name
symbolical of her change of life. Observe that R. Eleazar,

in comment on the passage, "And Isaac brought her into the tent—Sarah his mother", said that the form of Sarah was there revealed, and Isaac was comforted by virtue of this, as he looked at her image every day. But Abraham, although he married again, never entered Sarah's tent nor allowed that woman to enter there, for a handmaid may not be heir to her mistress. No other woman, in fact, ever appeared in Sarah's tent save Rebekah. And although Abraham knew that Sarah's image revealed itself there, he left the tent entirely to Isaac to behold each day his mother's form. This is indicated in the verse, AND ABRAHAM GAVE ALL THAT HE HAD UNTO ISAAC, where the expression "all that he had" indicates the form of Sarah that was installed in that dwelling. According to another explanation this verse indicates that Abraham transmitted to Isaac the exalted doctrine of the true faith, so that he should be attached to his rightful grade. BUT UNTO THE SONS OF THE CONCUBINES THAT ABRAHAM HAD ABRAHAM GAVE GIFTS. What sort of gifts were they ? They comprised the sides of the low grades, that is to say, the names of the powers of the unclean spirit, so as to complete the whole list of grades. (Isaac was raised above those grades by the power of the true faith.) "The sons of the concubines" are the sons of Keturah, who had formerly been a concubine and was now once more a concubine.' R. Hiya said that the term "concubines" here in the plural must be taken literally. AND HE SENT THEM AWAY FROM ISAAC HIS SON, so that they should not be on a par with Isaac. WHILE HE YET LIVED, that is, while Abraham was yet alive and vigorous, so that they should not complain against him after his death, and so that Isaac might strengthen himself in the side of rigour so as to prevail over them all and make them all submit to him. EASTWARD, UNTO THE EAST COUNTRY: for the reason that there are the haunts of the impure practitioners of magic and witchcraft. Observe this. It is written: "And Solomon's wisdom excelled the wisdom of all the children of the East" (1 Kings v, 10). Herein is an allusion to the descendants of the very children of Abraham's concubines, who, as already said, inhabit the mountains of the East, where they instruct the sons of men in the arts of magic and divination. It was this very land of the East from which came Laban and Beor and his son Balaam, who were all magicians.'

R. Hizkiah discoursed on the verse: *Who gave Jacob* [134*a*] *for a spoil, and Israel to the robbers? Did not the Lord, he against whom we have sinned, and in whose ways they would not walk?* (Is. XLII, 24). 'Observe,' he said, 'that since the destruction of the Temple, blessings have been withdrawn from the world, if one might say so, both on high and here below, so that all the lower grades are reinforced and exercise dominion over Israel on account of their sins. Now the verse just cited requires elucidation. For while it begins by speaking of Jacob and Israel in the third person, it goes off into the first, saying "he against whom *we* have sinned", and then reverts to the third person, saying "and *they* would not walk". The truth is that when the Sanctuary was destroyed and the Temple was burnt and the people driven into exile, the Shekinah left her home in order to accompany them into captivity. Before leaving, however, she took one last look at her House and the Holy of Holies, and the places where the priests and the Levites used to perform their worship. When she entered the land of exile she observed how the people were oppressed and trodden under foot by the nations, and she exclaimed, "Who gave Jacob for a spoil, etc. ?" And the reply of the people was: "he against whom we have sinned". Then the Shekinah echoed back: "And in whose ways they would not walk." So in the days to come, when the Holy One, blessed be He, will remember His people, the community of Israel, the Shekinah will return from exile first and proceed to her House, as the holy Temple will be built first. The Holy One, blessed be He, will then say to the Community of Israel: "Shake thyself from the dust, arise and sit down, O Jerusalem" (Is. LII, 2). She will enquire, "Whereto shall I go, since my House is destroyed, my Temple is burnt with fire ?" The Holy One, blessed be He, will then rebuild the Temple first, restore the Holy of Holies, build the city of Jerusalem and then raise her from the dust. So Scripture says: "The Lord doth build up Jerusalem" first, and then, "He gathereth together the dispersed of Israel", and afterwards, "Who healeth the broken in heart, and bindeth up their wounds" (Ps. CXLVII, 2, 3)—this being an allusion to the resurrection of the dead. Then will be fulfilled that which is written, "And I will put my spirit within you, and cause you to walk in my statutes, etc." (Ezek. XXXVI, 27).

'Blessed be the Lord for evermore !'

TOL'DOTH

Gen. XXV, 19–XXVIII, 9

R. Hiya once discoursed on the text: *Who can express the mighty acts of the Lord, or make all his praise to be heard?* (Ps. CVI, 2). 'When God', he said, 'resolved to create the world, He used the Torah as the plan both of the whole and the parts. Hence Scripture says: "Then I was by him as a nursling, and I was [134*b*] daily all delight" (Prov. VIII, 30), where the word *'amon* (nursling) may also be read *'oman* (architect, designer). When God was about to create man the Torah remonstrated, saying: "Should man be created and then sin and be brought to trial before Thee, the work of Thy hand will be in vain, for he will not be able to endure Thy judgement." Whereto God replied: "I had already fashioned repentance before creating the world." When God created the world, He said to it: "O world, world! Thou and thy order are founded only upon the Torah, and therefore I have created man in thee that he may apply himself to its study; otherwise I will turn thee into chaos again." Hence Scripture says: "I have made the earth and created man upon it" (Is. XLV, 12). The Torah in truth continually calls to the sons of men to devote themselves to its study, but none gives ear. Yet whoever labours in the Torah upholds the world, and enables each part to perform its function. For there is not a member in the human body but has its counterpart in the world as a whole. For as man's body consists of members and parts of various ranks all acting and reacting upon each other so as to form one organism, so does the world at large consist of a hierarchy of created things, which when they properly act and react upon each other together form literally one organic body. Thus the whole is organised on the scheme of the Torah, which also consists of sections and divisions which fit into one another and, when properly arranged together, form one organic body. This reflection led David to exclaim: "How manifold are thy works, O Lord! In wisdom hast thou made them all; the earth is full of thy creatures"

(Ps. CIV, 24). The Torah contains all the deepest and most recondite mysteries; all sublime doctrines, both disclosed and undisclosed; all essences both of the higher and the lower grades, of this world and of the world to come are to be found there, but there is no one [135*a*] to fathom its teachings. Hence it is written: "Who can express the mighty acts of the Lord, or make the whole of his praise to be heard ?" (Ps. CVI, 2). Solomon thought to penetrate to the innermost meanings of the Torah, but it baffled him and he exclaimed: "I said, I will get wisdom, but it was far from me" (Eccl. VII, 23). David said: "Open thou mine eyes, that I may behold wondrous things out of thy law" (Ps. CXIX, 18). We read of Solomon that he "spoke three thousand proverbs; and his songs were a thousand and five" (I Kings V, 12), and tradition explains this to mean that each of his proverbs admitted of a thousand and five interpretations. Now if this could be said of the words of mere flesh and blood like Solomon, must we not perforce believe that each of the words of the Torah spoken by the Holy One, blessed be He, contains proverbs, songs, and hymns innumerable, sublime mysteries, and truths of Divine Wisdom ? Hence: "Who can express the mighty acts of the Lord ?".'

'We derive also another lesson from this verse. It is written "And these are the generations of Isaac" (Gen. XXV, 19), and a few verses before (*Ibid.* 12) the text says, "And these are the generations of Ishmael", and goes on to enumerate twelve princes. Seeing that Isaac had only two sons, we might think that in this respect Ishmael was superior to him. But in truth it is just in allusion to Isaac that Scripture exclaims: "Who can express the mighty acts of the Lord ?" the term "mighty acts" being an allusion to Isaac. For Isaac begat Jacob, who in his own self excelled them all, and who further begat twelve tribes, through whom all both above and below were firmly established. Isaac was invested with the sanctity of the supernal world, whereas Ishmael was of the lower world. Hence it says: "Who can express the mighty acts of the Lord, or make the whole of his praise to be heard ?" the latter clause alluding to Jacob, as much as to say: "When the sun joins the moon innumerable stars are thereby illumined." '

AND THESE ARE THE GENERATIONS OF ISAAC, ABRA-
HAM'S SON. 'Why', asked R. Jose, 'should Isaac be
referred to just here, and here only, as "Abraham's son" ?
The reason is that with the death of Abraham Isaac assumed
the image of his father, so that anyone looking at him could
say "This is surely Abraham", and thus would be convinced
that "Abraham begat Isaac".'

R. Isaac rose from his bed one night [135*b*] to study the
Torah. R. Judah, who happened then to be in Caesarea, said
to himself at the same time: 'I will go and join R. Isaac in the
study of the Torah.' He accordingly set out along with his
youthful son Hizkiah. As he was nearing R. Isaac's threshold
he overheard him expound the verse: "And it came to pass
after the death of Abraham, that God blessed Isaac his son;
and Isaac dwelt by Beer-laḥai-roi" (Gen. xxv, 11). 'The connection between the two parts of this verse', he said, 'is obscure, but may be explained as follows. It was necessary that
God should bless Isaac, because Abraham had not blessed
him, and the reason why Abraham had not blessed him was
to prevent that blessing being transmitted to Esau. Hence the
task of blessing fell, so to speak, to the Almighty. The text
thus continues: "And Isaac dwelt by Beer-laḥai-roi" (lit. the
well of the living and seeing one), that is, as the Aramaic paraphrase has it, "the well where appeared the Angel of the
Covenant", to wit, the Shekinah, to which Isaac became
attached, thereby drawing upon himself the blessing of the
Almighty.' At that point R. Judah knocked at R. Isaac's door,
entered the room and joined him. R. Isaac said: 'Now, the
Shekinah herself is in our presence.' Said R. Judah: 'Your
exposition of the term *beer-laḥai-roi* is quite correct, but
there is more in it than you have said.' He then began to discourse thus. 'It is written: *A fountain of gardens, a well of
living waters, and flowing streams from Lebanon* (S. S. IV, 15).
"A fountain of gardens" is a description of Abraham; "a
well of living waters" is a description of Isaac, of whom it is
written: "And Isaac dwelt by the well of the living and seeing
one (*beer-laḥai-roi*)." The "well" is none other but the
Shekinah; "the living one" is an allusion to the Righteous
One who lives in the two worlds, that is, who lives above, in

the higher world, and who also lives in the lower world, which exists and is illumined through him, just as the moon is only illumined when she looks at the sun. Thus the well of existence literally emanates from "the living one" whom "it sees", and when it looks at him it is filled with living waters. (The word "living" is similarly used in the verse [136*a*] "And Benaiah the son of Jehoiada, the son of a living man" (II Sam. XXIII, 20), i.e. a righteous man who illumines his generation as the living Deity above illumines the universe.) So the well constantly looks to the "living one" to be illumined. Further, the statement that Isaac dwelt by Beer-laḥai-roi teaches the same lesson as the statement "And Isaac was forty years old when he took Rebekah" (Gen. XXV, 20), and abode with her and was united with her, symbolising in this way the union of darkness with night, as it is written: "His left hand under my head" (S. S. II, 6). Observe now that after Abraham's death Isaac remained in Kiriath-arba; how, then, it may be asked, can it say that he dwelt in Beer-laḥai-roi ? The answer is, to indicate that Isaac attached himself and held fast to that well in order to awaken the attribute of mercy, as already explained.'

R. Isaac discoursed on the verse: *The sun shineth forth and the sun cometh in and hasteth to his place where he ariseth* (Eccl. I, 5). ' "The sun shineth forth" from the supernal place where he is established, in order to cast his lustre on the moon, which only reflects the light of the sun; "and cometh in" in order to join the moon. "He goeth toward the South" (*Ibid.* I, 6), which is on the right and in which, therefore, his strength reposes (for all the strength of the body is on the right side); "and then turneth about to the North" (*Ibid.*), in order to impart light both to the one side and to the other. Further, "The wind turneth about continually and in its circuit" (*Ibid.*). Although the text here speaks of the wind and not of the sun, yet it is all one, and has the same inner meaning; all this is that the moon may be illumined from the sun and the two may be associated. Observe that when Abraham appeared in the world he embraced the moon and drew her near; when Isaac came he took fast hold of her and clasped her affectionately, as it says: "His left hand under my head" (S. S. II, 6).

But when Jacob came the sun joined the moon and she became illumined, so that Jacob was found perfect on all sides, and the moon was encircled in light and attained completion through the twelve tribes.'

R. Judah discoursed on the verse: *Behold, bless ye the Lord, all ye servants of the Lord, etc.* (Ps. cxxxiv, 1). 'This verse tells us', he said, 'that only those are truly worthy to bless the Almighty who are the servants of the Lord. For although it is true that every [136b] Israelite is regarded as fitted to bless the Almighty, yet only the servants of the Lord are worthy to offer those benedictions from which is diffused blessing in the upper and lower worlds. And who, then, are those servants of the Lord ? "They that stand in the house of the Lord in the night seasons" (*Ibid.*), to wit, those who rise at midnight and keep vigil in the study of the Torah: these do "stand in the house of the Lord in the night seasons", as at that time the Holy One, blessed be He, comes to disport Himself with the righteous in the Garden of Eden. Since, then, we are passing the night in expounding the Torah, let us say something about Isaac, whom we have just mentioned.'

R. Isaac then began his discourse on the verse: AND ISAAC WAS FORTY YEARS OLD WHEN HE TOOK REBEKAH ETC. 'The number "forty" here', he said, 'has an esoteric significance, to wit, that Isaac when he took Rebekah comprised in himself the union of North and South and fire and water. Further, as the rainbow exhibits three colours, green, white, and red, so Rebekah was three years old when Isaac took her; and he begat offspring when he was sixty years old, this being a ripe age for producing a child like Jacob who should be endowed with all good qualities, according to God's design. THE DAUGHTER OF BETHUEL THE ARAMEAN, OF PADAN-ARAM, THE SISTER OF LABAN THE ARAMEAN. Why all these details, seeing that it has already been stated: "And Bethuel begat Rebekah etc." ? (Gen. XXII, 23). It is to emphasise the fact that although she was brought up among sinful people, being the daughter of Bethuel, and a native of Padan-Aram, and the sister of Laban the Aramean, and thus came from a wicked environment, yet she did not follow their ways, but distinguished herself in good and righteous deeds.

Here a difficulty arises. If we could say that Rebekah was then twenty years old or more, or even thirteen years old, then we could indeed commend her for not imitating the conduct of her surroundings; but since, as previously said, she was only a child of three years, how can we ascribe to her any merit on this account?' R. Judah said in reply: 'Though she was but three years old, she had shown her character by what she did for Abraham's servant.' R. Isaac rejoined: 'In spite of all that she had done for him, one could not yet say positively that her character was really good. [137*a*] But we learn this from another source. It is written, "As a lily among thorns, so is my love among the daughters" (S. S. II, 2). The lily may be taken as symbolic of the Community of Israel, which in the midst of its multitudes resembles a rose among thorns. But there is a more esoteric explanation of the verse, as follows. Isaac was derived from the side of Abraham, who was the embodiment of supernal grace (*Ḥesed*), and acted graciously towards all creatures, though he himself represented the attribute of severity. Rebekah, on the other hand, originated from the side of severity, but broke away from her kith and kin and joined Isaac; and in spite of her origin, she was of a mild disposition and gracious bearing, so that in the midst of the severity which characterised Isaac she was "as a lily among thorns". And if not for her gentleness the world would not have been able to endure the severity inherent in Isaac. In this manner God constantly mates couples of opposing natures, one, for example, of a stern with one of a mild type, so that the world preserves its balance.'

R. Judah followed with a discourse on the text: AND ISAAC ENTREATED THE LORD FOR HIS WIFE. 'The term "entreated" (*vaye'tar*)', he said, 'implies prayer accompanied by offerings, on an analogy with a kindred term in the passage, "So the Lord was entreated for the land" (II Sam. XXIV, 25), where also the prayer was accompanied by offerings. It is written here first, "And Isaac entreated", and then "And the Lord let himself be entreated", indicating that a celestial fire descended to meet the fire ascending from below. According to another explanation, the term *vaye'tar* (and he entreated) is akin to *vayeḥtar* (and he dug), signifying that

Isaac in his prayer dug a tunnel, as it were, leading right up to the supernal department appointed over fecundity. He thus rose above the planetary influences (*mazzal*) in the same way as Hannah in her prayer, of whom it is written: "And she prayed unto ('*al*', lit. upon) the Lord" (1 Sam. 1, 10). Similarly, the term *vaye'ather* (and he let himself be entreated) implies that the Lord Himself cleared a way for Isaac's prayer, with the result that "Rebekah his wife conceived". Observe that Isaac lived with his wife for twenty years without having children, the reason being that God delights in the prayer of the righteous, who thereby attain to higher sanctity and purification. He therefore withholds from them [137b] their needs until they offer their supplications. Now observe that Abraham did not supplicate God for children, notwithstanding that Sarah was barren (for when he said "Behold, to me thou hast given no seed" (Gen. xv, 3), he did not mean it as a prayer, but as a mere statement of fact); but Isaac did offer up prayer on behalf of his wife, as he felt confident that he himself was not sterile. This confidence was based on his inspired knowledge that Jacob was destined to issue from him and produce twelve tribes, but he could not tell whether it would be from his present wife or from another. Hence he entreated the Lord for his *wife*, not for *Rebekah*.' The youthful son of R. Judah here asked his father: 'If that is so, why did not Isaac love Jacob as much as Esau, knowing as he did that the former would rear twelve tribes ?' 'That is a good question,' said his father, 'and the answer is as follows. All creatures of the same kind love one another and are drawn to one another. Now we are told that Esau "came forth ruddy", a colour emblematic of severity. There was thus an affinity between Isaac, the representative of severity on high, and Esau, the embodiment of severity here below; and through this affinity Isaac loved him above Jacob. Hence we read: "And Isaac loved Esau, because he did eat of his hunting", where the term *zayid* (hunting) suggests the same idea as the similar term in the verse: "Like Nimrod a mighty hunter (*gibbor zayid*) before the Lord" (Gen. x, 9).'

R. Isaac said: 'It is written: AND THE CHILDREN STRUGGLED TOGETHER WITHIN HER; AND SHE SAID, IF IT

BE SO, WHEREFORE DO I LIVE? AND SHE WENT TO ENQUIRE OF THE LORD. Whither did she go? To the Academy of Shem and Eber. "And the children struggled together within her", for there already Esau declared war against Jacob. The term *vayithrozzu* (and they struggled) is akin to a root meaning "to break", and thus it implies that they broke asunder and drifted away from each other. Observe that the one was of the side of him who rides the serpent, whilst the other was of the side of Him who rides on the sacred and perfect throne; of the side [138*a*] of the sun that illumines the moon. And observe further that because Esau was drawn after that serpent, Jacob dealt with him crookedly like the serpent, who is cunning and goes crookedly, as we read: "And the serpent was more cunning etc." (Gen. III, 1). Jacob then dealt with him after the manner of the serpent in order to draw him further serpentward, so that he should separate further from himself and thus not have any share with him either in this world or in the world to come; and our teachers have said, "When a man comes to kill you, kill him first." It is written of Jacob: "In the womb he took his brother by the heel" (Hos. XII, 4), that is, he drew him downwards by[1] the heel. So it says: AND HIS HAND HAD HOLD ON ESAU'S HEEL, i.e he put his hand on Esau's heel in order thereby to force him down. According to another explanation, the words "and his hand had hold" imply that he could not escape him entirely, but his hand was still clinging to his brother's heel. Esoterically speaking, the moon was obscured through the heel of Esau; hence it was necessary to deal with him cunningly, so as to thrust him downwards and make him adhere to the region assigned to him.'

AND HE CALLED HIS NAME JACOB. It was God who called him so. (So, too, it is written lower down, "Hath he not rightly called his name Jacob?" (Gen. XXVII, 36) and not "his name was called".) God saw that the primeval serpent was full of guile to do mischief, and so when Jacob appeared He said: "Behold, here is one who can stand up to him", and therefore He called him *Ya'kob*, akin to the term *vaya'kebeni*

---

[1] Al. "to the heel", i.e. to the lower grades.

(and he acted toward me with guile) (Gen. XXVII, 35). It has already been pointed out that the simple term *vayikra* (and he called), as when it says, "and he called unto Moses", points to the lowest grade (of the Sephiroth). At no time did Jacob receive a name from a human being. So in another passage we find: "And the God of Israel called him *El* (God)" (Gen. XXXIII, 20), signifying that the God of Israel called Jacob by the name of "*El*" (God), as though to say, "I am the God of the supernal world and be thou the God of the world below". Observe that Jacob knew that Esau was destined to ally himself to that tortuous serpent, and hence in all his dealings with him he conducted himself like another tortuous serpent, [138b] using all cunning devices; and so it was meet. The same idea was expressed by R. Simeon when, in expounding the verse, "And God created the great fishes, and every living creature that creepeth" (Gen. I, 21), he said: 'The "great fishes" are symbolic of Jacob and Esau, and "every living creature that creepeth" symbolises all the intermediate grades.' Verily Jacob was endowed with cunning to enable him to hold his own with that other serpent; and so it was meet. For the same reason every New Moon a goat is to be offered up so as to draw the serpent to his own place and thus keep him away from the moon. The same applies to the Day of Atonement, when a goat is to be offered. All this is cunningly devised in order to gain dominion over him, and make him impotent to do mischief. So Scripture says: "And the goat shall bear upon him all their iniquities into a land which is cut off" (Lev. XVI, 22), where the goat (*sa'ir*=Seir), as already explained, symbolises Esau. In all dealings with him cunning and craft are employed, in accordance with the words of the Scripture: "And with the crooked thou dost show thyself subtle" (Ps. XVIII, 27); and as the evil serpent is resourceful and crafty, trying to mislead the heavenly as well as the earthly beings, Israel anticipate him and counter him with similar ruses and devices so as to prevent him from working his evil will; just as Jacob, who was endowed with the true faith, in all his actions towards Esau had no aim but to prevent the serpent from defiling the Sanctuary or even approaching it, and so achieving dominion over the world. There was however, no need either for Abraham or for Isaac to use such tortuous ways, seeing that Esau, who was of the side of the serpent, had not yet appeared in the world. But Jacob, being the master of the household, had to counter the serpent, and to give him no chance to tarnish the Sanctuary of Jacob. Hence Jacob had need of such shifts more than any other person. Israel, therefore, was chosen as the portion of the heritage of the Holy One, blessed be He, as it is written: "For the portion of the Lord is his people, Jacob the lot of his inheritance" (Deut. XXXII, 9).

AND THE BOYS GREW. It was the side of Abraham which gave them their vitality, and his merit was their support. He trained them in observing the precepts, for so we read: "For I have known him, to the end that he may command his children etc." (Gen. XVIII, 19). R. Eleazar said: 'Each one of them took his own way, [139*a*] one to the side of true faith and the other to the side of idolatry; and they had already exhibited the same traits whilst in the womb of their mother, where each one of them inclined to his own side. Thus, whenever she was performing some good action or approaching a goodly spot in order to carry out some precept of the Torah, Jacob would gleefully thrust himself forward to come forth. But did she happen to pass near an idolatrous shrine, Esau would kick and struggle to come forth. Thus, when they were fully formed and emerged into the world, they separated, each one taking his own way and being drawn to the place befitting him.'

AND ISAAC LOVED ESAU, FOR THE HUNTER'S CUNNING WAS IN HIS MOUTH. So we translate in accordance with what has been said above. A MAN OF THE FIELD: this means that he was a highwayman who robbed and murdered people, while all the time pretending to his father that he was abroad performing his prayers. Again, he was a fieldman in that his portion was not cast in inhabited land but in wild and desolate places. It may be asked, how came Isaac to be unaware of Esau's evil deeds, seeing that the Shekinah was with him, as is proved by the fact of his subsequently blessing

Jacob. The truth is that the Shekinah, although continually with him, did not reveal to him Esau's evil career in order that Jacob should receive his blessing not by the will of Isaac, but solely by the will of the Holy One, blessed be He. So it was destined to be, and when Jacob entered into the presence of his father the Shekinah accompanied him, and Isaac thus felt that there was before him one who was worthy of being blessed; and blessed he was by the will of the Shekinah.

AND JACOB SOD POTTAGE; AND ESAU CAME IN FROM THE FIELD, AND HE WAS FAINT. R. Eleazar said: 'According to the received explanation, the pottage of lentils was a sign of mourning for the death of Abraham. But if so, we should have expected Isaac to have prepared it. The deeper explanation, therefore, is that Jacob cooked [139*b*] that pottage in virtue of his clear discernment of the side to which Esau adhered. Lentils form a red pottage which is cooling to hot blood. Hence Jacob purposely chose such a dish as a means of weakening the strength and power of Esau, and the effect was that Esau sold himself to Jacob as a slave and sold him his birthright. At that moment Jacob divined that for the sake of one he-goat that his descendants would bring as a sacrifice to Esau's grade, the latter would consent to be a slave to them and desist from attacking them.' R. Judah said: 'Of a like manner were Jacob's dealings with Laban, who was a magician, as it says: "I have observed the signs, and the Lord hath blessed me for thy sake" (Gen. XXX, 27); and notwithstanding that Jacob is designated a "simple man", this means only that he was so in his dealings with anyone who deserved to be treated gently; but where cunning and severity were necessary, he could use these also. For he was of a twofold character, and to him could be applied the words: "With the merciful thou dost show thyself merciful. . . . And with the crooked thou dost show thyself subtle" (Ps. XVIII, 26–27), just as required.'

AND THERE WAS A FAMINE IN THE LAND, BESIDE THE FIRST FAMINE, ETC. R. Judah discoursed here on the verse:

The Lord trieth the righteous; but the wicked and him that loveth violence his soul hateth (Ps. XI, 5). 'How goodly', he said, 'are the acts of the Holy One, blessed be He, all based upon justice and truth, as it says: "The Rock, his work is perfect; for all his ways are justice; a God of faithfulness and without iniquity, just and right is he" (Deut. XXXII, 4). For He did not punish Adam, the first man, until He had given him precepts to keep him in the right path and save him from defilement; and not until he was unmindful and transgressed the command of his Master was he punished. [140*a*] Even then God did not exact the full penalty from him, but was long-suffering with him and permitted him to survive for one day—to wit, a thousand years—save seventy years which Adam presented of his allotted time to King David, who had none of his own. In like manner, the Almighty does not mete out punishment to a man in strict accordance with the evil deeds to which he is addicted, or else the world could not endure. God is thus long-suffering with the righteous, and even more so with the wicked. He is forbearing with the wicked in order that they may change in their ways in complete repentance and so establish themselves in this world and in the world to come, as Scripture says: "Have I any pleasure, saith the Lord God, in the death of the wicked, and not rather that he should return from his way and live" (Ezek. XVIII, 23), i.e. that he may live in this world and in the world to come. The Almighty is also forbearing with the wicked for the sake of the goodly seed which may spring from them for the benefit of the world, as there issued from Terah that goodly scion, Abraham, who was a blessing for the world. But with the righteous God is strict, as He knows that they will turn aside neither to the right nor to the left, and therefore He puts them to the test; not for His own sake, since He knows the firmness of their faith, but so as to glorify them the more. It was for this purpose that God—as we read—"proved (*nissah*) Abraham" (Gen. XXII, 1), or, as we may also translate, "He raised his banner aloft throughout the world" [for the term *nissah* (he proved) implies the lifting of an ensign, as it is written: "Lift up an ensign (*nes*) over the peoples" (Is. LXII, 10). The text continues: "The Lord trieth the righteous" (Ps. XI, 5). For what reason ? Said R. Simeon: 'Because when God finds delight in the righteous, He brings upon them sufferings, as it is written: "Yet it pleased the Lord to crush him by disease" (Is. LIII, 10), as explained elsewhere. God finds delight in the soul but not in the body, as the soul resembles the supernal soul, whereas the body is not worthy to be allied to the supernal essences, although the image of the body is part of the supernal symbolism. [140b] Observe that when God takes delight in the soul of a man, He afflicts the body in order that the soul may gain full freedom. For so long as the soul is together with the body it cannot exercise its full powers, but only when the body is broken and crushed. Again, "He trieth the righteous", so as to make them firm like "a tried stone", the "costly corner-stone" mentioned by the prophet (Is. XXVIII, 16). "But the wicked and him that loveth violence his soul hateth." So we would naturally translate; but this is hardly admissible, and it is more probable that the verse alludes to that grade whence all souls derive their existence, and tells us that "that grade hateth the soul of the wicked man", not wanting it at all, neither in this world nor in the world to come. When God created Adam He gave him a precept for his well-being and endowed him with wisdom through which he rose to the higher grades of contemplation. But when Adam turned his thoughts to the lower world, he let himself be enticed by the evil tempter and clung to him, so that all that he had observed of the glory of his Master vanished from his mind. After him Noah at first was a man righteous and devout; but afterwards he also went downwards, and seeing the wine—wine a day old, not yet refined—"he drank of the wine, and was drunken, and he was uncovered within his tent" (Gen. IX, 21). Then came Abraham, who contemplated the wisdom and glory of his Master. In his time "there was a famine in the land; and Abram went down into Egypt to sojourn there" (*Ibid.* XII, 10), but subsequently he "went up out of Egypt, he and his wife and all that he had, and Lot with him, into the South" (*Ibid.* XIII, 1). That is, he ascended again to his own former grade, so that he came out unscathed as he went in. Then came Isaac, of whom it is written: "And there was a famine in the land, beside the first famine, etc." He went into Gerar and afterwards ascended again from thence unscathed. Thus God proves the righteous in order to glorify them in this world and in the world to come.

AND THE MEN OF THE PLACE ASKED HIM OF HIS WIFE; AND HE SAID: SHE IS MY SISTER. Like Abraham before him, he referred with these words to the Shekinah, which was with him as well as with Rebekah his wife; for like Abraham he carried out the injunction: "Say unto wisdom: Thou art my sister" (Prov. VII, 4). They were further entitled to call her sister in virtue of the verse, "My sister, my love, my dove, my undefiled" (S. S. V, 2), for it is for this that the righteous cleave to God.

AND IT CAME TO PASS, WHEN HE HAD BEEN THERE A LONG TIME . . . WITH REBEKAH HIS WIFE. The particle *eth* (with) indicates that it was the Shekinah that was with Rebekah. In any case it is not to be supposed that Abimelech saw Isaac having intercourse with his wife in the daytime, for this would be contrary to the dictum: "Israel are holy and they abstain from cohabitation in the daytime." But the truth is that Abimelech was an astrologer, and the window through which he looked was nothing but the planetary constellation. [The word "window" is similarly used in the passage: "Through the window she looked forth, and peered, the mother of Sisera" (Jud. V, 28).] Abimelech by this means discovered that, contrary to Isaac's assertion, Rebekah was his wife. So ABIMELECH CALLED ISAAC, AND SAID, ETC. R. Jose said: 'Abimelech would have behaved toward Isaac as he behaved toward Abraham, were it not that God had reproved him in the previous case. Note that when Abraham said, "Surely the fear of God is not in this place" (Gen. XX, 11), his reason for thinking so was that the people lacked faith, and had they possessed faith, he would have had no need to act as he did.' [141a] R. Eleazar said: 'The Shekinah does not abide outside the Holy Land, and that is what Abram meant by saying that "the fear of God is not in this place", namely, that this was not the place where the Shekinah could find abode. Isaac, however, held fast to the true faith under the inspiration of the Shekinah, which he saw residing, as it were, within his wife.'

AND ABIMELECH CHARGED ALL THE PEOPLE, SAYING: HE THAT TOUCHETH THIS MAN OR HIS WIFE SHALL SURELY BE PUT TO DEATH. Observe how long a respite God gave to this wicked people for the sake of the kindness that Abimelech showed to Israel's first ancestors. It was on this account that Israel could not touch them till many generations had elapsed. Abimelech thus did well to show kindness to Abraham in saying to him: "Behold my land is before thee: dwell where it pleaseth thee" (Gen. XX, 15). R. Judah said: 'Woe to the wicked who when they do a kindness never do it perfectly. Ephron, for instance, first said to Abraham: "Nay, my lord, hear me: the field I give thee and the cave that is therein, I give it thee, etc." (Gen. XXIII, 11). But later on he said: "A piece of land worth four hundred shekels, etc." (*Ibid*. 15); and then we read: "And Abraham weighed to Ephron the silver . . . current money with the merchant" (*Ibid*. 16). Similarly here, at first Abimelech said: "He that toucheth this man, etc", but later on he said, "Go from us, for thou art much mightier than we" (Gen. XXVI, 16).' R. Eleazar said to R. Judah: 'Abimelech's kindness to him consisted in his not taking anything from him, and sending him away with all his possessions intact, and then going after him to make a covenant with him.'

AND ISAAC DIGGED AGAIN THE WELLS, ETC. R. Eleazar said: 'In digging these wells Isaac acted fittingly, for he discerned from his knowledge of the mysteries of Wisdom that in this way he could attach himself more firmly to his faith. Abraham likewise made a point of digging a well of water. Jacob found the well already prepared for him, and he sat down by it. Thus they all looked for a well and strove through it to preserve their faith pure and undiminished. And nowadays Israel hold fast to the well through the symbolism of the precepts of the Torah, as when each day every Israelite performs the precept of the fringes in which he envelops himself, and of the phylacteries which he puts on his head and on his arm. All these have a deep symbolism, since God is found in the man who crowns himself with the phylacteries and envelops himself in the fringes. Hence, whoever does not envelop himself in the latter, nor crown himself with the former each day to invigorate himself in faith, makes it appear as though faith does not dwell within him, and fear of his Master has departed from him, and so his prayer is not as it should be. Hence our ancestors strengthened themselves in the true faith in digging the well, symbolic of the supernal well, which is the abode of the mystery of perfect faith.'

AND HE REMOVED FROM THENCE, AND DIGGED AN-OTHER WELL. R. Hiya discoursed on the verse: *And the Lord will guide thee continually, and satisfy thy soul in brightness, and make strong thy bones* (Is. LVIII, 11). 'The true believers', he said, 'have derived strength from this verse, where promise is made to them of the world to come, for the word "continually" includes both this world and the world to come. Again, the term "continually", which seems super-fluous, is an allusion to the continual burnt-offering which is offered at dusk, and is held firm underneath the arm of Isaac and is symbolic of the world to come. The term "guiding" is similarly used by David in the verse: "He guideth me in straight paths for his name's sake" (Ps. XXIII, 3). "And satisfy thy soul in brightness"; this is the "clear mirror" from the contemplation of which all souls obtain delight and benefit. "And make strong thy bones": these words do not seem to harmonise with what has gone before, which we have inter-preted of the souls of the righteous ascending on high. We interpret them, therefore, to allude to the resurrection of the dead, when the Holy One, blessed be He, will reconstitute the bones and restore the body to its former state. The soul will then derive stronger illumination from the "clear mir-ror", so as to illumine the body to the full extent of which it is capable. Hence: "And thou shalt be like a watered garden" (Is. LVIII, 11), that is, like the celestial garden whose supernal waters never fail, but flow on for ever and ever; [141*b*] "and like a spring of water, whose waters fail not" (*Ibid.*), alluding to the river that issues from Eden and flows on for all eternity. Observe that the "well of living waters" is a symbol within a symbol for guiding faith. There is the well which is the very source of the waters, and there is the well which is fed by that source of water. There are thus two grades, which are, however, really one with two aspects, male and female, in fitting union. The well and the issue of waters are one, designated by the name of "well", it being at once the supernal never-ceasing fountain and the well that is filled by it. And whoever gazes at that well gazes at the true object of faith. This is the symbol which the patriarchs transmitted in digging the well, in such a way as to indicate that the source and the well are indissoluble. AND HE CALLED ITS NAME REHOBOTH (lit. streets, broad places). By this he intimated that his descendants would one day tend that well in the fitting manner through the mystical potency of offerings and burnt-offerings (like Adam, when God "put him into the garden of Eden to dress it and keep it" (Gen. II, 15), to wit, by offerings and burnt-offerings), so that its springs should flow forth on every side, as Scripture says: "Let thy springs be dispersed abroad, and courses of water in the streets (*rehoboth*)" (Prov. v, 16). Hence here the name of Rehoboth (streets, broad places).'

R. Simeon here discoursed on the verse: WISDOM CRIETH ALOUD IN THE STREET, SHE UTTERETH HER VOICE IN THE BROAD PLACES (Prov. I, 20). 'This verse', he said, 'contains a deep mystical teaching. The term *hokhmoth* (lit. wisdoms) implies the superior Wisdom and the lesser Wisdom which is included in the superior Wisdom and abides therein. The superior Wisdom is an essence most recondite and concealed, unknown and unrevealed, as Scripture says: "Man knoweth not the price thereof, etc." (Job XXVIII, 13); and when it expands into a source of light, its illumination is that of the world to come, and that world is created by it: for so we have learned, that the world to come was created by the *Yod*, and there Wisdom remained hidden, the two being one. When God was crowned, it was through the mystery of the future world, as already said. There was joy at this illumination, but all was in silence without a sound being heard abroad. Wisdom then willed it to expand further, so that from that space there issued fire and water and air, as already said, from which there sprang up a voice which issued forth abroad and was heard, as already said. From that point onwards all is exterior (*huz*), whereas in the interior the voice is silent and not heard abroad. Once, however, the secret force has become audible, it is called "without" (*huz*). Hence it is incumbent on man to be zealous in searching after wisdom "in the wide places" (*ba-rehoboth*). This refers to the firmament, which contains all the luminous stars, and which constitutes the fountain of perennial waters, referred to in the verse: "And a river went forth from Eden to water the garden" (Gen. II, 10). And there "she uttereth her voice", both the superior and the lower Wisdom, which in truth are one. Solomon alluded to this in saying: "Prepare thy work without" (*ba-huz*), and make it ready for thee in the field" (Prov. XXIV, 27), where the word "without" is used as in the verse "Wisdom crieth out without", indicating the point from which man can commence to inquire and investigate, as it is written: "For ask now of the days past . . . and from one end of heaven unto another" (Deut. IV, 32). The "field" again is the "field which the Lord hath blessed" (Gen. XXVII, 27). When a man has penetrated into the mystery of Wisdom and perfected himself therein, then Solomon tells him to "build his house" (Prov. XXIV, 27), i.e. to cultivate his soul in his body, so as to attain perfection. Hence, when Isaac digged and prepared the well in peace he called it Rehoboth (wide places), and all was done in the right manner. Happy the righteous by whose works the Holy One sustains the world, as it says: "For the upright shall inhabit the land" (Prov. II, 21), where the term *yishkenu* (they will inhabit) may be read *yashkinu* (they shall cause to be inhabited).'

AND IT CAME TO PASS, THAT WHEN ISAAC WAS OLD, AND HIS EYES WERE DIM. R. Simeon said: 'It is written: *And God called the light day, and the darkness he called night* (Gen. I, 5). This verse has already been expounded, but there is yet more to be learnt from it. For all the works of the Almighty are manifestations of truth and contain deep lessons;

and all the words of the Torah assist faith and are deeply symbolical. Observe now that Isaac was not so fortunate as Abraham, whose eyes were not blinded nor dimmed. Herein is a profound lesson touching faith, as has already been explained elsewhere. By "the light" here is meant Abraham, who is the light of the day and whose light keeps on expanding [142*a*] and growing stronger like that of the day. Hence it is written: "And Abraham was old, advancing in days" (Gen. XXIV, 1), that is, in illumination, and as he grew older his light continued to expand, so that he was "shining more and more unto the perfect day" (Prov. IV, 18). On the other hand, "the darkness" is a description of Isaac, who represents darkness and night, and hence when he was old his eyes were dim, so that he could not see. He had to become enveloped in darkness in order to become attached to his own proper grade.' R. Eleazar his son came and kissed his hand. He said: 'So far I understand. Abraham was bathed in light from the side of his grade; whereas Isaac became wrapt in darkness from the side of *his* grade. But why is it written of Jacob: "And the eyes of Israel were heavy for age" (Gen. XLVIII, 10) ?' R. Simeon in answer said: 'It is written here "they were heavy", but not "they were dim"; and further, it is not written "for *his* old age", but "for old age", referring to the old age of Isaac, and implying that his eyes were heavy as a result of the side of Isaac, but still they were only so heavy as to prevent him seeing properly, but not entirely dim. Whereas Isaac's eyes were altogether dimmed, so that darkness settled upon him and night took hold of him, until to him could be applied the words, "And the darkness he called night." '

AND HE CALLED ESAU, HIS ELDER SON, who was derived from his own side of severe judgement, AND HE SAID: BEHOLD NOW, I AM OLD, I KNOW NOT THE DAY OF MY DEATH. R. Eleazar discoursed on the verse: *Happy is the man whose strength is in thee, etc.* (Ps. LXXXIV, 6). 'Happy is the man', he said, 'who holds fast to the Holy One and places his strength in Him. Like whom, for instance ? Shall we say, like Hananiah, Mishael and Azariah, when they boldly said to the

King of Babylon: "Behold, our God whom we serve is able to deliver us from the burning fiery furnace; and he will deliver us out of thine hand" (Dan. III, 17) ? Not so; for if God had not stood by them to deliver them, His name would not have been acclaimed holy as they declared it to be. But they themselves realized their mistake, and so they corrected themselves and said: "But if not, be it known unto thee, O King, etc." (*Ibid.* 18), that is, whether our God deliver us or not, be it known unto thee that we will not serve thy gods, etc. Tradition tells us that Ezekiel said something to them which opened their eyes, namely, that God would not stand by them if they expected reward. It was then that they began all over again, saying: "But if not, be it known unto thee, O King, etc." A man, therefore, should not confidently affirm: "God will deliver me or will do for me this or that"; but he should endeavour to fulfil the precepts of the Law and to walk in the path of truth, and then put his full trust in Him that He will help him thereto. For assuredly whenever a man sets out to purify himself he is helped thereto from on high. A man should thus put his trust in God and not anywhere else. Hence the expression "whose strength is in thee". The next words, "in whose heart are paths", indicate that a man should purge his heart of all strange thoughts, so as to make it like a path that leads straight to the desired destination. According to another interpretation, the word "strength" alludes to the Torah, of which we read: "The Lord gives strength unto his people" (Ps. XXIX, 11). It is thus here indicated that a man should study the Torah in single-hearted devotion to the Almighty, and whoever labours in the Torah from worldly motives had better not have been born. The word *mesilloth* also may be translated not "highways" but "extollings" (cf. the verse "Extol (*solu*) him that rideth upon the skies" (Ps. LXVIII, 5)). It thus alludes to the man who labours in the Torah with the object of extolling God and making Him the only object of devotion in the world. Observe that Jacob performed all his actions for the sake of God, and therefore God was always with him and did not ever remove His Presence from him. We know this from the fact that although Jacob was not present when Isaac called Esau his son, the Shekinah told Rebekah, who in her turn told Jacob.' R. Jose said: 'Observe that had Esau, God forbid, been blessed there and then, Jacob would never have been able to assert himself; but all was directed by Providence, and everything fell into its right place.'

AND REBEKAH LOVED JACOB, and so she sent for him and said to him: BEHOLD, I HEARD THY FATHER SPEAK UNTO ESAU THY BROTHER, SAYING . . . NOW THEREFORE, MY SON, HEARKEN TO MY VOICE, ETC. It was then the eve of Passover, a time when the evil tempter had to be removed, so as to restore to power the moon, to symbolise the true object [142b] of faith. Rebekah therefore prepared two dishes. R. Judah said: 'Herein were foreshadowed the two he-goats which the children of Jacob were in the future to offer, one for the Lord and the other for Azazel on the Day of Atonement. We see thus Rebekah offering "two kids of the goats", one for the supernal grade and the other with the object of subduing the grade of Esau, so as to deprive him of any power over Jacob. Hence "two kids of the goats", both of which Isaac tasted and ate of. Similarly, when it says "And he brought him wine, and he drank", the word "brought" intimates that the wine was fetched from a distant region, namely, from the region of Esau. R. Eleazar said: 'There is an allusion here to that wine in which is all kind of exhilaration, since Isaac and his side required to be exhilarated.'

AND REBEKAH TOOK THE CHOICEST GARMENTS OF ESAU, ETC. These were the garments of which Esau had despoiled Nimrod. They were precious garments which, originally belonging to Adam, in time came into the hands of Nimrod, who used them as his hunting dress, for so Scripture says: "He was a mighty hunter before the Lord" (Gen. x, 9). Then Esau went out into the field and made war against Nimrod, and slew him and possessed himself of those garments, as is hinted in the passage: "And Esau came in from the field, and he was faint" (*Ibid.* xxv, 29), that is, from killing, as in the passage, "for my soul fainteth before the murderers" (Jer. IV, 31). Now, Esau kept those garments in Rebekah's apartment, from whence he would fetch them whenever he went a-hunting. On that day, however, he went out into the field without them, and thus he stayed there longer than usual. Now when Esau put on those garments no aroma whatever was emitted from them, but when Jacob put them on they were restored to their rightful place, and a sweet odour was diffused from them. For Jacob inherited the beauty of Adam; hence those garments found in him their rightful owner and thus gave off their proper aroma. Said R. Jose: 'Can it really be so, that Jacob's beauty equalled that of Adam, seeing that, according to tradition, the fleshy part of Adam's heel outshone the orb of the sun? Would you, then, say the same of Jacob?' Said R. Eleazar in reply: 'Assuredly Adam's beauty was as tradition says, but only at first before he sinned, when no creature could endure to gaze at his beauty; after he sinned, however, his beauty was diminished and his height was reduced to a hundred cubits. Observe further that Adam's beauty is a symbol with which the true faith is closely bound up. This is hinted at in the passage: "And let the graciousness of the Lord our God be upon us" (Ps. XC, 17), as well as in the expression, "to behold the graciousness of the Lord" (*Ibid.* XXVII, 4). And Jacob assuredly participated of that beauty. The whole, then, is deeply symbolical.'

AND HE SMELLED THE SMELL OF HIS RAIMENT, AND BLESSED HIM. Observe that it is not written "*the* raiment", but "*his* raiment". This is explained by the text "Who coverest thyself with light as with a garment" (Ps. CIV, 2). The word "his" may also be understood to indicate that it was only when Jacob put them on that the garments emitted their sweet odour; and it was only the sweet odour diffused by them that made Isaac bless him, for only then did he feel that there was before him one deserving of the blessings, since otherwise all these divine aromas would not have accompanied him. Hence the sequence of the verse: AND HE SMELLED THE SMELL OF HIS RAIMENT, AND BLESSED HIM, AND SAID: SEE THE SMELL OF MY SON IS AS THE

SMELL OF THE FIELD WHICH THE LORD HATH BLESSED. The subject of the word "said" is, according to some, the Shekinah, according to others, Isaac himself. "The field which the Lord hath blessed" alludes to the "field of apple trees", the field which the patriarchs cherish and cultivate.

SO GOD GIVE THEE OF THE DEW OF HEAVEN, AND OF THE FAT PLACES OF THE EARTH, AND PLENTY OF CORN AND WINE. R. Abba said: 'We may bring into connection with this passage the verse: "A song of Ascents. In my distress I called unto the Lord and he answered me" (Ps. CXX, 1). Many songs and hymns did David utter before the Almighty for the purpose of perfecting his grade and making himself a name, as Scripture says: "And David got him a name" (II Sam. VIII, 13). But this song David recited when he contemplated this incident of Jacob.' R. Eleazar said: 'It was Jacob who uttered this psalm at the moment when his father said to him: "Come near, I pray thee, that I may feel thee, my son, whether thou be my very son Esau or not." That was [143*a*] a moment of great distress for Jacob, as he feared that his father would recognize him. We read, however: "And he discerned him not, because his hands were hairy, as his brother Esau's hands; so he blessed him." It was then that Jacob said: "In my distress I called unto the Lord, and he answered me. O Lord, deliver my soul from lying lips, from a deceitful tongue" (Ps. CXX, 1–2). The "lying lips" is a reference to the grade of Esau, which is so called because when the serpent brought curses into the world it was by means of cunning and crookedness. Observe that when Isaac said to Esau: "and go out into the field, and take me venison", he added, "I will bless thee before the Lord" (Gen. XXVII, 7). Now, had Isaac said simply, "that I may bless thee", there would have been no harm. But when he uttered the words "before the Lord", the Throne of Glory of the Almighty shook and trembled, saying: "Will the serpent now be released from his curses and Jacob become subject to them?".' At that moment the angel Michael, accompanied by the Shekinah, appeared before Jacob. Isaac felt all this, and he also saw the Garden of Eden beside Jacob, and so he blessed him in the presence of the angel. But when Esau entered there entered with him the Gehinnom, and thus we read: "And Isaac trembled very exceedingly", as until that time he had not thought that Esau was of that side. "And I have blessed him"—he then said—"yea, he shall be blessed". Jacob thus equipped himself with wisdom and cunning, so that the blessings reverted to himself who was the image of Adam, and were snatched from that serpent of "the lying lips" who acted and spoke deceitfully in order to lead astray the world and bring curses on it. Hence Jacob came with craft and misled his father with the object of bringing blessings upon the world, and to recover from the serpent what hitherto he had withheld from the world. It was measure for measure, as expressed in the verse: "Yea, he loved cursing, and it came unto him; and he delighted not in blessing, and it is far from him" (Ps. CIX, 17). Concerning him it is written: "Cursed art thou from among all cattle, and from among all beasts of the field" (Gen. III, 14). He remains in that curse for evermore, and Jacob came and took away from him the blessings; from the very days of Adam Jacob was destined to snatch from the serpent all those blessings, leaving him still immersed in the curses without the possibility of emerging from them. David also said concerning him: "What shall be given unto thee, and what shall be done more unto thee, thou deceitful tongue?" (Ps. cxx, 3). That is to say, of what benefit was it to the serpent that he brought curses upon the world? As the adage says: "The serpent bites and kills, and feels no satisfaction". "A deceitful tongue": in that he deceived Adam and his wife and brought evil upon them and upon the world, until Jacob came and took away from him all the blessings. "Sharp arrows of the mighty" (*Ibid.* 4) is an allusion to Esau, who nursed his hatred toward Jacob on account of these blessings, as we read: "And Esau hated Jacob because of the blessing, etc." So GOD GIVE THEE OF THE DEW OF HEAVEN, AND OF THE FAT PLACES OF THE EARTH, that is to say, blessings from above and from below in conjunction. AND PLENTY OF CORN AND WINE, in consonance with the text: "yet have I not seen the righteous forsaken, nor his seed begging bread" (Ps. XXXVII, 25). This, as we have laid down, was uttered by the Prince of the world; hence "plenty of corn and wine". LET PEOPLES SERVE THEE: alluding to the time when King Solomon reigned in Jerusalem, as it is written: "And all the kings of the earth etc. . . . And they brought every man his present" (II Chr. IX, 23–24). AND NATIONS BOW DOWN TO THEE, alludes to the time when the Messiah will appear, concerning whom it is written: "Yea, all kings shall prostrate themselves before him" (Ps. LXXII, 11). R. Judah said: 'The whole applies to the advent of the Messiah, of whom it is also written: "all nations shall serve him" (*Ibid*.).' BE (*heveh*) LORD OVER THY BRETHREN. The irregular form *heveh* (be), instead of *heyeh* or *tihyeh*, has a deep mystical signification, being composed, as it is, of the three letters which are the basis of faith: *Hé* at the first, *Vau* in the centre, then *Hé* following. Hence: "Be (*heveh*) lord over thy brethren", namely, to rule over them and subdue them at the time of King David. R. Jose said: 'These blessings apply to the time of the advent of the Messiah, since on account of Israel transgressing the precepts of the Torah Esau was able to take advantage of the blessing given to him, "thou shalt shake his yoke from off thy neck" (Gen. XXVII, 40).' R. Jose said: 'All these [143*b*] blessings were from the side of Jacob's portion, so that Jacob only received what was his own. Isaac desired to transfer them to Esau, but God brought it to pass that Jacob came into his own. Observe the parallelism. When the serpent brought curses upon the world God said to Adam: "Because thou hast hearkened unto the voice of thy wife . . . cursed is the ground for thy sake, etc." (Gen. III, 17), meaning that it should not bring forth fruit or any vegetation in proper measure. Corresponding to this curse we have here the blessing, "of the fat of the earth". Again, there it is written: "In toil thou shalt eat it" (*Ibid*.): here comes the corrective, "of the dew of heaven". There it says: "Thorns also and thistles shall it bring forth unto thee" (*Ibid*. 18)—here, "and plenty of corn and wine". There we have "In the sweat of thy face thou shalt eat bread" (*Ibid*. 19)—here, "Let peoples serve, and nations bow down to thee", tilling the earth and cultivating the field, as it is written: "And aliens shall be your plowmen and your vine-dressers"

(Is. LXI, 5). Jacob thus turned each curse into a blessing, and what he took was his own. God brought all this about so that Jacob should remain attached to his own place and portion, and that Esau should remain attached to *his* place and portion.'

R. Hizkiah questioned this exposition, saying: 'Do we not find that later on Esau received a similar blessing as regards the fat places of the earth and the dew of heaven, as we read: "Behold, of the fat places of the earth shall be thy dwelling, and of the dew of heaven from above" ?' Said R. Simeon in reply: 'The two blessings are not alike, being from entirely different grades. As regards Jacob it is written: "So God give thee", whereas as regards Esau it is written merely: "Of the fat places of the earth shall be, etc."; as regards Jacob it is written: "of the dew of heaven and of the fat places of the earth", but as regards Esau, "of the fat places" and then "of the dew of heaven". The difference between the two goes very deep. For the "dew of heaven" promised to Jacob is the supernal dew that flows from the Ancient of Days, and is therefore called "dew of heaven", namely, of the upper heaven, dew that flows through the grade of heaven, to fall on the "field of consecrated apples". Also, the earth mentioned in Jacob's blessing alludes to the supernal "earth of the living". Jacob thus inherited the fruit of the supernal earth and the supernal heaven. Esau, on the other hand, was given his blessings on earth here below and in heaven here below. Jacob obtained a portion in the highest realm, but Esau only in the lowest. Further, Jacob was given a portion both above and below, but Esau only here below. And although he was promised, "And it shall come to pass when thou shalt break loose, that thou shalt shake his yoke from off thy neck" (Gen. XXVII, 40), this was only to be here below, but regarding the upper world it is written: "For the portion of the Lord is his people, Jacob the lot of his inheritance" (Deut. XXXII, 9).'

Observe that as soon as Jacob and Esau commenced to avail themselves of their blessings, the former possessed himself of his portion on high, and the latter of his portion here below. R. Jose the son of R. Simeon, the son of Laqunia, once said to R. Eleazar: 'Have you ever heard from your father how it comes about that the blessings given by Isaac to Jacob

have not been fulfilled, while those given to Esau have all
been fulfilled in their entirety ?' R. Eleazar replied: 'All the
blessings are to be fulfilled, including other blessings with
which God blessed Jacob. For the time being, however,
Jacob took his portion above and Esau here below. But in
aftertime, when the Messiah will arise, Jacob will take both
above and below and Esau will lose all, being left with no
portion of inheritance or remembrance whatever. So Scripture says: "And the house of Jacob shall be a fire, and the
house of Joseph a flame, and the house of Esau for stubble,
etc." (Obad. i, 18), so that Esau will perish entirely, whilst
Jacob will inherit both worlds, this world and the world to
come. Of that time it is further written: "And saviours shall
come up on Mount Zion to judge the mount of Esau; and the
kingdom shall be the Lord's" (*Ibid.* i, 21), that is to say, the
kingdom which Esau has taken in this world shall revert to
God. For although God rules both above and below, yet for
the time being He has given to all the peoples each a portion
and an inheritance in this world; but at that time He will take
away dominion from all of them, so that all will be His, as it
is written, "And the kingdom shall be the Lord's". It will be
the Lord's alone, as it is further written, "And the Lord shall
be king over all the earth; in that day shall the Lord be One,
and his name One" (Zech. xiv, 9).'

AND IT CAME TO PASS AS JACOB WAS SCARCELY GONE
OUT, ETC. R. Simeon said: 'The double form *yaẓo yaẓa*
(lit. going out, went out) indicates that [144*a*] the Shekinah
went out with him. For it had entered along with Jacob, and
had been with him when he received his blessings and had
confirmed them. And when Jacob went out the Shekinah
went out with him, and hence the twofold expression *yaẓo
yaẓa*, implying a simultaneous going out of two.' AND
ESAU HIS BROTHER CAME IN FROM HIS HUNTING. It
was literally "his", devoid of any blessing, and the Holy Spirit
cried out to Isaac: "Eat thou not the bread of him that hath
an evil eye" (Prov. xxiii, 6). AND HE ALSO MADE SAVOURY
FOOD. . . . LET MY FATHER ARISE. He spoke in a rough
and overbearing manner, with no sign of politeness. Observe

the difference between Jacob and Esau. Jacob spoke to his father gently and modestly, as it says: "He came to his father and said: My father." He was careful not to startle him, and said in a tone of entreaty: "Arise, I pray thee, sit and eat of my venison." But Esau said: "Let my father arise", as though he were not addressing him personally. Also, when Esau entered the Gehinnom accompanied him, so that Isaac shook with fear, as it says: "And Isaac trembled, greatly, exceedingly." The word "exceedingly" is added to show that no such fear and terror had ever assailed Isaac since the day he was born; and not even when he lay bound on the altar with the knife flashing before his eyes was he so affrighted as when he saw Esau enter and the Gehinnom enter with him. He then said: Before thou camest, and I have blessed him. yea, and he shall be blessed, because he saw that the Shekinah had confirmed his blessings. According to another explanation, Isaac said: "And I have blessed him", and a heavenly voice answered: "Yea, and he shall be blessed." Isaac, indeed, wanted to curse Jacob, but the Holy One said to him: "O Isaac, thou wilt thereby be cursing thyself, since thou hast already pronounced over him the words, 'Cursed be every one that curseth thee, and blessed be every one that blesseth thee'." Observe that all, both above and below, confirmed these blessings, and even he who was the portion that fell to the lot of Esau consented to those blessings, and, moreover, actually himself blessed Jacob, as it is written: "And he said: Let me go for the day breaketh. And he said: I will not let thee go, except thou bless me" (Gen. xxxii, 27). The angel said "Let me go" because Jacob seized hold of him. You may wonder how could a man of flesh and blood take hold of an angel, who is pure spirit, as it is written: "Who makest spirits thy messengers, the flaming fire thy ministers" (Ps. civ, 4). But the truth is that when the angels, the messengers of the Holy One, descend to earth, they make themselves corporeal, and put on a bodily vesture like to the denizens of this world. For it is fitting not to deviate from the custom of the place where one happens to be, as has already been explained. We find it thus written of Moses when he ascended on high: "And he was there with the Lord forty days and forty nights; he did neither eat bread, nor drink water" (Ex. xxxiv, 28), in order not to deviate from the custom of the place to which he went. Similarly we read, as an example of the behaviour of angels on descending here below: "And he stood by them under the tree, and they did eat" (Gen. xviii, 8). So here, Jacob could only have wrestled with the angel after the latter had assumed a bodily vesture after the manner of a being of this world. The reason, too, why Jacob had to wrestle with him the whole of that night was because those beings possess dominion only in the night, and so, correspondingly, Esau dominates only during the exile, which is none other than night. During the night, therefore, the angel held fast to Jacob and wrestled with him; but as soon as day broke his strength waned, and he could no more prevail, so that Jacob got the upper hand, since Jacob's domination is in the daytime. (Hence it is written: "The burden of Dumah. One calleth unto me out of Seir: Watchman, what of the night? Watchman, what of the night?" (Is. xxi, 11). For the domination of Esau, who is identical with Seir, is only in the night.) The angel, therefore, feeling his strength ebb as the day broke, said: "Let me go, for the day breaketh." Jacob's answer, "I will not let thee go, except thou hast blessed me", [144*b*] is peculiar, since we should have expected "except thou *wilt* bless me". By using the past tense, however, Jacob as much as said: "except thou acknowledge those blessings with which my father blessed me, and wilt not contend against me on account of them". The angel, we are told, thereupon said: "Thy name shall be called no more Jacob, but Israel; for thou hast striven with God and with men, and hast prevailed" (Gen. xxxii, 29). By the name Israel he meant to imply: "We must needs be subservient to thee, since thou art crowned with thy might above in a supernal grade." "Israel shall be thy name"; assuredly so, for "thou hast striven with Elohim". By this name he apparently referred to himself, but he really had a deeper meaning, viz. "Thou hast striven to associate thyself with God in a close union, as symbolised by the junction of the sun and the moon." Hence he did not say "thou hast prevailed *over* God", but "*with* God", i.e. to unite closely with God.

R. Simeon here discoursed on the verse: *When a man's ways please the Lord, he maketh even his enemies to be at peace with him* (Prov. XVI, 7). 'How greatly', he said, 'is it incumbent on man to direct his path toward the Holy One, blessed be He, so as to observe the precepts of the Torah. For, according to our doctrine, two heavenly messengers are sent to accompany man in his path through life, one on the right and one on the left; and they are also witnesses to all his acts. They are called, the one, "good prompter", and the other, "evil prompter". Should a man be minded to purify himself and to observe diligently the precepts of the Torah, the good prompter who is associated with him will overpower the evil prompter, who will then make his peace with him and become his servant. Contrariwise, should a man set out to defile himself, the evil prompter will overpower the good prompter; and so we are agreed. Thus when a man sets out to purify himself, and his good prompter prevails, then God makes even his enemies to be at peace with him, that is to say, the evil prompter submits himself to the good prompter. Of this Solomon said: "Better is he that is lightly esteemed, and hath a servant" (Prov. XII, 9), the servant being the evil prompter. Hence inasmuch as Jacob put his trust in the Almighty, and all his actions were for His sake, God "made even his enemies to be at peace with him", to wit, Samael, who is the power and strength of Esau; and, he having made peace with Jacob and consented to the blessings, Esau also consented to them. For until Jacob was at peace with the chieftain of Esau, Esau was not at peace with Jacob. For in all cases power below depends on the corresponding power above.'

AND ISAAC TREMBLED VERY EXCEEDINGLY, AND SAID: WHO THEN (*epho*) IS HE . . .? The term *epho* (lit. here) is an allusion to the Shekinah that was present when Isaac blessed Jacob. Isaac thus as much as said: "Who is he that stood here and confirmed the blessings I conferred upon him? YEA, AND HE SHALL BE BLESSED, seeing that God approved of these blessings." R. Judah said: 'For having caused his father thus to tremble, Jacob was punished by being thrown into a similar tremor when his sons showed him Joseph's coat and said, "This have we found" (Gen. XXXVII, 32).' (Note that the word *epho* used by Isaac here is also used to herald the punishment of Jacob through the loss of Joseph, who, when sent to seek his brethren, said: "Where (*epho*) are they feeding the flock ?" (*Ibid.* 16); and this although God approved of the blessings.) AND ISAAC TREMBLED A GREAT TREMBLING. The term "great" is echoed by the phrase "and this great fire" (Deut. XVIII, 16), thus intimating that the Gehinnom entered along with Esau. VERY EXCEEDINGLY ('*ad me'od*): the term *me'od*, on an analogy with the same term in the clause, "and behold, it was very (*me'od*) good" (Gen. I, 31), alludes to the angel of death; hence the exclamation: "Who then is he . . . ?" [145*a*]

WHEN ESAU HEARD THE WORDS OF HIS FATHER, ETC. R. Hiya exclaimed: 'How much has Israel suffered on account of those tears which Esau shed before his father, in his desire to be blessed by him, out of the great regard he had for his father's words !' HAS ONE NOT RIGHTLY CALLED HIM JACOB ? The form of the expression, instead of the more natural "has not his name been called", indicates the contempt with which Esau uttered the words. FOR HE HATH SUPPLANTED ME THESE TWO TIMES. The word "these" (*ze*) implies that the supplanting was of the same character on both occasions, since the word *bekhorathi* (my birthright) consists of the same letters as *birkhathi* (my blessing). The word *ze* has a similar force in the sentence: "Surely we had now (*ze*, lit. this) returned a second time" (Gen. XLIII, 10), where the letters of the word *shavnu* (we had returned) can be transposed to form *boshnu* (we are put to shame), as much as to say: "if we delay longer, we shall both return and be ashamed". Job made use of a similar word-play when he said: "And thou holdest me for thine enemy" (*oyeb*) (Job XIII, 24), as much as to say: "Thou hast turned about *Iyob* (Job) into *oyeb* (enemy)." Similarly here, Esau said: "He first took my birthright (*bekhorathi*), and now he turned the same about into my blessing (*birkhathi*), which he has also taken from me."

Behold, I have made him thy lord ... and what then shall I do for thee, my son? By the word *epho* (then, lit. here) he implied that there was no one there to approve of a blessing for him. Isaac thus blessed him with worldly goods; he surveyed his grade and said, "And by thy sword shalt thou live", as much as to say: "This is just what suits you, to shed blood and to make war." It was for this reason, as R. Eleazar explains, that he first said to him: "And what then shall I do for thee ?", seeing that I behold in thee harshness, the sword and blood, but in thy brother the way of peace. Then he added "my son", as if to say, "my son thou surely art, and I transmit to thee all this". Hence, by thy sword shalt thou live and thou shalt serve thy brother. This has not yet been fulfilled, seeing that Esau has till now not yet served Jacob, since Jacob did not desire it at the time, and, indeed, himself many times called him "my master". The reason is that Jacob gazed into the distant future and therefore deferred the fulfilment of the blessings to the end of days, as already said.

As R. Hiya and R. Jose were once walking together, they noticed R. Jesse the Elder coming up behind them. So they sat down and waited for him until he came up to them. As soon as he joined them they said, 'Now we shall journey with godspeed.' As they proceeded, R. Hiya said: ' "It is time to do for the Lord" (Ps. cxix, 126).' R. Jose thereupon began to discourse on the verse: *She openeth her mouth with wisdom, and the law of kindness is on her tongue* (Prov. xxxi, 26). 'The word "wisdom" ', he said, 'signifies the *Beth* of the word *bereshith* (in the beginning), as already explained elsewhere. The *Beth* is closed in on one side and open on the other. It is closed in on one side as symbolic of that which is written: "And thou shalt see my back" (Ex. xxxiii, 23), and open on the other side so as to illumine the higher worlds. (It is also open on one side in order to receive from the higher worlds, like a hall in which guests gather.) For that reason it is placed at the beginning of the Torah, and was later on filled in. Again, "She openeth her mouth with wisdom", for so the word *bereshith* is rendered in the Chaldaic version, *behokhmetha* (with wisdom). "And the law of kindness (*hesed*) is on her tongue", i.e. in her subsequent utterances, as it is written: "And God said: Let there be light, and there was light." The "mouth" again is an allusion to the *Hé* of the Divine Name, which contains the Whole, which is both unrevealed and revealed, and comprises both the higher and the lower emanations, being emblematic of both. "She openeth her mouth with wisdom", inasmuch as, though herself hidden and absolutely unknowable, as it says, "And it is hid from the eyes of all living, and kept close from the fowls of the air" (Job xxviii, 21), yet when she begins to expand by means of the Wisdom to which she is attached and in which she resides, she puts forth a Voice which is the "law of kindness" (*hesed*). Or again, the "mouth" can be taken as alluding to the final *Hé* of the Divine Name, which is the Word that emanates from Wisdom, while the "law of kindness on her tongue" signifies the Voice which is above the Word, controlling it and guiding it, [145*b*] since speech cannot be formed without voice, as has been agreed.'

R. Hiya then followed with a discourse on the verse: *I wisdom dwell with prudence, and find out knowledge of devices* (Prov. viii, 12). ' "Wisdom" here', he said, 'alludes to the Community of Israel; "prudence" signifies Jacob, the prudent man; and "knowledge of devices" alludes to Isaac, who used devices for the purpose of blessing Esau. But since wisdom allied itself with Jacob, who was possessed of prudence, it was he who was blessed by his father, so that all those blessings rested on him and are fulfilled in him and in his descendants to all eternity. Some have been fulfilled in this world, and the rest will be fulfilled on the advent of the Messiah, when Israel will be one nation on earth and one people of the Holy One, blessed be He. So Scripture says: "And I will make them one nation on earth" (Ez. xxxvii, 22). And they will exercise dominion both on high and here below, as it is written: "And, behold, there came with the clouds of heaven one like unto a son of man" (Dan. vii, 13), alluding to the Messiah, concerning whom it is also written: "And in the days of those kings shall the God of heaven set up a kingdom, etc." (*Ibid.* ii, 44). Hence Jacob desired that the blessings should be reserved for that future time, and did not take them up immediately.'

R. Jesse then followed with a discourse on the verse: *But fear not thou, O Jacob my servant, neither be dismayed, O Israel, etc.* (Jer. XLVI, 27). 'When Jacob', he said, 'rose to leave his father, he became aware that he would not be able to avail himself of the blessings till a long time had elapsed, and he was greatly dismayed. A voice then went forth and said: "But fear not thou, O Jacob . . . for I am with thee" (*Ibid.* 27-28), i.e. I will not forsake thee in this world. "For, lo, I will save thee from afar" (*Ibid.*), i.e. at the time for which thou hast reserved those blessings, "and thy seed from the land of their captivity" (*Ibid*), that is to say: "Although Esau has already taken possession of his blessing and so will enslave thy children, I will free them from his hands, and then thy children will be masters over them." "And Jacob will return" (*Ibid.*), i.e. he will return to his blessings, "and he will be quiet and at ease" (*Ibid.*) from the kingdoms of Babylonia, Media, Greece, and Edom, which have enslaved Israel, "and none shall make him afraid" (*Ibid.*), for ever and ever.'

The three then proceeded on their way, when R. Jose remarked: 'Truly all that God does in the world is an emblem of the divine Wisdom and is done with the object of manifesting Wisdom to the sons of men, so that they should learn from those works the mysteries of Wisdom, and all is accomplished according to plan. Further, all the works of God are the ways of the Torah, for the ways of the Torah are the ways of the Holy One, blessed be He, and no single word is contained in it but is an indication of ever so many ways and paths and mysteries of divine Wisdom. Did not Rabban Johanan evolve three hundred legal decisions, through esoteric allusions, from the verse: "And his wife's name was Mehetabel, the daughter of Matred, the daughter of Mezahab" (Gen. XXXVI, 39)—decisions which he revealed only to R. Eleazar ? This shows that each incident recorded in the Torah contains a multitude of deep significations, and each word is itself an expression of wisdom and the doctrine of truth. The words of the Torah, then, are all sacred, revealing wondrous things, as we read: "Open thou mine eyes, that I may behold wondrous things out of thy law" (Ps. CXIX, 18). Here is a proof. When the serpent had subverted Adam and his wife, and infected her with impurity, the world fell thereby in a state of defilement, and was laid under a curse, and death was brought into it. So the world had to be punished through him until the tree of life came and made atonement for man and prevented the serpent from ever again having dominion over the seed of Jacob. For each time the Israelites offered up a he-goat the serpent was subdued and led captive, as already said. Hence Jacob brought his father two he-goats (*se'irim*), one to subdue Esau, who was hairy (*sa'ir*), and the other to subdue the grade to which Esau was beholden and to which he adhered, as has been said already. And it is through this that the world will be preserved until a woman will appear after the pattern of Eve and a man after the pattern of Adam, who will circumvent and out-manœuvre [146a] the evil serpent and him who rides on him, as explained elsewhere.'

R. Jose further discoursed as follows: *And Esau was a cunning hunter . . . and Jacob was a perfect man, dwelling in tents* (Gen. XXV, 27). 'In which way was he "perfect" ? In that he was "dwelling in *tents*", i.e. that he held fast to the two sides, to that of Abraham and that of Isaac. In dealing with Esau he advanced from the side of Isaac, as already said, and in the spirit of the passage: "With the merciful thou dost show thyself merciful . . . and with the crooked thou dost show thyself subtle" (Ps. XVIII, 26–27). But when he came to receive the blessings, he came with help from on high, and with support from both Abraham and Isaac, and thus all was prescribed by wisdom, as already said above. For Jacob conquered the serpent with prudence and craft, but chiefly by means of the he-goat; and although the serpent and Samael are the same, yet he also conquered Samael by another method, as described in the passage, saying: "and there wrestled a man with him until the breaking of the day. And when he saw that he prevailed not against him" (Gen. XXXII, 25–26). Observe how great Jacob's merit must have been. For as his adversary was intent on destroying him completely, and that night was the night when the moon was created, it was doubly unpropitious for Jacob, who remained behind all alone. For we have been taught that a man should not go out alone in the night time; how much less then in the night when the lights were created,[1] since the moon is defective, and on such a night the evil serpent is specially powerful. Samael thus came and attacked him, in order to destroy him utterly. Jacob, however, had strong support on all sides, on the side of Isaac and on the side of Abraham, both of whom constituted the strength of Jacob. When Samael attacked Jacob's right he saw there Abraham equipped with the strength of day, being of the side of the Right, the same being Mercy (*Hesed*). When he attacked his left, he saw there Isaac with the strength of stern judgement. When he attacked in front, he found Jacob strong on either side by reason of those surrounding him, and thus we read: "And when he saw that he prevailed not against him, he touched the hollow of his thigh" (Gen. XXXII, 26), that is, a part that is outside of the trunk and one of its supports. Hence, "the hollow of Jacob's thigh was strained" (*Ibid.*). When day appeared and night departed, Jacob's strength increased and Samael's waned, so that the latter said: "Let me go, for the moment of the recital of the morning hymn had arrived", and it was therefore necessary for him to depart. He thus confirmed Jacob's blessings and added to them one blessing more, as it says: "And he blessed him there" (*Ibid.* 30).

'Many were the blessings which Jacob received at different times. First he obtained blessings from his father, through the exercise of craft; then a blessing from the Shekinah, at the time when he returned from Laban, as we read, "And God (*Elohim*) blessed Jacob"; another blessing he received from that angel, the chieftain of Esau; and then his father blessed him when he set out for Padan-Aram, saying, "And God Almighty bless thee. . . ." (Gen. XXVIII, 3). When Jacob saw himself equipped with all these blessings, he deliberated within himself, saying, "Of which of these blessings shall I avail myself now?" He decided to make use for the time being of the least of them, which was the last; for although in itself it was powerful, yet Jacob thought that it was not so strong in promises of dominion in this world as the others. Jacob hence

---

[1] i.e. the fourth night of the week.

said: "Let me take this blessing to use for the time being, and the others I will reserve against the time when I and my descendants after me will be in need of them—the time, that is, when all the nations will assemble to exterminate my offspring from the world." To Jacob may be applied the words of the Scripture: "All nations compass me about, verily, in the name of the Lord I will cut them off. They compass me about, yea, they compass me about. . . . They compass me about like bees, etc." (Ps. cxviii, 10-12). Here we have three times the words "compass me about", corresponding to the three remaining benedictions: his father's first blessing, then God's blessing, and thirdly the blessing of the angel. Jacob said: "Those blessings will be needed at that time for use against all those kings and nations: I shall therefore reserve them for that time, but now to cope with Esau this blessing will suffice me." He was like a king who had at his disposal a numerous and powerful army with skilled leaders, able and ready to engage in warfare with the most powerful [146b] adversary. Being once informed that a highway robber was infesting the country, he merely said, "Let my gate-keepers set out to deal with him." "Of all thy legions," he was asked, "hast thou no others to send but these gate-keepers ?" "To cope with the robber these will suffice," he answered, " whereas all my legions and military leaders I have to keep in reserve for the time when I will need them to meet my powerful adversaries." Similarly Jacob said: "For dealing with Esau these blessings will suffice me, but the others I will keep in reserve against the time when my children will need them to withstand all those monarchs and rulers of the earth." When that time will come all those blessings will become operative, and the world will be established on a firm foundation. From that day onward that kingdom will gain the ascendancy over all other kingdoms, and it will endure for ever, as it is written: "It shall break in pieces and consume all these kingdoms, but it shall stand for ever" (Dan. ii, 44). This is "the stone that was cut out of the mountain without hands, etc." (*Ibid*. 45). The same stone is alluded to in the words: "From thence, from the Shepherd, the stone of Israel" (Gen. xlix, 24). This stone is the Community of Israel, alluded to in the verse:

"And this stone, which I have set up for a pillar, etc." (Gen. XXVIII, 22).' R. Hiya cited the following verses in regard to Jacob's blessings: ' "A remnant shall return, even the remnant of Jacob" (Is. X, 21). 'This is a reference', he said, 'to the remainder of the blessings. It is further written: "And the remnant of Jacob shall be in the midst of many peoples (i.e. all the peoples, and not Esau alone), as dew from the Lord, as showers upon the grass" (Micah v, 6).' R. Yesa said: 'It is written: "A son honoureth his father, and a servant his master" (Mal. I, 6). Such a son was Esau, for there was not a man in the world who showed so much honour to his father as he did, and this it was that procured him dominion in this world. The "servant honouring his master" is typified by Eliezer the servant of Abraham, as already explained elsewhere. So, too, the tears which Esau shed made Israel subject to him, until the time when they will return unto the Holy One with weeping and with tears, as it says, "They shall come with weeping, etc." (Jer. XXXI, 9). And then will be fulfilled the prophecy: "And saviours shall come up on Mount Zion, to judge the Mount of Esau, and the kingdom shall be the Lord's" (Ob. I, 21). Blessed be the Lord for evermore.'

VAYEẒE

Gen. XXVIII, 10–XXXII, 3

AND JACOB WENT OUT FROM BEER-SHEBA AND WENT
TOWARD HARAN. R. Hiya drew a parallel between this
statement and the verse: *The sun ariseth, and the sun goeth
down, and hasteth to his place where he ariseth* (Eccles. I, 5).
'The sun arising', he said, 'is parallel to Jacob when in Beer-
sheba; and "the sun going down" to Jacob on his way to
Haran, when, as we read, "he tarried there all night, because
the sun was set"; and as the "sun hasteth to his place [147*a*]
where he ariseth", so Jacob "lay down in that place to sleep".
Observe that although the sun illumines all quarters of the
world, yet he travels only in two directions, as we read: "He
goeth toward the South, and turneth about unto the North"
(Eccles. I, 6), one being the right and the other the left. Every
day, too, he emerges from the East, turns to the South, then to
the North, then toward the Western side, and finally is
gathered unto the West. As the sun emerges from the East, so
Jacob went out from Beer-sheba, and as the sun turns toward
the West, so Jacob went toward Haran.' R. Simeon said that
Jacob "went forth" from the ambit of the Land of Israel, and
he "went into" another sphere, as is implied in the sentence,
"and he went toward Haran" (lit. strange, alien). R. Hiya
said: 'When the sun goes down to the West, the West is
called the place of the sun and his throne, the place in which
he abides, and to which he gathers in all his radiance. This
accords with the Rabbinic dictum that God puts on phylacteries, that is, He takes up all the supernal crowns, to wit the
emblem of the supernal Father and the emblem of the supernal Mother (these being the phylactery worn on the head),
and then He takes up the Right and the Left, thereby carrying
the whole.' R. Eleazar said: 'The "Beauty of Israel" takes up
the whole, and when the Community of Israel is drawn toward the world on high, it also carries the whole, the male
world of the Holy One as well as the female world [147*b*] of
the Holy One; for just as all the lights radiate from the one,

so the other carries the whole, one world being a representation of the other. Hence Beer-sheba (lit. well of seven) signifies the Jubilee year, *be'er* (well) symbolising a Sabbatical year; and the sun shines only from the Jubilee year. Hence "Jacob went out from Beer-sheba and went unto Haran", that is toward the West, which is identical with the Sabbatical year.' R. Simeon said: 'Beer-sheba symbolises the Sabbatical year, and Haran the year of *'orlah*, inasmuch as he issued from the sphere of holiness into an alien sphere, since he was fleeing from his brother, as already explained.' But when he arrived at Bethel, which is still within the holy sphere, it is written:

AND HE LIGHTED UPON THE PLACE. R. Hiya said: 'This is the place mentioned in the verse, "and he hasteth to his place" (Eccl. I, 5). AND TARRIED THERE ALL NIGHT, BECAUSE THE SUN CAME, i.e. came to illumine it, as it says: "he hasteth to his place where he shines". AND HE TOOK OF THE STONES OF THE PLACE. This is an allusion to the twelve precious and wondrous stones of the upper layer, of which it is written, "Take you . . . twelve stones" (Josh. IV, 3), and underneath which there are thousands and myriads of hewn stones. Hence it says "of the stones", and not simply "the stones". AND PUT THEM UNDER HIS HEAD (lit. heads). The plural form shows that we should refer the "his" not to Jacob but to the place, and understand the "heads" to be the four cardinal points of the world: he arranged the stones three to the [148*a*] North, three to the West, three to the South, and three to the East, and that place or spot was above them so that it should be established on them. Thereafter he LAY DOWN IN THAT PLACE TO SLEEP, for now that the couch was properly arranged, he, namely the sun, lay down on it. Thus the words "and he lay down in that place to sleep" are parallel to the text: "the sun ariseth and the sun comes in".'

Whilst R. Isaac was one day sitting at the entrance of the cave of Apikutha, a man passed by with his two sons. Said one of them to the other: 'The sun is most powerful when it is in the South, and were it not for the wind which tempers the heat, the world could not exist.' Said the younger brother:

'If not for Jacob, the world could not subsist. For when the unity of God is proclaimed by his sons with the verse, "Hear, O Israel, the Lord our God, the Lord is one" (Deut. VI, 4), which is an expression of perfect and absolute oneness, then Jacob their father joins them, and takes possession of his house, where he abides in close association with his fathers, so that male and female become united.' Said R. Isaac to himself: 'I will join them and listen to what they have to say.' He accordingly went along with them. The man then commenced to discourse on the verse: *Arise, O Lord, unto thy resting place, thou and the ark of thy strength* (Ps. CXXXII, 8). 'David,' he said, 'when he uttered these words, was like a man saying to a king, "Let your Highness arise and proceed to his abode of rest." Moses also addressed God similarly when he said: "Arise, O Lord, and let thine enemies be scattered" (Num. X, 35). The difference between the two is this. Moses spoke like a man giving orders in his own household, and so, as it were, bade the Lord to make war against His enemies; whereas David solicited Him to retire to His place of rest, and in accordance with the rules of etiquette included in his invitation both the King and His Consort. Hence he said: "Arise, O Lord, unto thy resting place, thou and the ark of thy strength", so as not to separate them. From David's conduct on this occasion we learn that anyone who invites a king should strive to entertain him in some novel [148b] fashion, so as to afford him special pleasure. If, for instance, it is the king's wont to be entertained by ordinary clowns and jesters, he should provide for him specially refined and courtly entertainers. Thus, when David invited the King and His Consort, he replaced the customary entertainers of the King with a higher order. So he said: "Let thy priests be clothed with righteousness, and let thy saints sing songs" (Ps. CXXXII, 9). Now the Levites were the regular musicians of the King, but David, having extended an invitation to Him, deviated from the normal practice and provided priests and saints to entertain Him. God said to him: "David, I do not wish to burden thee overmuch." Said David in reply: "O my Master, when Thou art in Thy palace, Thou doest according to Thy will, but now that I have invited Thee, it is for me to arrange matters, and it is my will to bring before Thee these, although it is not their usual task." From here we learn again that in his own house a man may arrange things as he pleases, but when invited out he must be at the command of his host, and conform to his desires. For when David substituted the priests for the Levites, God assented to his wish. David further said: "For thy servant David's sake turn not away the face of thine anointed" (*Ibid.* 10), as much as to say: "Let not the arrangements I have made be annulled." God said to him: "David, even my vessels I will not make use of, but will use thine instead." Nor did God stir from there until He had bestowed upon him a multitude of gifts, as it is written: "The Lord swore unto David in truth; he will not turn back from it: of the fruit of thy body will I set upon thy throne" (*Ibid.* 11).' R. Isaac went up to the man and kissed him, saying: 'It was worth my while to come hither if only to hear this.'

The elder son of the man then discoursed thus: *And Jacob went out from Beer-sheba, and went unto Haran.* 'Jacob', he said, 'acted in conformity with the verse: "Therefore shall a man leave his father and his mother, and shall cleave unto his wife" (Gen. 11, 24). Or again, his action may be regarded as symbolical of a later time when Israel left the Sanctuary and were driven into exile among the nations, as described in the text: "And gone is from the daughter of Zion all her splendour" (Lam. 1, 6), as well as in the passage, "Judah is gone into exile because of affliction" (*Ibid.* 3).' The younger son then began to discourse thus: *And he lighted upon the place, and tarried there all night, etc.* 'Even a king,' he said, 'when he desires to visit his consort, should coax her and use words of endearment, and not treat her as a mere chattel; and though he should have a golden couch with embroidered coverings in a grand palace, and she prepares for him a bed on a floor of stones with a straw mattress, it is incumbent on him to leave his own couch and lie down on hers, so as to give her satisfaction, and so that their hearts may be united, without any constraint. We learn this lesson from this text, which tells us that when Jacob went unto her, he "took from the stones of the place . . . and lay down in that place to sleep", showing that he loved even the stones of that place.'

R. Isaac wept for joy, and said: 'Seeing that such pearls are in your possession, how can I help following you ?' The man said to him: 'You must leave us, as we have to go to the town to celebrate the wedding of this my son.' R. Isaac then said: 'I must then needs go my own way.' [149a] He then went and repeated the expositions he had heard to R. Simeon, who remarked: 'They indeed spoke well, and all they said about God has been affirmed by us. Moreover, these expositions come from the mouths of the descendants of R. Zadok the invalid. He was called invalid because he fasted forty years, praying that Jerusalem should not be destroyed in his life-time. He used to discover within each word of the Torah profound lessons, from which he deduced the proper rules for the conduct of life.' Said R. Isaac: 'Not many days elapsed before I again met that man, accompanied by his younger son. I said to him: "Where is your other son ?" He said: "I had him married, and he is with his wife." Then, recognising me, he said: "I swear to you that I refrained from inviting you to the marriage of my son for three reasons: first, because I did not know you, and, since the style of an invitation must accord with the rank of the recipient, I was afraid lest you might happen to be a great man and I should unwittingly offend your dignity; secondly, I thought ou might be in a hurry, and so I did not wish to inconvenience you; and thirdly, I did not wish to put you to shame in the presence of the company of guests, as it is a custom with us that whoever sits at table with the bride and bridegroom gives them presents and gifts." I said to him: "God give you credit for your good intentions." I further asked him his name, and he said: "Zadok the Little." On that occasion I learnt from him thirteen profound lessons in the Torah, and from his son I learnt three, one concerning prophecy, one concerning dreams, and one concerning the difference between prophecy and dreams. He said that prophecy is of the male world, whereas dreams are of the female world, and from the one to the other is a descent of six grades. Prophecy is from both the right side and the left side, but dreams are only from the left side. Dream branches out into many grades in reaching here below; hence dreams are universally diffused throughout the world, each man seeing the kind of dream that answers to his own grade. Prophecy, on the other hand, is confined to its own region.' [149b]

AND HE DREAMED. It may be asked, how came Jacob, the holy man, the perfection of the Patriarchs, to have a vision only in a dream, and that in such a holy spot ? The reason is that Jacob at that time was not yet married, and that Isaac was still alive. It is true that we find him subsequently saying: "and I saw in a dream" (Gen. XXXI, 10), at a time when he was already married. But that was due to the inferiority of the place, as well as to the fact that Isaac was still alive. So when he came into the Holy Land with all the tribes, with "the foundation of the house, the mother of the children rejoicing", we read, "and God spake unto Israel in the visions of the night" (Gen. XLVI, 2)—not "dream", but "visions", which are of another and higher grade. Dreams are transmitted through the medium of Gabriel, who is the sixth in rank of inspiration; but a vision comes through the grade of the *Hayyah* that rules in the night. True, it says in one place, "Gabriel, make this man to understand the vision" (Dan. VIII, 16). The reason there is that a dream is more precise than a vision, and may explain what is obscure in a vision, and therefore Gabriel was sent to explain to Daniel what was obscure in his vision. A "vision" (*mar'eh*=vision, or mirror) is so called because it is like a mirror, in which all images are reflected. (Thus we read: "And I appeared . . . as *El Shaddai*" (Ex. VI, 2), this grade being like a mirror which showed another form, since all supernal forms are reflected in it.)

AND BEHOLD A LADDER SET UP ON THE EARTH. This ladder signifies the grade on which the other grades rest, to wit, the "Foundation of the world". AND THE TOP OF IT REACHED TO HEAVEN, so as to be attached to it. For this grade is the conclusion of the Body standing between the upper and the lower world in the same way as the sign of the covenant is situated at the end of the trunk of the body, between the thighs. AND BEHOLD, THE ANGELS OF GOD ASCENDING AND DESCENDING ON IT; this alludes to the

Chieftains who have charge of all the nations, and who ascend and descend on that ladder. When Israel are sinful, the ladder is lowered and the Chieftains ascend by it; but when Israel are righteous, the ladder is removed and all the Chieftains are left below and are deprived of their dominion. Jacob thus saw in this dream the domination of Esau and the domination of the other nations. According to another explanation, the angels ascended and descended on the top of the ladder; for when the top was detached, the ladder was lowered and the Chieftains ascended, but when it was attached again, the ladder was lifted and they remained below. But it comes to the same thing.

It says of Solomon that" In Gibeon the Lord appeared to him in a dream by night" (1 Kings III, 5). [150*a*] Here we have "appearing" and "dream" combined, to show that there was there a mingling of two grades, a higher and a lower, the reason being that Solomon had not then yet attained his full development. But when he had perfected himself it is written of him, "And God gave Solomon wisdom" (*Ibid.* v, 9), also" And Solomon's wisdom excelled, etc." (*Ibid.* 10); for the moon then reached its fullness and the Temple was built, and thus Solomon saw wisdom eye to eye and had no need of dreams. After he sinned, however, he was beholden again to dreams as before. Hence it says that "God appeared unto him twice" (*Ibid.* XI, 9)—twice, that is, in dreams, for communications through wisdom he had every day. Moreover, the dream-medium of Solomon excelled that of all other men inasmuch as it was a mingling of grade with grade, of vision with vision. In his later days, however, darkness fell upon him on account of his sins, and the moon waned because he observed not the holy covenant and gave himself up to strange women. This was the condition God made with David, saying: "If thy children keep my covenant . . . . their children also for ever shall sit upon the throne" (Ps. CXXXII, 12), where the expression "for ever" is of the same import as the phrase "as the days of the heaven above the earth" (Deut. XI, 21). And since Solomon did not keep the covenant properly, the moon began to wane, and so in the end he was beholden again to dreams; and likewise Jacob was beholden to dreams, as explained before.

And behold, the Lord stood (*nitsab*) upon it, etc. Here Jacob discerned the essential unity of the object of faith. This is implied in the term *nitsab* (firmly knit), which implies that Jacob saw all grades stationed as one on that ladder so as to be knit into one whole. And inasmuch as that ladder is situated between two sides, God said to him: I am the Lord, the God of Abraham thy father, and the God of Isaac, these two being respectively of the two sides, one of the right and the other of the left. According to another explanation, the Lord was standing over *him*, to wit, over Jacob, so as to form the Divine Chariot, with the Community of Israel, embodied in Jacob, as the uniting link in the midst, between the right and the left. That Jacob was in the midst is proved by the fact that the text here calls Abraham "thy father", but not Isaac, thus showing that Jacob was next to Abraham; and hence the text naturally continues: The land whereon thou liest, showing that the whole formed one sacred Chariot. Here Jacob saw that he was to be the crown of the patriarchs. The words "the God of thy father Abraham and the God of Isaac" show that Jacob was attached to either side and holding fast to both of them. But as long as he was not married this fact is not disclosed in the text, save to those who can read between the lines. After he married and begat children, however, it was openly stated, as it is written: "And he erected there an altar, and the God of Israel called him *El* (godlike)". From here we learn that whoever is incomplete below remains incomplete on high. Jacob was an exception, yet he too before marriage was not perfected openly; or rather, he only foresaw that he eventually would be perfected. It is true, God had already said to him, "And, behold, I am with thee, and will keep thee whithersoever thou goest." This, however, only implies that God's care and protection were always with him in the hour of need, in this world; but as regards the higher world, he was not sure of it till he had perfected himself.

And Jacob awakened out of his sleep, and he said: Surely the Lord is in this place, and I knew it not. How, we may ask, could he have known ?

The truth is, however, that he meant much the same as Saul when he said: "and I have not entreated the Presence of the Lord" (1 Sam. XIII, 12). What Jacob really said was: "And I have not known *Anokhi* (I, i.e. the Shekinah)"; as much as to say: "Behold all this revelation has been vouchsafed to me whilst yet I have not reached the stage of a knowledge of *Anokhi* (I) and of entering under the wings of the Shekinah, so as to attain perfection". Similarly, Rebekah said: "If it be so, what boots me *Anokhi* (I) ?" (Gen. XXV, 22), because she saw every day the splendour of the Shekinah, [150*b*] but when she felt the pains of approaching childbirth, "she went to enquire of the Lord" (*Ibid.*), that is, she proceeded from the Shekinah grade to another grade, identical with the Lord (Jehovah). Hence Jacob said: "Have I seen all this without knowing *Anokhi?*", because he was single, and had not yet come under the wings of the Shekinah. Straightway:

AND HE WAS AFRAID, AND SAID: HOW FULL OF AWE IS THIS PLACE. The word "place" here has a twofold significance. It refers in the first instance to the place mentioned by Jacob in the preceding verse; but it also refers to the mark of the holy covenant, which should not be left inoperative. (These two significations, however, are only two aspects of one and the same idea.) Jacob then said: THIS IS NONE OTHER THAN THE HOUSE OF GOD, implying: "This is not to remain idle; its covenant is not meant to exist in isolation. It is in sooth a godly abode, to be used for the promotion of fecundity and for receiving blessing from all the bodily organs. For indeed this is THE GATE OF HEAVEN, or, in other words, the gate of the Body, the gate assuredly through which pass the blessings downwards, so that it is attached both on high and below: on high, as being the gate of heaven, and below, as being none other than the house of God." Hence "he was afraid, and said: How full of awe is this place !" But mankind (it may be added) pay no regard to its preciousness, so as thereby to become perfect on high and here below.'

The father of the youth went up to him and kissed him. R. Isaac said: 'When I heard him speak thus, I wept and said:

Blessed be the Merciful One who has not allowed divine Wisdom to perish from the world. I followed them until we entered the next town, a distance of three parasangs. Hardly had they arrived in the town when the man had his son affianced. I said to him: "You act upon your own words." I also repeated the remark of R. Simeon, that all these verses are allegorical and have a profound significance. When I repeated all this in the presence of R. Simeon, he remarked to me that I should not think that all this exposition was merely the youth's own idea: it contains recondite thoughts which bear the seal of divine Wisdom.'

AND JACOB VOWED A VOW, SAYING: IF GOD WILL BE WITH ME, ETC. Said R. Judah: 'After receiving all these promises, how could Jacob still say, "*If* God will be with me, etc."? What Jacob meant, however, was this: "Some dreams are true and some not, so if this dream should come true, and God will really be with me as I have dreamt, then "the Lord shall be to me for God", that is, I shall draw blessings from the well-spring of the universal stream towards the region called *Elohim*.' For Israel being in the centre take first of the original well-spring, and after the bounty reaches them they pass it on toward that region. Hence we may render: "and the Lord shall be toward me, first, and afterwards the whole will be drawn toward *Elohim*": i.e. in the same way as *Elohim* will fulfil for me all these good promises, so will I draw toward Him from my region all those blessings and will make Him the all-comprehensive uniting force. When will that be? "When I come back to my father's house in peace", when I shall be settled in my own grade, in the grade of peace so as to make perfect my father's house, then "will the Lord be toward me, toward *Elohim* (God)".' According to another explanation, Jacob meant: "I desire to come back to my father's house in peace, because there is the Holy Land, and there I will become perfected, and the Lord shall be my God. In that place will I duly rise from this grade to another grade, and there I will engage myself in His worship." R. Hiya adduced here the verse: *The tale of iniquities is too heavy for me; our transgressions, thou wilt pardon them* (Ps. LXV, 4).

'The two halves of the verse', he said, 'do not seem to fit one another. The truth is, however, that David first prayed for himself and then for mankind in general, as though to say, "I know my own sins, but there are a great number of sinners in the world whose sins are much more grievous than mine; this being so, both mine [151*a*] and theirs, all our transgressions, thou wilt pardon them." For when sinners become numerous in the world, they go up to the place where the records are kept, as it is written, "there is a sitting in judgement and the books are open" (Dan. VII, 10). That book stood, as it were, over the head of David, and hence he said, "The tale of iniquities is too heavy for me, and therefore", he went on, "our transgressions thou wilt pardon them". Jacob, being in a similar condition, felt distrustful, not of God, but of himself, and he feared lest his sins should prevent him from returning in peace and deprive him of God's providential care. THEN SHALL THE LORD BE MY GOD: i.e. should I return in peace, I shall not care even if the attribute of divine mercy becomes justice towards me, inasmuch as I will worship Him continually.' R. Aha said that Jacob's words amounted to saying: 'Now I have no need of severity, but when I will return to my father's house, I will link myself with that attribute also.' Said R. Jose: 'That is not so, but what Jacob practically said was: Now I require the attribute of divine justice to guard me (against my enemies) until I return in peace to my father's house, but then I will combine mercy with justice, and bind all attributes in a firm unity.'

AND THIS STONE, WHICH I HAVE SET UP FOR A PILLAR, SHALL BE GOD'S HOUSE: seeing that all will be then united into one, and this stone will be blessed from the right and from the left, from on high and from below, for the reason that I will give the tenth of everything. We should have expected here, instead of *Elohim*, the name *Jehovah*, as in the text: "to prepare chambers in the house of the Lord (*Jehovah*)" (II Chr. XXXI, 20), also: "Let us go unto the house of the Lord (*Jehovah*)" (Ps. CXXII, 1). But in truth, the name *Elohim* here points to the tribunal which represents the attribute of justice on its two supernal sides, on the side of the

Jubilee year, known as Living God (*Elohim Ḥayyim*), and on the side of Isaac, expressed simply by the term "God" (*Elohim*). R. Eleazar said: 'The Jubilee Year, although it dispenses judgement, is yet altogether pervaded with mercy and is the source of universal joy and gladness. But "the house of God (*Elohim*)" represents rigorous judgement only, on the side of the left, either for good, in consonance with the text, "His left hand be under my head" (S. S. II, 6), or for evil, as it says, "Out of the North the evil shall break forth upon all the inhabitants of the land" (Jer. I, 14). Well then may it be called "the house of God (*Elohim*)".' R. Simeon said: ' "The house of God (*Elohim*)" signifies the same as "the city of the great king" (Ps. XLVIII, 3). Verily the supernal world is not only "King", but a "Great King", and that is what is meant here.'

R. Hiya and R. Hizkiah were once sitting underneath a tree in the field of Ono. R. Hiya fell into a slumber and beheld Elijah. He said to him: 'The whole field is illumined with your presence.' Elijah answered: 'I am come to tell you that Jerusalem is about to be laid waste together with all the towns of the sages, for the reason that Jerusalem is the embodiment of judgement, and is preserved by judgement, and now judgement demands its destruction; and Samael has already been given power over it and over its mighty ones. I have therefore come to advise the sages thereof so that they may try to obtain for Jerusalem some years of grace. For so long as knowledge of the Torah is found therein it will be spared, the Torah being the tree of life by which all live. But when the study of the Torah ceases below, the tree of life disappears from the world. Hence so long as the sages cling to the Torah, Samael has no power over them, as Scripture says: "The voice is the voice of Jacob, but the hands are the hands of Esau" (Gen. XXVII, 22). The voice is the Torah, which is termed the voice of Jacob, and so long as that voice pours forth, the utterance also dominates and prevails (over the hands of Esau). Hence the study of the Torah should never cease.' R. Hiya [151*b*] then awoke, and they went and told the sages. Said R. Jesse: 'We all know this, and so it is written: "Except the Lord keep the city, the watchman waketh in vain" (Ps. CXXVII, 1), as much as to say: "It is those who labour in the Torah who preserve the Holy City, and not the warriors and men of might".'

AND HE LOOKED, AND BEHOLD A WELL IN THE FIELD, ETC. R. Judah discoursed on the verse: *A psalm* (*mizmor=* song, hymn) *of David when he fled from Absalom his son* (Ps. III, 1). 'The companions', he said, 'have been perplexed by the title "song" given to this psalm. When his own son rose up against him, David should rather have uttered a lamentation, since a little hurt from one's kin is worse than a great hurt from a stranger. The truth, however, is that David was apprehensive lest the punishment for his sons might be remitted to the next world, and so when he found that it was being exacted from him in this world he rejoiced. Further, he was comforted by the fact that many, superior to himself, had had to flee alone, like Jacob, who "fled into the field of Aram" (Hos. XII, 13), all alone, and Moses, who fled from the face of Pharaoh (Ex. II, 15), also alone; whereas he was accompanied by all the nobility and the valiant men of the land and the chiefs of Israel, who stood on his right hand and on his left to guard him on all sides. Seeing himself thus favoured, David broke out into song.' R. Judah further remarked: 'The fugitives mentioned above in the course of their wanderings all came across that well. Why not David also? The reason is that it was at that time at enmity with him, whereas it welcomed Jacob and Moses and was eager to approach them, and as soon as it saw them its waters rose to meet them, like a woman rejoicing to greet her husband. Why, it may be asked, was not Elijah when he fled also met by the well? The reason is that Elijah is beneath the well and not above it, as Moses and Jacob were, and hence he is an angel who executes messages. So when it says that "Jacob looked, and behold, a well in the field", there is here an inner meaning, to wit, that he discerned the supernal well which corresponds to the well below. This is borne out by the next words: THREE FLOCKS OF SHEEP LYING THERE BY IT. Since they were only [152*a*] three, why is it written, "And thither were all the flocks gathered"? But in truth the three allude to the South, the East, and the North, the South on one side, the North on the other, and the East between them, all three standing by that well, holding fast to it and filling it. Why all this ? FOR OUT OF THAT WELL THEY WATERED THE FLOCKS, the allusion being the same as in the text: "They give drink to all the *Hayyoth* of the field" (Ps. CIV, 11). Further, the words AND THITHER WERE ALL THE FLOCKS GATHERED, can be illustrated from the passage: "All the rivers run into the sea" (Eccl. I, 7). AND THEY ROLLED THE STONE FROM THE WELL'S MOUTH: i.e. they dispelled from it the rigidity of hard judgement, which congeals it as it were into stone, from which water cannot flow. For when those rivers arise, the South, which is on the right, gathers strength and prevents the North from solidifying the water. For a large river, with a great volume of water, does not become frozen and congealed so soon as a small river with a small volume of water. Hence when those rivers arrive, the South, which is the right, puts forth its strength and the waters thaw and are loosened, so as to flow onward and give drink to the flocks, as it says, "they water the *Hayyoth* of the field" (Ps. CIV, 11). Then "they put the stone back upon the well's mouth in its place", because the world has need of its judgement so as thereby to punish the guilty.

Observe that Jacob, when he sat by the well and saw the water rising up toward him, knew that there he would meet his destined wife; and so it was, as Scripture says: WHILE HE WAS YET SPEAKING WITH THEM, RACHEL CAME WITH HER FATHER'S SHEEP. AND IT CAME TO PASS WHEN JACOB SAW RACHEL, ETC. It was the same with Moses, who, when he sat down by the well, as soon as he saw the water rising toward him knew that there he would meet his destined wife; and so indeed it turned out, as we read: "And the shepherds came and drove them away, etc." (Ex. II, 17), with the result that there he met with Zipporah. [152b] It was the well that served as medium to both of them. Observe that in this section the term "well" (*be'er*) is mentioned seven times, which indicates the identification of this well with "Beer-Sheba" (the well of seven). In the narrative of Moses, on the other hand, the well is mentioned only once, when it says, "and he sat down by the well" (*Ibid.* 15). The reason is that Moses completely separated himself from his house here below, whereas Jacob did not separate himself at all. Moses adhered to one, the one of which we read: "My dove, my undefiled, is but one, she is the only one of her mother" (S. S. VI, 9). Moses thus was master of the house and ascended on high; hence of him it is written: "and he sat upon (*'al*) the well", whereas of Jacob it is merely written, "and he saw, and behold a well in the field".

[The following is an alternative exposition of this section. AND JACOB WENT OUT FROM BEER-SHEBA, AND WENT TOWARD HARAN. R. Abba discoursed on the verse: *Happy are they that keep justice, that perform acts of charity (zedakah) at all times* (Ps. CVI, 3). 'Happy are Israel', he said, 'to whom the Holy One, blessed be He, gave the Law of truth so that they should exert themselves in its study day and night, as whoever exerts himself in the study of the Torah achieves complete freedom, even from death, which can no more prevail over him, as already explained elsewhere. For whoever exerts himself in the study of the Torah and lays hold of it, lays hold of the tree of life; and whoever relaxes his hold of the tree of life, behold the tree of death overshadows him and takes hold of him. So Scripture says: "If thou relaxest in the day of adversity, thy strength is narrow indeed" (Prov. XXIV, 10), signifying that whoever relaxes in the study of the Torah, in the day of adversity his strength (*Koah-KoH*=the strength of *KoH*) is narrow indeed, to wit, the strength of *KoH* that continually follows on the right of the man that walks in the ways of the Torah, and forms his constant guard, so that the evil power is prevented from approaching him and is powerless to accuse him. But of him who turns aside from the ways of the Torah and relaxes his hold of it, it is said: "narrow indeed is the strength of *KoH*", as the evil power, represented by the left, obtains dominion over that man and thrusts aside that *KoH*, so that he has no room to move. According to another interpretation, the term "*zar*" (narrow) signifies here "adversary"; for when a man holds fast to the ways of the Torah he is beloved both on high and below, and is the favourite of the Holy One, blessed be He, as we read: "And the Lord loved him" (II Sam. XII, 24); but when a man turns aside from the ways of the Torah, then *ẓar koḥekoh*, that is, the strength of *KoH* becomes his enemy, and makes the evil one obtain dominion over him so as to accuse him in this world and the world to come. For the evil one, who is the same as the evil tempter, dominates the world from many sides, and exercises great power therein; he is indeed the very same mighty serpent through whom Adam fell into sin, and who entices mankind to draw him unto themselves until he draws out their souls. Now his power is over the body, and when he obtains that power over the body, the soul departs because the body has become defiled. To obtain that dominion over the body, however, the evil one must receive authorisation. Further, many evil powers come forth from his side to dominate the world. According to our teachers, all the affairs of the world come under their rule, as he has subordinates and ministers who interfere in all the activities of the world. Hence he is called the "left end". For, as already explained, there is a right end and a left end; and this left end is identical with the "end of all flesh". It is called "the end of all flesh", but not "the end of all spirit". Each is an "end" in the mystical sense, but one presides over flesh, the other over spirit, the latter being the inner one, the former the outer one; one being right, the other left, one being holy, the other defiled, as already explained elsewhere. Now observe a deep and holy mystery of faith, the symbolism of the male principle and the female principle of the universe. In the former are comprised all holinesses and objects of faith, and all life, all freedom, all goodness, all illuminations [153*a*] emerge from thence; all blessings, all benevolent dews, all graces and kindnesses—all these are generated from that side, which is called the South. Contrariwise, from the side of the North there issue a variety of grades, extending downwards, to the world below. This is the region of the dross of gold, which comes from the side of impurity and loathsomeness and which forms a link between the upper and nether regions; and there is the line where the male and female principles join, forming together the rider on the serpent, and symbolised by Azazel. Now from thence there spread many grades which dominate the world, all of them presenting sides of defilement and acting as chieftains and prefects in the world. Observe that Esau, when he emerged into the world, was red all over like a rose, and was hairy after the pattern of a goat (*sa'ir*), and from such a being came forth chieftains and prefects, fully armed, who dominate the world. This has already been explained elsewhere. Observe now the verse previously cited: "Happy are they that keep justice", to wit, they who keep the faith of the Holy One, blessed be He, since God is justice, so that a man should be on his guard not to turn aside but to keep to the way of justice, as God is justice and all His ways are justice. The verse proceeds: "that exercise charity (*zedakah*) at all times". The words "at all times" cannot be taken quite literally, but refer to those who endeavour to follow the ways of the Torah and dispense charity to those who are in need of it. For when charity is given to the poor, its effect is felt both on high and here below. For that charity ascends on high and reaches to the region of Jacob, who is the supernal chariot, and causes blessings to flow toward that region from the very fountain of fountains; and from that charity he causes blessings to flow in abundance to all the lower beings and to all chariots and hosts. All these are blessed and increase in illumination, as is befitting, for they all are comprehended within the term "time" (*'eth*). This, then, is the meaning of the words "that do charity in the whole of time". Observe that as long as Israel were in the Holy Land they drew the blessings from on high to below, but after they went forth from the Holy Land they came under a strange power and blessings were withheld from the world. Jacob was at first under sacred jurisdiction, but when he departed from the land he entered into a strange jurisdiction. And before he came under a strange jurisdiction the Holy One, blessed be He, appeared unto him in a dream, and he saw wonderful things, and holy angels accompanied him until he sat down by the well; and when he sat by the well the waters thereof rose toward him, as a portent that he would there meet his wife, and the same thing happened to Moses. The inward significance of the matter is that the well only rose when it saw its affinity, to form with him a union.']

AND JACOB WENT ON HIS JOURNEY, AND CAME TO THE LAND OF THE CHILDREN OF THE EAST (Gen. XXIX, 1). R. Abba said: 'Since Laban dwelt in Haran, why did Jacob go further on ? That Laban dwelt in Haran we know from the verses: "And Jacob said unto them: My brethren, whence are ye ? And they said: Of Haran are we. And he said: Know ye Laban the son of Nahor ? And they said: We know him" (*Ibid.* 4–5). The truth, however, is that Jacob said to himself: "I wish to enter into communion with the Shekinah, or in other words, I desire to marry. Now, when the servant was sent to take a wife for my father, he found a well of water through which he met my father's destined wife. But, behold, in this place I have found neither spring, nor well, nor any water at all." Straightway he proceeded further, and came to "the land of the children of the East", where he found a well, as already said, and where he encountered his wife.' Said R. Eleazar: 'That place was assuredly Haran, but the well was in an outlying field, and that is why it says that "Rachel ran and told her father" (*Ibid.* 12).' R. Eleazar further remarked: 'Since Jacob had to find his wife by the well, why did he not meet there Leah, who was to be the mother of so many tribes ? The answer is that it was not the will of God that Leah should be espoused to Jacob openly, and in fact he married her without his knowledge, as it is written: "And it came to pass in the morning that, behold, it was Leah" (*Ibid.* 25). It was also in order to rivet his eye and heart on the beauty of Rachel, so that he should establish his principal abode with her. [153b] How did Jacob know that she was Rachel ? We must suppose that the shepherds told him, as it is written, "and, behold, Rachel his daughter came with the sheep" (*Ibid.* 6).'

AND HE SAID: I WILL SERVE THEE SEVEN YEARS FOR RACHEL THY YOUNGER DAUGHTER. Why should Jacob have mentioned seven years rather than ten months or one year ? For one thing, Jacob did not want people to say that he lusted after Rachel's beauty. Also he knew that the wisdom of the moon requires a septennate; and all the seven supernal years hovered over Jacob before he married Rachel, so that his association with her should accomplish its true purpose. For Jacob, before his marriage, first made his own all those years, so that when at last he came to her he should be as it were the heaven to her earth. Hence it says: AND THEY SEEMED UNTO HIM BUT A FEW DAYS. The inner meaning of the word *ahadim* (few, lit. united) is that all those seven years resembled in his eyes those superior years that are bound together so as to form a complete whole and an inseparable unity. The verse continues: FOR THE LOVE HE HAD FOR HER, that is, his desire to reproduce the supernal pattern. R. Abba said: 'Jacob assuredly served seven years in order to join himself to the Sabbatical Year.' R. Eleazar said: 'Observe that the Jubilee Year, wherever mentioned, symbolises that which is undisclosed (to the human mind), whereas the Sabbatical Year symbolises the disclosed. So when Jacob had served the first seven years, a voice went forth and said: O Jacob, it is written: "from one world to the other world" (Ps. CVI, 48). The one world is the upper world, which is veiled, the category of the Jubilee Year. From thence is the starting point; for those which are veiled and undisclosed are from the category of the Jubilee Year.' Hence they were hidden from Jacob, who thus mistakenly thought that his own seven years were from the Sabbatical septennate. Their inwardness was hidden from him in order that he should make a beginning from the highest world, from the Jubilee cycle which is undisclosed. And after the years symbolic of the Jubilee cycle, which is undisclosed, had passed, he served the years of the Sabbatical septennate which are disclosed. He was thus crowned with the two worlds and laid hold of both of them.

Observe that Leah bore six sons and one daughter. That was in the order of things, since six world-directions were stationed above her, and so the six sons and one daughter formed a symbol of the grades. Rachel bore two righteous ones, and this was also in order, since the Sabbatical septennate is placed perpetually between two Righteous Ones, as it is written: "The righteous ones shall inherit the land" (Ps. XXXVII, 29), one Righteous One on high and one below. From the one on high there is a flowing out of upper waters, and from the one below there is a reciprocal welling up of water from the female principle toward the male principle in a perfect ecstasy. There are thus a Righteous One on this side and a Righteous One on that side; and as the male principle above is situated between two female principles, so the female principle below is situated between two Righteous Ones. Hence Joseph and Benjamin represent the two Righteous Ones. Joseph merited to be the (symbol of the) Righteous One on high in virtue of his having kept under guard the sign of the holy covenant. Benjamin was the Righteous One below, so that the Sabbatical septennate was crowned between Righteous Ones, to wit, Joseph the righteous and Benjamin the righteous.

It may be asked, was Benjamin indeed a righteous man? Yes, he was, in that he never in his life transgressed in regard to the sign of the holy covenant. It is true, however, that he was never exposed to a temptation like that of Joseph. If so, why was he called righteous? The reason is that during the whole time of Jacob's mourning for the loss of Joseph he abstained from conjugal intercourse. But, it may be said, when Joseph was carried off, was not Benjamin a mere child? What, then, is the point of saying that he abstained from con- jugal intercourse? The answer is that he abstained from con- jugal intercourse even after he was married. But again we may ask, how is this to be squared with the tradition that Joseph, when he came down to Egypt, asked him whether he had a wife and children, and he answered, "Yes, and they are all named in memory of my brother, to wit, Bela and Becher, and Ashbel, Gera, and Naaman, etc." (Gen. XLVI, 21). How, then, can it be said that he abstained from conjugal relations? The truth, however, is that Benjamin had no children at that time, but he had begotten them already when the brethren went (finally) to Egypt. Benjamin, then, assuredly observed conjugal abstinence all the time his father mourned for Joseph, saying: "Behold, my brother Joseph constituted the sign-of-the-holy-covenant of my father, that sign being the end of the bodily trunk. Now that he is lost I have to guard [154*a*] the place of my brother". One may still object that at the time when Joseph was lost Benjamin had not yet proved himself righteous, and he did not, in fact, do so until the time when he withstood temptation. But the truth is that Jacob knew that Joseph would guard that place, and the others obtained that knowledge from Jacob. It was for that reason that he prolonged his stay with Laban until his body, as it were, was made complete, the completion being constituted by the sign of the holy covenant. Hence it is written: "And it came to pass when Rachel had borne Joseph, etc." (*Ibid.* XXX, 25), Jacob having said to Laban in so many words, "Now that my body has been made complete I am desirous of going." In this way Benjamin knew that his brother was righteous, and he trod in his footsteps. And after Joseph had been found he returned home, had conjugal intercourse, and begat children. God thus declared him righteous here below and Joseph righteous above.

It was thus in the order of things that Rachel bore two sons and Leah six sons and a daughter; and the first seven years were thus veiled from Jacob as they represented the Jubilee cycle; and whilst in intention serving the Sabbatical seven years, which are of the disclosed realm, Jacob in reality served the Jubilee cycle which belongs to the undisclosed realm. So Scripture says: "And Jacob served seven years for Rachel", the term seven years being unqualified, implying that he served for Rachel seven years of the supernal order, and he thus laid hold of both worlds. From here we learn that only through the disclosed can a man reach the undisclosed. If it is asked, how can the first seven years correspond to the Jubilee cycle, seeing that in regard to the latter it is written, "seven times seven years" (Lev. XXV, 8), and here there are no seven times, the answer is that the seven times are represented in the seven days of festivity with which Jacob celebrated his marriage with Leah. The number was thus made complete, since each day may be regarded as sevenfold, in harmony with the verse, "Seven times a day do I praise thee, because of thy righteous ordinances" (Ps. CXIX, 164), and the seven years were thus to be multiplied by the seven days. But, it may be said, Jacob should have first served the Sabbatical septennate and attached himself to the grade of the Sabbatical year. The answer is that since in intention he did serve them, the effect was the same as if he had served them in reality.' R. Abba then came up to R. Eleazar and kissed him, saying: 'Blessed be the Merciful One for the exposition of this verse. Concerning such a privilege, it is written: "The Lord was pleased for his righteousness' sake, to make the Torah great and glorious" (Is. XLII, 21).' R. Eleazar said further:' What has been said about Leah having borne six sons and one daughter and Rachel having borne two sons is assuredly correct; but how do the sons of the concubines fit into the scheme ? They constitute, as it were, the four joints, the so-called hinder parts, alluded to in the statement: "and all their hinder parts were inward" (I Kings VII, 25). For the right arm contains three joints, the middle one of which is the largest and projects backwards, being as it were outside the body. There is a similar joint in the left arm, as well as in the right thigh and in the left thigh; and when the whole is properly arranged, all of them look inward, in fulfilment of the statement, "all their hinder parts were inward". Now all the other joints are in the line of the body, but these protrude outside the arms and the thighs. Correspondingly, the sons of the handmaids, although they are within the number, yet are not of the same rank as the sons of Rachel and Leah, and thus remain outside. According to another explanation, these four are the joints by which all the others are moved.' R. Abba remarked: 'So assuredly it is, and thus the whole is properly constructed.'

AND THE LORD SAW THAT LEAH WAS HATED. R. Eleazar said: 'It is written: "Who sets aright the foundation ('*aqereth*, lit. barren woman) of the house, a joyful mother of children. Hallelujah" (Ps. CXIII, 9). "The foundation of the house" is an allusion to Rachel, whereas by "a joyful mother of children" is meant Leah. According to another explanation, the "foundation of the house" is an allusion to the Sabbatical year, which constitutes the basis of this world; and "a joyful mother of children" signifies the Jubilee year, on which depend the joy and gladness of all the worlds; and this verse comprehends them all in a sacred symbolism, and hence the concluding word, "Hallelujah". We can now understand why it says here that "Leah was hated". This seems strange, in view of the fact that children of a hated woman are of a low type, whereas all Leah's children were of a high type. But the truth is that the Jubilee is a veiled world nothing of which [154*b*] is disclosed to human intelligence; hence Jacob was wholly unaware of it. Now the lower world is intelligible, and is the starting point for the ascending grades. Just as the Supernal Wisdom is a starting point of the whole, so is the lower world also a manifestation of Wisdom, and a starting point of the whole. This world, therefore, is named "Thou" (*attah*), being symbolic of the Sabbatical year, and is intelligible, whereas the upper world, symbolic of the Jubilee, is named He (*hu'* = he, or it), as it is wholly veiled from human understanding. Hence there is an inner significance in the words "and he lay with her that (*hu'*) night". Hence, too, it is written: "And the Levite shall serve *hu* (him)" (Num. XVIII, 23), so as to draw blessings for every one from it, namely from the upper world, which remains for ever veiled. Jacob, however, had no mind to attach himself to the undisclosed, but only to the disclosed, in harmony with the recondite meaning of the verse, "and he shall cleave to his wife" (Gen. II, 25). Also, from the words: "And the Lord saw that Leah was hated" we may learn that a man is not naturally tempted by his mother, and that hence he may remain alone with his mother in any place whatever without any scruple. Observe that it was for the sake of Jacob that the world became firmly established. (For though we have said elsewhere that it was for the sake of Abraham, the truth is that it was for the sake of Jacob that Abraham was firmly established, as it is written: "Thus saith the Lord, concerning the house of Jacob who redeemed Abraham" (Is. XXIX, 22).) For at first God built up worlds and destroyed them, and only when Jacob came did the worlds take their final form, and were not again demolished as heretofore. So Scripture says: "But now thus saith the Lord that created thee, O Jacob, and he that formed thee, O Israel" (Is. XLIII, 1). Israel is also called "son" to God, as it is written: "Israel is my son, my first-born", also, "Let my son go that he may serve me" (Ex. IV, 22–23). There is also the same allusion in the verse: "What is his name, and what is his son's name, if thou knowest" (Prov. XXX, 4).'

AND SHE CALLED HIS NAME REUBEN (lit. see, a son). She did not give him a more specific name, because he was to form a group with the other two, Simeon and Levi. The name Levi, being akin to the term *loyoth* (joining) (1 Kings VII, 30), signifies the perfect combination of them into one scheme. R. Judah said that the same idea is implied in the phrase: "The excellency of dignity, and the excellency of power" (Gen. XLIX, 3), which is rendered in the Chaldaic paraphrase: "Birthright, priesthood, and kingdom", kingdom belonging to the side of power (*Geburah*). Hence the name Reuben, implying "son" (*ben*), simply. R. Abba said that the birth of that triad, as implied in the name Reuben, was the goal towards which Leah strove, as indicated in her utterance: "Now this time will my husband be joined unto me, because I have borne him three sons" (Gen. XXIX, 34), that is, three joined together as one. Observe now that the Heavenly Throne consists of our three patriarchs, to whom King David was subsequently joined, making together a tetrad, symbolic of the Divine Tetragrammaton. Correspondingly we have Reuben, Simeon, and Levi, to whom later on there was joined Judah, who inherited the kingship. Hence the significance of the passage: "This time will I praise the Lord. Therefore she called his name Judah. And she left off bearing", the reason being that now all the four supports of the Heavenly Throne were completed. (Why did she say: "this time will I praise the Lord" in regard to this son and not in regard to any of the others? The truth is that we learn from here that as long [155*a*] as the Community of Israel is in exile the Divine Name remains incomplete.) Observe that with the birth of three sons the Heavenly Throne was not yet made complete until Judah was born; hence only then Leah said, "This time will I praise the Lord", and not in regard to any of the other sons; and hence again the term *vatha'amod* (and she left off, lit. stood), implying that the Heavenly Throne stood then firm on its supports. (This term also indicates that up to that point there is unity, but below that is the world of separation.) As for the two other sons born subsequently with the same characteristics, these were united with the others, constituting together a unity symbolic of the six directions of the world.

Observe further that all the twelve tribes are the integral parts of the Community of Israel in this world, to give full strength to the supernal light, enveloped in blackness, and restore the root principle of the Whole to its place. All the worlds are built on the same pattern; and through this relation the lower world was completed on the pattern of the upper world. By the birth of Issachar and Zebulun there was made complete the number six, symbolic of the six directions of the world. Then again the four sons of the handmaids were associated with them, they being, as it were, the four joints that were linked with them, as already explained. So Scripture says of them: "and their hinder parts were inward" (I Kings VII, 25), to wit, although they were the sons of the handmaids, yet they belonged inward. R. Hizkiah said: 'We have affirmed that what the lower world produces belongs to the category of separation, as it is written "and from thence it was parted" (Gen. II, 11). If so, what about Joseph and Benjamin? How can you say that they belonged to the same world as the others, since they did not issue from the upper world, and what the lower world brings forth is for the lower world and not for the upper world; and, if so, they are separated from the others, since it has been laid down that whatever the lower world produces belongs to the category of separation.' R. Abba came up and kissed him and said: 'This is a real difficulty, since it is true that the upper world becomes perfected by the twelve which properly belong to it. But it can be solved esoterically as follows. At every moment the Righteous One both leaves and enters the lower world. Hence he is built up in this place, while his root is above. Thus he is always present in the lower world.[155*b*] It is written: "And it came to pass as her soul (*nafshah*) was in departing, for she died" (Gen. XXXV, 18). Now the Righteous One is both in and out of this lower world. When he enters it he does so as symbolised by Joseph the righteous; and when he leaves it he does so as symbolised by Benjamin. Hence it says in connection with the birth of Benjamin: "And it came to pass as her soul (*nafshah*) was in departing—for she died", where "her soul" alludes to the Righteous One that was departing, to wit, Benjamin. She called him Ben-oni (son of my sorrow), thinking that what she bore belonged to the lower world, the world of separation, thus leaving only eleven as belonging to the upper world. His father, however, called him Benjamin (son of the right hand) (*Ibid.*), implying that he ascended on high to the upper world; for when Joseph disappeared Benjamin took his place. Thus did the Righteous One both enter the lower world and leave it. Hence Joseph and Benjamin and all the others completed the number of twelve, who formed a unity after the supernal pattern.'

THIS TIME WILL I PRAISE THE LORD. R. Simeon adduced here the verse: "I will praise the Lord with my whole heart (*lebab*), with the council of the upright, and with the congregation" (Ps. CXI, 1). 'The intensified form *lebab* (heart) is used here', he said, 'to show that David desired to praise the Lord with his whole being, including both his good prompter (*yetser-tob*) and his evil prompter (*yetser-ra‘*), or, in other terms, the right side and the left side, the heart (*lebab*), being symbolic of South and North. By the phrase "with the council of the upright" David implied the other directions, making up the six directions of the world, after the supernal pattern; "the congregation" is a reference to the realm of Judah, the term *‘edah* (congregation) being akin to the term *‘eduth* (testimony) in the passage, "and my testimony (*ve-‘edothi*) that I shall teach them" (Ps. CXXXII, 13), as well as to the vocable *‘od* (yet) in the passage, "but Judah yet (*‘od*) ruleth with God, etc." (Hos. XII, 1). On the other hand, in the verse: "I will praise thee with my whole heart (*libi*), toward Elohim will I sing praise unto thee" (*Ibid.* CXXXVIII, 1), David addressed himself to one single realm, designated Elohim[1], singing praises to the grade associated with the right

---

[1] The grade Malkuth, or Kingdom.

side. Observe that Judah embraced all sides, having taken hold of the South as well as of the East; himself issuing from the left side, with his beginning in the North, he took hold of the South, since his turnings were to the right, and attached himself to the body. Hence Leah's words: "This time I will praise the Lord." The words, "And she stood still not to bear any more" imply that there was now a firm standing, that all was now in order, since the Heavenly Throne was now (with the birth of Judah) made complete.'

R. Simeon was once walking in the country when he met R. Abba and R. Hiya and R. Jose. When he saw them he said: 'We ought to have here some new expositions of the Torah.' So the three of them sat down for a time. When he was about to go, each one of them in turn discoursed on a Scriptural text. R. Abba took the verse: *And the Lord said unto Abram, after that Lot had separated from him: Lift up now thine eyes, etc.* (Gen. XIII, 14). 'Did Abraham then', he asked, 'inherit only so much of land as was within his range of vision and no more —a mere three, four, or, at most, five parasangs ? This would contradict the next verse saying: "for all the land which thou seest to thee I will give it" (*Ibid.* 15). But the truth is that in surveying the four directions of the world he saw the whole land, since the four directions embrace the whole world. Furthermore, God raised him high above the Land of Israel [156*a*] and made him see how it is bound up with the four cardinal points. Abram thus looked over the whole of the land. In a similar way, whoever sees R. Simeon sees the whole world, sees the delight of the upper world and the lower world.' R. Hiya followed with the text: "The land whereon thou liest, to thee will I give it, and to thy seed" (Gen. XXVIII, 13). 'Did God, then', he asked, 'promise him no more than that spot, a mere four or five cubits ? The truth, however, is that God at that moment folded up the whole of the land of Israel within those four cubits, so that that spot comprised the whole land. Now, if the whole land can be so concentrated, how much more truly may it be said that R. Simeon, who is the light of the world, is of equal worth with the whole world !' R. Jose then took the passage: "This time will I praise the Lord." 'Was it not', he asked, 'equally incumbent on her to praise God for the birth of her other sons ? But the truth is that Judah, in virtue of being the fourth son, was the completion of the Heavenly Throne. Judah alone is thus the mainstay of the Heavenly Throne and is its truest support. For this very reason, moreover, was he called Judah (*YHVDH*), a word which contains the Divine Name with the addition of the letter *Daleth* (four), pointing to the four supports of the Heavenly Throne. With how much greater force can this be said of R. Simeon, who illumines the whole world with the light of the Torah, and who kindles the light of many lamps !'

AND REUBEN WENT IN THE DAYS OF WHEAT HARVEST, AND FOUND MANDRAKES IN THE FIELD. R. Isaac discoursed on the verse: *How manifold are thy works, O Lord ! In wisdom hast thou made them all; the earth is full of thy creatures* (Ps. CIV, 24). 'Who', he said, 'can count the works of the Almighty, inasmuch as there are hosts upon hosts, and legions upon legions of beings, each differing from the other, all existing simultaneously ? For just as the one hammer-blow causes sparks to fly off in all directions, so God brought into being simultaneously manifold species and hosts, each differing from the other, without number. The world was brought into being by a word and a breath together, as it is written: "By the word of the Lord were the heavens made, and all the host of them by the breath of his mouth" (Ps. XXXIII, 6). One is inoperative without the other, but from their combined action there came into being hosts upon hosts and legions upon legions, and all simultaneously. Now when God was about to create the world, He produced a secret spark from which there issued and radiated all the lights which are disclosed. First there spread from it those lights which constitute the upper world. Then it continued its radiation, and the Artificer made it into a light without brightness, and thus He made the lower world. And by reason of its being a light, but without illumination, it feels itself attracted towards [156b] the upper world. Now it is that light without illumination which through its attachment to the upper world brought into being all those legions and hosts of existences, all the multitudinous species, of which it is written, "How manifold are thy works, etc." And whatever is on earth has its counterpart on high, there being no object, however small, in this world but what is subordinate to its counterpart above which has charge over it; and so whenever the thing below bestirs itself, there is a simultaneous stimulation of its counterpart above, as the two realms form one interconnected whole. This may be illustrated from the verse: GIVE ME, I PRAY THEE, OF THY SON'S MANDRAKES. It was not the mandrakes that made Rachel bear children, but God used them as an instrument for procuring the birth of a child, Issachar, who should hold fast to the Torah more than all the other tribes. For Rachel at first held fast to Jacob and did not let him go to Leah, as it is written: "Is it a small matter that thou hast taken away my husband?" But afterwards Rachel said: "Therefore he shall lie with thee to-night for thy son's mandrakes." Thus the mandrakes were responsible for the birth of Issachar, through whom the fragrance of the Torah ascended to the presence of the Almighty, in harmony with the words: "The mandrakes give forth fragrance" (S. S. VII, 14); and thus it is further written: AND HE LAY WITH HER THAT (*hu*) NIGHT, where the term *hu* (he) points assuredly to Him of the supernal world, which, as already explained, is hidden absolutely. For the Torah came forth from the upper world, which is everywhere pointed to by the vocable *hu* (He), indicating a realm undisclosed. Now Issachar took hold of the Torah, which is called the tree of life, meaning life of the upper world, which is called *hu* (he) and not *attah* (thou). It is clear that it was not the mandrakes that opened Rachel's womb, seeing that it is written "and God hearkened to her, and opened her womb"—God, and no other. For although the mandrakes are endowed with a certain power above, yet that power cannot influence the birth of children, inasmuch as children depend on fate (*mazzal*) and nothing else. However, the mandrakes also are a help to [157*a*] women who are slow in child-bearing but not barren, the latter being under the influence of *mazzal*.'

AND LEAH WENT OUT TO MEET HIM, AND SAID: THOU

MUST COME IN UNTO ME, ETC. This language appears on the surface to be immodest, but really it is a proof of Leah's modesty that she said nothing in the presence of her sister, but went out to meet Jacob, and there told him in a low tone that, though he properly belonged to Rachel, yet I HAVE SURELY HIRED THEE, and have obtained permission from Rachel; and in order that he might not become confused in the sight of Rachel, she spoke to him outside and not in the house. Moreover, one door of Leah's tent faced on the road, and she brought him in by that door before he could enter into the tent of Rachel, so that she should not say anything in the presence of Rachel, which would have been immodest. She further reflected that should Jacob once enter Rachel's tent, it would not be right for her to make him leave it; she therefore intercepted him outside. Leah went to all this trouble because the Holy Spirit stirred within her, and she knew that all those holy tribes would issue from her; and she thus hastened the hour of union in her loving devotion to God, and under the same inspiration she called them by names with deep symbolical meanings.

As R. Hiya and R. Jose were once walking on the road, the latter said: 'Every time we walk together and discuss matters pertaining to the Torah, God performs for us miracles, and now that we have a long road before us let us occupy ourselves in the Torah and so God will join us.' R. Hiya then opened with the verse: *In the first month, on the fourteenth day of the month at even, ye shall eat unleavened bread* (Ex. XII, 18). 'This unleavened bread', he said, 'is called in another place "bread of affliction" (Deut. XVI, 3), an expression on which the companions have commented as follows. When Israel were in Egypt they were under an alien power; and when God desired to bring them near unto Himself, He assigned them the region of the bread of *'oni* (affliction), the term *'oni* admitting also of the reading *'ani* (poor), and thus pointing to King David, who said of himself: "for I am poor (*'ani*) and needy" (Ps. LXXXVI, 1). Now this bread of affliction is called *maẓẓah* (unleavened bread), symbolic of the female principle, which without the male principle is, so to speak, in poverty. Thus Israel were first brought near the grade symbolised by *maẓẓah*.

But afterwards God caused them to enter other grades, until the male principle joined the female principle, and so *mazzah* received the addition of the letter *vau*, symbolic of the male principle, and became converted into *mizvah* (command, precept). So Scripture says: "For this commandment" (Deut. xxx, 7): first *mazzah* (unleavened bread), then *mizvah* (commandment).'

Whilst they were going along they heard a voice saying: 'Ye tent-dwellers who take a crooked path, turn to the high ground and do not descend by the path leading downwards.' R. Jose said: 'This proves that God is guarding our way.' They then took the mountain path and ascended a hill that was situated between huge rocks, saying to themselves: 'Since God desires us to take this road, we are sure to see something of note, or experience some miracle.' They went on and sat down by a cleft in the rock, and were amazed to see a man suddenly emerge from it. 'Who art thou?' said R. Jose. 'I belong to the denizens of *Arqa*,' he answered. 'Are there human beings there?' they asked. 'Yes,' he answered, 'and they sow and reap. Some of them are of a strange appearance, different from my own; and the reason I ascended to you is to learn from you the name of the earth wherein ye dwell.' 'This earth', R. Jose replied, 'is called *erez*, namely, the *erez* (land) of life, of which it is written: "As for the earth (*erez*), out of it cometh bread" (Job xxvIII, 5), implying that only out of this earth cometh bread, but not out of any other, or if it does come, it is not bread of any of the seven kinds.' The man thereupon returned to his place, leaving them astonished. They said: 'Assuredly, God wishes to recall something to our minds through this incident.' R. Hiya then said: 'Assuredly so. Now in regard to the verse you have just cited, I remember that my grandfather pointed out to me an excellent idea in connection with the unleavened bread, namely, that God first gave Israel that bread from the land of life and afterwards He gave them bread from heaven; and so we have affirmed. He further said that a [157*b*] man born into this world knows nothing until he tastes bread, and only then is there an awakening in him of intelligence and power of discernment. In the same way, when Israel left Egypt they were devoid of all knowledge until God made them taste bread of that earth called *erez*, of which it says: "As for the earth (*erez*), bread cometh of it." Then Israel began to know and to recognise God. God, however, desired that they should know also of that place which is the fitting counterpart of this earth, but they were not able to do so until they tasted bread from that place, to wit, heaven, as it says: "I will cause to rain bread from heaven for you" (Ex. XVI, 4). It was only then that they attained to a knowledge and a vision of that realm.' R. Jose came up to R. Hiya and kissed him, saying: 'Assuredly this was the reflection of which God desired to remind us. We learn, then, that the preliminary to Israel's knowledge was bread.' They then arose and proceeded on their way. Whilst walking they noticed two Damascene plums, a male and a female, which led R. Jose to remark: 'There is no species which is not divided into male and female. Further, whatever being exists on dry land has its counterpart in the sea.'

R. Jose discoursed on the verse: AND JACOB CAME FROM THE FIELD IN THE EVENING, AND LEAH WENT OUT TO MEET HIM. 'According to tradition,' he said, 'she knew of his coming through the braying of an ass, and hence Scripture says: "Issachar is an ass large-boned" (Gen. XLIX, 14), where the word *garem* (large-boned) can also be read *garam* (he caused), signifying that the ass was a cause of his birth. Leah said to herself: I assuredly know that should Jacob once enter Rachel's tent I shall not be able to get him out again. I will therefore await him here so that he may enter my tent. FOR I HAVE SURELY HIRED THEE WITH MY SON'S MAN-DRAKES. She mentioned the mandrakes to Jacob, because she thought this would predispose him in her favour, on account of their efficacy for childbirth. Jacob, however, knew that it did not depend on the mandrakes but on heaven. By the words "for I have surely hired thee", Leah may have referred to the Torah, which Jacob embodied. Or she may have meant literally his own self, as much as to say: [158*a*] "I have hired thee so that I may bear thy very image." From here we learn that whoever studies diligently the Torah in-herits the world to come and the inheritance of Jacob. For the name Issachar may be divided into the two words *yesh sakher* (there is a reward), found in the verse: "there is a reward to thy work" (Jer. XXXI, 16), and again: "There is (*yesh*) an inheritance for those that love me, and I will fill their treasures" (Prov. VIII, 21).'

BECAUSE I HAVE BORNE HIM SIX SONS. R. Hizkiah said: 'The six sons prefigured the upward and downward and the four directions of space, and the purpose of prolonging the word *ehad* (in reciting the Shema) is to acclaim God as King on high and below and in the four directions of the world, and so truly one.' R. Hizkiah further said: 'A distinction is to be drawn between "mountains of separation" (S. S. II, 17) and "mountains of spices" (*Ibid.* VIII, 14). The latter are typified by the six sons of Leah, who included within themselves the other six sons, thus constituting all the twelve, with Leah presiding, as it were, over them, in fulfilment of the passage: "the mother of the children is joyful. Praise ye the Lord" (Ps. CXIII, 9). It is therefore written "thou shalt not take the dam with the young" (Deut. XXII, 6), for the reason that she represents the undisclosed world, and hence: "thou shalt in any wise let the dam go, but the young thou mayest take unto thyself" (*Ibid.* 7), inasmuch as she symbolises the world that is absolutely concealed, while "the young thou mayest take unto thyself" in harmony with the verse: "For ask now of the days past, etc., and from the one end of heaven unto the other" (*Ibid.* IV, 22). Now, all these are called "mountains of spices", whereas all which is underneath is called "the mountains of separation", in allusion to the passage: "and from thence it was parted and became four heads" (Gen. II, 10).' R. Jesse said: 'The sons of the handmaids represented the four joints which were necessary for the perfecting of the whole.' R. Eleazar remarked: 'It was for that reason that these joints project outwards, despite the fact that they are all organic parts of the body, which otherwise is perfectly straight; and thus all the tribes ascend as a testimony on high, as Scripture says: "Whither the tribes went up, even the tribes of the Lord, as a testimony unto Israel, to give thanks unto the name of the Lord" (Ps. CXXII, 4).' R. Eleazar further cited the verse:

AND IT CAME TO PASS WHEN RACHEL HAD BORNE JOSEPH, ETC. 'With the birth of Joseph, Jacob saw that the adversary of Esau had appeared, and he therefore made ready to depart. Observe further that Joseph gave, as it were, fixity to Jacob, corresponding to the *Ẓaddik* in whom the Body ends, and so he merited in particular to be called righteous. So when Jacob saw that the Body was made complete, his body conceived the desire to depart, the completion of the body being the sign of the covenant. But for all that it was Benjamin who completed the number of the twelve tribes. Why, then, it may be asked, did Jacob, knowing that the number of the tribes was not yet full, not wait for the birth of Benjamin to complete the number ? The reason is that Jacob was guided by a further consideration. "It is clear", he said, "that if the number of the tribes will be completed here, then divine perfection will rest upon them in the appropriate manner; but in this land it is not desirable that they should attain perfection, but only in the Holy Land." The proof that all the twelve tribes together effect the full realisation of the lower world is to be seen in the fact that immediately Benjamin was born Rachel died, and this lower world fell into its proper place, and attained through them perfect realisation. Hence Benjamin had to be born in the Holy Land and not elsewhere. So Scripture says: "And as for me, when I came from Paddan, Rachel died unto me in the land of Canaan" (Gen. XLVIII, 7). Rachel thus died there, and her place was filled by this lower world, which assumed its rightful place in a completed House. But as long as Rachel was alive the lower world could not be made perfected through them. If it is asked why Leah did not die at the same time, the answer is that the House was in the lower world, and from it all were to be brought to full self-realisation, but it was not in the upper world. This was the reason that Leah did not die at that time. Moreover, all that concerned Leah is kept under a veil, as she typified the upper world, which is veiled and undisclosed; and this is another reason why Leah's death is not divulged like that of Rachel. It is in accordance, too, with this difference between the upper and the lower worlds that Leah was buried away from sight in the cave of Machpelah; whereas Rachel was buried by the open road. Hence it is that all blessings are from two worlds, the disclosed and the undisclosed, though the whole originates from the upper world; [158b] and when we offer blessings to God we invariably associate Him with the two worlds in such words as: "Blessed be the Lord, the God of Israel, from one world even unto the other world" (Ps. CVI, 48). It is for this reason that the upper world is named *Hu* (He), whereas the lower world is named *Attah* (Thou), because it is blessed from the upper world through the Righteous One. Thus Scripture says: "Blessed be the Lord out of Zion, who dwelleth in Jerusalem, etc." (Ps. CXXXV, 21): assuredly it is out of Zion that He is blessed. Observe that we similarly find the divine Name repeated twice in: "The Lord, the Lord . . . merciful and gracious" (Ex. XXIV, 6), alluding to the two worlds, the hidden and the revealed; and this explains the tonal pause between the two. But for all that, the one world and the other form together an absolute unity.'

AND IT CAME TO PASS, WHEN RACHEL HAD BORNE JOSEPH, ETC. R. Judah said: 'Jacob, as a straightforward man, did not wish to leave save by the permission of Laban. In the end, it is true, he did depart without asking Laban's permission, but this was because he feared that Laban would not let him go, and in consequence the last of the twelve tribes would be born in an alien land. Hence, when he saw that the time had come for Benjamin to be born, he fled, as it is written: SO HE FLED WITH ALL THAT HE HAD. For as soon as Benjamin was born, the Shekinah attached herself to the company of the tribes and made her home with them. And Jacob, through his knowledge of the mystic symbolism, was aware that as soon as the twelve tribes should be complete the Shekinah would make them her adornment and attach herself to them, and that Rachel would die and the Shekinah would take possession of the House. Our tradition tells us that the lower world was assigned to Jacob in the same way as it was later to Moses, but this could not be accomplished until there were the full twelve tribes in the House to whom the Shekinah could attach herself. It was then that Rachel was removed, and the Shekinah took up her abode in the House with all the tribes, and become the foundation of the House. Assuredly, "He sets in her place the foundation of the House" (Ps. CXIII, 9). Jacob thus said: "The time has now arrived for the number of the twelve tribes to be completed, so that the upper world will be due to descend into the House to become attached to them, and this poor woman (Rachel) will be thrust out to make room for it. Should she die here, I shall never be able to get away. Moreover, this is not the land where it is fitting that the House should be made complete." Hence AND IT CAME TO PASS, ETC.' R. Simeon, on hearing all this exposition, said: 'Assuredly all R. Judah's expositions are excellent, but this excels them all. Jacob might indeed have departed at once, but he delayed until Rachel was pregnant with Benjamin. Then he fled without asking permission, so as not to linger there any more and so that his union with all the tribes might be effected in the fitting place.'

R. Abba said: 'We read of Moses that "he went and returned to Jethro his father-in-law, etc." (Ex. IV, 18). Now Moses, who was the shepherd of Jethro's flock and lived with him as Jacob with Laban, when he wished to go away first obtained his permission; why, then, did not Jacob, being so upright a man, obtain permission from Laban before leaving him? The truth is, as tradition teaches us, that Jacob feared lest Laban might employ all sorts of devices to make him remain with him longer, as he had done at first. Moses, however, had nothing of the kind to fear from Jethro. Laban was a magician, and in all his dealings with Jacob used magical arts. But Jacob did not wish to remain there any longer, since God had said to him: "Return unto the land of thy fathers, etc." (Gen. XXXI, 3). Jacob thus did not wish to stay and transgress the command of his Master.'

R. Abba further discoursed on the verse: *For the Leader; of the sons of Korah, upon Alamoth. A song* (Ps. XLVI, 1). 'This verse,' he said, 'if properly considered, will be found to contain a deep mystical allusion. And, indeed, all the songs and hymns sung by the sons of Korah were ancient songs and hymns sung anew; and all the songs and hymns sung by David and his associates contain deep allusions of wisdom. Now God has made the lower world after the pattern of the upper world, and all the arrangements laid down by David and Solomon and by all the true prophets were [159a] after the supernal pattern. Observe that in the same manner as there are watches of the night on earth, so are there in heaven relays of angels who sing praises to their Master and intone hymns continually; they all stand ranged in rows, facing each other, and producing one harmony of song and praise. Thus the companions have interpreted the phrase "upon Alamoth. A song". The term "Alamoth", according to them, has a meaning similar to its homonym in the verse: "There are threescore queens, and fourscore concubines, and maidens (*'alamoth*) without number" (S. S. VI, 8), whilst the phrase "without number" finds its echo in the passage: "Is there any number in his armies?" (Job XXV, 3). Hence "maidens without number" all standing in rows upon rows, facing each other, to sing hymns and praises to their Master. These are called "the maidens of song" because there are other maidens who do not chant hymns like these. There are three orders (of singers) arrayed on each one of the four sides of the world, and each order again is subdivided into three sub-orders. The first order on the East contains thus three orders each with three sub-orders, amounting altogether to nine, each of which comprises thousands and tens of thousands of angels. All these nine orders are guided by a signal of engraved letters to which they constantly look up. The same procedure is followed by the rest of the orders, all of whom are similarly guided by engraved letters. Furthermore, they are arrayed in a series of ranks one above the other, all of them chanting praises in unison; and when those letters soar high in the air the chief of them gives the command and a melodious chanting is raised. Then one letter flies up from the lower world, rising and descending, until two letters fly down to meet it; they then join together into a group of three, corresponding to the letters YHV ,which are the three letters within the "illuminating mirror". The two supernal letters which rise aloft are intertwined the one within the other, expressing the union of mercy and severity. Hence they are two, and are of the upper world, symbolising the male principle. On the other hand, the one that ascended from below and joined them symbolises the female principle, and thus is embraced by the two, in the same way as the female is embraced by two arms, the right and the left, so that a unity is formed which is both male and female. For when the world was created it was the supernal letters that brought into being all the works of the lower world, literally after their own pattern. Hence, whoever has a knowledge of them and is observant of them is beloved both on high and below.' R. Simeon said: 'All these letters consist of male and female merging together into one union, symbolical of the upper waters and the lower waters, which also form one union. This is the type of perfect unity. Hence, whoever has a knowledge of them and is observant of them, happy is his portion in this world and in the world to come; as therein is contained the root principle of true and perfect unity. Now, the three orders on each side act in perfect unison, being truly symbolical of the supernal order. The second order on the South consists also of three orders each with three sub-orders, forming a total of nine, as said above. As for the letters, they are distributed on all the sides, so as to become united later, inasmuch as there are letters of the female principle and letters of the male principle, the two classes of which come together to form a unity symbolical of the mystery of the complete divine Name. The third order on the North also comprises three orders each with three sub-orders, amounting to nine. The total number of orders on all three sides thus amounts to twenty-seven, [159*b*] corresponding to the twenty-seven letters, inclusive of the five final letters. These twenty-seven letters distributed over the three sides consist of nine letters of the female principle which join and become united with the other eighteen letters, as has been explained, all being carried out in proper order. Observe that after the pattern of the supernal letters there are other letters here below, the upper letters being large ones and the lower letters small ones, but both of the same pattern. And they both contain the mystery of the male principle and the female principle, which together form a perfect unity.'

AND GOD (*Elohim*) REMEMBERED RACHEL. The name

Elohim is used here because Rachel was still dependent upon a "lucky star", and therefore also the term remembering (*zakhar*) is used here. Of Sarah, however, it is written that "the Lord visited (*paqad*) her" (Gen. XXI, 1), because she did not depend on a lucky star, and so in her case all forces were combined. The reason why in her case the term "visiting" (*paqad*) is used, is that "remembering" had already preceded, and the key to child-birth had already been handed over, as it were, to the lower-world force, God having declared: "But my covenant will I establish with Isaac, whom Sarah shall bear unto thee at this time, etc." (*Ibid.* XVII, 21). Since, then, Isaac had been "remembered" in the higher sphere, he now was noticed within the sphere of the female principle under the process of "visiting", so as to effect a unity of both forces. R. Hiya here discoursed on the verse: *And moreover I have heard the groaning of the children of Israel, whom the Egyptians keep in bondage; and I have remembered my covenant* (Ex. VI, 5). 'The expression "remembering" is used here', he said, 'because it was a process taking place on high, above the starry course (*mazzal*), and in virtue of the male principle, coming on top of the process of "visiting", which operates in exile, here below, in virtue of the female principle. In a similar sense it is written: "And God remembered Rachel", which has a meaning similar to that of the passage: "and I remembered my covenant". Now, if we say that the term "visiting" is used only of the female principle (the Shekinah), we are met with a difficulty in the text: "I have surely visited you". For how could the Shekinah speak thus, seeing that she was herself in exile, and, in fact, how could she appear to Moses at all ? But in truth there is a deep significance in this passage. For as the sun, although his centre is in heaven, yet spreads his power and might throughout the earth, so that the whole earth is full of his glory, so, as long as the Temple was in existence, the whole earth, to wit, the Holy Land, was full of God's glory; but now that Israel is in exile, the Shekinah is on high, but still her might surrounds Israel so as to shield them, even when they are in a strange land. For the Shekinah is both here below and on high. The Shekinah on high abides in the twelve holy chariots and the twelve supernal *Hayyoth;* the lower Shekinah is among the twelve holy tribes, and thus the upper Shekinah and the lower Shekinah are intertwined, and both operate together and simultaneously. Now, when Israel is in exile, the upper Shekinah is not complete because the lower Shekinah is not complete, and that is what is meant by the Shekinah being in exile when Israel is in exile. It is like a king who has lost a son, and who as a sign of his mourning turns over his couch and spreads thistles and thorns on its underside and then lays himself down on it. Similarly when Israel went into exile and the Temple was destroyed, God took thorns and thistles and put them underneath Him, as it were, as it is written: "And the angel of the Lord appeared unto him in a flame of fire out of the midst of a thorn-bush" (Ex. III, 2), the reason being that Israel was in exile. It was now "visiting", as the "remembering" had taken place already, as it says: "And I remembered my covenant." First, then, there was a "remembering", which was now followed by a "visiting", [160*a*] the "visiting" completing the previous "remembering". Similarly with Sarah it says: "And the Lord visited Sarah." But here in the case of Rachel, since she had not yet been "remembered" before, it does not say "visited" but "remembered", a term concerned with luck or fate (*mazzal*).'

R. Judah and R. Hizkiah were once going from Cappadocia to Lydia, the former riding whilst the latter was on foot. R. Judah dismounted and said: 'From now onward let us occupy ourselves with expositions of the Torah, in harmony with the injunction: "Ascribe ye greatness unto our God" (Deut. XXXII, 3).' Said R. Hizkiah: 'It is a pity we are not three, as then one could have expounded while the other two chimed in.' R. Judah rejoined: 'This only applies to the recital of benedictions, one mentioning the name of the Holy One, blessed be He, and the other two responding, in harmony with the verse: "When I proclaim the name of the Lord, ascribe ye greatness unto our God" (*Ibid.*); but in regard to the Torah, even two may sit together and praise the Almighty for the great boon of the Torah.' R. Hizkiah then asked: 'Why are three required for the recital of benedictions?' His companion replied: 'I have just explained, but in truth there is a mystic virtue in the number three for pronouncing the praises of the Almighty, as in this way the blessings are established through a supernal symbolism.' Whilst they were proceeding on their way, R. Judah said: 'We have learned that there is a remembering for good and a remembering for evil; a visiting for good and a visiting for evil. Examples of remembering for good are: "But I will for their sakes remember the covenant of their ancestors" (Lev. XXVI, 45); "And God remembered Noah" (Gen. VIII, 1); "And God remembered his covenant" (Ex. II, 24). An example of remembering for evil is: "So he remembered that they were but flesh" (Ps. LXXVIII, 39). Visiting for good we find in: "I have surely visited you" (Ex. III, 16); visiting for evil we find in, "Then will I visit their transgression with the rod, and their iniquity with strokes" (Ps. LXXXIX, 33). In all these verses there are mystic references. All those remembrances and visitations for good refer to grades of the true object of faith embracing male and female, the one under remembrance, the other under visiting, both being for good. Contrariwise, the remembrance and visitation for evil refer to the other side (*sitra ahra*), with allusions to strange gods, and similarly embracing male and female in one union: the one (male) under remembrance, the other (female) under visitation, both unceasingly intent on evil. There are thus two parallel and opposing influences. From the one there flows all the inspiration of true Faith and all supernal sanctifications; from the other flows whatever is evil, all kinds of death and all sorts and conditions of mischief in the world.' R. Hizkiah said: 'Assuredly it is so. Happy is he whose portion is firmly established on the good side, and who does not incline himself to the other side, but is delivered from them.' Said R. Judah: 'Assuredly it is so, and happy is he who is able to escape that side, and happy are those righteous who are able to wage war against that side.' R. Hizkiah asked: 'How ?' R. Judah, in reply, began to discourse on the verse: *For by wise guidance thou shalt make thy war, etc.* (Prov. XXIV, 6). 'This war', he said, 'alludes to the war against the evil side, which man must combat and overcome, so as to be delivered from it. It was in this way that Jacob dealt with Esau, who was on the other side, so as to outwit him by craft, as was necessary in order to keep the upper hand of him from the beginning to the end, as befitted. Moreover, the beginning and the end fitted into one another, the beginning being "my birthright" (*bekhorathi*), while the end concerned "my blessing" (*birkhothi*), so that the two victories were embodied in two vocables of similar sound. Happy thus is he who escapes them and obtains mastery over them. Observe, again, that remembrance and visitation for good go together in the true faith, and happy is he who strives after true faith in accordance with that which is written: "They shall walk after the Lord, who shall roar like a lion, etc." (Hos. XI, 10).' Said R. Hizkiah: 'Assuredly it is so. Observe that when a man prays, he should not say: "O remember me and visit me", since remembrance and visitation can be for evil as well as for [160*b*] good, and the evil forces are ready to take the word out of the mouth of the suppliant, and thus to make remembrance of the sins of that man and bring punishment on him. Unless, indeed, he be a perfectly righteous man, so that when search is made for his sins he will be unaffected. It was so with Nehemiah when he said: "Remember me, O my God, for good" (Nehem. XIII, 25). Again, when a man prays, it is best that he should merge himself in the general mass of the community. We may take example from the Shunammitess and her answer to Elisha. It happened to be the day of the New-Year on which the heavenly Court sits in judgement over the world, and God is called King of Judgement, when Elisha spoke to her, and hence he asked her: "Wouldst thou be spoken for to the King?" (II Kings IV, 13). But she answered: "I dwell among mine own people" (*Ibid.*), as much as to say: "I have no desire to be marked out on high, but only to be counted among the multitude, and not to stand out apart from them." It is thus requisite for a man to mingle himself among the mass and not to isolate himself, so that no special notice may be taken of his sins, as already explained.'

R. Judah discoursed on the verse: *Have the gates of death been revealed to thee? Or hast thou seen the gates of the shadow of death?* (Job. XXXVIII, 17). 'God', he said, 'addressed these words to Job when He saw him perplexed by the problem of divine justice. Job had said: "Though he slay me, yet will I trust in him (*lo*) (*Ibid.* XIII, 15). The word *lo* is written with an *aleph*, meaning "not", and is read as with a *vau*, meaning "in Him". God said in reply to him: "Am I the one that kills the sons of men ? Have the gates of death been revealed to thee ? And seest thou the gates of the shadows of death ? There are ever so many gates open on that side, over which death ruleth, hidden away from the sons of men, who know them not." There are here mentioned both "death" and "the shadow of death". These are a pair, the one being the angel of death, the other his rider,[1] who also is his protecting shadow and strength, the two being linked together and forming but one being. All the grades that issue from them and are attached to them form their "gates". Corresponding to the gates on high, of which it is written: "Lift up your heads, O ye gates, etc." (Ps. XXIV, 7), and which are called rivers and brooks flowing through the six directions of the world, there are these gates of death and the shadow of death emanating from the other side, forming certain grades that rule over the world. The "gates of death" and the "gates of the shadow of death" are female and male combined into one. Hence, in answer to Job's complaints: "As the cloud is consumed and vanisheth away, so he that goeth down to the grave shall come up no more" (Job VII, 8), and so forth, God said to him: "Are those gates revealed unto thee as being all in my power, and destined one day to be destroyed from off the world, as it is written: 'He shall swallow up death for ever' ? (Is. XXV, 8.)" '

AND GOD (*Elohim*) REMEMBERED RACHEL, AND GOD (*Elohim*) HEARKENED UNTO HER AND OPENED HER WOMB. The name *Elohim* (God) is mentioned here twice, once to represent the male world and the other the female world, the two having been necessary, since the birth of children depends on fate (*mazzal*). Now when Rachel was moved to name her son Joseph, saying, " The Lord add to me another son", Jacob knew that it was she that was destined to complete the number of the tribes, whilst she herself would not

---

[1] The grade *Geburah*.

survive; hence he desired immediately to leave, but he could not carry out his wish. When, however, Benjamin was about to be born, Jacob fled and departed thence, so that the House should not be made complete and the world of holiness become bound up with it in a strange land. So Scripture says: "And the Lord said unto Jacob: Return unto the land of thy fathers, and to thy kindred; and I will be with thee" (Gen. XXXI, 3). God, in effect, said to him: "Until now Rachel was with thee, being the basis of the House; henceforward I will be with thee and will carry on the House with thee in its complement of the twelve tribes". The same idea is implied in the verse: "And as for me, when I came from Paddan, Rachel died unto me ('*alai*, lit. upon me")" (Gen. XLVIII, 7). By the word '*alai* (on me) Jacob meant to say, "it was on account of me and through me that she was thrust out and another one came and took over the house so as to inhabit it with me".

AND HE SAID: APPOINT (*naqebah*) ME THE WAGES, AND I WILL GIVE IT. R. Isaac said: "The term *naquebah* (appoint, akin to *neqebah*=female) signifies that the wicked Laban said to himself, "I see that Jacob has an eye only for females, [161*a*] for the sake of whom he will serve me." He therefore said in effect: "Behold, a female shall be thy wage as before; tell me on what female thou hast cast thine eyes, and I will give her to thee in return for thy service." AND JACOB SAID: THOU SHALT NOT GIVE ME AUGHT. Jacob practically said: "Far be it from me ! For in all my acts I am zealous for the glory of the Holy King, and hence thou shalt not give me aught, as my mind is not set on that, but if thou wilt do this thing for me, etc." '

AND HE REMOVED THAT DAY THE HE-GOATS. R. Eleazar quoted here the verse: *Lord, who shall sojourn in thy tabernacle. . . . He that walketh in perfection, and worketh righteousness, and speaketh truth in his heart* (Ps. XV, 1–2). ' "He that walketh in perfection",' he said, 'refers to Abraham, who, after he had circumcised himself, was called "perfect"; "and worketh righteousness" refers to Isaac; "and speaketh the truth" refers to Jacob, who indeed attached himself to the truth. If that is so, why then did he act towards Laban in this way? The reason is that Jacob wanted to see if the hour was propitious for him, for it is permissible for a man to test his luck before returning to his land. If he finds fortune favourable, well and good; but if not, let him not stir before his luck is in again. It is written: SO SHALL MY RIGHTEOUSNESS WITNESS AGAINST ME HEREAFTER, ETC., for he did not attempt to obtain from Laban anything for nothing, but he acted throughout honestly and uprightly, and, moreover, he asked Laban for permission to depart. Hence Laban himself said: I HAVE OBSERVED THE SIGNS, AND THE LORD HATH BLESSED ME FOR THY SAKE. For Laban tested Jacob by all manner of divinations, and found that he brought him luck; through Jacob he obtained each month a hundred sheep and a hundred lambs and a hundred he-goats more than his flock was wont to produce.' R. Abba said: 'Jacob brought him in a thousand sheep and a thousand lambs and a thousand he-goats extra every month. This is proved by the verse: FOR IT WAS LITTLE WHICH THOU HADST BEFORE I CAME, AND IT HATH INCREASED ABUNDANTLY: AND THE LORD HATH BLESSED THEE FOR MY SAKE. For a blessing from on high never results in less than a thousand of each kind. So that there was a surplus of a thousand in Laban's ewes, and the same in his lambs, and in his goats, until he acquired great wealth, and all through Jacob. But when Jacob came for his recompense, he only obtained ten of each kind, and even this he considered great riches. What a small part then did he take for himself of all that he contributed for the benefit of Laban, and even that he had to force from him, as it were, by means of the rods which he placed against the flock. Observe how Jacob in his simplicity did everything possible to satisfy Laban, and while bringing him all this wealth, he only asked for the spotted and speckled. But for all that Laban consented to this, he would not in the end let him have them, but he took ten of each kind and sent them to him through his sons, saying: "Take these, and whatever they will bear of the sort you said shall be yours." It is thus written: "And your father hath deceived me" (Gen. XXXI, 7), and also, "and thou hast changed my wages ten times" (*Ibid.*

41), the term *monim* (times, akin to minim = kinds) indicating ten of each kind. So whatever agreement Laban made with Jacob, he went back on his word and took from him everything, until God had compassion on him, so that he wrested what was his own from him by force, as it were.' R. Eleazar remarked that all these verses contain deep lessons, based on what we have learned from tradition, to wit, that some blessings from above are obtained by action, some by speech, and others by devotion. So that whoever wishes to draw down to himself blessings must exercise prayer, which consists of speech and devotion; yet there are blessings that cannot be obtained by prayer, but only by action.

Observe that Jacob, the simple man, acted throughout with wisdom. AND HE SET THE RODS—we read—WHICH HE HAD PEELED OVER AGAINST THE FLOCKS IN THE GUT-TERS IN THE WATERING TROUGHS. This was all done with esoteric wisdom so as to draw benedictions from the chief well-spring that waters all the supernal grades which were his lot and portion. The rods were symbolic of the grades embodying judgement, which he had "peeled", that is, the severity of which he had mollified. "In the gutters" (*rehatim*) finds its echo in the passage: "The king is bound to the gutters (*rehatim*)" (S. S. VII, 5), [161*b*] indicating that the supernal King is tied and bound to those supernal aque-ducts whence flow benedictions for all, "Flowing in the watering troughs"; to wit, in the rivers and brooks that flow on until they reach their final reservoir. Again, "where the flocks came to drink" is parallel with the verse: "They give drink to every animal of the field, the wild asses quench their thirst" (Ps. CIV, 11), both alluding to the reservoir, the gather-ing place of all the waters whereto all resort to drink. "And they were heated" (*vayeḥamnah*). When the north wind blows, the waters become frozen, they stop flowing, so that no one comes to drink of them. This is the time when judgement im-pends over the world, and the cold of the North freezes the waters. But when the south wind arises, the waters become warmer, and, the ice being melted, flow on their way, and all come to drink of them; for the southern warmth having caused the waters to thaw, all come to drink with relish the waters after they have been freed from the icy grip of the North. Thus all that Jacob did contained a deep symbolic purpose. Further it is written:

AND JACOB TOOK RODS OF FRESH POPLAR, ETC. R. Eleazar discoursed here on the verse: *For the Lord hath chosen Jacob unto himself and Israel for his own treasure* (Ps. CXXXV, 4). 'From the actual words of the original', he said, 'we could not tell whether it was the Lord who chose Jacob or vice-versa. That the former is meant we know from the parallel verse which says: "For the portion of the Lord is his people, Jacob the lot of his inheritance" (Deut. XXXII, 9). Nevertheless, it is also true that Jacob on his part, too, has chosen his heritage and his portion, and, rising above all intermediate grades, has taken for his lot "rods of fresh poplar" (*libneh*= white), symbolic of the white grade of the Right side, and "of the almond and of the plane-tree", symbolic of the red grade of the Left side; "and peeled with streaks in them", signifying that he removed severity from the Left, and linked the Left with the Right, while he entered between and laid hold of both of them together, so that there resulted one united blend of two colours, but at the same time "making the white appear", i.e. predominate over the red. Why all this ? So as to draw to the grade which was his own portion blessings from the universal well-spring, and to place that grade, which is the third, "in the gutters in the watering-troughs", as has been already explained. Now from these operations of Wisdom blessings flow to the lower world, and all worlds are watered and beatified, as it says: "In the morning he devoureth the prey" (Gen. XLIX, 27), and after that: "and at even he divideth the spoil" (*Ibid.*), so that the blessings pass [162*a*] to all the lower worlds. Jacob, too, took his portion of those blessings that rested upon him in this world, inasmuch as he is the portion and lot of the Holy One, blessed be He.'

R. Jesse the Younger was a frequent visitor at the school of R. Simeon. Referring one day to the verse: "Blessings are upon the head of the righteous" (Prov. X, 6), he asked: 'Why does it say "upon the head of the righteous", and not simply "upon the righteous" ?' R. Simeon in answer said: 'This is

an allusion to the Holy Crown, as has been explained elsewhere. Or again, the "head of the righteous" can be an
allusion to Jacob, who received the blessings and transmitted
them to the Righteous One, from whom they were diffused
to all sides, so that all worlds were blessed. We have, however,
affirmed that "Righteous" is the name given to the place of
the covenant whence there issue fountains abroad, and just as
the aperture of a wine cask through which the wine is drawn
is called the top or head of the cask, so is this spot called "the
head of righteous", when it wells forth into the female.
Furthermore, whoever succeeds in keeping unsullied the
sign of the holy covenant, and observes the precepts of the
Torah, is called righteous, and is so called from the crown of
his head to the sole of his foot; and when blessings flow into
the world they rest upon his head, from whence they are
diffused throughout the world, through the medium of the
holy and worthy sons whom he brings up.' R. Jesse further
cited the verse, *I have been young, and now am old; yet have I
not seen the righteous forsaken* (Ps. XXXVII, 25). 'These words,'
he said, 'according to our teaching, were uttered by the
Chieftain of the world, who concentrated in them more
wisdom than most people would think.' R. Simeon said to
him: 'My son, that is quite true, as it deals with the subject
of holy union. It is a laudation of this unity, in which day is
never found without night, for night is ever found in day.
Now the Righteous One holds fast to the upper world and
also to the lower world. As for the words "nor his seed begging bread", the meaning is that when the seed flows forward,
he does not court the Female, since she abides with him and
never parts from him, and hence is ever in a state of readiness
for him. For the seed does not flow save when the Female is
present, [162b] and their mutual desires are blended into one
indissoluble ecstasy. Hence he has no need to ask for consent.'
R. Jesse remarked: 'This surely is not the case during the
time of exile.' R. Simeon rejoined: 'As regards the seed it is,
since it is written "his seed" but not he himself; that is, the
outpouring of the blessings only occurs when there is close
union of the female with the male. It may be asked then, does
the assertion, "and I have not seen a righteous forsaken"

apply to the time of exile ? The truth is that the Righteous One is always closely bound to the upper world and so far is never abandoned. Thus at one time, that is, at the time of exile, the Righteous One is not forsaken from the side of the upper world, to which he holds fast, whilst at another time he is not forsaken from the two sides, holding fast to both, the upper and the lower worlds, so that in fact he is never forsaken.'

This *Zaddik* is also called "the firmament of the heaven" (Gen. 1, 17). For there are two similar firmaments, one at the beginning and one at the end of the series of eight. The top one is the eighth firmament, the one in which there are set all the lesser and the greater stars. It is the undisclosed upper firmament which upholds the totality of things and from which all existence flows. This is the eighth firmament counting from below, and is thus the top one and the starting-point from which all things receive their existence. Correspondingly there is an eighth firmament counting from above, in which also are set all stars and lights and lamps. This firmament supports the whole and forms the end of the whole. Thus the top firmament and the end firmament are of the same pattern, forming together the river that flows on perennially so that the end is already enclosed in the beginning. Hence it says: "And God set them in the firmament of heaven." For what purpose ? "To give light upon the earth." There is, however, a difference between the two firmaments, for while the upper one sustains and nourishes the upper world in which it is set and all those upper sides, the lower firmament sustains and nurtures the lower world and all those lower sides. It may be asked, what is meant here by the "upper world", seeing that the upper eighth firmament, which is hidden and undiscoverable, is itself the upper world and is so called ? But the truth is that while it itself forms the upper world proper, all those that emanate from it are also designated by that name. It is the same with those that emanate from the lower world, they also being designated by its name. Yet all of them form one unity. Blessed be He for ever and ever ! It is written: *The trees of the Lord have their fill, the cedars of Lebanon which he hath planted; Wherein the birds make their nests; as for the stork* (*ḥasidah*), *the fir trees are her house* (Ps. CIV, 16–17). The allusion of Lebanon has been explained already elsewhere. The birds also are the two referred to in many places [163*a*] as those from which there emerge hosts of other birds. They themselves, however, are superior, as emanating from Lebanon, which is in the supernal realm. They are hinted at in the words "Laban had two daughters". The "fir-trees" are the six supernal sons, symbolic of the six directions of the world, as already explained elsewhere. In them "the stork has made her house". Why is it called here by the feminine form *ḥasidah* (stork, lit. filled with mercy) ? The truth is that this upper world is really of the female principle, but we usually give it a masculine name (*ḥesed*), inasmuch as in its unfolding it is the source whence all beneficence and all light come forth. And thus, as it is *ḥasidah*, there springs from it *ḥesed* (mercy), which is the primordial light referred to in the statement: "And God said, Let there be light" (Gen. I, 3). It is thus that region of which it says: "fir-trees are her house", where the word *beroshim* (fir-trees) may be read *berashim* (at the heads, or head), signifying that there is another world (*Geburah*) which has its habitation below and constitutes the Court of Justice of this world. It is to this that we can refer such expressions as: "And it repented the Lord . . . and it grieved him at his heart" (*Ibid.* V, 6), or "the fierce anger of the Lord", for in the realms above there resides only light spreading life all around. Hence the dictum: "there is no grief in the presence of God". Hence, too, it is written: "Serve the Lord with gladness; come before his presence with singing" (Ps. C, 2), the word "Lord" alluding to the upper world, and the word "presence" to the lower world. Happy are Israel in this world and in the world to come. So Scripture says: "Happy art thou, O Israel, who is like unto thee ? A people saved by the Lord, the shield of thy help, and that is the sword of thy excellency ! etc." (Deut. XXXIII, 29).

AND HE SET THE RODS WHICH HE PEELED IN THE GUTTERS, ETC. Said R. Eleazar: 'There are sinners who either neglect altogether the words of the Torah, or if they do cast an eye on them, think them mere foolishness. But in truth the foolishness is in their own minds, since all the words of the Torah are sublime and precious, and of every word it is written: "She is more precious than rubies; and all the things thou canst desire are not to be compared with her" (Prov. III, 15). Woe to all these foolish and senseless people, when the Holy One, blessed be He, will demand an account from them for the insult done to the Torah and they will be punished for having rebelled against their Master. So Scripture says: "For it is no empty thing for you" (Deut. XXXII, 47), implying that if it is an empty thing, its emptiness is from you yourselves, seeing that all the things one can desire are not to be compared with her. How can they say that the Torah is an empty thing seeing that Solomon said: "If thou art wise, thou art wise for thyself" (Prov. IX, 12), implying that whoever becomes wise in the Torah benefits himself thereby ? Thus the Torah is filled with all riches and no one can add thereto even one letter. "But if thou scornest, thou alone shalt bear it" (*Ibid.*), since the worth of the Torah will be in no wise diminished thereby, and the scorning will only recoil on the head of the scorner so as to cause him to perish in this world and in the world to come. Observe now. When the supernal letters are joined together and attach themselves to that grade which is the last of all the supernal holy grades, and it becomes filled from them and enriched with blessings from the upper world, this same grade is in readiness to "water all the flocks" according to their requirements, each one being watered both with judgement and mercy. Now Jacob desired to institute evening prayer and so restore the light of the moon and water her and enrich her with blessings on all sides. Hence it is written, "And he set the rods, etc." These rods signify severity and force, which issue from the supernal *Geburah*. So Jacob, in his desire to put himself right with that grade, "set the rods", that is, he removed all the influences of severity and force symbolised by the rods, and "placed them in the gutters", to wit, those four gutters[1] that stand underneath "the well, which the princes digged" (Num. XXI, 18), the well which was filled from those supernal rivers and fountains; for when water comes forth out of that sacred well,

---

[1] i.e. the four *Ḥayyoth*, v. Ezek. I, 5.

these four receive the whole of it, they being called gutters (*rehatim*=swift runners) for that reason, and to that source [163*b*] they all come to drink, taking of those implements of severity and force what is fitting for each. So it says: "over against the flocks". Further it is written, "and they conceived" (lit. grew hot); that is to say, when they are invested with power to punish, they become heated thereby, and then they set out to roam to and fro in the world and closely inspect the ways of men, whether for good or for evil. Further we read: "And the flocks became heated at the sight of the rods", inasmuch as these rods become hot and take charge of the judgements to be meted out to the world, and the sons of men receive their punishments through them, as we read: "The sentence is by the decree of the angels, and the decision by the word of the holy ones" (Dan. IV, 14).'

R. Hiya discoursed on the verse: *My soul cleaveth unto thee; thy right hand holdeth me fast* (Ps. LXIII, 9). 'King David', he said, 'could speak thus because his soul ever clave to God, and he had no care for worldly matters, and therefore God supported him and never let him go; and so it is with every man who cleaves to God. Or again, David may have meant these words as a prayer that his grade should be crowned in the supernal realm, for when that grade clings to the supernal grades to ascend after them, then the right hand of God lays hold of it, raises it, and unites it to itself, as we read: "And thy right hand would hold me" (Ps. CXXXIX, 10), also: "And his right hand should embrace me" (S. S. VIII, 3). Hence David's words: "Thy right hand holdeth me fast." Of him who does hold fast to the Holy One, blessed be He, it is written: "His left hand should be under my head, and his right hand should embrace me" (*Ibid.*), an expression indicative of perfect attachment and union.'

When the water pours into those gutters, they are filled on all four sides, so that all the flocks can be watered each from its proper side. Now when Jacob essayed to perfect his grade, he chose for himself the right side which befitted him, and allowed the left side which did not befit him to part from him, as it is written: "and he put his own droves apart, and put them not unto Laban's flocks". "Apart", that is, by himself, so that he should not avail himself of alien idols of the other sides. Happy the portion of Israel of whom it is written: "For thou art a holy people unto the Lord thy God, and the Lord hath chosen thee, etc." (Deut. XIV, 2). Now Jacob was the crown of the patriarchs and their epitome, summing them all up within himself, and he therefore set about to restore the light of the moon, as well as to institute the evening prayer; and all this work was well becoming him, as thereby he perfected all those sides of holiness which belonged to his side, and separated his portion from the portion of the other nations. The former are the supernal sides, sanctified with the supernal sanctities, whilst the latter are utterly defiled and unclean. So that Jacob, as already explained, "put his own droves apart"; that is, he prepared himself for the adoption of a faith which should keep him apart, as it is written: "and the Lord hath chosen thee to be his own treasure out of all peoples" (Deut. XIV, 2); "and put them not unto Laban's flock", that is, he did not place his portion and lot with them. Jacob thus, being the perfection of the patriarchs, established the true faith, and separated his own portion and lot from that of other peoples. To such an action could be applied the words: "But ye that did cleave unto the Lord your God are alive every one of you this day" (*Ibid.* IV, 4). Said R. Abba: 'Happy is the portion of Israel, who are exalted above the idolatrous nations, in virtue of their grade being above on high, whereas the grade of the idolatrous people is down below. The former are of the side of holiness, the latter of the side of uncleanness; they are on the right, the others on the left. But when the Temple was destroyed, then it could be said, "He hath drawn back his right hand" (Lam. II, 3), wherefore also it is written: "Save me with thy right hand and answer me" (Ps. LX, 7); and the left side has since been gathering force and uncleanness, and will continue to do so until God shall rebuild the Temple and establish the world on its right foundation, and the right order shall be restored, and the side of uncleanness shall pass out of the world, as it says: "and I will cause the unclean spirit to pass out of the land" (Zech. XIII, 2), [164*a*] also: "He will swallow up death for ever" (Is. XXV, 8). God will then remain alone, as it is written: "And the idols shall utterly pass away" (*Ibid.* 11, 18), also: "and the Lord alone shall be exalted in that day" (*Ibid.* 17). He alone, then, will be left, as it is written: "And there was no strange God with him" (Deut. XXXII, 12), the unclean host being then extirpated from the world, so that both in the upper world and in the lower world there will be no other left save God alone, with Israel, the holy people, worshipping Him. For Israel will then be designated holy, as it is written: "And it shall come to pass, that he that is left in Zion, and he that remaineth in Jerusalem, shall be called holy, even every one that is written unto life in Jerusalem" (Is. IV, 3). There will thus be one and only one King on high and below, and one and only one people to worship Him, as it is written: "And who is like thy people Israel, a nation one in the earth . . . ?" (I Chron. XVII, 21).'

R. Isaac and R. Jesse were once walking together on the road. Said R. Jesse: 'Behold, the Shekinah is near us. Let us therefore engage in an exposition of the Torah, since whoso occupies himself with the Torah draws Her nearer to himself.' R. Isaac then began a discourse on the verse: *The Lord liveth, and blessed be my Rock, and exalted be the God of my salvation* (Ps. XVIII, 47). 'This verse', he said, 'has a recondite meaning. We know that God is called "the living one". But this verse indicates that the perfectly righteous man also is called "living one", so that there is a righteous living one on high, and correspondingly a righteous living one here on earth. On high it is God who is called "living one", and here below it is the righteous man who is called "living one", as it is written: "And Benaiah the son of Jehoiada, the son of a living man"[1] (II Sam. XXIII, 20). He was so called because he was a righteous man, and the righteous man is called "living one". The words "blessed by my Rock" have the same reference, since the Living One and the Blessed One are never parted, and when united are called "well of living waters"; the one flows in, and the other is filled therewith. "And exalted be the God of my salvation"; this indicates the supernal world, which is high and exalted over all, inasmuch

---

[1] According to the *K'tib.*

as from it everything springs, even all the outpouring by which the well is filled, receiving therefrom blessings to spread light among all the dwellers of the lower world. And when the whole is filled properly, then "exalted will be the Rock of salvation".' R. Jesse then discoursed on the verse: *He withdraweth not his eyes from the righteous; but with kings upon the throne he setteth them for ever, and they are exalted* (Job XXXVI, 7). 'When', he said, 'the domination of the wicked ceases and they perish from the world, then the righteous obtain dominion, as it says: "He preserveth not the life of the wicked, but giveth to the poor their right" (*Ibid.* 6). The words, "He withdraweth not from the righteous his eye" are parallel to the text, "The eyes of the Lord are toward the righteous" (Ps. XXXIV, 16). "But with kings upon the throne"; these are the kings who are, as it were, united to their thrones, and whom He setteth for ever so that they remain immovably established. "And they are exalted", to wit, to rule over the world so that the throne remains firmly established on its supports. Or, again, it may mean that they raise the throne and set it up on high so that it should become united to its proper place and there should thus be a complete unity.'

Whilst they were proceeding on their way they caught sight of a man coming towards them, with a child riding on his shoulders. Said R. Isaac: 'This man is without doubt a Judean, and he wants to give people a chance to do a good action.' Said R. Jesse: 'Let us be the first to take advantage of the opportunity.' When he came up to them, R. Jesse asked him: 'Whereto is the saffron pot set on the path?' The man replied: 'So as to afford people an opportunity of doing a pious action; for I have two sons who were taken captive by a brigand who passed through my native town, and now I am on the road in order to afford people the opportunity of doing a good action.' The two thereupon availed themselves of the occasion and gave him food to eat. The Judean then began a discourse on the verse: *My food which is presented unto me for an offering made by fire, of a sweet savour unto me, shall ye observe to offer unto me in due season* (Num. XXVIII, 2). 'The offering brought unto the Holy One, blessed be He, every day,' he said, 'was for the purpose of feeding the world and providing sustenance both for the upper world and the lower world, inasmuch as the upper world moves in response to the lower world, with the result that every one is supplied according to his due. The words, "My food which is presented to me as an offering", are paralleled by the verse, "I have eaten my honeycomb with my honey; I have drunk my wine with my milk" (S. S. v, 1); and "made by fire" by the words: "Eat, O friends, drink, yea, drink abundantly, O beloved" (*Ibid.*). Now, if God assigns food above in order that therefrom food may be dispensed below, with how much more reason must he who offers food for the preservation of a soul be rewarded, in that God will bless him and direct to him sustenance from on high, so that the world will receive blessings for his sake!' R. Isaac remarked: 'Assuredly this is the inner meaning of the verse.' R. Jesse said: 'This incident assuredly bears out the admonition of the Sages that no man should ever treat slightingly another man, for this man has occasioned us a double privilege.'

The stranger then continued his discourse on the above verse, but in the name of [164*b*] R. Eleazar. 'The accusative particle "*eth*" here,' he said, 'alludes to the Community of Israel; the "offering" is a connecting link (between high and low); "my food" is an allusion to the food that descends from on high in response to the stirring here below; "as a fire offering" includes all the other hosts which receive their necessary sustenance each one in proper measure; "of a sweet savour unto me" signifies the uniting of the whole in one bond of unity and good will so as to form an emblem of the upper world; "shall ye observe to offer unto me in due season" alludes to the time when Abraham bestirred himself to do the will of God, regarding which it is written: "And Abraham rose early in the morning" (Gen. XXII, 3), and also to the time when Isaac was bound on the altar, which was at eventide.' Said R. Jesse: 'In that case, we should rather have expected the plural "seasons".' The Judean in reply said: 'At the time of the sacrifice, fire and water are intermingled and become one, and hence it says "season" and not "seasons". The expression "ye shall observe to offer unto me" is used in connection with this offering only, the reason being that this offering ascends to the highest grade in an intermingling of the Right and the Left, symbolised by Abraham and Isaac.' Said R. Jesse: 'If only to hear this, it was worth our while coming here. Happy are Israel in this world and in the world to come! In regard to this it is written: "Thy people are all righteous, they shall inherit the land for ever; the branch of my planting, the work of my hands, wherein I glory" (Is. LX, 21).'

NOW LABAN WAS GONE TO SHEAR HIS SHEEP, ETC. R. Jose said: 'The teraphim were idols, so called out of contempt, the name being akin to the word *toreph* (obscenity). The proof that they were idols is found in Laban's question: "Wherefore hast thou stolen my gods ?" as well as in Jacob's words: "With whomsoever thou findest thy gods, etc." For Laban was a great sorcerer who practised all kinds of magical arts, and it was by such means that he learnt all that he wished to know.' R. Hiya said that the powers of the idol were derived from wizardry; R. Jose, from divination. R. Judah said: 'They were derived from a close observance of the times and moments for striking and for holding off. At one moment the craftsman would use his hand to beat it into shape, and another he would relax. Hence the term *teraphim*, akin to *hereph* (relax) (II Sam. XXIV, 16). For when the craftsman was making it, the man who knew the proper seconds and hours stood over him, saying now "strike", and now "stay". There is no other work which requires to be timed in this way. Now, this magic idol was continually uttering evil counsel, and prompting to mischief. Rachel thus feared lest it should counsel her father to do mischief to Jacob, and by reason of her contempt for the idol she placed it underneath her, so that it was not able to speak; for whenever it was consulted they used to sweep and clean up before it. The teraphim were a male and a female image, and a number of ceremonies had to be performed before them before they would speak. Hence Laban delayed three days before pursuing, as he was unaware of Jacob's flight, as it says: AND IT WAS TOLD LABAN ON THE THIRD DAY THAT JACOB WAS

FLED.' R. Judah further said: 'Laban prepared himself in two ways: he equipped himself with all his magical arts and also with ordinary weapons in order to destroy Jacob, as it is written: "An Aramean was going to destroy my father" (Deut. XXVI, 5). So when God saw that he intended to destroy Jacob, He warned him, saying: TAKE HEED TO THYSELF THAT THOU SPEAK NOT TO JACOB EITHER GOOD OR BAD. This is borne out by Laban's words: IT IS IN THE POWER OF MY HAND TO DO YOU HURT, to wit, through his magical arts. Observe that Laban covered in one day a distance that took Jacob seven days, and all in order to destroy him utterly; first because he had fled, and secondly for the loss of the teraphim. Now, as regards Rachel, although her purpose was to wean her father from idolatry, yet she was punished by not surviving to bring up Benjamin or even to live with him a single hour; and all on account of the pain she caused her father, notwithstanding her good intention.' R. Isaac said: 'All this reproof which Jacob administered to Laban served to make him acknowledge the Holy One, blessed be He, as is proved from Laban's words: SEE, GOD IS WITNESS BETWIXT ME AND THEE. But observe that it is further written: THE GOD OF ABRAHAM, AND THE GOD OF NAHOR . . . JUDGE BETWIXT US. This indicates that, sinner as he was, he reverted to his former idolatrous worship, for after invoking the God of Abraham, he immediatey added "the God of Nahor".' [165*a*] AND JACOB SWORE BY THE FEAR OF HIS FATHER ISAAC. Why by "the fear of Isaac" and not by the God of Abraham ? Because he did not wish to trouble, as it were, the right-hand grade for the sake of Laban; furthermore, it is not right for a man to swear, even a true oath, by the most high realm. R. Jose said: 'Truly, Jacob's oath was most appropriate to the occasion. For he said to himself: "Behold, he has invoked the God of Abraham, but left out the name of my father; let me therefore make up the deficiency." Hence he swore by the "fear of his father Isaac". Another explanation is that Jacob desired to bring the grade of severity on to his side to assist him against Laban.'

AND JACOB WENT ON HIS WAY, AND THE ANGELS OF
GOD MET HIM. R. Abba discoursed on the verse: *Male and
female created he them, etc.* (Gen. v, 2). 'How incumbent it is
upon us', he said, 'to study intently the words of the Torah !
Woe to those whose heart is obdurate and whose eyes are
blinded ! Behold, the Torah is calling unto them, saying:
"Whoso is thoughtless, let him turn in hither; as for him that
lacketh understanding, she saith to him: Come, eat, of my
bread, and drink of the wine which I have mingled" (Prov.
IX, 4–5). But there is no one to pay attention to her. Observe
that this verse contains sublime mysteries, it has an inner and
an outer meaning. Thus, one meaning is that the sun and
moon are closely united, as is implied in the passage: "The
sun and the moon stand still in *her* habitation" (Hab. III, 11);
and another is that Adam and Eve were created as a united
pair; and since they were coupled together, God blessed
them. For blessing does not reside save in a spot where there
are male and female. Observe that when Jacob set out on his
journey to Haran he was all by himself, not yet having married. What does Scripture say of that occasion ? "And he
lighted upon (*vayifga'*=entreated) the place, etc." (Gen.
XXVIII, 11), and he was only promised deliverance in a dream.
But now that he was married and was coming with all the
tribes, heavenly legions entreated and supplicated him, as it
were, for we read: "And the angels of God met (*vayifge'u*=
entreated) him." Whereas before it was he who entreated the
"place", now it was they who entreated him, for the reason
that it was for the sake of Jacob and the tribes that they were
watered from the great sea. Moreover, whereas before he saw
them only in a dream of the night, now he saw with open eyes
and in full daylight, as it is written: AND JACOB SAID
WHEN HE SAW THEM: THIS IS GOD'S CAMP, ETC. [165*b*]
How, it may be asked, did he recognise them ? The answer is
that they were the same angels whom he had seen in his
dream. Hence he called them *Mahanaim* (two camps),
indicating the camp which had appeared to him on high and
the camp which appeared now below. Why did they appear
unto him to entreat him ? Because the Shekinah accompanied
him in order to bear along his household, and she was also

awaiting the birth of Benjamin so as to make her home with Jacob as pre-ordained. It is in allusion to this that Scripture says: "And Jacob shall again be quiet and at ease, and none shall make him afraid" (Jer. xxx, 10). Blessed be the Lord for evermore. Amen and Amen !'

VAYISHLAH

Gen. XXXII, 4–XXXVI, 43

AND JACOB SENT MESSENGERS (lit. angels), ETC. R. Judah discoursed on the text: *For he will give his angels charge over thee, to keep thee in all thy ways* (Ps. XCI, 11). 'According to the companions,' he said, 'the moment a child is born into the world, the evil prompter straightway attaches himself to him, and thenceforth brings accusations against him, as it says, "sin coucheth at the door" (Gen. IV, 7), the term "sin" being a designation of the evil prompter, who was also called sin by King David in the verse: "and my sin is ever before me" (Ps. LI, 5). He is so called because he makes man every day to sin before his Master, never leaving him from the day of his birth till the end of his life. But the good prompter first comes to man only on the day that he begins to purify himself, to wit, when he reaches the age of thirteen years. From that time the youth finds himself attended by two companions, one on his right and the other on his left, the former being the good prompter, the latter the evil prompter. These are two veritable angels appointed to keep man company continually. Now when a man tries to be virtuous, the evil prompter bows to him, the right gains dominion over the left, and the two together join hands to guard the man in all his ways; hence it is written: "For he will give his angels charge over thee, to keep thee in all thy ways." '

R. Eleazar applied this verse to Jacob when God assigned to him companies of angels as an escort because he came with the full number of tribes, forming with them a godly company. Hence it says: "And Jacob went on his way, and the angels of God met him" (Gen. XXXII, 2), as already explained. Here, therefore, when he was delivered from the hands of Laban and dissociated himself from him, the Shekinah joined him, and sacred camps came to encircle him, so that [166*a*] "Jacob said when he saw them, etc." (*Ibid.* 3). It was from these angels that he sent a mission to Esau, as it says: "And Jacob sent angels" (*mal'akhim*).' R. Isaac said: 'Why, in one place in the Psalms does it say "The *angel* of the Lord encampeth round about them that fear him and delivereth them" (Ps. XXXIV, 8), in the singular, and in another place, "For he will give his *angels* charge over thee" (*Ibid.* XCI, 11), in the plural? The reason is that the term "angels" is a reference to angels proper, whereas in the verse: "The angel of the Lord encampeth", the reference is to the Shekinah, as in the verse: "And the angel of the Lord appeared unto him in a flame of fire out of the midst of a bush" (Ex. III, 2). Thus "the angel of the Lord encampeth round about those who fear him" to deliver them; and when the Shekinah abides within a man, ever so many holy legions rally round him. David uttered this verse when he escaped from Achish the king of Gath, because the Shekinah encompassed him and delivered him from Achish and his people, and all those who assailed him. It is written in the same connection: "And he feigned himself mad (*vayitholel*) in their hands" (1 Sam. XXI, 14). The term *vayitholel* here, in place of the more usual *vayishtagea'*, contains an allusion to the kindred term used formerly by David when he said: "For I was envious of the madmen (*holelim*)" (Ps. LXXIII, 3). God thus said in effect to David: "As thou livest, since thou enviest madmen, thou thyself wilt yet be driven to play the madman"; and so it came to pass when he was brought before Achish and his life was in danger; he then "feigned himself mad (*vayitholel*) in their hand", that is, he behaved like one of those madmen (*holelim*) whom he had once envied; and only then did the Shekinah come to his rescue. How, it may be asked, could this be, seeing that the Shekinah abides only in her own heritage, the Holy Land? The answer is that from there only she bestows blessings, but for purposes of protection she is to be found elsewhere also. So here, when Jacob departed from Laban, all the holy legions surrounded him, so that he was not left by himself.'

R. Hizkiah asked: 'If that was so, how came Jacob, as stated later, to be "left alone" (Gen. XXXII, 25)?' Said R. Judah in reply: 'Because he exposed himself deliberately to danger, and therefore the angels deserted him. It was to this that he alluded when he said: "I am not worthy of all the mercies and of all the truth which thou hast shown unto thy servant" (*Ibid.* 11).' R. Isaac said that the reason why they departed was to leave him alone with the chieftain of Esau, who came down to him with divine permission; and they meanwhile went off to chant the hymns for which the hour was then due and to sing the praises of the Holy One, blessed be He, and afterwards they returned to Jacob. "Now I am become two camps": to wit, the camp of the Shekinah and his own household, so that he was complete on all sides, having his portion both with the white and with the red. R. Eleazar said: 'The sages have stated that on that night and at that hour the power of Esau was in the ascendant, and therefore Jacob was left alone, or, from another aspect, the sun was left alone, the light of the moon having been obscured. Nevertheless, the guardianship of Providence did not leave him entirely, so that his antagonist prevailed not against him, as it says: "And when he saw that he prevailed not against him . . .". He looked to Jacob's right, and there his gaze met Abraham; he turned to his left, and there he saw Isaac; he looked at Jacob's body, and he saw that it was a fusion of the two sides, and so he touched the hollow of his thigh, which is a pillar adjoining the body but is outside the body. In this way, then, the angel encompassed Jacob on all sides to deliver him; and when the Shekinah came down to abide with him, there joined him multitudinous hosts and legions; and it was of those angels that he sent a party to Esau.'

AND JACOB SENT ANGELS. Said R. Abba: 'What induced Jacob to make advances towards Esau? Would he not have done better to leave him alone? The truth is that Jacob said to himself: "I am well aware that Esau has great respect for his father and would never cause him any vexation, and so I know that I have no ground to fear him so long as my father is alive. Let me, therefore, effect a reconciliation with him whilst my father is alive." Straightway, then, Jacob "sent angels before him".' R. Simeon opened a discourse on the verse: *Better is he that is lightly esteemed, and hath a servant, than he that playeth the man of rank, and lacketh bread* (Prov.

XII, 9). 'This verse', he said, 'speaks of the [166*b*] evil prompter, who lays plots and unceasingly brings up accusations against a man. He puffs up a man's heart, encouraging him to arrogance and conceit, and induces him to twirl his hair and carry his head high, until he obtains an ascendancy over him and drags him down to Gehinnom. Better, therefore, is one who is "lightly esteemed" and who does not follow the evil prompter, but remains humble in heart and spirit and submits himself to the will of the Holy One, blessed be He. The evil prompter is bowed down before such a one, and so far is he from obtaining the mastery over the man that it is the man who obtains the mastery over him, as it says, "but thou mayest rule over him" (Gen. IV, 7). Such a man is better than he who "playeth the man of rank", who has a high opinion of himself, twirls his hair and is full of conceit, as already mentioned above, but "lacketh bread", to wit, the true faith, which is referred to as "the bread of his God" (Lev. XXI, 22) (*Ibid.* 6). Again, "he who is lightly esteemed" is exemplified in Jacob, who humbled himself before Esau so that the latter should in time become his servant, in fulfilment of the blessing: "Let people serve thee, and nations bow down to thee, etc." (Gen. XXVII, 29). For Jacob's time had not yet arrived, as he deferred it to the future, and in the immediate present he "esteemed himself lightly". But in the proper time "he that playeth the man of rank" will become the servant to him "that lacketh bread", to the man who was allotted "plenty of corn and wine" (*Ibid.* 28). Jacob knew that it was for the time being necessary for him to humble himself before Esau, and so made himself as one who "esteemed himself lightly". And, moreover, he displayed therein more craft and subtlety than in all his other dealings with Esau; and had Esau realised this, he would rather have taken his own life than come to such a pass. Jacob thus acted throughout with wisdom, and to him can be applied the words of Hannah: "They that strive with the Lord shall be broken in pieces ... and he will give strength unto his king, etc." (I Sam. II, 10).'

AND HE COMMANDED THEM, SAYING: THUS SHALL

YE SAY UNTO MY LORD ESAU: THUS SAITH THY SER-
VANT JACOB: I HAVE SOJOURNED WITH LABAN, AND
STAYED UNTIL NOW. He began by representing himself as
Esau's servant, in order that the latter's thoughts might be
diverted from the blessings which he had received from his
father, and the enjoyment of which he was postponing for a
future time, as already said. R. Judah said: 'What was Jacob's
object in saying to Esau, "I have sojourned with Laban" ?
What had this to do with his message to Esau ? The reason
was that Laban the Aramean was famous throughout the
world as a master magician and sorcerer whose spell no man
could escape. He was, in fact, the father of Beor, who was the
father of Balaam, mentioned in Scripture as "Balaam the son
of Beor, the soothsayer" (Josh. XIII, 22). But for all Laban's
skill and pre-eminence in sorcery and magic, he could not
prevail over Jacob, though he employed all his arts to destroy
him, as it says: "An Aramean designed to destroy my
father" (Deut. XXVI, 5).' R. Abba said: 'All the world knew
that Laban was the greatest of wizards and sorcerers and
magicians, and that no one whom he wished to destroy could
escape from him, and that it was from him that Balaam learnt
all his skill—Balaam, of whom it is written: "for I know that
he whom thou blessest is blessed, and he whom thou cursest
is cursed" (Num. XXII, 6). Thus Laban and his magic were
universally feared. Hence Jacob's first intimation to Esau
was, "I have sojourned with Laban"; and lest Esau should
think that it was merely a month, or, at most, a year, he added:
"and I stayed until now"—a space of twenty years. And lest
Esau should think that he had achieved nothing of consequence, he added: "And I have oxen and asses", these being
the symbols of two grades of severity that are never combined
together save to bring suffering on the world. (This is the
underlying reason of the precept: "Thou shalt not plow with
an ox and an ass together" (Deut. XXII, 10)). Further, "and
flocks, and men-servants, and maid-servants", these being
symbolic of the lower crowns whom God slew in Egypt, in
the form of "the first-born of cattle, the first born of the
captive" (Ex. XII, 29), and "the first-born of the maid-
servant" (*Ibid.* XI, 5). Straightway Esau was seized with fear

and went forth to meet him. Indeed, he was as much afraid of Jacob as Jacob was afraid of him. Jacob was like a traveller who hears that robbers are lying in wait for him on the road. Meeting another man, he asks him to whom he belongs, and he replies: "I am a member of such and such a band of robbers". "Get thee hence," exclaims the wayfarer, "for I have about me a snake who kills anyone that approaches me." The man then returns to the chief of the brigands and warns him, saying: "A man is coming along this way who has about him a snake which bites anyone who approaches him [167*a*] and kills him." Hearing this, the chief of the brigands says: "I had better go out to meet that man and make peace with him." When the wayfarer sees him coming he exclaims: "Woe is me, he is going to kill me." So he commences to bow and prostrate himself before him, whereupon the brigand regains his self-assurance, thinking: "If he had with him such a dangerous snake as he said, he would not have bowed so much to me. But since he does bow so much before me, I will not kill him." In the same way Jacob sent word to Esau, saying: "I have sojourned with Laban and stayed until now", as much as to say: "I have stayed with him twenty years, and I have brought with me a deadly snake who slays people with his bite." Esau, on hearing this said: "Woe is me, who can stand up before him ?" for he was afraid that Jacob would kill him with his mouth. He therefore went forth to meet him and to make peace with him. But Jacob, we read, as soon as he saw him, "was greatly afraid and distressed", and when he approached him he commenced bowing and kneeling before him, as it says: "and bowed himself to the ground seven times, until he came near to his brother". Esau then said to himself: "Had he really been so well equipped as he said, he would not have bowed before me", and he again began to carry himself haughtily.

It is written in regard to Balaam: "And God came unto Balaam at night" (Num. XXII, 20). Similarly in regard to Laban it is written: "And God came to Laban the Aramean in a dream of the night, and said unto him: Take heed to thyself that thou speak not to Jacob either good or bad" (Gen. XXXI, 24). Instead of the words "that thou *speak not*", we

should have expected here "that thou *do* no evil to Jacob"·
But the truth is that Laban in his pursuit after Jacob did not
intend to contend against him with armed force, as he was
well aware that Jacob and his sons were more than a match
for him, but he designed to kill him with the power of his
mouth. Hence: "that thou speak not", and not "that thou do
not". It is also written: "It is in the power of my hand to do
you hurt" (Gen. XXXI, 29). Laban knew this from the warning
given him, as he himself continued: "But the God of your
father spoke to me, etc." (*Ibid.*). And this is the very testimony which God commanded the Israelites to pronounce, as
it is written: "And thou shalt testify and say before the Lord
thy God: An Aramean intended to destroy my father, etc."
(Deut. XXVI, 5). Of Balaam it is further written: "and he went
not as at other times, to meet enchantments" (Num. XXIV, 1),
this being his wont, since he was an adept in divinations.
Laban also said: "I have observed the signs" (Gen. XXX, 27),
that is to say, he tested Jacob's fortune by means of his
divinations, and when he set out to destroy him he also intended to accomplish his end by the same power of magic and
sorcery, but God did not permit him. And it was in allusion
to this that Balaam his grandson said: "For there is no enchantment with Jacob, neither is there any divination with
Israel" (Num. XXIII, 23), as much as to say: "Who can prevail against them, seeing that when my grandfather sought to
destroy their ancestor by means of enchantments and sorceries, he did not succeed, as he was not permitted to curse
him ?" Laban, indeed, employed against Jacob all the ten
kinds of magic and divination of the flashing of the underworld crowns, but could do him no hurt, as it is written: "and
he changed my wages ten times, but God suffered him not to
hurt me" (Gen. XXXI, 7), where the term *monim* (times) is akin
to the term *minim*, signifying "kinds". These ten kinds of
witchcraft are alluded to in the verse saying: "There shall
not be found among you . . . one that useth divination, a
soothsayer, or an enchanter, or a sorcerer, or a charmer, or
one that consulteth a ghost or a familiar spirit, or a necro-
mancer" (Deut. XVIII, 10–11). R. Jose said: 'Divination and
enchantment are two different arts of the same potency.

Balaam made use of divination against Israel, as it says: "with divinations in their hand" (Num. XXII, 7). Laban, on the other hand, used enchantments against Jacob, but neither of them succeeded. Hence Balaam said: "For there is no enchantment with Jacob, neither is there any divination with Israel" (*Ibid.* XXIII, 23), the first half of the verse alluding to the days of Laban, the other half to the time of Balaam himself. Balaam said in effect to Balak: "How can anyone prevail against them, seeing that all the divinations and sorceries residing in our crowns derive their potency from the flashing of the supernal sovereignty, which is attached to them, as it is written: 'The Lord his God is with them, and the shouting for the King is among them" (*Ibid.* 21).' R. Judah said: 'Far be it from us to imagine that Balaam knew aught of the supernal sanctity, [167b] seeing that God did not choose any people or tongue to make use of His glory save His holy children, to whom he said: "sanctify yourselves therefore, and be ye holy" (Lev. XI, 44). Only those who are themselves holy are permitted to make use of holy things; and it is only Israel who are holy, as it is written: "For thou art a holy people" (Deut. XIV, 2), that is, thou alone art holy, but no other people. Contrariwise, those who are impure are brought into contact with impurity and become more impure, and of such it is written: "he is unclean; he shall dwell alone; without the camp shall his dwelling be" (Lev. XIII, 46); for impurity calls unto impurity, as it says: "and he shall cry unclean, unclean" (*Ibid.* 45), where the text admits of the rendering, "and unclean calls to unclean", that is, seeks out its own kind.'

R. Isaac said: 'Was it becoming for a holy man like Jacob to admit that he had contaminated himself with Laban and his enchantments ? Was this anything to his credit ?' R. Jose said to him: 'Although R. Judah has given an explanation, I agree with you that we should seek another. For we find a somewhat similar difficulty in Jacob's words: "I am Esau thy first-born" (Gen. XXVII, 19), where also we may ask: "Was it becoming for a righteous man like Jacob to assume the name of the impure Esau ?" I will answer both these difficulties. There is a tonal pause after the word "I-am" (*anokhi*) in this passage, so that what Jacob really said was: "I am (who I am, but) Esau (is) thy first-born", as already explained elsewhere. Similarly here Jacob meant to say: "Do not pay any regard to the blessing which my father gave, nor imagine that it has been fulfilled in me. For he blessed me saying, 'be lord over thy brethren', whereas of a truth 'I am thy servant Jacob, to my lord Esau'. Again, he blessed me with 'plenty of corn and wine', but I have no stock of these, but 'oxen, and asses and flocks', and am only a shepherd in the field. Of the blessing 'of the dew of heaven, and of the fat places of the earth', nothing has been fulfilled in me, seeing that 'I have sojourned with Laban', being merely a sojourner, without so much as a house that I can call my own, let alone the fatness of the earth." The whole of Jacob's message was thus calculated to divert Esau's regard from those blessings, so that he should not quarrel with him over them.' R. Abba said: 'It is written of Jacob that he was "a perfect man, dwelling in tents" (Gen. xxv, 27). The designation "perfect man" was given him because he resided in the two supernal Tabernacles and embodied in himself both this side and that side, and thus was made complete. His language must not be construed into an admission that he had contaminated himself with the enchantments of Laban, and, with all due respect to R. Judah, his heart was pure and full of thankfulness for the kindness and the truth that God had shown him. Thus Jacob's message to Esau amounted to saying: "Everyone knows what kind of a man Laban is, and that no one can escape him. Yet I stayed with him twenty years, and though he contended with me and sought to destroy me, yet God delivered me from his hand." Jacob's purpose in all his words was to prevent Esau from thinking that the blessings had been fulfilled, and so from nursing a grudge against himself. Regarding such conduct Scripture says: "For the ways of the Lord are right, etc." (Hos. xiv, 10), also: "Thou shalt be whole-hearted with the Lord thy God" (Deut. xviii, 13).'

AND THE ANGELS RETURNED TO JACOB, SAYING: WE CAME TO THY BROTHER ESAU, AND MOREOVER HE COMETH TO MEET THEE, AND FOUR HUNDRED MEN

WITH HIM. The word "Esau" after "thy brother" seems to be superfluous, since Jacob had no other brothers. It was, however, a hint to Jacob not to think that Esau had retraced his steps and entered on the path of rectitude, but that he was still the same wicked Esau as of old. And moreover "he cometh to meet thee", and that not by himself, but having "four hundred men with him". Why all these details ? Because God always delights in the prayer of the righteous, and He crowns Himself, as it were, with their supplications. So we affirm that the angel in charge of the prayers of Israel, Sandalphon by name, takes up all those prayers and weaves out of them a crown for the Living One of the worlds. All the more, then, must we believe that the prayers of the righteous, in which God takes delight, are made into a crown for Him. Seeing that Jacob had with him legions of holy angels, it may be asked why he was afraid. The truth is that the righteous rely not on their merits but on their prayers and supplications to their Master. R. Simeon said: 'The prayer of a congregation ascends to the Almighty, and He is crowned therewith, because it comprises many hues and directions, wherefore it is made into a crown to be placed on the head of the Righteous One, the Living One of the worlds; whereas the prayer of an individual is not many-sided and presents only one hue, and hence is not so complete and acceptable as the prayer of a congregation. Jacob was many-sided, and therefore God craved for his prayer, and hence it is written: "Then Jacob was greatly afraid and was distressed".' R. Judah cited here the verse: "Happy is the man that feareth alway; but he that hardeneth his heart shall fall into evil" (Prov. XXVIII, 14). [168*a*] 'Happy is the people of Israel', he said, 'in whom the Holy One, blessed be He, finds delight, and to whom He has given the Torah of truth that thereby they may merit life eternal. For whoso labours in the Torah is vouchsafed from heaven the best life, and is taken up into the life of the world to come, as it is written: "for that is thy life, and the length of thy days" (Deut. XXX, 20); also, "and through this thing ye shall prolong your days" (*Ibid*. XXXII, 47), implying life in this world and in the world to come.' R. Eleazar said: 'Whoever labours in the Torah for its own sake will not die through the agency of the evil prompter (the same being the serpent and the angel of death), inasmuch as he holds fast to the tree of life and relaxeth not. For this reason the bodies of the righteous who have laboured in the Torah remain undefiled after death, since the spirit of defilement does not hover over them. How came it, then, that Jacob, who was the tree of life itself, as it were, was afraid of Esau, who surely could not prevail against him ? Had he not, too, the promise: "And, behold, I am with thee" (Gen. xxviii, 15) ? And had he not further protection in the escort of the host of holy angels, of whom it says, "and the angels of God met him" (*Ibid.* xxxii, 2) ? The reason, however, of his fear was that he did not wish to rely on a miracle, as he did not consider himself deserving that a miracle should be wrought on his behalf. The cause of his self-mistrust was that he had not rendered filial service to his father and mother as he should have done, and that he had not devoted himself to the Torah, and, further, that he had married two sisters. But, in truth, a man should always go in fear and offer up prayer to the Almighty, as it says: "Happy is the man that feareth alway".

'It was the prayers offered up by the patriarchs that sustained the world, and by them are upheld all who dwell therein; and the merits of the patriarchs will never be forgotten, inasmuch as they form the support of the upper and the lower realms; and Jacob's support is firmer than that of all the others. Hence it is that when the children of Jacob are oppressed, God looks at the image of Jacob and is filled with pity for the world. This is hinted in the passage: "Then will I remember my covenant with Jacob" (Lev. xxvi, 42), where the name Jacob is spelt *plene*, with a *vau*, which is itself the image of Jacob. To look at Jacob was like looking at the "clear mirror". According to tradition, the beauty of Jacob was equal to that of Adam, the first man.' R. Jose said: 'I have heard it said that he who sees in his dream Jacob robed in his mantle enjoys length of life.' R. Simeon said: 'We have learnt that no life-portion was originally assigned to David, but Adam gave him seventy years of his own; and so David lived seventy years, whilst Adam lived a thousand years less seventy; thus the first thousand years included the lives of both Adam the first man and King David. The Scripture', he said, 'alludes to this in the verse, "He asked life of thee, thou gavest it him; even length of days for ever and ever" (Ps. XXI, 5). For when God created the Garden of Eden and placed in it the soul of King David, He saw that it possessed no life-portion of its own, and cast about for a remedy. So when He created Adam the first man, He said, "Here, indeed, is the remedy"; and so it was that from Adam were derived the seventy years that David lived. Further, each of the patriarchs conceded him some years of his own life, that is to say, Abraham and Jacob and Joseph, but not Isaac, because King David belonged to the same side as himself. Abraham allowed him five years of the hundred and eighty years which he was properly entitled to live, so that he lived only a hundred and seventy-five years, five years less than his due. Jacob was also due to live in this world as many years as Abraham, but he lived [168*b*] only a hundred and forty-seven years. Thus, Abraham and Jacob between them conceded to David thirty-three years. Then Joseph should have lived a hundred and forty-seven years like Jacob, his father, but he fell short of that number by thirty-seven years. These, with the other thirty-three, completed the seventy years allotted to David, which were thus transferred to him out of the lives of the patriarchs. The reason why Isaac did not transfer to him any years like the others was that he was himself wrapt in darkness, and David came from the side of darkness, and he who is in darkness possesses no light whatever, nor any life: it is for that reason that David possessed no life at all of his own. But those others, being possessed of light, could afford light to King David, who was beholden to them for light and for life, since of the dark side he had no life at all. Hence Isaac did not come into the reckoning. Why, it may be asked, was Joseph's contribution greater than those of the other two together ? It was because Joseph was reckoned the equivalent of the other two, since he was called "the righteous", and he was better able than the others to illumine the moon, and hence he conceded to King David a greater share of life than all the others.

'To protect himself against Esau, Jacob resorted to prayer and did not rely upon his merit, since he desired to keep this in reserve for the benefit of his descendants in the future, and not to use it up now against Esau. Hence he now offered up his prayer to the Almighty, and did not rely upon his merits, nor ask for deliverance for their sake. Hence we read: AND HE SAID: IF ESAU COME TO THE ONE CAMP, AND SMITE IT, THEN THE CAMP WHICH IS LEFT SHALL ESCAPE. It was for this reason that he "divided the people that was with him . . . into two camps". Now the Shekinah never departed from the tent of Leah nor from the tent of Rachel. Jacob knew, therefore, that they were under the protection of the Almighty, and so he put the handmaids and their children foremost, saying to himself: "If Esau slays them, well, he will slay them, but as regards the others I have no fear, since the Shekinah is with them." Hence it says: THEN THE CAMP WHICH IS LEFT SHALL ESCAPE. Having taken this step, he next resorted to prayer, as it is written: And Jacob said, O GOD OF MY FATHER ABRAHAM, AND GOD OF MY FATHER ISAAC, O LORD, WHO SAIDST UNTO ME: RETURN UNTO THY COUNTRY, AND TO THY KINDRED, AND I WILL DO THEE GOOD.' R. Jose discoursed on the verse: *A prayer of the poor, when he fainteth (ya'atof) and poureth out his complaint before the Lord* (Ps. CII, 1). He said: 'As has been laid down in many places, this psalm was composed by King David when he contemplated the plight of the poor man, and that was when he fled from his father-in-law. It was then that he composed a "prayer of the poor", as much as to say: "Behold, this is the prayer a poor man offers up to the Almighty, and one which should ascend in advance of all other prayers." The phrase, "a prayer of the poor", finds its parallel in the expression: "A prayer of Moses, the man of God" (*Ibid.* XC, 1), the one alluding to the phylactery of the head, the other to that of the arm, the two being inseparable and of equal importance. The reason why the prayer of the poor is admitted first into the presence of the Almighty is indicated in the verse: "For he hath not despised nor abhorred the lowliness of the poor, etc." (*Ibid.* XXII, 25). According to another exposition, the term "a prayer" is an allusion to Moses; "of the poor" to David; "when he fainteth" (*ya'atof*= is covered) to the moon when it is hidden and the sun is concealed from it. Observe that the prayer of other people is just a prayer, but the prayer of a poor man breaks through all barriers and storms its way to the presence of the Almighty. So Scripture says: "And it shall come to pass, when he cries unto me, that I will hear; for I am gracious" (Ex. XXII, 26); also: "I will surely hear their cry" (*Ibid*. 22). David continues: "and poureth out his complaint before the Lord", like one who protests against the judgements of the Almighty.'

R. Eleazar said: 'The prayer of the righteous is an object of joy for the Community of Israel, [169a] who weave out of it a crown by which to adorn themselves before the Holy One, blessed be He. Hence God holds it in special affection: He longs, as it were, for the prayer of the righteous, when they are in straits, because they know how to appease their Master.'

Note the words of Jacob's prayer: O GOD OF MY FATHER ABRAHAM, AND GOD OF MY FATHER ISAAC, O LORD, WHO SAIDST UNTO ME: RETURN. Various strands are here fitly interwoven. "O God of my father Abraham" symbolises the Right; "God of my father Isaac" symbolises the Left; while by the words "Who saidst unto me" Jacob interwove himself between the two.

I AM NOT WORTHY OF ALL THE MERCIES. The connection of those words with what precedes is as follows. Jacob said in effect: "Thou hast promised me to deal well with me, but I know that all thy promises are conditional. Now, behold, I possess no merits, so that I am not worthy of all the mercies and of all the truth which Thou hast shown unto Thy servant; and all that Thou hast done for me until this day Thou hast done not for sake of my merits but for Thine own sake. For behold, when first I crossed the Jordan, fleeing from Esau, I was all alone, but Thou hast shown unto me mercy and truth, in that I have now crossed with two companies." Up to this point Jacob was reciting the praises of the Almighty; he then proceeded to pray for his requirements. From Jacob all men can take example, when offering prayer, first to recite the praises of their Master, and only then to present their petition. So Jacob, after praising the Lord, continued: "Deliver me, I pray thee, from the hand of my brother, from the hand of

Esau; for I fear him, lest he come and smite me, the mother with the children." Here, too, is a lesson that in praying a man should state in precise terms what he requires. Thus Jacob commenced: "Deliver me, I pray thee," and since it might be said that he had already been delivered from the hand of Laban, he added "from the hand of my brother"; and since, again, the term "brother" covers all relatives, he added "from the hand of Esau"; and yet again, lest it should be urged that he had no need of such a delivery, he continued: "for I fear him, lest he come and smite me, the mother with the children"; all this in order that there should be no possibility of misunderstanding.

AND THOU SAIDST: I WILL SURELY DO THEE GOOD, ETC. We find King David closing a prayer with the words: "Let the words of my mouth and the meditation of my heart be acceptable before thee" (Ps. XIX, 15), the former of these clauses referring to what he had actually said explicitly, and the latter to his inner thoughts which he had only half expressed. This division of prayer into clearly expressed and half-expressed desires corresponds to a distinction in the divine grades, the clearly expressed prayer being addressed to the lower grade, the meditation of the heart to the higher and inner grade. Jacob divided his prayer similarly; first he stated what he desired distinctly, then he left his thought only half expressed, in the words alluding to the promise made to him, "and I will make thy seed as the sand of the sea, which cannot be numbered for multitude". There was here an underlying thought which was best left unexpressed. This division was necessary, as explained, so as to make the unification complete. Happy are the righteous who know how to express fittingly the praises of their Master, as a preliminary to their prayer. Of them it is written: "And he said unto me: Thou art my servant, Israel, in whom I will be glorified" (Is. XLIX, 3).

AND JACOB WAS LEFT ALONE, ETC. R. Hiya discoursed on the verse: *There shall no evil befall thee, neither shall any plague come nigh thy tent.* (Ps. XCI, 10). 'When God', he said, 'created the world, He made on each day [169b] the work appropriate for that day. This has already been explained. Now on the fourth day the lights were created; but the moon was created without light, since she diminished herself. This is implied in the phrase "Let there be lights", wherein the term *meoroth* (lights) is written defectively (less the letter *vau*), as it were *me'eroth* (curses); for as a result of the moon's diminution, occasion was granted to all spirits and demons and hurricanes and devils to exercise sway, so that all unclean spirits rise up and traverse the world seeking whom to seduce; they haunt ruined places, thick forests and deserts. These are all from the side of the unclean spirit, which, as has been said, issues from the crooked serpent, who is, indeed, the veritable unclean spirit, and whose mission is to seduce man after him. Hence it is that the evil prompter has sway in the world, following men about and employing all manner of ruses and seductions to turn them aside from the paths of the Holy One, blessed be He. And in the same way as he seduced Adam and thereby brought death into the world, so does he ever seduce men and cause them to defile themselves; and whoever allows himself to be defiled draws upon himself the unclean spirit and clings unto him, and numerous unclean influences are at hand to defile him, so that he remains polluted in this world and in the world to come. Contrariwise, should a man strive to purify himself, the unclean spirit is foiled and can no longer dominate him. Thus it is written: "No evil shall befall thee, neither shall any plague come nigh thy tent".' R. Jose said: ' "Evil" here alludes to Lilith (night-demon), and "the plague" to the other demons, as has been explained elsewhere.' R. Eleazar said: 'It has been taught that a man should not go out alone at night, and especially when the time of the creation of the moon recurs and it is without light. For at that time the unclean spirit, which is the same as the evil spirit, is at large. Now, the term "evil" here is an allusion to the evil serpent, while "the plague" alludes to him who rides on the serpent, so that evil and plague work together. It is true, we have also been taught that the term "plague" signifies "the plagues of the sons of man", which issued from Adam. For during all those years that Adam kept away from his wife, unclean spirits came and conceived from him, and bore offspring, which are called "plagues of the off-spring of Adam"; and it has been affirmed that when a man is sleeping and is not in control of himself, he is assailed by an unclean spirit and sometimes by a number of unclean female spirits who draw him unto themselves, conceive from him and give birth to spirits and demons. These sometimes appear in the form of human beings, save that they have no hair on their heads. It is therefore incumbent on a man to be on his guard against them and not to let himself be contaminated by them, but to follow the paths of the Torah. For there is no man falls asleep on his bed in the night-time but he has a foretaste of death, in that his soul (*neshamah*) departs from him; and since his body is left without the holy soul, an unclean spirit comes and hovers upon it and it becomes defiled. It has already been said elsewhere that a man should not pass his hands over his eyes when he wakes in the morning on account of the unclean spirit hovering over his hands. Now, although Jacob was beloved by the Almighty, yet when he was left alone a strange spirit immediately came and joined battle with him.' R. Simeon said: 'It is written of Balaam, "and he went *shefi* (to a bare height)" (Num. XXIII, 3). The word *shefi* signifies "alone", and it is also akin to the term *shefifon*, in the phrase "*shefifon* (a horned snake) in the path". So Balaam went alone, like a snake that goes alone and lurks in by-paths and lanes, with the object of attracting to himself the unclean spirit. For he who walks alone at certain periods, and in certain places, even in a town, attracts to himself the unclean spirit. Hence no one should ever go on a lonely road, even in a city, but only where people are about, nor should a man go out in the night-time, when people are no longer about. It is for a similar reason that it is written: "his body shall not remain all night upon the tree" (Deut. XXI, 23), [170*a*] so as not to leave the dead body, which is alone, without the spirit, above ground in the night. The wicked Balaam, however, for that very reason went alone like the serpent, as already explained.'

AND THERE WRESTLED (*vaye'oveq*) A MAN WITH HIM. R. Joshua the son of Levi said: 'From the word *behe'ovqo* (in his wrestling) we learn that they raised a dust with their feet which reached the Throne of Glory, as this word finds a parallel in the phrase "the dust (*'abaq*) of his feet" (Nahum I, 3). The angel here mentioned was Samael, the chieftain of Esau, and it was right that his dust should rise to the Throne of Glory which is the seat of judgement.' R. Simeon said: 'This dust (*'abaq*) was not ordinary dust, but ashes, the residue of fire. It differs from dust proper in that it is sterile and unproductive, whereas dust (*'afar*) is that from which all fruit and vegetation spring and is common to the lower and higher existences.' R. Judah remarked: 'If so, how can we explain the passage: "He raiseth up the poor out of the dust" (I Sam. II, 8) ?' R. Simeon replied: 'The dust possesses nothing of its own, hence it is from the dust that the poor man has to be raised who possesses nothing of his own either. At the same time the dust is the source of all fruitfulness and of all the produce of the world, and from it have been formed all things in the world, as it is written: "all are of the dust and all return to dust" (Eccl. III, 20), including, according to tradition, even the solar sphere. But the dust called *abaq* is forever barren, and hence, as the term *vaye'obeq* ("and he wrestled", or "raised the dust") implies, the man came up, riding, as it were, upon that dust, in order to contest Jacob's right.'

UNTIL THE BREAKING OF THE DAY; this being the moment when his dominion passed away and vanished. The same will happen in the time to come. For the present exile is like the night, and in that night the barren dust rules over Israel, who are prostrate to the dust; and so it will be until the light will appear and the day will break; then Israel will obtain power, and to them will be given the kingdom, as they are the saints of the Most High. So Scripture says: "And the kingdom and the dominion, and the greatness of the kingdoms under the whole heaven, shall be given to the people of the saints of the Most High; their kingdom is an everlasting kingdom, and all dominions shall serve and obey them" (Dan. VII, 27).

AND HE SAID: LET ME GO, FOR THE DAY BREAKETH. AND HE SAID: I WILL NOT LET THEE GO, EXCEPT THOU

BLESS ME. R. Judah discoursed on the verse: *Who is she that looketh forth as the dawn, fair as the moon, clear as the sun, terrible as an army with banners?* (S. S. VI, 10). 'This verse', he said, 'refers to Israel, at the time when the Holy One, blessed be He, will raise them up and bring them out of captivity. At that time he will first open for them a tiny aperture of light, then another somewhat larger, and so on until He will throw open for them the supernal gates which face on all the four quarters of the world. And, indeed, this process is followed by God in all that He does for Israel and the righteous among them. For we know that when a man has been long shut up in darkness it is necessary, on bringing him into the light, first to make for him an opening as small as the eye of a needle, and then one a little larger, and so on gradually until he can endure the full light. It is the same with Israel, as we read: "By little and little I will drive them out from before thee, until thou be increased, etc." (Ex. XXIII, 30). So, too, a sick man who is recovering cannot be given a full diet all at once, but only gradually. But with Esau it was not so. His light came at a bound, but it will gradually be withdrawn from him until Israel will come into their own and destroy him completely from this world and from the world to come. Because he plunged into the light all at once, therefore he will be utterly and completely exterminated. Israel's light, on the other hand, will come little by little, until they will become strong. God will illumine them forever. All then will ask: "Who is she that looketh forth like the dawn", this being a reference to the first tiny streak of the dawn, then "fair as the moon", the light of the moon being stronger than that of the dawn, and then "clear as the sun", that is, a still stronger light, and finally "terrible as an army with banners", expressive of the light in its full strength. For, just as when the dawn emerges from the darkness its light at first is faint, but gradually brightens till full daylight is reached, so when God will bestir Himself to shine upon the Community of Israel, He will first shed on them a streak of light like that of the daybreak which is still black, then increase it to make it "fair as the moon", then "clear as the sun", until it will be "tremendous as an army with banners", as already explained.' [170b]

Now in connection with Jacob it is not written: "for daybreak has *come (ba')*", but "for daybreak has *gone up ('alah)*". For at the moment when daybreak arrived, the Chieftain summoned all his strength and struck out at Jacob in order thereby to impart power to Esau; but as soon as the blackness of the dawn passed the light came on and Jacob's power increased; for his time had then arrived to come into the light, as it is written: "And the sun rose upon him as he passed over Peniel." In the next words, AND HE LIMPED UPON HIS THIGH, there is a hint that after Israel in exile have endured many sufferings and pains, when daylight rises upon them and they attain to rest and ease they will in their memory go through again their past sufferings and afflictions and will wonder how they could have endured them. So Jacob, after "the sun had risen upon him", was "limping upon his thigh", vexing himself for what had befallen. But when the blackness of the early dawn passed he made a great effort and grasped his opponent, whose strength at the same time gave out, his dominion being only during the night, whereas Jacob has ascendancy in the daytime. Hence he said: LET ME GO, FOR THE DAY BREAKETH, so that, as he might have added, "I am now in thy power".

R. Hiya said: 'Had Jacob's strength not failed him at that spot (the sinew that shrank) he would have prevailed against the angel so completely that Esau's power would then have been broken both on high and below.' R. Simeon remarked: 'Ezekiel the prophet said: "As the appearance of the bow that is in the cloud in the day of rain, so was the appearance of the brightness round about. This was the appearance of the likeness of the glory of the Lord. And when I saw it I fell upon my face, etc." (Ez. I, 28). This verse illustrates the difference between the other prophets and Moses, of whom it is written, "And there hath not arisen a prophet since in Israel like unto Moses" (Deut. XXXIV, 10). For Moses gazed into the clear mirror of prophecy, whereas all the other prophets looked into a hazy mirror. [171*a*] Moses received the divine message standing and with all his senses unimpaired, and he comprehended it fully, as it is written: "even manifestly, and not in dark speeches" (Num. XII, 8); whereas other prophets fell on their faces in a state of exhaustion and did not obtain a perfectly clear message. All those prophets thus failed to realise fully what God had in store for Esau in the future, with the exception of the prophet Obadiah, who, being himself a proselyte, originating from the side of Esau, was able to receive a full message with regard to Esau. The reason why all the prophets except Moses were thus weak was that "he touched the hollow of Jacob's thigh through the sinew of the thigh-vein"—the sinew that draws to the thigh all its energy; the energy of the thigh was thus broken, and Jacob remained "limping upon his thigh", and hence the rest of the prophets, with the exception of Moses, could not retain their faculties during a vision and grasp it fully. Now just as the prophets were thus weakened, so when scholars are not encouraged and no one gives them pecuniary support the Torah is forgotten from one generation to another and its strength is weakened, those who toil in it having no support, and the sinful kingdom increases in power with each day. Much evil therefore results; since, as the upholders of the Torah become weaker, strength is thereby gained by him who has no legs to stand upon. For when God said to the serpent, "upon thy belly shalt thou go" (Gen. III, 14), the serpent had his supports and legs cut off so that he was left with nothing to stand on. But when Israel neglect to support the Torah, they thereby provide him with supports and legs on which to stand firm and upright.

Many were the stratagems and cunning devices to which the serpent-rider resorted on that night against Jacob. For he well knew that "the voice is the voice of Jacob, but the hands are the hands of Esau" (Gen. XXVII, 22), so that whenever the voice of Jacob is interrupted, the hands of Esau are reinforced. He therefore cast about on all sides for means of interrupting his voice, but he found him strong on all sides, his arms strong on both sides and firmly upheld between them, and the Torah firmly entrenched therein. Seeing, therefore, that he could not prevail against him, he "touched the hollow of his thigh". For he knew that when the supports of the Torah are broken, the Torah itself is shaken; hence he thought that in this way he should reap the benefit of what their father had said, namely: "And it shall come to pass when thou shalt break loose, that thou shalt shake his yoke from thy neck" (*Ibid.* 40). His whole purpose in contending with Jacob was to break the force of the Torah, and when he saw that he could not strike at the Torah itself, he weakened the power of its upholders; for without upholders of the Torah there will be no "voice of Jacob", and the hands of Esau will operate. Jacob, on seeing this, as soon as day broke, seized hold of him and did not let him go, so that he blessed him and confirmed to him those blessings, and said to him: "Thy name shall be called no more Jacob (*Ya'aqob*=supplanter), but Israel (*Yisrael*=princehood and strength), so that no one can prevail against thee." Now, from that serpent issue numerous hosts which disperse themselves on every side to prowl about the world. It is incumbent, therefore, upon us to preserve in a complete state the sinew of the thigh-vein, for although the serpent-rider touched it, it retained its vitality, and we require its strength to establish ourselves in the world and to make good the words: "For thou hast striven with God and with men, and hast prevailed." When the adversary sees that that part is not broken or consumed, his own strength and courage is broken [171*b*] and he can no more do any harm to the sons of Jacob. It is for that reason that we are forbidden to give that part (of an animal) to anyone to eat and may not benefit of it in any way. R. Jesse the elder connected the word "touched" in this clause with the same word in the verse: "He that toucheth the dead, even any man's dead body, etc." (Num. XIX, 11). 'Just as in the latter case', he said, 'there is defilement, so here defilement is implied, that part of the body being an object of defilement, so that we may not put it to any use whatever.' Blessed be the Merciful One who gave the Torah to Israel, whereby to merit this world and the world to come, as it is written: "Length of days is in her right hand; in her left hand are riches and honour" (Prov. III, 16).

AND HE HIMSELF PASSED OVER BEFORE THEM, AND BOWED HIMSELF TO THE GROUND SEVEN TIMES, UNTIL HE CAME NEAR TO HIS BROTHER. Said R. Eleazar: 'It is written, "For thou shalt bow down to no other god, for the Lord, whose name is Jealous, is a jealous God" (Ex. xxxiv, 14). Now, Jacob was the consummation of the patriarchs, who was selected as the choicest portion of the Almighty, and was brought specially near to Him and was perfected above and below. How came it, then, that such a man should bow down to the wicked Esau, who was of the side of another god, so that bowing down to him was the same as bowing down to another god ? The proverb, it is true, says, "When a fox is in honour, bow down to him." This, however, could not apply to Esau, who was like another god, belonging to that side and that portion to whom Jacob would in no way bow down. A similar difficulty arises with the verse: "And thus ye shall say: All hail ! (*leḥay*, lit. to the living one) and peace be both unto thee, and peace be to thy house, and peace be unto all that thou hast" (1 Sam. xxv, 6). Now, inasmuch as, according to our teaching, it is forbidden to give the first greeting to a wicked man, how could David have sent such a message to Nabal ? There, however, the explanation is that David in reality addressed his words to God, as is implied in the expression *leḥay* (to the Living One), although Nabal misunderstood them as addressed to himself. Similarly, when we read: "And Israel bowed himself upon the bed's head" (Gen. xlvii, 31), we are not to suppose that he bowed down in worship to his son, but that his obeisance was directed towards the spot where the Shekinah rested. So in this passage, the words: "and he himself passed over before them" refer to the celestial Shekinah who went before Jacob in order to afford him the promised protection from on high. When Jacob became aware of this he thought it incumbent on him to make obeisance towards the Holy One, blessed be He, who was going, as it were, in front of him, and so "he bowed himself to the ground seven times, until he came near to his brother". Mark that it is not written, "and he bowed down to Esau", but simply "he bowed down", implying that he did so because he saw the Holy One, blessed be He, going before him, not that he made obeisance by way of worship to anyone else. Everything was thus in order. Happy are the righteous all of whose actions are for the glory of their Master, and with the object that they themselves should turn neither to the right nor to the left.'

AND ESAU RAN TO MEET HIM, AND EMBRACED HIM, AND FELL ON HIS NECK AND KISSED HIM; AND THEY WEPT. The word *zavaro* (his neck) is used here instead of the more usual *zavorav;* while dots are placed over the letters of the word *vayishoqehu* (and he kissed him). Said R. Isaac: 'Many are the methods by which the Scripture conveys recondite allusions, yet with a common purpose. It is written: "But the wicked are like the troubled sea; for it cannot rest, and its waters cast up mire and dirt" (Is. LVII, 20). This verse may be applied to Esau, all of whose actions were wicked and sinful. His approaches to Jacob on this occasion were insincere, as is shown by the signs mentioned above. The "neck" here is an allusion to Jerusalem, which is indeed the neck of the universe, and the singular form *zavaro* is used instead of the regular dual form *zavorav* as a hint that the seed of Esau would one day fall upon and destroy one of the two Temples. Again, the dots above the word *vayishaqehu* (and he kissed him) indicate that he kissed him reluctantly. The verse: "but the kisses of an enemy are importunate" (Prov. XXVII, 6) has been applied by our teachers to Balaam, who, although he blessed Israel, did it against his will; but Esau provides another illustration.' R. Jose said: 'It is written: "For thou hast smitten all my enemies upon the cheek, thou hast broken the teeth of the wicked" (Ps. III, 8), and there is a tradition which reads here *shirbabtha* (thou hast lengthened) instead of *shibbartha* (thou hast broken), to indicate that Esau's teeth were suddenly lengthened to prevent him from biting.' We read further: AND THEY WEPT; both the one and the other with good cause, [172*a*] as the companions have expounded. For Esau was so evilly disposed to Jacob that even at that very time he was planning how to afflict him and bring accusations against him in the distant future. Hence they wept: Jacob for fear lest he might not escape from his brother's onslaught, and Esau to think that his father was still alive, so that he was unable to do any harm to Jacob.' R. Abba said: 'Assuredly

Esau's wrath was allayed at the moment he beheld Jacob, since his chieftain had confirmed Jacob's claims, and therefore it would have been vain for Esau to vent his wrath. For all the affairs of this world depend on what is done above, and whatever is agreed upon above is accepted below, and no power can be exercised below until power is granted above. Thus one world depends always on the other.'

LET MY LORD, I PRAY THEE, PASS OVER BEFORE HIS SERVANT; AND I WILL JOURNEY ON GENTLY, ETC. R. Eleazar said: 'This bears out what we said before, namely, that Jacob did not wish as yet to avail himself of the first blessings that he received from his father, not one of which had so far been fulfilled, since he reserved them for the end of days when his descendants should need them in their struggle against the nations of the world. Hence, when Esau said: "Let us take our journey, and let us go", that is, "let us share together this world and rule it in partnership", Jacob replied: "Let my lord, I pray thee, pass over before his servant", as much as to say: "Have thou first thy dominion of this world, and I will journey on gently, and reserve myself for the world to come and for the latter days that flow on gently . . . 'until I come unto my lord unto Seir', i.e. I will endure subjection to thee until my time will come to rule over the mount of Esau, as it is written: 'And saviours shall come up on mount Zion to judge the mount of Esau; and the kingdom shall be the Lord's' " (Oba. 1, 21).'

AND JACOB JOURNEYED TO SUCCOTH, AND BUILT HIM A HOUSE, AND MADE BOOTHS FOR HIS CATTLE. THEREFORE THE NAME OF THE PLACE IS CALLED SUCCOTH. R. Hiya discoursed on the verse: *Except the Lord build the house, etc., except the Lord keep the city, etc.* (Ps. CXXVII, 1). He said: 'When God resolved to create the world, He produced out of the primordial lamp of scintillation a nucleus that flashed forth from the midst of darkness and remained on high while the darkness went below. It flashed along through a hundred paths and ways, some narrow and some broad, until the House of the world[1] was made. This House forms the centre of the universe, and it has many doors and vestibules on all its sides, sacred and exalted abodes where the celestial birds build their nests, each according to its kind. From the midst of it rises a large tree, with mighty branches and abundance of fruit providing food for all, which rears itself to the clouds of heaven and is lost to view between three rocks, from which it again emerges, so that it is both above and below them. From this tree the house is watered. In this house are stored many precious and undiscovered treasures. Thus was the house built and completed. That tree is visible in the day-time but is hidden at night, whereas the house becomes manifest in the night and is hidden by day. As soon as darkness sets in and all the doors on all sides are closed, innumerable spirits fly about, desiring to know what is in it. They pass between the birds, bringing their credentials, they flit about and see many things, until the darkness by which the house is enveloped is aroused and sends forth a flame and strikes with mighty hammers, causing the doors to be opened, and splitting the rocks; then the flame goes up and down and strikes the world with blows that resound above and below. Then a [172b] herald ascends, attaches himself to the ether, and makes proclamation. That ether emerges from the pillar of cloud of the inner altar, and spreads itself out into the four quarters of the world. A thousand thousand stand at the left side and a myriad of myriads stand at the right side. And the herald stands in his place and makes loud proclamation. Then innumerable are those who chant hymns and make obeisance; and two doors open, one on the South and one on the North. The house then is lifted up and is fastened between the two sides, whilst hymns are chanted and songs of praise ascend. Then some enter silently whilst the house is lit up on every side with six lights, brilliant and resplendent, and from thence flow out six rivers of balsam from which all the "animals of the field" are watered, as it says: "They give drink to every animal of the field, the wild asses quench their thirst, etc." (Ps. CIV, 11). They thus continue

---

[1] By 'house of the world' here seems to be meant the 'world of emanation', which is 'central', as being least penetrable to the intelligence.

singing praises until daybreak. At daybreak, the stars, the constellations and their hosts all commence to chant songs of praise and hymns, as we read: "When the morning stars sang together, and all the sons of God shouted for joy" (Job XXXVIII, 7). Now observe the words: "Except the Lord build the house they labour in vain that build it." This is a reference to the Most High King who constantly builds the house and perfects it, but only when acceptable worship ascends from below in due form. Then again the words "Except the Lord keep the city, the watchman waketh but in vain" refer to the time when the darkness of the night sets in and armed companies roam to and fro in the world, and the doors are shut, and the city is guarded on all sides so that the uncircumcised and the unclean may not come near it. So it says: "For henceforth there shall no more come unto thee the uncircumcised and the unclean" (Is. LII, 1), since God will one day remove them from the world. Who, then, is the uncircumcised and who is the unclean? They are both one, the same that seduced Adam and his wife to follow him and so bring death into the world. He, too, will continue to defile this house until such time as the Holy One, blessed be He, will cause him to vanish from the world. Hence: "Except the Lord keep the city, etc."

'Observe that Jacob "journeyed to Succoth", whereas Esau "returned that day on his way unto Seir", each one taking the road toward his own side. Esau betook himself toward the side of Seir, that is, toward the "strange woman", the strange god, which are both designated by the name Seir; whereas Jacob journeyed to Succoth (lit. tabernacles), a name indicative of the true faith. "And built him a house", to wit, the House of Jacob.' Said R. Eleazar: 'Here is an indication that Jacob instituted evening prayer. We read further: "and he made booths (*succoth*) for his cattle"; these were other tabernacles which he made for guarding them, but the former *succoth* were his own portion.'

AND JACOB CAME PERFECT (*shalem*): perfect in every respect; the same allusion is contained in the words: "In Shalem (lit. in perfection) also he set his tabernacle" (Ps.

LXXVI, 3). For faith became his constant companion when he attained perfection, when he was crowned in the spot appropriate to him; and then also that Tabernacle was crowned along with him who was the perfection of the patriarchs, being completed by his sons. He was thus perfect on all sides: perfect on high, perfect below, perfect in heaven and perfect on earth. Perfect on high in that he was the consummation of the patriarchs, the glory of Israel; perfect below, through his holy sons; perfect in heaven and perfect on earth, so that "in perfection also he set his tabernacle".

AND DINAH THE DAUGHTER OF LEAH WENT OUT. The companions have remarked that there exist a variety of grades and sides on high, each one different from the other, *serpents* of all sorts, one kind endeavouring to gain dominion over the other and to devour prey, each according to its kind. From the side of the unclean spirit ever so many grades branch out, and all of them lie in wait to bring accusations against each other. Hence it is written: "Thou shalt not plow with an ox and an ass together" (Deut. XXII, 10), inasmuch as when these are joined together they bring accusations against mankind. Observe further that the great desire of the unclean grades is to find matter of charge against the holy sides. Thus, since Jacob was a holy man, they all lay in wait for him and contended with him. First the serpent bit him when he touched the hollow of his thigh, and now the ass bit him. Then it was Jacob himself who opposed the serpent, now it was Simeon and Levi, who belonged to the side [173*a*] of stern judgement, who stood up against the ass and prevailed over him and completely subdued him, as we read: "And they slew Hamor (lit. ass) and Shechem his son with the edge of the sword." Now Simeon, who was under the zodiacal sign of ox (Taurus), set upon the ass so as to prevent the two from joining, as then the latter would have set upon him. All came to contend with Jacob, who, however, was delivered from them and afterwards obtained dominion over them. Then came the one who is designated ox, and made himself perfect among the asses, that is, among those who were of the side of the ass. For Joseph was designated ox, and of the Egyptian the Scripture says: "whose flesh is as the flesh of asses" (Ez. XXIII, 20). It was for this reason that the sons of Jacob later on fell among those asses, inasmuch as the ox was joined with them; and they bit them to the bone until Levi arose as on the former occasion, and scattered and subdued them, and utterly broke their force. He also removed the ox from them, as it is written: "And Moses took the bones of Joseph with him" (Ex. XIII, 19). Observe that when Simeon assailed the ass (*Hamor*) on the first occasion he first made them see blood —the blood of circumcision—and after that "they slew all the males". God dealt in the same way through the hand of the Levite, Moses, with those other asses, the Egyptians. He first showed them blood and afterwards "the Lord slew all the first-born in the land of Egypt" (*Ibid.* XII, 29). In connection with Hamor it is written: "They took their flocks and their herds and their asses, etc."; in connection with those other asses it is written: "jewels of silver and jewels of gold, and raiment" (*Ibid.* 35), also: "And a mixed multitude went up also with them; and flocks and herds, even very much cattle" (*Ibid.* 38). In the same way, too, as Simeon withstood this one ass, Levi withstood that company of asses. They all conspired against Jacob the holy man and essayed to bite him, but he together with his sons stood up against them and subdued them. But now that Esau is biting him and his children, who will stand up against him ? Jacob and Joseph, one on one side and the other on the other side. So Scripture says: "And the house of Jacob shall be a fire, and the house of Joseph a flame, and the house of Esau for stubble, etc." (Oba. 1, 18).

And they journeyed; and a terror of God was upon the cities that were round about them, and they did not pursue after the sons of Jacob. R. Jose said: 'They all came together, but when they commenced to gird on their arms a terror seized them and they left them alone. Hence "they did not pursue after the sons of Jacob".'

Put away the strange gods, etc. These were the silver and gold vessels that they had taken from Shechem, and on which were engraved images of their gods. R. Judah said: 'Their idols themselves were made of silver and gold, and Jacob hid them there in order that his children should not make use of the side of idolatry, as a man is forbidden to have any benefit whatsoever from it.'

As R. Judah and R. Hizkiah were once walking together on the road, the latter said: 'It is written: "And he took the crown of Malcam from off his head; and the weight thereof was a talent of gold, and in it were precious stones; and it was set on David's head" (II Sam. XII, 30). Now, we have been taught that "Milcom the abomination of the Ammonites" (I Kings XI, 5) is the same as Malcam in this verse. How, then, was this crown permitted to be set on David's head? And further, why is it called "abomination", whereas other idols are referred to as "gods of the peoples", "strange gods", and the like?' R. Judah replied: 'Indeed, other idols are also called abominations, as we read: "And ye have seen their abominable things and their idols" (Deut. XXIX, 16). As regards the identification of Malcam with Milcom, this is certainly correct; nevertheless David was able to use the crown of Malcam because Ittai the Gittite, before he became a proselyte, broke it, that is to say, he disfigured the image which was on it, and so made its use permissible,[1] and it was set on David's head. The idol of the Ammonites was a serpent graven deep on that crown, and for that reason it was called abomination.' R. Isaac said that the order "put away the strange gods" referred to the other women who brought with them on their persons all their ornaments. Hence it is written: AND THEY GAVE UNTO JACOB ALL THE FOREIGN GODS, to wit, of those women. AND JACOB HID THEM [173b] so that his people should not derive any benefit whatever from the side of idolatry.

Observe the complete devotion of Jacob to the Almighty, as shown by his words: AND LET US ARISE, AND GO UP TO BETH-EL, AND I WILL MAKE THERE AN ALTAR UNTO GOD, WHO ANSWERED ME IN THE DAY OF MY DISTRESS, AND WAS WITH ME IN THE WAY WHICH I WENT. From

---

[1] According to the Rabbinical rule: "An idolater can render his do null and void."

these last words we learn that it is incumbent on a man to praise God and to give Him thanks for any miracle or any kindness that He has shown him. Observe that first Jacob said: "let *us* arise and go up to Beth-El", thus associating his children with him; but then: "and *I* will make there an altar", and not "*we* will make". The reason was that this task devolved upon him alone, since it was he who had passed through all those tribulations from the time when he fled from his brother, whereas his sons were not born until after. Hence he did not associate them with him. R. Eleazar said: 'From here we learn that he to whom a miracle is vouchsafed must himself offer thanks; just as he who has eaten a meal should say grace, and not one who has eaten nothing.'

AND HE BUILT THERE AN ALTAR, ETC. There is no mention here of libation or offering. The reason is that Jacob's intention was only to complete the grade which required completion, to wit, to join the lower grade, referred to by the word "altar", to the upper, referred to by the word "Lord". Hence he only built an altar and did not offer drink-offerings or burnt-offerings. AND CALLED THE PLACE EL-BETH-EL: a name analogous to the Most High Name, inasmuch as when there is a plenitude of light, then "like mother, like daughter", the two becoming one. BECAUSE THERE GOD WAS (lit. were) REVEALED UNTO HIM: the word *Elohim* (God) here is an allusion to the seventy who are always attendant on the Shekinah, there being seventy thrones round the Shekinah. Hence: "there God was revealed unto him", indicating the same place of which it is written: "And behold, the Lord stood beside him" (Gen. XXVIII, 13).

AND GOD WENT UP FROM HIM IN THE PLACE WHERE HE SPOKE WITH HIM. R. Simeon said: 'From here we learn that Jacob formed the Holy Chariot together with the other patriarchs; further, that Jacob constitutes the supernal Holy Chariot which will restore the full light of the moon, and that he forms a Chariot by himself, as implied in the statement: "And God went up from him". It is written: "For what great nation is there, that hath God so nigh unto them,

as the Lord our God is whensoever we call upon him ?"
(Deut. IV, 7). How dear', he exclaimed, 'must Israel be to
the Almighty, seeing that there is no nation or language
among all the idol-worshippers that has a god to hearken unto
them, whereas the Holy One, blessed be He, is ready to
receive the prayers and supplications of Israel in their hour
of need, to hearken to their prayers for the sake of their
grade.'

AND GOD SAID: THY NAME SHALL BE CALLED NO
MORE JACOB, BUT ISRAEL SHALL BE THY NAME; AND
(he) CALLED HIS NAME ISRAEL. The subject of "and
called" is the Shekinah, as in the expression: "And (he) called
unto Moses": whereas the name "God" earlier in the sentence refers to the higher grade. The name Israel was given
him in virtue of his having achieved perfection, and so by this
name he was raised to a higher grade and was made perfect in
that name. As R. Eleazar and R. Jose were once walking on
the road, the latter said to R. Eleazar: 'Assuredly it is as you
said, that Jacob was the consummation of the patriarchs and
that he was attached to all the sides and so his name was
called Israel. But how comes it that God afterwards again
called him many times by the name of Jacob, and that he is
commonly called Jacob just as before ?' R. Eleazar replied:
'That is a good question. To find an answer, consider the
verse: "The Lord will go forth as a mighty one, he will stir
up jealousy like a warrior" (Is. XLII, 12). Why say *as* a
mighty one, seeing that He is a mighty one; and why say
like a warrior, seeing that He is a warrior ? But the truth is
that, as we have learned, the name *Jehovah* (Lord) is everywhere expressive of the attribute of mercy. Now, assuredly,
[174*a*] God is named *Jehovah* (Lord), as it is written: "I am
the Lord *Jehovah*" (*Ibid.* 8). Yet we see that at times His
name is called *Elohim* (God), which is everywhere expressive
of judgement. The explanation is that when the righteous are
numerous among mankind, He is called by the name of
Jehovah (Lord), the name which implies mercy, but when
sinners abound, He is called by the name of *Elohim* (God).
Similarly with Jacob. When he is not among enemies, or in a

strange land, his name is Israel, but when he is among enemies or in a strange land he is called Jacob.' R. Jose rejoined:
'This does not quite solve the difficulty, seeing that it is
written: "thy name shall no more be called Jacob", and yet
all the time we do call him Jacob; as for your remark that he
is only called Jacob when among enemies or in a strange land,
do we not find it written: "And Jacob dwelt in the land of his
father's sojournings in the land of Canaan" (Gen. XXXVII, 1),
which was not a strange land ?' R. Eleazar replied: 'Just as
the names "Lord" and "God" indicate different degrees, so
the names Jacob and Israel indicate different degrees; and as
for the words "thy name shall no more be called Jacob", that
signifies merely that Jacob should not be his fixed name.'
Said R. Jose: 'If that is so, how is it that the name of Abraham
became fixed after God had said: "Neither shall thy name
any more be called Abram, but thy name shall be Abraham"
(*Ibid.* XVII, 5).' R. Eleazar replied: 'It is because there it is
written: "but thy name shall be (*vehayah*), that is, always,
whereas here it is written: "but Israel shall be (*yihyeh*) thy
name", that is, at least on one occasion, if not oftener. When,
however, his posterity were crowned with priests and Levites,
and were raised to high degrees, he was invested with the
name of Israel in perpetuity.'

Whilst they were walking, R. Jose said to R. Eleazar: 'It
has been said that with Rachel's death the house was transferred to Her who required to be adorned with twelve tribes.
Nevertheless, why should Rachel have died immediately after
the birth of Benjamin ?' R. Eleazar in reply said: 'It was in
order that the Shekinah should be duly crowned and take her
place in the house as "a joyful mother of children". With
Benjamin, the Shekinah was equipped with the full twelve
tribes, and with him the kingdom of heaven began to be made
manifest on earth. Now the beginning of any manifestation is
brought about with strain, and involves a doom of death
before it can become established. Here, when the Shekinah
was about to assume her rightful place and to take over the
house, the doom fell upon Rachel. Similarly, when the kingdom was about to be made manifest on earth, it commenced
with a judgement, and the kingdom was not established in its

place until a doom had fallen upon Saul, in accordance with his deserts; and only then was it established. It is a general rule that beginnings are rough, whereas the subsequent course is smooth. Thus, on New Year's day (*Rosh-hashana*) the year opens with severity, as the whole world passes under judgement, each individual according to his deeds, but soon after comes relief and forgiveness and atonement. The reason is that the beginning is from the left side, and so it brings harsh judgements, until the right side is aroused and ease follows. In time to come God will first treat the idolatrous nations gently and indulgently, but afterwards with severity and stern judgement. So Scripture says: "The Lord will go forth as a mighty one, he will stir up jealousy as a warrior; he will cry, yea, he will shout aloud, he will prove himself mighty against his enemies" (Is. XLII, 13); which interpreted means that first He will manifest Himself as *Jehovah* (the Lord), in His attribute of mercy, then as a mighty one, but not in His full might, then as a warrior, but not in His full war panoply, and finally, His whole might will become manifest against them in order to exterminate them, so that "he will cry, yea, he will shout aloud, he will prove himself mighty against his enemies." Again, it is written: "Then shall the Lord go forth, and fight against those nations, as when he fighteth in the day of battle" (Zech. XIV, 3). Also: "Who is this that cometh from Edom with crimson garments from Bozrah? etc." (Is. LXIII, 1).'

AND IT CAME TO PASS, AS HER SOUL WAS IN DEPART-ING—FOR SHE DIED—THAT SHE CALLED HIS NAME BEN-ONI; BUT HIS FATHER CALLED HIM BENJAMIN. R. Judah discoursed on the verse: *The Lord is good, a stronghold in the day of trouble; and he knoweth them that take refuge in him* (Nahum I, 7). 'Happy', he said, 'is the man who finds his strength in the Holy One, blessed be He, since His strength is invincible. The Lord is indeed "good to all" (Ps. CXLV, 9), "a stronghold", wherein is salvation, as we read: "He is a stronghold of [174*b*] salvation" (*Ibid.* XXVIII, 8); "in the day of trouble", to wit, in the day of Israel's oppression at the hand of other nations. Now of him who relaxes his hold of the Holy One, blessed be He, it is written: "If thou art faint in the day of adversity, thy strength is straitened" (Prov. XXIV, 10), and the only way of holding firmly to God is to hold firmly to the Torah; for whosoever holds firmly to the Torah holds firmly to the tree of life, and, as it were, adds strength to the community of Israel. But if he relaxes his hold of the Torah, then, as it were, he presses hard the Shekinah, which is the strength of the world. Again, when a man relaxes his hold of the Torah and walks in the wrong path, ever so many enemies are ready at hand to act as his accusers in the day of trouble, nay, even his own soul, which is his power and strength, turns against him, and becomes his enemy, so that it may be said of him "thy strength becomes an enemy" (*zar*=enemy, or straitened).' Said R. Abba: 'When a man follows the guidance of the Torah and walks in the straight path, many are the advocates that rise up to say a good word for him. Thus we read: "If there be for him an angel, an intercessor, one among a thousand, to vouch for man's uprightness; then he is gracious unto him, and saith: Deliver him from the pit, I have found a ransom" (Job XXXIII, 23, 24). These verses', continued R. Abba, 'present a difficulty. Is not everything revealed before God, that He should require an angel to point out to Him the good or bad that is found in a man, so that only when a man has defenders on his side to recall his merits before Him, and no accusers, then He is gracious unto him, and saith: "Deliver him from going down into the pit, I have found a ransom"? But the language of the text, if properly considered, contains the answer. For it would have sufficed to say: "If there be for him an angel"; who, then, is the "intercessor, one among a thousand"? It is one of the angels appointed to follow man on his left side. There are a thousand such, as it says, "A thousand may fall at thy side, and ten thousand at thy right hand" (Ps. XCI, 7). Now "one among a thousand" is a designation of the evil prompter, who is the outstanding figure of the thousand on the left, since he is the one who ascends on high and obtains authorisation. Hence, if a man walks in the way of truth and the evil prompter becomes his servant, according to the words, "Better is he that is lightly esteemed, and hath a servant" (Prov. XII, 9), then he ascends on high and becomes the man's advocate, pleading his merits before God, whereupon God says: "Deliver him from going down into the pit." Nevertheless, the evil prompter does not return empty-handed, since another man is delivered into his power, one whose sins he has already set forth, and this one is a ransom for the other man. This is what is meant by the words: "I (God) have found a compensation" (for thee, the accuser). According to another interpretation, the ransom consists in the merits of the man, through which he is freed from the pit and from death. It is therefore incumbent on a man to walk in the path of truth so that the accuser should be turned into his defender. A similar procedure is employed by Israel on the Day of Atonement, when they tender a he-goat to the evil prompter and so engage his attention until he ascends and gives testimony before the Almighty, in their favour. Thus Solomon says: "If thine adversary be hungry, give him bread to eat, and if he be thirsty, give him water to drink" (*Ibid.* xxv, 21), referring to the evil prompter. The words: "The Lord is good, a stronghold in the day of trouble" apply to Jacob when Esau came forward to accuse him, and the words: "and he knoweth them that put their trust in him" were exemplified when the trouble of Dinah befell him. Observe that the accuser attacks a man only in time of danger; and so it was on account of Jacob having delayed to fulfil his vows which he had made to God that the accuser came forward against him, [175*a*] selecting the moment when Rachel's life was in danger. "Behold," he said, "Jacob has made vows and has not paid them; he has wealth and children and is short of nothing, yet he has not paid his vow that he made before Thee; and Thou hast not punished him." Then straightway "Rachel travailed and she had hard labour", the term "hard" indicating that a severe doom was issued on high at the instigation of the angel of death.'

AND RACHEL DIED. We have seen that Jacob, at the time Esau came up to him, put the handmaids and their children foremost, and Leah and her children after, and Rachel and

Joseph hindermost. Why did he put Rachel hindermost ? Because he feared that the wicked Esau might observe her beauty and assail him on account of her. It is written further: "Then the handmaids came near, they and their children, and they bowed down. And Leah also and her children came near, and bowed down", the females before the males. But in regard to Rachel it is written: "and after came Joseph near and Rachel", that is, Joseph in front of his mother, so as to protect her. And here Rachel was punished at the hand of the evil prompter, who availed himself of the moment of danger and brought accusations against her; and Jacob was punished for not having paid his vow. Jacob felt this blow more acutely than all the other sufferings that befell him. That her death was due to him we learn from his words: "Rachel died upon me" (Gen. XLVIII, 7), or, as we may translate, "on account of me", i.e. through my not having paid my vows. R. Jose said: 'It is written: "the curse that is causeless shall come home" (Prov. XXVI, 2). This signifies that the curse of a righteous man, even if pronounced under a misapprehension, once uttered is caught up by the evil prompter to be used at a moment of danger. Now Jacob said to Laban: "With whomsoever thou findest thy gods, he shall not live" (Gen. XXXI, 32); and although he was unaware that it was Rachel who had stolen them, the Satan (adversary) who perpetually dogs the footsteps of the sons of men, seized on that utterance. Hence we are taught that a man should "never open his mouth for the Satan", inasmuch as the latter is sure to take hold of his utterance and use it to bring accusations on high and below; all the more so if it is the utterance of a righteous man or a sage. These, then, were the true causes of Rachel's death.'

AND IT CAME TO PASS, AS HER SOUL DEPARTED—FOR SHE DIED. R. Abba said: 'What need is there to state that she died, after it says that her soul departed ? The object is to make it clear that her soul did not return again to her body, as sometimes happens with some people. Thus we read: "And his spirit returned unto him"; also: "And their heart departed" (Gen. XLII, 28); or: "My soul departed" (S. S. v, 6); again: "until there was no soul left in him" (1 Kings xvii, 17). But when Rachel's soul passed out, it did not return, and so she died.'

AND SHE CALLED HIS NAME BEN-ONI (the son of my sorrow), in reference to the doom that was pronounced against her; but Jacob turned him round and attached him to the right (*Benyamin*=the son of the right hand), as the West (of which Benjamin was symbolic) needed to be bound up with the right. Thus, although he was Ben-oni (the son of sorrow), derived from the side of chastisement, yet was he also Benjamin (the son of the right), as the mother was bound up with the right and was buried by the road, as explained elsewhere. Rachel's death and burial-place are recorded, but neither the death nor the burial-place of Leah is recorded; and this although the matriarchs have a joint symbolism, which has been explained elsewhere.

AND JACOB SET UP A PILLAR UPON HER GRAVE. R. Jose said: 'He did this in order that her burial-place should never be forgotten until the day when God shall raise the dead to life. This is borne out by the phrase: "unto this day", which means until that great day.' R. Judah said: 'It means, until the day when the Shekinah will return with the exiles of Israel to that spot, as it is written: "And there is hope for thy future, saith the Lord; and thy children shall return to their own border" (Jer. xxxi, 17). This is the oath which God swore unto her; and Israel are destined, when they return from exile, to stop at Rachel's grave and weep there as she wept over Israel's exile. It is thus written: "They shall come with weeping, and with supplications will I lead them" (*Ibid.* 9); also: "for thy work shall be rewarded" (*Ibid.* 16). And at that [175b] time Rachel who lies on the way will rejoice with Israel and with the Shekinah. The Companions have thus expounded all this.'

AND IT CAME TO PASS, WHILE ISRAEL DWELT IN THAT LAND, THAT REUBEN WENT AND LAY WITH BILHAH HIS FATHER'S CONCUBINE; AND ISRAEL HEARD OF IT. NOW THE SONS OF JACOB WERE TWELVE. R. Eleazar said: 'The term dwelt (*sh'kon*) indicates that Leah and Rachel had died by that time, and the house had been taken over by the new mistress (the Shekinah). In spite of the words of the text, we are not to suppose that Reuben really lay with Bilhah. The truth is that during the lives of Leah and Rachel the Shekinah hovered over them; and now that they had died the Shekinah never departed from the house, but took up there her abode, namely, in the tent of Bilhah; nor would it have been found there had not Jacob formed a new union of male and female. But Reuben, in his displeasure at seeing Bilhah filling his mother's place, came and disarranged the couch; and because the Shekinah rested on it, it is written, "And he lay with Bilhah".' R. Jesse said that Reuben laid himself down to sleep on that couch, thus showing disrespect to the Shekinah. Hence Reuben was not excluded from the list of the tribes; and so Scripture relates that "the sons of Jacob were twelve", commencing with Reuben, Jacob's first-born, thus putting him at the head of the tribes.

R. Judah discoursed on the verse: *For the ways of the Lord are right, and the just do walk in them; but transgressors stumble therein* (Hos. XIV, 10). 'All the ways of God', he said, 'are right and true, but mankind know not and regard not what it is that keeps them alive. Hence "the just do walk in them", because they know the ways of God, and they devote themselves to the Torah; for whoever devotes himself to the Torah knows those ways and follows them without turning either to the right or the left. "But transgressors do stumble therein", to wit, the sinners, since they labour not in the Torah nor regard the ways of the Almighty, and know not in which way they are walking. And since they are thoughtless and do not study the Torah, they stumble in their ways in this world and in the world to come. Now the soul of one who has laboured in the study of the Torah, when it leaves this world, ascends by the ways and paths of the Torah—ways and paths familiar to them. They who know the ways and paths of the Torah in this world follow them in the other world when they leave this world. But those who do not study the Torah in this world and know not its ways and paths, when they leave this world know not how to follow those ways and paths, and hence stumble therein. They thus follow other ways which are not the ways of the Torah, and are visited with many chastisements. Of him who devotes himself to the Torah, on the other hand, it is written: "When thou liest down, it shall watch over thee; and when thou awakest, it shall talk with thee" (Prov. VI, 22). "When thou liest down", to wit, in the grave, the Torah shall watch over thee against the judgement of the other world; "and when thou awakest", that is, when the Holy One, blessed be He, will awake the spirits and souls so as to bring the dead to life again, it shall talk with thee, the Torah will speak in defence of the body, so that those bodies which laboured to keep the Torah as required will rise up. These it is who will be the first to rise up, and of whom it is written: "And many of them that sleep in the dust of the earth shall awake, some to everlasting life, etc." (Dan. XII, 2), for the reason that they occupied themselves with everlasting life, which is the Torah. Further, all the bodies of those who have devoted themselves to the Torah will be preserved, and the Torah will protect them, inasmuch as at that time the Holy One, blessed be He, will raise up a wind from all four quarters of the world, a wind specially prepared to bring to life all those who have laboured in the Torah so that they should live for ever. It may be asked here, what of the dead who were revived by the prophet's invocation, "Come from the four winds, O breath" (Ez. XXXVII, 9), and who yet did not survive, but died a second time ? The answer is that at that time, although the wind was compounded of all four winds, it did not come down to give them permanent life, but only to demonstrate the mode in which God will one day bring the dead to life, namely, by a wind [176*a*] formed in this fashion. So that although those who were then resurrected turned again into bones, since their resurrection was only meant as a proof to the world that God will one day raise the dead to life, we may still believe that at the proper time the righteous will be resurrected for an everlasting life. For the Torah itself will stand by each one of those who have occupied themselves in the study of the Torah, recounting his merits before the Almighty.' R. Simeon said: 'All the words of the Torah, and all the doctrine of the Torah to which a man devotes his mind in this world, are ever before the Almighty, and at that time the Torah will recount how the man devoted himself to the Torah in this world, and thereat such men will all rise for everlasting life, as we said already.' Thus, "the ways of the Lord are right, and the just do walk in them; but transgressors do stumble therein."

R. Hiya cited in this connection: "Now Eli was very old; and he heard all that his sons did unto all Israel, and how that they lay with the women that did service at the door of the tent of meeting" (1 Sam. 11, 22). 'Are we to believe', he said, 'that the priests of the Lord actually did such a thing ? And what, in fact, were their sins as recorded by the Scripture ? Merely that they "dealt contemptuously with the offering of the Lord" (*Ibid.* 17), and that "the custom of the priests with the people was that, when any man offered sacrifice. . . . Yea, before the fat was made to smoke, the priest's servant came, and said to the man that sacrificed: Give flesh to roast for the priest. . . . Nay, but thou shalt give it to me now, and if not, I will take it by force" (*Ibid.* 16). In fact, they only took those portions that belonged to the priests, and it was only because they treated lightly the offerings that they were punished. Yet here Scripture states that "they lay with the women that did service at the door of the tent of meeting". Assuredly they could not have committed so grave a sin, and that in so sacred a place, without the whole of Israel arising and slaying them. The truth is that what they did was to prevent the women from entering and offering their prayers until the other sacrifices had been offered, because their offerings were of a kind in which the priests had no portion. It is this action of preventing them from entering the sanctuary which is described by the words: "they lay with the women, etc." Similarly, in the case of Reuben, we should not dream of taking literally the words "and he lay with Bilhah". What he did was to prevent her from performing her conjugal duty to his father, and this was the object of his disarranging his father's couch; and, moreover, he did it in the presence of the Shekinah; for the Shekinah is always present whenever marital intercourse is performed as a religious duty; and whoever obstructs such a performance causes the Shekinah to depart from the world. So Scripture says: "Because thou wentest up to thy father's bed; then profanedst thou that one that went up to my couch" (Gen. XLIX, 4). Hence it is written: "that Reuben went and lay with Bilhah, his father's concubine; and Israel heard of it. Now the sons of Jacob were twelve"; that is to say, they were all included in the number, and their merit was in no wise abated.'

R. Eleazar asked: 'Why do we find in this verse first the name Israel and then the name Jacob ? The reason may be given as follows. Reuben said to himself: "My father was intended to raise twelve tribes and no more, yet now he is about to beget more children. Does he then wish to disqualify us and replace us with others?" So straightway he disarranged the couch and prevented the intended intercourse, thereby slighting, as it were, the honour of the Shekinah that hovered over that couch. Hence it is written first "and *Israel* heard", since it was by that name that he was exalted among the twelve hidden ones which are the twelve pure rivers of balsam, and then "and the sons of *Jacob* were twelve", alluding to the twelve tribes by whom the Shekinah was adorned and whom the Torah again enumerated [176b] as before, implying that they were all of them holy, all of them considered by the Shekinah worthy to behold the sanctity of their Master; for had Reuben really committed the act mentioned, he would not have been included in the number. For all that, he was punished by being deprived of the birthright and by its transference to Joseph, as we read: "And the sons of Reuben, the first-born of Israel—for he was the first-born; but forasmuch as he defiled his father's couch, his birthright was given unto the sons of Joseph" (1 Chron. VI). We see from this how all that God does is planned with profound wisdom, and every act of a man leaves its imprint and is preserved before the Almighty. For on the night when Jacob went in to Leah, all his thoughts were centred upon Rachel, and from that intercourse, and from the first germ, and under that intention Leah conceived; and we have affirmed that had not Jacob been unaware of the deception, Reuben would not have entered into the number. It is for that reason that he did not receive a name of special significance, but was simply called

Reuben (*reu-ben*=behold, a son). But for all that, the intended effect was produced, and the birthright reverted to the eldest son of Rachel, as originally purposed. Thus everything came right in the end, for all the works of the Almighty are based on truth and right.'

R. Hizkiah one day found R. Jose cooking a dish from which grease was dripping on to the fire, sending up a cloud of smoke. He said then to him: 'If the pillars of smoke which used once to ascend from the top of the altar had continued to go up like this smoke, wrath would not have descended on the world and Israel would not have been exiled from their land.' R. Jose then opened a discourse on the verse: *Who is this that cometh out of the wilderness like pillars of smoke, perfumed with myrrh and frankincense, with all powders of the merchant* (S. S. III, 6). 'When Israel', he said, 'were journeying in the wilderness, the Shekinah went in front of them, as it is written: "And the Lord went before them by day in a pillar of cloud, to lead them the way; and by night in a pillar of fire, to give them light" (Ex. XIII, 22). They on their side followed its guidance; wherefore it is written: "Thus saith the Lord: I remember thee the affection of thy youth, the love of thine espousals; how thou wentest after me in the wilderness, etc." (Jer. II, 2). The Shekinah was accompanied by all the clouds of glory, and when it journeyed the Israelites took up their march, as it says: "And whenever the cloud was taken up from over the tent, then after that the children of Israel journeyed, etc." (Num. IX, 17). And when the Shekinah ascended, the cloud also ascended on high, so that all men looked up and asked: "Who is this that cometh out of the wilderness like pillars of smoke?" For the cloud of the Shekinah looked like smoke because the fire which Abraham and his son Isaac kindled clung to it and never left it, and by reason of that fire it ascended both as cloud and smoke; but for all that it was "perfumed", or, as we may also translate, "bound up with myrrh and frankincense", that is, with the cloud of Abraham on the right and with the cloud of Isaac on the left. The words "with all powders of the merchant" allude to Jacob, or, according to another explanation, to Joseph, whose bier accompanied the Israelites in the wilderness, and the designation *rokhel* (merchant or tale-bearer) is given to him because he brought evil reports of his brethren to their father; or, again, because just as the seller of spices keeps his herbs and spices in bundles, so Joseph through one action kept the whole of the Torah, since all the precepts of the Torah are bound up with the preservation of the holy covenant in its integrity. The Shekinah was thus leagued with Abraham, Isaac, and Jacob together with Joseph, inasmuch as the two latter are one in essence, each one being the image of the other, as indicated in the words: "These are the offspring of Jacob: Joseph" (Gen. XXXVII, 2). Now, when the Israelites dwelt in their land and brought offerings, they all drew themselves nearer to God in manner due; and when the work of sacrifice was performed and the smoke of the altar ascended in a straight column, they knew that it had kindled [177a] the lamp which they desired to kindle, and so all faces shone and all lamps were lit. But since the destruction of the Temple not a day passes but is visited with wrath and rage, as it says: "and God hath indignation every day" (Ps. VII, 12), and joy has departed from on high and from below, and Israel have gone into exile and are subject to other gods, and the words of Scripture have been fulfilled, saying: "and there thou shalt serve other gods" (Deut. XXVIII, 64). Why all this ? "Because thou didst not serve the Lord thy God with joyfulness, and with gladness of heart, by reason of the abundance of all things. Therefore shalt thou serve thine enemy, etc., in want of all things" (*Ibid.* XXVIII, 47–48). And so it will be until God will arise and redeem them from among the nations, as we read. "then the Lord thy God will turn thy captivity, and have compassion upon thee, and will return and gather thee from all the peoples, whither the Lord thy God hath scattered thee. If any of thine that are dispersed be in the uttermost parts of heaven, from thence will the Lord thy God gather thee, etc." (*Ibid.* XXX, 3–4).'

NOW THESE ARE THE GENERATIONS OF ESAU—THE SAME IS EDOM. The Scripture does not enumerate the sons of Esau until after it has recorded the death of Isaac, whereas Jacob's sons were enumerated long before. The reason for the distinction is this. Esau had neither portion nor inheritance nor lot in Isaac, but only Jacob and his sons. Jacob and his sons are therefore the portion of the Holy One, blessed be He, and they enter into the reckoning; but Esau, who was not of the portion of the side of true faith, made up his account, as it were, after the death of Isaac, and his portion parted and took its course to another region. Observe that after Isaac died and Esau retired to his own side, it is written: "And Esau took his wives . . . and went into a land away from his brother Jacob", that is, he relinquished to Jacob both the capital and the profit, or, in other words, the bondage of Egypt and the land, and he sold his own portion in the cave of Machpelah, and went away from the land and from the true faith, abandoning all completely. Observe, then, how much Jacob's portion was thus enhanced in every respect, in that Esau did not remain with him, but parted from him and went away to his own portion and lot, so that Jacob was left in possession of the heritage of his father and of his ancestors. Hence: "and he went into a land away from his brother Jacob", the last phrase indicating that he had no desire for Jacob's portion or inheritance or his meed of faith. Happy the portion of Jacob, of whom the Scripture says: "For the portion of the Lord is his people, Jacob the lot of his inheritance" (*Ibid.* XXXII, 9).

AND THESE ARE THE KINGS THAT REIGNED IN THE LAND OF EDOM, BEFORE THERE REIGNED ANY KING OVER THE CHILDREN OF ISRAEL. R. Jesse discoursed on the verse: *Behold, I make thee small among the nations, thou art greatly despised* (Ob. I, 2). 'When God', he said, 'made the world, He divided it into seven regions corresponding to the seventy Chieftains whom He placed in charge over the seventy nations, assigning to each the nation appropriate to him, as we read: "He set the borders of the peoples, according to the number of the children of Israel" (Deut. XXXII, 8); and of all those Chieftains who were given charge over the other nations no one is so much despised before Him as the Chieftain of Esau. The reason of this is that the side of Esau is the side of defilement; and the side of defilement is despicable before the Holy One, blessed be He, as it springs from those base grades that are behind the empty millstones of the red custodians. Hence, God said to it: "Behold, I make thee small among the nations; thou art greatly despised", as it is written: "upon thy belly shalt thou go, and dust shalt thou eat all the days of thy life" (Gen. III, 14), and also: "cursed be thou from among all cattle, and from among all beasts of the field" (*Ibid.*) Observe that the lower grades form a hierarchy, one above the other, and each different from the other, yet all linked and interlocked with each other. So is kingdom separate from kingdom, yet is each linked to the other. All the grades are held, as it were, by one chain of a certain measurement, which in its turn is divided into three smaller chains which reach down and are tied to the stars and planets, so that each grade is assigned one [177b] star or planet. Those stars in their turn operate under the grades above. Every grade has thus charge of its own proper region, and, when they diverge, a chain is formed by which each grade is bound to its proper side. The sides of the unclean grades, which are on the left side, diverge all of them into numerous ways and paths and distribute their power to thousands and myriads in the lower world; and in reference to this it was said to Edom: "Behold, I make thee small among the nations; thou art greatly despised." Now, in the text, "And these are the kings that reigned in the land of Edom", the words "in the land" indicate the side of his grade, that is, the grade of Esau, since it is written: "Esau— the same is Edom." All these things were thus from the side of the unclean spirit; and they were "before there reigned any king over the children of Israel", inasmuch as they embody the grades that stand first at the lower gates. It was this that Jacob had in mind when he said "Let my lord, I pray thee, pass over before his servant" (Gen. XXXIII, 14), since Esau's grades were the first to gain an entrance. They thus reigned before there was any king over Israel, for as yet the time had not arrived] for the kingdom of heaven to enter into power and to league itself with the children of Israel. When it did, it began with the least of the tribes, which was Benjamin, as it says: "There is Benjamin, the youngest, ruling them, etc." (Ps. LXVIII, 28), and with him the kingdom began to advance. After that the kingdom came into its own place and was established, never to be removed.'

R. Hiya discoursed on the verses: *Yet now hear, O Jacob my servant, and Israel, whom I have chosen; thus saith the Lord that made thee and formed thee from the womb, who will help thee: Fear not, O Jacob my servant, and thou Jeshurun, whom I have chosen* (Is. XLIV, 1–2). 'Observe', he said, 'how God has promised Israel in many places to make them worthy of the world to come, as He has not chosen for his portion any other people or language, but only Israel. It was for this purpose that He gave them the Torah of truth, by whose means they may live virtuously and learn the ways of the Holy One, blessed be He, so that they may inherit the Holy Land; for whoever is thought worthy of the Holy Land has a portion in the world to come. So Scripture says: "Thy people also shall be all righteous, they shall inherit the land for ever" (*Ibid.* LX, 21). Now, in the verses above quoted three grades are mentioned: first Jacob, then Israel, and finally Jeshurun. Jacob and Israel have been explained. Jeshurun suggests the word *shur* (row, side) and indicates that he has his rank on this side and on the other. The three names, though representing different grades, are really the same. Jacob is called "my servant" because sometimes he is like a servant who has orders from his master and is eager to execute his will. We read elsewhere: "the Lord that created thee, O Jacob, and he that formed thee, O Israel" (*Ibid.* XLIII, 1), and in the above verse we read: "Thus saith the Lord that made thee." We have thus herein the terms "created", "formed", and "made", which represent different grades, one above the other, but which all are essentially one. Happy the portion of Israel in whom the Holy One, blessed be He, finds delight above all the nations who worship idols, of which it is written: "They are vanity, a work of delusion; in the time of their visitation they shall perish" (Jer. X, 15). That will come to pass on the day when God will destroy them from the world, so that He alone will remain, as it says: "And the Lord alone shall be exalted in that day" (Is. II, 11).'

R. Judah discoursed on the verse: *Fear not, thou worm*

Jacob, and ye men of Israel; I help thee, saith the Lord, and thy Redeemer the Holy One of Israel (*Ibid.* XLI, 14). 'Observe', he said, 'that all the Gentiles have been placed by the Almighty under the charge of certain tutelary Chieftains, as already stated, and that they all follow their own gods, as it is written: "For all the peoples walk each one in the name of its god" (Micah IV, 5); and they are addicted to bloodshed and warfare, to robbery, violence, and fornication, [178a] and other kinds of wickedness, and use all their power to injure and do harm. Israel, on their part, have no force or power to overcome them save in their mouth, like to the worm which has no strength or power except in its mouth, by which, however, it wears through everything. Hence Israel are called "worm". Or again, as the silkworm, that precious creature which produces from itself a fine thread out of which is woven the costliest kingly raiment, leaves behind before it dies a seed out of which it comes to life as before; so Israel, although they seemingly die, always re-emerge and persist in the world as before. So Scripture says: "Behold, as the clay in the potter's hand, so are ye in my hand, O house of Israel" (Jer. XVIII, 6). The term *homer* (clay) signifies in reality the material of glass which, when broken, can be refounded and made whole as before. "Fear not . . . men of Israel", they being the tree of life, for since the children have engrafted themselves on the tree of life, they will arise from the dust and will be established in the world as one united people to worship the Holy One, blessed be He, in harmony with the words: "That they may call upon the name of the Lord, to serve him with one consent" (Zeph. III, 9).'

R. Eleazar and R. Isaac were one day travelling on the road together when the time for the reading of the Shema arrived. R. Eleazar paused and recited the Shema and said his prayer. After he had finished, R. Isaac said to him: 'Have we not learnt that before a man starts on a journey he must first ask leave from his Master and offer up his prayer?' R. Eleazar said in reply: 'When I left it was not yet time either for the reading of the Shema or for saying prayers. Now that the sun has risen I have said my prayer. But all the same, before commencing my journey I did offer a prayer to Him and consulted

Him, as it were. I, however, did not say this prayer because I have been occupied in studying the Torah since midnight, and from the early dawn up to now it was not yet the time for prayer, for while the morning is still dark the Wife is conversing with her Husband, being about to retire to her tent, where her maidens keep her company. Hence no man should then interrupt them and break in with other words. Now, however, that the sun has risen it is the time for prayer, as it is written: "'They shall fear thee with the sunrise" (Ps. LXXII, 5), which indicates the close connection between fear of God, or devotion, and the light of the sun, which makes it incumbent on man not to part them, but to associate them together.' The two then proceeded on their way, until they arrived at a field, where they sat down. Raising their eyes, they saw a mountain, on the top of which they discerned strange creatures moving about. R. Isaac began to tremble. Said R. Eleazar to him: 'Why are you afraid?' He answered: 'Because this mountain looks so formidable and on it are strange creatures, which I fear will attack us.' R. Eleazar then said to him: 'Whoever is afraid of his sins has cause to fear. Those creatures are not of the dangerous kind that haunt the mountains.' He then began to discourse on the verse: AND THESE ARE THE CHILDREN OF ZIBEON: AIAH AND ANAH—THIS IS ANAH WHO FOUND THE YEMIM IN THE WILDERNESS. 'In regard to this verse,' he said, 'it is agreed that these *yemim* are not the same as the Emim mentioned in the verse: "The Emim dwelt therein aforetime . . . but the children of Esau succeeded them" (Deut. II, 10–11). They were an unnatural kind of being which was first created from the side of evil spirits and goblins at the moment when the Sabbath was about to be sanctified, and they remained unsubstantial and bodiless, since neither the sixth day nor the seventh day would own them. [178b] When, however, Cain was driven from the face of the earth and dwelt in the land of Nod, they spread from his side and became corporeal, but not for any length of time. They are therefore called *yamim* (days), spelt in the same way as *yemim* here, without a *yod*, in allusion to the fact that they appear occasionally to men as they haunt the mountains, and for one moment in the day assume bodily shape, but forthwith lose it again. Anah found them and they taught him to bring bastards into the world. For Anah himself was a bastard, the offspring of an incestuous intercourse between Zibeon and his own mother; and this came about through the side of the unclean spirit that attached itself to him. Those and numerous other monstrous beings of many varieties are derived from that side and roam about in the wilderness and can be seen there, as the wilderness is a desolate place and therefore is a suitable haunt for them. For all that, whoever walks in the ways of the Holy One, blessed be He, and fears Him, has no cause to fear them.' The two then went on and ascended the mountain. Said R. Isaac: 'Are they found in all desert mountains like these ?' Said R. Eleazar: 'That is so, but of all those who labour in the Torah it is written: "The Lord shall keep thee from all evil; he shall keep thy soul. The Lord shall guard thy going out and thy coming in, from this time forth and for ever" (Ps. CXXI, 7–8).'

R. Eleazar discoursed on the verse: *Hallelujah* (praise ye the Lord). *I will give thanks unto the Lord with my whole heart, in the council of the upright, and in the congregation.* (Ps. CXI, 1). 'King David', he said, 'daily devoted himself to the worship of the Almighty, and he would rise at midnight and sing hymns and songs of praise and thanksgiving, so as to establish his place in the kingdom above. For as soon as the north wind began to blow at midnight he knew that the moment had come when God rose, as it were, to disport Himself with the righteous in the Garden of Eden; so he arose at that moment and busied himself with songs and thanksgivings until the morning. For, as we have affirmed, when the Holy One, blessed be He, appears in the Garden of Eden, He and all the righteous in the Garden of Eden listen to the voice of the suppliant, as we read: "The companions hearken for thy voice, cause me to hear it" (S. S. VIII, 13); and, moreover, a thread of grace is woven round him during the day, as it is written: "By day the Lord will command his lovingkindness, and in the night his song shall be with me" (Ps. XLII, 9). And furthermore, all the words of the Torah which one utters in the night ascend and are woven into a garland before the Almighty. King David therefore devoted himself during the night to the service of his Master. Observe the heading Hallelujah (praise ye the Lord), for we have learned that of all the titles that David affixed to his songs and hymns, the most excellent was Hallelujah, embracing as it does in one single word the name of God and the call to praise, the name being Yah, and the praise coming from the Community of Israel, who continually compose thanksgivings to the Holy One, blessed be He, as we read: "O God, there is no silence for thee; hold not thy peace, and be not still, O God" (Ps. LXXXIII, 2), because the Community of Israel continually arranges and offers up its thanksgivings to Him. Now we read further: "I will give thanks unto the Lord with my whole heart (*lebab*)", that is, as already explained, with the good and the evil prompter, who are always with a man: "in the council of the upright, and in the congregation" is an allusion to Israel, who are adorned with all grades—priests and Levites, the just and the pious. It is the same congregation of which we read: "God standeth in the congregation of God" (Ps. LXXXII, 1). Hence a man should continually offer praise to God, since He takes delight in songs and hymns, and when a man knows how to offer praise to God in the proper manner, He accepts his prayer and delivers him, as we read: "I will set him on high, because he hath known my name . . . With long life will I satisfy him, etc." (*Ibid*. XCI, 14–16).'

R. Jose discoursed on the verse: *Thou art my hiding-place; thou wilt preserve me from the adversary; with songs of deliverance thou wilt compass me about. Selah (Ibid. XXXII, 7).* 'It is God', he said, 'who is a hiding-place and a shield to the man that walks in the ways of the Torah; such a man is covered by the shadow of His wings so that no one can do him mischief. "Thou wilt preserve me from the adversary"; that is, from the adversary on high and from the adversary here below, both of whom are one and the same evil prompter, [179*a*] who is the opponent above and the opponent below; and if not for the evil prompter, man would have no adversary in the world. "With songs of deliverance thou wilt compass me about" is an allusion to those songs that possess grades of potency to save; with which, therefore, "Thou wilt compass me about" to afford me deliverance when on a journey. (This verse is efficacious whether read forwards or backwards.) Observe that all the songs and hymns that David sang contain deep allusions of wisdom, because he composed them under the inspiration of the Holy Spirit, which alone it was that prompted him.'

R. Eleazar discoursed on the verse: *Thou didst thrust sore at me that I might fall; but the Lord helped me (Ibid.* CXVIII, 13). 'We should have expected', he said, ' "*they* did thrust sore at me" instead of "*thou* didst, etc." But, in truth, this alludes to the "other side" that continually thrusts at a man, and tries to seduce him and lead him astray from God; the same is, indeed, the evil prompter who follows man about. It is to him that David addressed the words, "thou didst thrust sore at me", seeing that he endeavoured by means of all sorts of afflictions to turn him aside from God. David thus said: "Thou didst thrust sore at me—to cause me to fall into Gehinnom—but the Lord helped me—so that I was not delivered into thy hand." It is, hence, incumbent on a man to be on his guard against the evil prompter, so that he shall not obtain the mastery over him; such a man God guards in all his ways, as it is written: "Then shalt thou walk in thy way securely, and thou shalt not dash thy foot" (Prov. III, 23), also: "When thou goest thy step shall not be straitened; and if thou runnest thou shalt not stumble" (*Ibid.* IV, 12); and also: "But the path of the righteous is as the light of dawn, that shineth more and more unto the perfect day" (*Ibid.* IV, 18).'

Said R. Judah: 'Happy are Israel whom the Holy One, blessed be He, preserves in this world and in the world to come, as it is written: "Thy people also shall be all righteous, they shall inherit the land for ever" (Is. LX, 21). Blessed be the Lord, for evermore. Amen and Amen !'

VAYESHEB

Gen. XXXVII, 1–XL, 23

AND JACOB DWELT IN THE LAND OF HIS FATHER'S SOJOURNINGS, IN THE LAND OF CANAAN. R. Hiya discoursed on the verse: *Many are the ills of the righteous, but the Lord delivereth him out of them all* (Ps. XXXIV, 20). 'Many, indeed', he said, 'are the adversaries with whom a human being has to contend from the day that God breathes into him a soul in this world. For as soon as he emerges into the light of day, the evil prompter is at hand in readiness to join him, according to our interpretation of the verse: "Sin coucheth at the door" (Gen. IV, 7). In proof whereof note that the beasts from the day they are born are able to take care of themselves, and avoid fire and similar dangers, whereas man, on the other hand, seems to feel at first a natural propensity to throw himself into the fire, the reason being that the evil prompter dwells within him and from the beginning lures him into evil ways. So Scripture says: "Better is a poor and wise child than an old and foolish king, who knoweth not how to receive admonition any more" (Eccl. IV, 13). The "child" here signifies the good prompter, who is so called because he is, as it were, a youngster by the side of man, whom he does not join till he is at the age of thirteen years, as elsewhere affirmed. He is better, then, than "an old and foolish king", to wit, the evil prompter, who is called king and ruler over the sons of men, and who is assuredly old, since, as already said, so soon as a man is born and sees the light of day he [179*b*] attaches himself to him; and he is foolish, not knowing how to receive admonition, since, as Solomon says of him also, "the fool walketh in darkness" (*Ibid.* II, 14). Indeed, he comes from the very quarry of darkness, and light is for ever a stranger to him.' R. Simeon said: 'It has been laid down that the "poor child" here is the good prompter, the same as he who said of himself: "I have been young, and now am old" (Ps. XXXVII, 25). He is called "poor child", as he has no possession whatever of his own, and is called "youth" for the reason that he is constantly renewed in the same way as the moon; also he is wise, since wisdom dwells within him. He is better than the "old king", who is the evil prompter, as already said, since from his first emergence he has never rid himself of his impurity, and he is foolish in that all his steps are toward the evil ways, and he turns the sons of men from the right path, employing all kinds of pretexts to divert them from the good way to the evil. And he hastens to join man on the very day he is born, in order that man may come to believe in him, and that when the good prompter arrives later he may be loth to believe him and think him a burden. Similarly our teachers have defined a "cunning wicked man" to be one who comes first to the judge and pleads his cause before his opponent arrives; as Scripture says: "He that pleadeth his cause first seemeth just, etc." (Prov. XVIII, 17). In the same way the evil prompter is cunningly wicked, as we read: "And the serpent was more cunning, etc." (Gen. III, 1), and so he arrives first to take up his abode with man, and make his case plausible to him, so that when his fellow, that is, the good prompter, arrives, he finds himself obnoxious to man, and is not able to raise his head, as though he were bowed down with a heavy burden, because of that cunningly wicked one who has got the start of him. Hence the words of Solomon: "the poor man's wisdom is despised, and his words are not heard" (Eccl. IX, 16), because the other has anticipated him. Hence for a judge to receive the pleadings of one litigant in the absence of the other is like acknowledging strange gods. But the way of the righteous judge is to wait till "his neighbour cometh and searcheth him out" (Prov. XVIII, 17). Similarly the righteous man is he who does not put credence in the evil prompter, but first waits for the arrival of the good prompter. For neglecting to do this the sons of man will stumble in the world to come. The righteous man, on the other hand, endures in this world many trials for not believing in and not associating himself with the evil prompter, but the Holy One, blessed be He, delivers him from all ills, as it says: "Many are the ills of the righteous, but the Lord delivereth him out of them all" (Ps. XXXIV, 20). For God finds delight in such a man and delivers him from all ills in this world and in the world to come. Happy is his portion ! See how many ills befell Jacob in his effort not to be drawn to the evil prompter, and to keep himself far from his portion; and for this he endured many afflictions and ills without respite.' R. Hiya applied to Jacob the verse: *I was not at ease, neither was I quiet, neither had I rest; but trouble came* (Job. III, 26). 'How many ills and sufferings,' he said, 'one after another come upon the righteous in this world that they may merit the world to come. Jacob was one of them, and could say of himself, "I was not at ease" in the house of Laban, from whom I could not escape; "neither was I quiet" on account of Esau, through the pain inflicted on me by his Chieftain, and later on through fear of himself; "neither had I rest" in the affair of Dinah and Shechem; "but trouble came", to wit, the trouble and confusion of the loss of Joseph, which was the worst of all, on account of his love for Joseph.'

AND JACOB DWELT IN THE LAND OF HIS FATHER'S SOJOURNINGS, IN THE LAND OF CANAAN. [180*a*] R. Jose discoursed here on the verse: *The righteous perisheth, and no man layeth it to heart, and godly men are taken away, none considering that the righteous is taken away from the evil to come* (Is. LVII, 1). 'When God', he said, 'surveys the world and finds it misbehaving and meet for chastisement, He first removes from it any righteous man that is present in it, so that chastisement should be visited on all the others and there should be none to shield them. For as long as there is a righteous man in the world chastisement cannot befall it, as we learn from Moses, of whom it is written: "Therefore he said that he would destroy them, had not Moses his chosen stood before him in the breach, etc." (Ps. CVI, 23). God thus first removes the righteous from the world, and only then collects His account, as it were. We thus translate the conclusion of the verse: "the righteous is taken away *before* (*mipné*) the evil to come", that is, before the evil is due to befall. (According to another interpretation, "from the evil to come" is an allusion to the evil prompter.) Observe now that although the *galuth* was already due in the life-time of

Jacob, yet because he was a righteous man—the perfection of the patriarchs—the sentence was postponed; for whilst he was alive punishment could not befall the world, and even the famine of Egypt ceased on his arrival. Neither did the exile really commence during the life-time of Joseph, since he was the image of his father, but as soon as he died the captivity began in earnest, as it says: "And Joseph died . . . come, let us deal wisely with them . . . and they made their lives bitter with hard service, in mortar and in brick, etc." (Ex. I, 6–14). Similarly, wherever a righteous man exists, God for his sake shields the world, and during his life-time no chastisement falls on the world; and so we affirm.'

AND JACOB DWELT IN THE LAND OF HIS FATHER'S SOJOURNINGS. The term *m'gure* (sojournings) can be rendered "apprehensions", being akin to the term *magor* in the phrase *magor misabib*, "a terror on every side" (Jer. VI, 25), and so indicates that Jacob passed all his life in fear and anxiety.

THESE ARE THE GENERATIONS OF JACOB: JOSEPH, ETC. When Jacob was brought to rest in Joseph, and so the sun was united with the moon, then there commenced a production of offspring, the progenitor being Joseph. For it is that perennially flowing stream which fructifies the earth and from which generations are propagated in the world. For the sun, even when he approaches the moon, cannot cause vegetation without the help of that grade which goes under the name of Righteous (*Zaddik*). It was, then, Joseph who was the grade of Jacob to bear fruit and bring forth offspring in the world. Hence: "These are the generations (*tol'doth*, lit. offspring) of Jacob: Joseph." Or, again, we may take the words to signify that whoever looked at Joseph thought he was looking at Jacob. Hence this form of expression is used only in connection with Joseph and not with any other of Jacob's sons—it is not written, for instance, "These are the offspring of Jacob: Reuben", the reason being that Joseph was the exact image of his father.

BEING SEVENTEEN YEARS OLD. R. Abba said: 'This number of seventeen is significant, corresponding as it does to the seventeen years of joy and honour which Jacob lived in Egypt, with all his sons round him and Joseph as king, and which God vouchsafed him in return for the years during which he mourned for Joseph, and did not see him.'

R. Hiya discoursed on the text: *Therefore hearken unto me, ye men of understanding: Far be it from God that he should do wickedness; and from the Almighty that he should commit iniquity. For the work* [180b] *of man will he requite unto him, and cause every man to find according to his ways* (Job XXXIV, 10–11). 'God,' he said, 'in creating the world, meant it to be based on justice, and all that is done in the world would be weighed in the scales of justice, were it not that, to save the world from perishing, God screened it with mercy, which tempers pure justice and prevents it from destroying the world. The world is thus governed in mercy and thereby is able to endure. But, you may ask, is not a man often punished by God undeservedly? The answer is, as has been affirmed, that when suffering befalls a righteous man, it is on account of the love which God bears to him. He crushes his body in order to give more power to his soul, so that He may draw him nearer in love. For it is needful that the body should be weak and the soul strong, that so a man may be beloved of God, as the Companions have affirmed, that the Holy One inflicts suffering on the righteous in this world in order that they may merit the world to come. But he who is weak of soul and strong of body is hated of God. It is because God has no pleasure in him that He inflicts no pain upon him in this world, but permits his life to flow smoothly along with ease and comfort, in that for any virtuous act he may perform he receives his reward in this world, so that no portion should be left him in the next world. This is in accordance with Onkelos's paraphrase of the text: "And he repayeth them that hate him to their face" (Deut. VII, 10), which reads: "And he repayeth them that hate him in this world." The righteous man, then, who is continually broken in body is the beloved of the Holy One, blessed be He.

Now various difficulties are raised by this statement. In the first place we know that the Shekinah does not dwell amid sad surroundings, but only where there is cheerfulness. For this reason Elisha said: "But now bring me a minstrel, and so it came to pass that when the minstrel played, the hand of the Lord came upon him" (II Kings III, 15), and we learn the same lesson from Jacob, from whom the Shekinah departed during the years that he was grieving for Joseph, but to whom it returned as soon as the glad tidings about Joseph reached him, when, as it says, "the spirit of Jacob their father revived" (Gen. XLV, 27). That being so, where, we may ask, is the cheerful spirit in the righteous man who is broken in body, seeing that he is tormented by his sufferings? And further, do we not know of many righteous men, beloved by the Almighty, who were never a prey to acute suffering or physical weakness? Why this discrimination? Why should these be physical wrecks and the others hale and hearty? One explanation given is that the latter were born of righteous parents, whereas the former, although themselves righteous, were not children of righteous parents. But the facts are against this, since we see many righteous men who are the sons of righteous parents, and who nevertheless are afflicted with bodily ills and are lifelong sufferers. But there is a deep mystery involved here, inasmuch as all the ways of God are based on truth and righteousness. In connection with this verse I have found in the books of the ancients a mystical doctrine, and next to it another mystical doctrine, both being in essence one and the same. It amounts to the following. There is a period when the moon is defective, judgement being visited upon her, and the sun being concealed from her. Now it is the moon that at all times and seasons releases souls to enter the sons of men—she having previously gathered them for the purpose. Of those souls, then, which she releases during the period that she is under sentence, every one will always be the victim of degradation and poverty and suffer other chastisements, irrespective of whether he be sinful or righteous. (Prayer, however, can avert any sentence of punishment.) But those souls which the moon sends forth when she is in the grade of completeness, and the perennially flowing stream plays about her, are destined to enjoy abundance of all good things—of riches, children, and bodily health—and all on account [181a] of the allotment (*mazzal*) that flowed forth and joined itself to that grade in order to be perfected and blessed by it. We see thus that all things are dependent on allotment (*mazzal*), according to the dictum: "Children, life, and livelihood do not depend on a man's merits, but on *mazzal*." Hence all those who are sorely afflicted in this world in spite of being truly righteous suffer through the mischance of their soul; but in compensation the Holy One, blessed be He, has compassion on them in the world to come.' R. Eleazar said: 'All the acts of the Almighty are in accordance with justice, and His purpose is to purify that soul from the scum that adheres to it in this world, so as to bring it into the world to come. When the body is crushed the soul is purified, and so God brings pains and sufferings on the righteous man in this world in order that he may gain life everlasting. In this regard it is written: "The Lord trieth the righteous, etc." (Ps. XI, 5).'

R. Simeon said: 'It is written: "Only he shall not go in unto the veil, nor come nigh unto the altar, because he hath a blemish; that he profane not my holy places, because I am the Lord who sanctify them" (Lev. XXI, 23). When the perennial stream releases human souls, and the Female becomes pregnant, they all range themselves within the edifice. Now all those that go forth at the period when the moon is defective by reason of the evil serpent, although pure and holy, become bruised and defective in whatever place they reach, and have to undergo pain and suffering. And these are the souls in whom the Holy One finds delight in spite of their being sad instead of joyful. Esoterically speaking they are a counterpart of something above, the body being impaired and the soul being within after the supernal pattern, each corresponding to each, and these are the souls that require to be renewed with the renewal of the moon, and hence it is written concerning them: "And it shall come to pass, that from one new moon to another, and from one Sabbath to another, shall all flesh come to worship before me" (Is. LXVI, 23), the word "all" signifying that these souls will be renewed wholly with the renewal of the moon. For they are partners, as it were, with the defective moon, for which reason she dwells in them always, without leaving them, in allusion to which the Scripture says: "I dwell . . . with him also that is of a contrite and humble spirit . . . to revive the heart of the contrite ones" (Is. LVII, 15), also: "The Lord is nigh unto them that are of a broken heart" (Ps. XXXIV, 19). These verses refer to those who are fellow-sufferers with the moon in her defect, and regarding whom it is fitly said, "to revive the heart of the contrite ones", that is, to make those who participated in the sufferings of the moon also participate in the new life to be bestowed on her in the future. Such sufferings undergone by them are called "sufferings in token of love". Happy is their portion in this world and in the world to come when they will be privileged to be partners with her, in allusion to which it is written: "For my brethren and companions' sakes, etc." (*Ibid.* CXXII, 8).'

R. Simeon further discoursed on the text: *Behold, my servant shall prosper, he shall be exalted and lifted up, and shall be very high* (Is. LII, 13). 'Happy is the portion of the righteous', he said, 'to whom the Holy One reveals the ways of the Torah that they may walk in them. This verse contains an esoteric meaning. When God created the world, He made the moon, and made her small, for she possesses no light of her own, but because she accepted her diminution she receives reflected light from the sun and from the other superior luminaries. Now, as long as the Temple existed, Israel were assiduous in bringing offerings, which together with all the other services performed by the priests, Levites, and Israelites had for their object to weave bonds of union and to cause luminaries to radiate. But after the Temple was destroyed there was a darkening of the lights, the moon ceased to receive light from the sun, the latter [181b] having withdrawn himself from her, so that not a day passes but is full of grievous distress and afflictions. The time, however, will come for the moon to resume her primordial light, and in allusion to this it is written: "Behold, my servant will prosper." That is to say, there will be a stirring in the upper realms as of one who catches a sweet odour and stands alert. "He shall be exalted", from the side of the most exalted luminaries; "and lifted up", from the side of Abraham; "and shall be high", from the side of Isaac; "very", from the side of Jacob. At that time, then, the Holy One will cause a stirring on high with the object of enabling the moon to shine with her full splendour, as we read: "Moreover the light of the moon shall be as the light of the sun, and the light of the sun shall be sevenfold, as the light of the seven days" (*Ibid.* xxx, 26). There will thus be added to the moon an exalted spirit whereby all the dead that are in the dust will be awakened. This is the esoteric meaning of "my servant", viz. the one that has in his hand the key of his Master.

So, too, in the verse: "And Abraham said unto his servant, etc." (Gen. xxiv, 2), the servant is an allusion to the moon as already explained. Also, the servant is identical with Metatron, who is the servant and messenger of his Master, and who was, as we read further, the elder of his house, the same who is alluded to in the text: "I have been young, and now am old" (Ps. xxxvii, 25). "That ruled over all that he had"; this applies to the same Metatron by reason of his displaying the three colours, green, white, and red. "Put, I pray thee, thy hand under my thigh"; this is symbolic of the foundation of the world, for this servant was destined to bring to life again the dwellers in the dust, and to be made the messenger by the spirit from on high to restore the spirits and souls to their places, to the bodies that were decomposed underneath the dust. We read further: "and I will make thee swear (*veashbe'akha*) by the Lord, the God of heaven", the term *veashbe'akha* implying that the servant will be invested with the mystery of the seven (*sheba'*) celestial lights which constitute the mystery of sublime perfection. Further: "that thou shalt not take a wife for my son of the daughters of the Canaanites." The "wife" is an allusion to the body lying underground, and "to my son" is an allusion to the soul, inasmuch as all the souls that issue from the celestial ever-flowing river are the children of the Holy One, blessed be He. The servant is thus bidden "not to take a wife for my son of the daughters of the Canaanites", or, in other words, not to take for a soul any of the bodies of the idolatrous nations whom the Holy One will in the future shake out of the Holy

Land, as we read: "and the wicked be shaken out of it" (Job XXXVIII, 13), as one shakes dust from his garment. The servant is further bidden: "But thou shalt go unto my country, and to my kindred." "To my country" has already been explained; "to my kindred" is an allusion to Israel. Observe now what is written further: "And the servant took ten camels." The "servant" we have already identified; "ten camels" represent the ten grades over which the servant exercises dominion, and which are after the supernal pattern; "of the camels of his master", to wit, an exact pattern of the superior degrees, as already said; "having all goodly things of his master's in his hand", to wit, all the supernal spirits that emerge from the supernal luminaries; "and he arose and went to Aram-Naharaim", to wit, the spot in the Holy Land where Rachel wept at the time the Temple was destroyed. "And he made the camels to kneel down without the city by the well of water", that is, he fortified the energy of the souls before their entering into the bodies for their revival; "at the time of evening", to wit, the eve of Sabbath, [182*a*] which is the sixth millennium, the same period as that alluded to in the text: "and to his labour until the evening" (Ps. CIV, 23), also in the words: "for the shadows of the evening are stretched out" (Jer. VI, 4). We read further: "at the time that women go out to draw water", to wit, the time when those who drew the waters of the Torah will rise from the dead before the rest of mankind, in virtue of their having taken hold of the tree of life. Further: "and the daughters of the men of the city came out to draw water", to wit, the bodies will come forth, as we read: "and the earth will throw up the shades" (Is. XXVI, 19), implying that the earth will in future give up all the bodies lying therein, "to draw water", that is, to receive the soul in a perfected state. Further: "So let it come to pass, that the damsel to whom I shall say, Let down thy pitcher, that I may drink." It is one of our affirmations that every soul that occupied itself in this world in the study of the deep mysteries of Divine Wisdom, when it goes to heaven is raised to a high grade, high above those who remained in ignorance; and it is they who will rise from the dead first. The words, then, "Let down thy pitcher, etc."

signify the inquiry which the servant will make of each soul regarding her occupation in this world. We read, then, "and she will say, Drink, and I will give thy camels drink also", that is, do thou drink first, and afterwards I will give drink to the other grades, for although those grades drink from the same source, they ultimately derive their sustenance from the religious activity of the righteous who knew how to serve their Master properly, for it is the righteous who know how to supply proper sustenance to each grade. "The same be the woman", it says further, "that thou hast appointed for the son of my master"; that assuredly is the body destined for that superior soul. Observe that it has been said before that the desire of the male towards the female forms a soul, and the desire of the female towards the male rises upwards to unite with the soul and form one being. The woman is thus the body which is destined for the association of the soul that is derived from the male. These bodies, then, are destined to rise first, as we said already, and then all the others in the other lands will be raised in a complete state and will be renewed with the renewal of the moon, and the world will be restored to its primeval state, in allusion to which it is written: "Let the Lord rejoice in his works" (Ps. CIV, 31). Hence we read: "Behold, my servant will understand", that is, he will know how to restore the souls, each one to its place. "He shall be exalted and lifted up and shall be very high", from the side of all the superior grades as said above. The next verse says: "According as many were appalled at thee—so marred was his visage unlike that of a man" (Is. LII, 14). According to our exposition, when the Temple was destroyed and the Shekinah went into exile into strange lands, then "behold, their *Erelim*[1] cry without, the angels of peace weep bitterly" (*Ibid.* XXXIII, 7), for all wept and mourned for the Shekinah that was exiled from her place, and in the degree that she became altered from what she was, to the same degree her Master withdrew his light and became altered from what he was, as it is written: "The sun was darkened in his going forth" (*Ibid.* XIII, 10). Hence: "so marred was his visage." According to another interpretation, the words, "so marred

---

[1] A kind of angel.

was his visage unlike that of a man" are illustrated by the verse: "I clothe the heavens with blackness, and I make sackcloth their covering" (*Ibid.* L, 3). For after the Temple was destroyed the heavens did not retain their former illumination. Esoterically speaking, benediction does not abide save where male and female are together, and since at that time [182*b*] the male was not with her, all the souls that issued then were not the same as they had been when the sun was in union with the moon, as already said. This union is symbolized by the relation of Joseph to Jacob, as expressed in the verse, "These are the generations of Jacob: Joseph." This form of expression implies that Jacob's image was completely reproduced in Joseph, and that whatever happened to the one happened to the other also, the two being parallel and having the same esoteric symbolism.'

AND JOSEPH BROUGHT EVIL REPORT OF THEM UNTO THEIR FATHER. This has been interpreted to mean that he accused them to his father of eating flesh cut from a living animal; he also accused the sons of Leah of having treated with contempt the sons of the handmaids. How, it may be asked, could they have done this, seeing that the sons of the handmaids were reckoned in the twelve tribes ? Or how could they have eaten flesh from a living animal, seeing that this was distinctly forbidden to the sons of Noah in the words: "Only flesh with the life thereof, which is the blood thereof, shall ye not eat" (Gen. IX, 4) ? The truth is, however, that it was only Joseph's talk, and he was punished for it. R. Judah said: 'The evil report of them that Joseph brought was that they cast their eyes on the daughters of the land, which was equivalent to providing sustenance to the unholy degrees that proceed from the unclean side.'

NOW ISRAEL LOVED JOSEPH MORE THAN ALL HIS CHILDREN, BECAUSE HE WAS THE SON OF HIS OLD AGE; AND HE MADE HIM A COAT OF MANY COLOURS. Said R. Eleazar: 'It is written: "Come, my people, enter thou into thy chambers, and shut thy doors about thee; hide thyself for a little moment, until the indignation be overpast"

(Is. XXVI, 20). God holds Israel in affection above the idolatrous nations, and on that account He warns them and puts them on their guard in all their deeds. There are three periods in a day during which the world is liable to chastisement, and at each of these periods it behoves a man to be specially on his guard. These are well known and are specified elsewhere. Furthermore, at a time when judgement is at work upon the world and death rages in a city, a man should not walk by himself in the open street, as already mentioned above, but he should shut himself in after the example of Noah, who shut himself within the ark so that he should not be met by the destroying angel. Hence: "Come, my people, enter into thy chambers, and shut thy doors about thee", so as not to be exposed to the destroying angel; "hide thyself for a little moment", until the indignation be overpast, as after the moment of judgement is passed the destroying angel has no more power to harm. And it is because God holds Israel in affection and draws them near to Himself that all the idolatrous nations hate Israel; for they see themselves kept at a distance whilst Israel are brought near. Similarly it was by reason of the love that Jacob showed towards Joseph above all his other sons that they conspired to slay him, though he was their own brother. How much greater, then, must be the enmity of the idolatrous nations towards Israel !' Observe the consequences that followed the excessive love shown to Joseph by his father: he was exiled from his father, and his father joined him in exile, and along with them [183a] the Shekinah also went into exile. It is true that the exile was really the consequence of a divine decree; yet the proximate cause was the coat of many colours which he made for him specially.

AND JOSEPH DREAMED A DREAM, ETC. On the subject of dreams, R. Hiya discoursed on the text: *And he said: Hear now my words: If there be a prophet among you, I the Lord do make myself known unto him in a vision, I do speak with him in a dream* (Num. XII, 6). 'God', he said, 'has brought into existence a series of grades, one higher than the other, one drawing sustenance from the other, some on the right, others on the left, all arranged in a perfect hierarchy. Now all the prophets drew their inspiration from one side, from the midst of two certain grades which they beheld in a "dull mirror", as it says: "I do make myself known unto him in a vision", the word "vision" denoting, as has been explained, a medium reflecting a variety of colours; and this is the "dull mirror". The dream, on the other hand, is a sixtieth part of prophecy, and so forms the sixth grade removed from prophecy, which is the grade of Gabriel, the supervisor of dreams. Now a normal dream proceeds from that grade, and hence there is not a dream that has not intermingled with it some spurious matter, so that it is a mixture of truth and falsehood. Hence it is that all dreams follow their interpretation, as it is written: "And it came to pass, as he interpreted to us, so it was" (Gen. XLI, 13); for since the dream contains both falsehood and truth, the word has power over it, and therefore it is advisable that every dream should be interpreted in a good sense.'

R. Hiya further discoursed on the text: *In a dream, in a vision of the night, when deep sleep falleth upon men, in slumberings upon the bed; then he openeth the ears of men, and by their chastisement sealeth the decree* (Job XXXIII, 15–16). 'When a man retires to rest,' he said, 'it behoves him first to acknowledge the Kingdom of Heaven[1] and then to say a short prayer. For when a man goes to bed and sleeps, his soul leaves him and soars aloft. God then reveals to the soul through that grade which presides over the soul future events, or things which correspond to a man's own thoughts, so as to serve as an admonition to him. For no revelation comes to man when his body is in full vigour, but an angel communicates things to the soul, and the soul transmits them to the man; dreams, then, originate on high when souls leave the bodies, each one taking its own route. There is a graduated series of the intimations by which deeper knowledge is conveyed to men, dreams forming one grade, vision another grade, and prophecy a third grade, in a rising series.

AND JOSEPH DREAMED A DREAM, AND HE TOLD IT TO HIS BRETHREN. AND THEY HATED HIM THE MORE

---

[1] i.e. to recite the Shema.

FOR HIS DREAMS. From this we learn that a man should not tell his dream save to a friend, otherwise the listener may pervert the significance of the dream and cause delay in its fulfilment. Joseph communicated his dream to his brethren, and they caused its fulfilment to be delayed for twenty-two years. Thus we find it written: AND HE SAID UNTO THEM, HEAR, I PRAY YOU, THIS DREAM [183*b*] WHICH I HAVE DREAMED. We see here how he begged his brethren to listen to him, and insisted on telling them his dream, which, had they given it another meaning, would have been fulfilled accordingly. But they said to him: "Shalt thou indeed reign over us ? or shalt thou have dominion over us ?" and with these words they sealed their own doom.

R. Hiya and R. Jose used to study with R. Simeon. R. Hiya once put to him the following question: 'We have learnt that a dream uninterpreted is like a letter undeciphered. Does this mean that the dream comes true without the dreamer being conscious of it, or that it remains unfulfilled ?' R. Simeon answered: 'The dream comes true, but without the dreamer being aware of it. For nothing happens in the world but what is made known in advance either by means of a dream or by means of a proclamation; as it has been affirmed. that before any event comes to pass in the world it is announced in heaven, whence it is broadcast into the world. So Scripture says: "For the Lord God will do nothing, but he revealeth his counsels unto his servants the prophets" (Amos. III, 7). This refers to the time when there were prophets in the world; when prophets were no more, their place was taken by the Sages, who, in a sense, even excelled the prophets; and in the absence of Sages things to come are revealed in dreams, and if not in dreams, through the medium of the birds of heaven; and so we have laid down.'

AND HIS BRETHREN WENT TO FEED THEIR FATHER'S FLOCK IN SHECHEM. R. Simeon said: 'The dots on the top of the particle *eth* in this sentence indicate that the Shekinah accompanied them by reason of their being a band of ten. (They were only ten because Joseph was not with them and Benjamin remained at home on account of his tender age.) Hence, when they sold Joseph they were in the company of the Shekinah, and, furthermore, they associated the Shekinah with them in their oath (not to reveal the affair of Joseph); and until the fate of Joseph became known, the Shekinah did not rest on Jacob. The proof that the Shekinah accompanied the brethren is the verse of the Psalms which speaks of "the tribes of the Lord, a testimony unto Israel" (Ps. CXXII, 4), a title which shows that they were all of them righteous and devout, constituting the support of the whole world, both on high and below.' R. Simeon further discoursed on the text: *I rejoiced when they said unto me: Let us go unto the house of the Lord* (*Ibid.* CXXII, 1). 'This verse has been explained', he said, 'as follows. David was minded to build the House of God, but he was commanded to leave the task to his son, as we read: "Now it was in the heart of David my father to build a house for the name of the Lord . . . nevertheless thou shalt not build the house; but thy son that shall come forth out of thy loins, he shall build the house for my name" (I Kings VIII, 18–19). The whole of Israel knew of this and they used to say: "When is David going to die so that Solomon his son may arise and build the House, and we shall be able to say, 'Our feet are standing within thy gates, O Jerusalem' (Ps. CXXII, 2), for we will then go up and offer sacrifices?" But although David knew that they were impatient for his death, yet he rejoiced to hear them speak thus on account of his son, who would take his place in carrying out the command to build the House. David thus commenced to sing its praises and said: "Jerusalem that art builded as a city that is compact together" (*Ibid.* CXXII, 3). According to our teachers, God fashioned the lower Jerusalem on the model of the heavenly Jerusalem, the one exactly facing the other, as it is written: "the place, O Lord, which thou hast made for thee to dwell in, the Sanctuary, O Lord, which thy hands have established" (Ex. XV, 17). The expression "that art builded" indicates that God will in time to come cause the upper Jerusalem to descend below; this is further proved by the phrase "as a city that is compact (*she-ḥubrah*) together", where the term *ḥubrah* (lit. she is joined), written in the singular, indicates that the Mother has joined the

o

Daughter and the two are become as one. We read further: "Whither the tribes went up", they being the support of the world and the upholding of the lower world, and even of the upper world, as it says: "even the tribes of the Lord, as a testimony unto Israel", the term "Israel" having its esoteric significance; for they, being the support of the lower world, act as a testimony to the upper world, and all in order "to give thanks unto the name of the Lord" (Ps. cxxii, 4), i.e. to acknowledge the name of God in all directions.' [184*a*]

AND ISRAEL SAID UNTO JOSEPH: DO NOT THY BRETHREN FEED THE FLOCK OF SHECHEM? COME, AND I WILL SEND THEE UNTO THEM. How came it that Jacob the perfect man, who loved Joseph above all his sons and knew that all his brethren hated him, sent him to them ? The truth is that he harboured no suspicion of them, knowing them to be all righteous; but God brought all this about in order to fulfil the decree pronounced "between the pieces" (Gen. xv, 17). We have found it stated in ancient books that the sons of Jacob were anxious to obtain dominion over Joseph before he went down into Egypt, because they knew that if he should go down there first before they obtained dominion over him the Egyptians would obtain dominion over Israel in perpetuity; but by selling Joseph as a slave they made themselves his masters, and since he later on rose to power and the Egyptians became his slaves, Israel became masters of all. Joseph was the symbol of the heavenly covenant, and so long as he was alive the covenant of the Shekinah remained with Israel in perfect harmony, but as soon as Joseph departed the covenant of the Shekinah together with Israel was plunged into captivity, as it says: "Now there arose a new king over Egypt, who knew not Joseph" (Ex. 1, 8). It was all fittingly ordained by Providence.

AND A CERTAIN MAN FOUND HIM: this was Gabriel, of whom we read: "the man Gabriel, whom I had seen in the vision at the beginning" (Dan. ix, 21). AND, BEHOLD, HE WAS WANDERING: indeed he was wandering both literally and metaphorically; he trusted his brethren and sought their affection but could not gain it, and he was looking for them but could not find them. Hence: AND THE MAN ASKED HIM, SAYING: WHAT SEEKEST THOU? AND HE SAID: I SEEK MY BRETHREN. . . . AND THE MAN SAID: THEY ARE DEPARTED HENCE, ETC. R. Judah discoursed on the text: *O that thou wert as my brother, that sucked the breast of my mother! When I should find thee without, I would kiss thee; yea, and none would despise me* (S. S. VIII, 1). 'The Companions', he said, 'interpret this verse as being addressed by the Community of Israel to the King to whom peace belongs. She said to Him: "O that thou wert as my brother", to wit, as Joseph towards his brethren, to whom he said: "Now, therefore, fear ye not; I will sustain you and your little ones" (Gen. L, 21), and whom he provided with food and fed in time of famine. According to another explanation, the phrase "as my brother" refers to Joseph, who was in the relation of a brother towards the Shekinah, with whom he was intimately associated—"that sucked the breast of my mother", this expresses the perfect affection between them; "when I should find thee without", to wit, in exile, in a strange land, "I would kiss thee", so that spirit should join spirit; "yea, and none would despise me", despite my dwelling in a strange land. Observe that although when Joseph fell into their hands they did not act towards him as brothers, yet when they fell into his hands he did act towards them as a brother, as it is written: "And he comforted them, and he spoke kindly unto them" (Gen. I, 21).

AND THEY SAID ONE TO ANOTHER (lit. one man to his brother). These are Simeon and Levi, who were truly brothers in all respects, both being descended from the side of rigorous judgement; and hence it was that their anger was the anger that causes death in the world, as it says: "Cursed be their anger, for it was fierce, and their wrath, for it was cruel" (*Ibid.* XLIX, 7). For there are two species of anger. There is anger which is blessed on high and below, and is called "blessed" (*barukh*), as explained in connection with the sentence: "Blessed be Abram of God Most High, Maker of heaven and earth" (*Ibid.* XIV, 19); and there is anger which is accursed on high and is called "cursed" (*arur*), and regarding this it is written: "Cursed be thou from among all cattle, and from among all beasts of the field" (*Ibid.* III, 14), as well as "Cursed be their anger for it was fierce." This is the recondite significance of the two mounts Gerizim and Ebal set aside for the blessing and the curse (Deut. XI, 29), the two mounts corresponding to these two grades; and hence one is called cursed and the other blessed. Simeon and Levi both belonged to the side of severity, from which side, in its extreme manifestation, issues the anger which is under a curse. All anger issues from the side of rigorous judgement, but in two directions, [184b] one referred to as blessed, the other as cursed. Similarly, from the side of Isaac there issued two sons, one of whom was blessed and the other cursed on high and below; the two separated, each going off towards his own side, the one making his abode in the Holy Land, the other on Mount Seir, being as he was "a cunning hunter, a man of the field" (Gen. XXV, 27). The latter had his home in the desert, in regions of waste and desolation, while the former "dwelt in tents" (*Ibid.*), all being fitly ordained. Hence it is that there are two grades, "blessed" and "cursed", each ranged on its own side. From the one issue all blessings in the upper and the lower worlds, all beneficence, all light, all deliverance, all redemption; whilst the other is the source of all curses, all wars and bloodshed, all desolation and evil, and all defilement.

R. Simeon said: 'It is written: *I will wash my hands in innocency; so will I compass thine altar, O Lord* (Ps. XXVI, 6). The inner implication of this verse has been explained as follows. Every man has a foretaste of death during the night, because the holy soul then leaves him, and the unclean spirit rests on the body and makes it unclean. When, however, the soul returns to the body, the pollution disappears, save from the man's hands, which retain it and thus remain unclean. Hence a man should not pass his hands over his eyes before washing them. When he has washed them, however, he becomes sanctified and is called holy. For this sanctification two vessels are required, one held above and the other placed beneath, so that he may be sanctified by the water poured on his hands from the vessel above. The lower vessel, then, is the vessel of uncleanness, receiving as it does the water of contamination, whilst the upper vessel is a medium of sanctification. The upper one is to be referred to as "blessed", the lower as "cursed". Further, the water of contamination should not be emptied in the house, in order that no one may come near it; for it forms a gathering-place for the elements of the unclean side, and so one may receive injury from the unclean water. Neither may a man pronounce a benediction before the pollution is removed from his hands. Thus, before he sanctifies his hands of a morning, a man is called unclean, and after that he is called clean. For this reason one should not allow water to be poured over his hands save by a man who has already washed his own hands, in harmony with the precept: "And the clean person shall sprinkle upon the unclean" (Num. XIX, 19). We see that the one with his hands washed is the clean person, the other the unclean. Similarly with the two vessels, the upper and the lower, the one being the holy vessel, the other the unholy. Nor is it permitted to put the polluted water to any use, or even to let it stay overnight in the house, but it must be emptied in a spot where people do not pass, as it is liable to cause harm through the unclean spirit that clings to it. It is quite permissible, however, to let it flow down a slope into the earth. It must not be given to witches, as by means of it they can do harm to people. One should, then, avoid this water, since it is water of curse, and the Holy One desires to purify Israel so that they may be holy, as it is written: "And I will sprinkle clean water upon you, and ye shall be clean; from all your uncleannesses, and from all your idols, will I cleanse you" (Ez. XXXVI, 25).'

AND THEY TOOK HIM AND CAST HIM INTO THE PIT. R. Judah here discoursed on the text: *The law of the Lord is perfect, restoring the soul* (Ps. XIX, 8). 'The study of the Torah', he said, 'procures for a man life in this world and in the world to come, so that he gains the two worlds; and even he that studies the Torah for worldly motives and not purely for its own sake as he ought to, gains a good reward in this world, and escapes punishment in the other. The Scripture says: "Length of days is in her right hand; in her left hand are riches and honour" (Prov. III, 16). There is, indeed, length of days for him who devotes himself to the Torah for its own sake. For such a one there is length of days in the other world, where days are indeed days. [185*a*] And further: "in her left hand are riches and honour", which means good reward in this world. Moreover, if a man has devoted himself to the Torah for its own sake, when he departs this world the Torah goes before him and proclaims his merit, and shields him against the emissaries of punishment. When a man's body is laid in the grave, the Torah keeps guard over it; it goes in front of his soul when it soars upwards, breaking through all barriers until the soul reaches its proper place; and it will stand by the man at the time when he is awakened at the resurrection of the dead, in order to defend him against any accusations. Thus Scripture further says: "When thou liest down, it shall watch over thee; and when thou awakest, it shall talk with thee" (*Ibid.* VI, 22). The "lying down" is an allusion to the time when man's body is lying in the grave and is being judged there; the Torah will then protect him; whilst "when thou awakest", that is, when the dead will rise from the dust, "it shall talk with thee", that is, plead thy cause.' R. Eleazar interpreted the clause "it shall talk with thee" to mean that when they rise from the grave the Torah will not be forgotten of them, but they will know it much as they did when they left this world. For their Torah will be preserved from that time, will penetrate within them, and will talk, as it were, within their very inwards; and moreover, they will be more adept than they were previously, so that points which formerly baffled them in spite of all their labour will now be fully comprehended by them, the Torah itself speaking within them. Hence: "when thou awakest, it will talk with thee".' R. Judah said: 'In a similar way, whoever devotes himself to the study of the Torah in this world will be privileged to study in the world to come; and so we affirm. On the other hand, the man who fails to study the Torah in this world, and so walks in darkness, when he leaves this world is taken and cast into Gehinnom, a nethermost place, where there will be none to pity him, a place called "tumultuous pit, miry clay" (Ps. XL, 3). Hence, of him who has not devoted himself to the study of the Torah in this world, but has besmirched himself with the offscourings of this world, it is written: "And they took him and cast him into the pit", that is, into Gehinnom, a place where those who have not laboured in the Torah are brought to judgement. "And the pit was empty", in the same way as he was empty: why so ? "Because there was no water" (i.e. Torah) in him. Observe, too, how great is the punishment for neglect of the study of the Torah, seeing that Israel were not exiled from the Holy Land save for having abandoned the Torah, as it is written: "Who is the wise man that may understand this ? . . . Wherefore is the land perished ? . . . And the Lord saith: Because they have forsaken my law, etc." (Jer. IX, 11).' R. Judah derived the same lesson from the verse: "Therefore my people are gone into captivity, for want of knowledge" (Is. V, 13), that is, because they have not applied themselves to the study of the Torah, which is the foundation of the upper and the lower worlds, as it says: "Were it not for my covenant enduring day and night, I would not have appointed the ordinances of heaven and earth" (Jer. XXXIII, 25).

AND THEY CAST HIM INTO THE PIT. There is a hint here that they cast him ultimately among the Egyptians, a place where there was no sign of true faith. R. Isaac said: 'Seeing that the pit contained serpents and scorpions, how could Reuben have advised that Joseph should be cast into it in order that "he might deliver him out of their hand, to restore him to his father" ? Had he no fear of the serpents and scorpions attacking Joseph ? And if they did, how could he deliver him out of their hand, to restore him to his father ? But the truth is that Reuben perceived the intense enmity of the brethren towards Joseph and how intent they were on killing him, and he therefore thought that it was better for him to fall into the pit of serpents and scorpions than to be delivered into the hands of enemies who would have no mercy on him. Hence the saying: "Rather should a man throw himself into a fire or a pit full of serpents and scorpions, than be delivered into the hands of his enemies." [185b] The reason is that in a place infested with serpents and scorpions, if the man be righteous, God may possibly perform a miracle for him, or it may happen that the merits of his ancestors may stand him in good stead and he will be delivered. But of those who are delivered into the hands of their enemies, few indeed are able to escape. Hence the expression "that he might deliver him out of their hand", as much as to say "Let him be delivered, at any rate, out of their hand, and if he is to die in the pit, then it cannot be helped." Observe the great piety of Reuben. He knew well the ruthlessness of Simeon and Levi when acting and planning in conjunction, as witnessed by their treatment of Shechem, where they not only slew all the males, but took all their little ones and their wives, all their silver and gold, all their cattle and precious vessels, and everything else they found in the city, and even everything which was in the field, as we read: "and that which was in the city and that which was in the field they took" (Gen. XXXIV, 28). Reuben thus said to himself: "If such a great city as that could not escape them, should this youth fall into their hands they will not leave of him a single shred." Hence he said: "He must at all costs be rescued from them, since they will leave no sign of him for his father to see again; whereas here, if he is killed, his body, at any rate, will remain for me to bring back to my father." Hence the words: "to bring him back to his father", that is, even if he die there. Hence, too, Reuben's words: "The child is not", that is to say, not even a dead child did I find. Observe his tactfulness in saying "Let *us* not take his life," and not "Do not *ye* take his life." Now Reuben was absent when Joseph was sold, as the brethren had each in turn to attend one day on their father, and that day happened to be Reuben's turn. He was anxious lest on that day Joseph should disappear, and therefore at once HE RETURNED UNTO THE PIT. BUT BEHOLD JOSEPH WAS NOT IN THE PIT;—not even dead—AND HE RENT HIS CLOTHES. AND HE RETURNED UNTO HIS BRETHREN AND SAID: THE CHILD IS NOT, ETC. For even Reuben did not know that Joseph had been sold. As already said, the brothers associated the Shekinah with them in the oath of secrecy, and so Reuben did not learn of it until Joseph made himself known to his brethren. Reuben's attempt to save Joseph's life was all the more disinterested, because he knew that the birthright had been taken away from him and given to Joseph, for we thus find that Moses interceded on his behalf, praying: "Let Reuben live, and not die" (Deut. XXXIII, 6), i.e., let him live in this world and not die in the world to come; and this prayer was prompted by this action of Reuben and also by his repentance for that other action.[1] For whoever repents of his sin, God preserves in this world and in the world to come.

AND THEY TOOK JOSEPH'S COAT, AND THEY KILLED A HE-GOAT, ETC., the reason being, as has been laid down, that the blood of a he-goat resembles that of a human being. We learn from this passage how particular God is with the righteous, even when they act correctly. For although Jacob acted fittingly in bringing a he-goat to his father, who was of the side of severity, yet because he thereby deceived his father, he was punished through that other he-goat, the blood of which his sons brought for the purpose of deceiving him. Of Jacob it is written: "And she put the skins of the kids of the goats upon his hands, and upon the smooth of his neck" (Gen. XXVII, 16); correspondingly, we read of his sons: "and they dipped the coat in the blood", with the object of deceiving him. It was measure for measure. Likewise, there we read: "And Isaac trembled very exceedingly" (*Ibid.* 33), and as a punishment Jacob trembled when his sons uttered the words: "know now whether it is thy son's coat or not". [186*a*] R. Hiya added: 'There it is written: "whether thou be my very son Esau or not ?" (*Ibid.* 21): correspondingly, here it is written, "whether it is thy son's or not". We thus find that the Almighty is particular with the righteous to a hairbreadth.' R. Abba said: 'When the brethren perceived the pain they had caused their father, they were stricken with remorse and cast about to ransom Joseph at all costs, if so be they could discover his whereabouts. But when they found that they were unable to do so, they turned on Judah, who

---

[1] i.e. the affair of Bilhah.

hitherto had been king over them, and deposed him from his high estate. Hence it is written: "And it came to pass at that time, that Judah went down from his brethren." '

R. Judah discoursed here on the text: *The Lord also thundered in the heavens, and the Most High gave forth his voice; hailstones and coals of fire* (Ps. XVIII, 14). 'When God', he said, 'created the world, He constructed for it seven pillars by which it was to be upheld. So Scripture says: "Wisdom hath builded her house, she hath hewn out her seven pillars" (Prov. IX, 1). These in turn are upheld by one grade from among them called "the Righteous One, the everlasting foundation" (*Ibid.* X, 25). Further, when the world was created, it was started from that spot which is the culmination and perfection of the world, the central point of the universe, which is identical with Zion, as it is written: "A psalm of Asaph. God, God the Lord hath spoken and called the earth from the rising of the sun unto the going down thereof. Out of Zion, the perfection of beauty, God hath shined forth" (Ps. L, 2). That is to say, God started the earth from Zion, from the spot where faith culminates in its full perfection. Zion is thus the citadel and central point of the universe, from which it began to be fashioned and from which the whole world is nourished. This lesson is esoterically indicated in our text. For Zion and Jerusalem, while one, represent two degrees, the one being the channel of judgement, the other of mercy; first there issues from one the sound of mercy, and afterwards there comes forth from the other the voice of judgement, the two forming the source from which the paths of judgement and mercy issue and diverge. Hence the expression "And the Lord also thundered in the heavens" indicates judgement, while "the Most High gave forth his voice" refers to mercy, and "hailstones and coals of fire" signify water and fire, that is, mercy and judgement commingled.'

Observe that when Judah was born, it is written: "and she left off bearing" (Gen. XXIX, 35), the reason being that Judah constituted the fourth of the four supports of the Heavenly Throne. But here it is written: AND JUDAH WENT DOWN FROM HIS BRETHREN, that is, from his position as their king, because Joseph had been taken down into Egypt, as explained.

AND JUDAH SAW THERE A DAUGHTER OF A CERTAIN CANAANITE. The term Canaanite has been explained by the Companions.

AND SHE CONCEIVED, AND BORE A SON; AND HE CALLED HIS NAME ER. Judah had three sons, and the only one who survived was Shelah. R. Eleazar and R. Jose and R. Hiya were once walking together. Said R. Jose to R. Eleazar: 'Why is it that of the first son of Judah it is written: "and *he* called his name Er", whereas of the other two it is written: "and *she* called his name Onan", "and *she* called his name Shelah"?' R. Eleazar replied: 'There is a deep mystic allusion in these sentences, which explains all. Thus Judah going down from his brethren symbolizes the moon becoming obscured and descending from the perfected grade to another grade to which the serpent becomes associated, as is indicated in the statement: "and he turned into a certain Adullamite, whose name was Hirah". Then we read: "And she conceived, and bore a son; and he called his name Er." The name *'Er* is a reversal of the letters *ra'* (evil), for he was evil, having issued from the side of the evil prompter. The accusative particle *eth* (the) inserted before his name likewise [186b] hints at the emergence of another grade, that of impurity and defilement, from which grade Er was born. Nor was the defect made good until afterwards, when Shelah appeared. It says further: "And Er, Judah's first-born, was evil in the sight of the Lord", where the term "evil" finds its echo in the sentence: "for the imagination of man's heart is evil from his youth" (Gen. VIII, 21). Er was evil in that he shed blood, by spilling the seed on the ground, and therefore the Lord slew him. After that it is written:

AND JUDAH SAID UNTO ONAN: GO IN UNTO THY BROTHER'S WIFE, ETC. R. Simeon opened here a discourse with the text: *I have roused up one from the north, and he is come, from the rising of the sun one that calleth upon my name;*

and he shall come upon rulers as upon mortar, and as the potter treadeth clay (Is. XLI, 25). 'How foolish', he said, 'are the sons of men who neither know nor care about the ways of the Almighty, their eyes being closed as in sleep. God made man after the supernal pattern, each limb corresponding to something in the scheme of Wisdom. For when the whole body of man had been duly shaped with all its members, God associated Himself with him and put a holy soul into him, so as to teach man to walk in the ways of the Torah and to observe His commandments in order that he might attain to his full perfection. Hence, while the holy soul is still within man's body, it is incumbent on him to multiply the image of the King in the world. There is herein an esoteric thought involved, namely, that just as the celestial stream flows on for ever without ceasing, so must man see that his own river and spring shall not cease in this world. And so long as a man is unsuccessful in his purpose in this world, the Holy One, blessed be He, uproots him and replants him over and over again. Observe, then, the meaning of the words: "I have roused up one from the north, and he is come", where the rousing alludes to the rousing and stirring up of the desire of a man for mating in this world, which originates from the North, whilst the words "and he is come" allude to the holy soul which descends from on high, whence God sends it, and comes into this world to enter into a man, as said above. "From the rising of the sun" alludes to the place of that celestial ever-flowing river, whence the soul issues and is illumined: "and there come rulers as mortar" signifies the heavenly forces which cause a rousing in the souls above corresponding to the stirring of the man in his body. For it is for this purpose that God creates souls in couples and sends them down to the world, so that there may be companionship both on high and below, and the well-spring of all may be blessed. God made man that he should steadfastly walk in His ways, and never cut off his fount and well-spring; for if a man cuts off his well-spring on earth and causes it to dry up, it is as though he causes the waters of the celestial river to fail, as described in the words: "The waters fail from the sea, and the river is drained dry" (Job XIV, 11). For inasmuch

as man has been established in this world after the pattern of
the upper world, he whose well-spring ceases to produce
through his not taking a wife is beyond remedy, and of him
it is said: "That which is crooked cannot be made straight"
(Eccl. I, 15). On the other hand, he who has taken a wife but
has not been blessed with offspring can be redeemed by his
near relative, that is, by his brother. He who dies without
leaving children will not enter within the curtain of heaven
and will have no share in the other world, and his soul will
not be admitted to the place where all souls are gathered and
his image will be cut off from there. Of such a one it is
written: "And this soul will be cut off from before me." Such
being the case, God has provided for such a man a redeemer
[187*a*] to redeem him out of the hands of the destructive
angels, to wit, his brother who is near to him. So Scripture
says: "If brethren dwell together, etc." (Deut. XXV, 5–10);
also: "Go in unto thy brother's wife, and perform the duty
of husband's brother unto her, etc." For the soul of such a
man does not enter before the presence of the Holy One,
blessed be He, but remains without, since he has not succeeded in radiating light in this world by means of the body.
He who has not succeeded in this place must go to another
place where he may have better fortune. When wood smoul-
ders without any flame, if it is struck it flares up and throws
out light. Man is compared to wood, as it says: "for the tree
of the field is man" (*Ibid.* XX, 19). Now a man who eats and
drinks and marries, but is not blessed with children, is like
the wood that burns without giving off any light, that is, his
soul has not been illumined in its present body but has remained in darkness. It is written: "He created it not a waste,
he formed it to be inhabited" (Is. XLV, 18), that is, God made
man for this purpose, and so dealt kindly with the world.
Observe the Scriptural text: "And Abraham took another
wife, and her name was Keturah" (Gen. XXV, 1). Herein is
an allusion to the soul which after death comes to earth to be
built up as before. Observe that of the body it is written:
"And it pleased the Lord to crush him by disease; to see if
his soul would offer itself in restitution, that he might see his
seed, and prolong his days, and that the purpose of the Lord

might prosper by his hand." (Is. LIII, 10). That is to say, if the soul desires to be rehabilitated then he must see seed, for the soul hovers round about and is ready to enter the seed of procreation, and thus "he will prolong his days, and the purpose of the Lord", namely the Torah, "will prosper in his hand". For although a man labours in the Torah day and night, yet if his source remains fruitless, he will find no place by which to enter within the heavenly curtain. As has been pointed out, a well of water, if not fed by its source and spring, is no well, since the well and the source are one and they have a joint symbolism. It is written: "It is vain for you that ye rise early, and sit up late, ye that eat the bread of sadness; so he giveth unto his beloved sleep" (Ps. CXXVII, 2). Precious, indeed, are the words of the Torah, each one containing sublime and holy mysteries, as has been affirmed, that when God gave the Torah to Israel, He gave it to them with all its sublime and holy treasures. The words: "It is vain for you that ye rise early" are addressed to those who are single, not exhibiting the proper union of male with female. In vain they rise early, as we read: "There is one that is alone, and he hath not a second . . . yet, there is no end of all his labour" (Eccl. IV, 8). In vain, too, they "sit up late", or, as we may translate, they "postpone rest", as woman is assuredly man's repose. They are addressed as "ye that eat the bread of sadness", for the man who has children eats his bread in good cheer and gladness of heart; but to him that has no children, the bread he eats is bread of sadness: "so he giveth unto his beloved sleep", the beloved being he whose wellspring is blessed, and to whom the Holy One vouchsafeth sleep in the other world, as we read: "and thou shalt lie down, and thy sleep shall be sweet" (Prov. III, 24), for he has a share in the world to come; the man will thus lie down and be blessed with the world to come. "There is one that is alone" (Eccl. IV, 8) is an allusion to the man who is improperly alone, without a wife; "and he hath not a second", no one to uphold him, no son to establish his name in Israel, or to bring him to his due meed; "yet there is no end of all his labour", as he is always labouring, day and night; "neither is his eye satisfied with riches" (*Ibid.*) and he has not the sense to reflect: "for whom, then, do I labour and bereave my soul [187b] of pleasure ?" (*Ibid*.) You may say that he has pleasure in that he eats and drinks and feasts every day; but it is not so, inasmuch as his soul (*nefesh*) does not share in his pleasure, so that assuredly he bereaves his soul of pleasure, of the blissful illumination of the world to come; for it is left stunted without attaining its full and proper growth. For God cares for His works, and so desires that a man should be set right and not perish from the world to come, as already said.'

R. Hiya put the following question: 'What is the position of a man who is just and upright and occupies himself with the study of the Torah day and night, and devotes himself wholly to the service of the Almighty, and yet is not blessed with children in this world despite all his effort, or who has children and they die—what is his position in the world to come ?' R. Jose replied: 'His good deeds and the Torah will shield him in the world to come.' R. Isaac said: 'Of such it is written: "For thus saith the Lord concerning the eunuchs that keep my Sabbaths, and choose the things that please me, and hold fast my covenant: even unto them will I give in my house and within my walls a monument and a memorial, better than sons and daughters; I will give them an ever-lasting memorial that shall not be cut off" (Is. LVI, 4–5), so that these have a share in the world to come.' Said R. Jose: 'All this is perfectly correct. But what of the following problem ? Suppose there is a perfectly righteous man who has all these qualities and duly perfects himself, yet dies without issue. Now, seeing that he will inherit his place in the world to come, will his wife require to marry his brother or not? If she has to do so, then the marriage will be purposeless, seeing that the other brother inherits his own place in the other world. The truth, however, is that she must still marry the brother, because we cannot say definitely whether the departed was really perfect or not. And in any case her second marriage is not purposeless, since it can serve to redeem some other righteous man who has died without children and has had no ransomer. The passage quoted above continues: "Two are better than one; because they have a good reward for

their labour" (Eccl. IV, 9), alluding to those who have performed the duty of leaving children in this world, for whose
sake they inherit a portion in the world to come. So God has
planted trees in this world; if they prosper, well and good,
and if not, He uproots them and replants them time after
time. All the ways of the Holy One are thus for the purpose
of achieving the good and the perfection of the world.'

GO IN UNTO THY BROTHER'S WIFE, AND PERFORM
THE DUTY OF A HUSBAND'S BROTHER UNTO HER. Judah
and all the other tribes were already cognisant of this duty,
the main purpose of which is expressed in the sentence: "and
raise up seed to thy brother", as that seed is needed for the
purpose of putting things right by growing into human shape
and form and thus preventing the stock from being severed
from its root. And when all has been put right, then those
concerned receive praise in the other world, as the Holy One
is pleased with them. Hence it says: "Wherefore I praised
the dead that are already dead more than the living that are
yet alive; but better than they both is he that hath not yet
been, who hath not seen the evil work that is done under the
sun" (*Ibid.* IV, 2–3). That is to say: I praised the dead that
are already dead more than the living that have returned
(from the other world) to the days of their youth; but better
than they both is he that has not yet returned to the days
of his youth, as he has no need to rectify and to suffer for his
former sins; for the Holy One [188*a*] has already given him
a fitting place in the other world. Happy the portion of the
just who walk in the way of truth. Of them it is written: "The
righteous shall inherit the land" (Ps. XXXVII, 29).

AND THE THING WHICH HE DID WAS EVIL IN THE SIGHT
OF THE LORD; AND HE SLEW HIM ALSO. R. Hiya discoursed here on the text: *In the morning sow thy seed, and in
the evening withhold not thy hand; for thou knowest not which
shall prosper, this or that, etc.* (Eccl. XI, 6). 'It behoves a man',
he said, 'to be well on his guard against sin, and to be heedful
in his actions before the Holy One, blessed be He; for numerous messengers and chieftains roam about the world,

spying out the works of the sons of man, to which they bear witness, and all of which are recorded in a book. Now of all the sins which defile a man, that which defiles him the most, both in this world and in the world to come, is the sin of spilling one's seed (semen). A man guilty of this sin will not enter within the Heavenly Curtain, and will not behold the presence of the Ancient of Days. So we learn from the recurrence of the word "evil" here and in the verse: "For thou art not a God that hath pleasure in wickedness; evil shall not sojourn with thee" (Ps. v, 5). It was on account of this sin, too, that the prophet said to the people, "your hands are full of blood" (Is. I, 15). Happy the portion of him who fears his Master, and is on his guard against the evil habit, keeping himself pure so as to persevere in the fear of his Master. Observe, then, the admonition saying: "In the morning sow thy seed." This alludes to the period when a man is in his prime and in the flower of youth, when he sets out to bring forth offspring from the woman destined for him. Then is the proper time for rearing children, as it says: "As arrows in the hand of a mighty man, so are the children of one's youth" (Ps. CXXVII, 4), as the father can then teach them the ways of the Holy One and so gain reward in the world to come, as it is written: "Happy is the man that hath his quiver full of them; they shall not be put to shame, when they speak with their enemies in the gate" (*Ibid.* 5), i.e. in the next world when the accusers bring their indictment against him, since there is no greater reward in the next world than that of the man who has trained his children in the fear of their Master and in the ways of the Torah. So it is written of Abraham: "For I have known him, that he will command his children and his household after him, that they may keep the way of the Lord, to do righteousness and justice" (Gen. XVIII, 19); and it was that merit which bestood him against all the accusers in the other world. Further: "and in the evening withhold not thy hand", that is to say, from begetting children even in old age, "for thou knowest not which shall prosper", that is which shall stand up in thy defence in the other world; and in regard to this it is written: "Lo, children are a heritage of the Lord" (Ps. CXXVII, 3), where the phrase "heritage of the Lord" is an allusion to the "bundle of souls" in the world to come, and the passage indicates that it is children that make a man worthy of entering that heritage of the Lord. Hence happy is the man who is blessed with them and who trains them in the ways of the Torah.

AND SHE PUT OFF FROM HER THE GARMENTS OF HER WIDOWHOOD. Tamar was the daughter of a priest, and it can hardly be imagined that she set out with the intention of committing incest with her father-in-law, since she was by nature chaste and modest. She was indeed virtuous and did not prostitute herself, and it was out of her deeper knowledge and wisdom that she approached Judah, and a desire to act kindly and faithfully (towards the dead). And it was because her act was based on a deeper knowledge that God aided her and she straightway conceived. So that it was all ordained [188*b*] from on high. If it is asked, why did not God cause those sons to be born from some other woman, the answer is that Tamar was necessary for this purpose, and not any other woman. There were two women from whom the seed of Judah was to be built up, from whom were to descend King David, King Solomon, and the Messiah, viz. Tamar and Ruth. These two women had much in common. Both lost their first husbands, and both took similar steps to replace them. Tamar enticed Judah because he was the next-of-kin to her sons who had died, and "she saw that Shelah was grown up, and she was not given unto him for wife". Ruth similarly enticed Boaz, as it says, "and she uncovered his feet and laid her down" (Ruth III, 7), and afterwards she bore him Obed. Now we do not ask why Obed was not born from another woman, for assuredly Ruth was necessary for that purpose to the exclusion of any other woman. From these two women, then, the seed of Judah was built up and brought to completion, and both of them acted piously, and had for their aim to do kindness toward the dead, for the proper establishment of the world subsequently. And this bears out our exposition of the verse "Wherefore I praise the dead that are already dead" (Eccl. IV, 2), for whilst their first husbands were alive there was no merit in them, but afterwards they were good for something, and so these two women exerted themselves to do kindness and truth with the dead; and God aided them in that work, and all was done fittingly. Happy is he who exerts himself in the study of the Torah day and night, as it says: "but thou shalt meditate therein day and night, that thou mayest observe to do according to all that is written therein; for then thou shalt make thy ways prosperous, etc." (Jos. I, 8).

AND JOSEPH WAS BROUGHT DOWN TO EGYPT, AND POTIPHAR BOUGHT HIM, ETC. The expression "was brought down" indicates that God approved of the act, so as to bring to fulfilment the announcement made to Abram between the pieces: "thy seed shall be a stranger, etc." (Gen. XV, 13). AND POTIPHAR BOUGHT HIM, for a sinful purpose.

R. Hizkiah discoursed on the text: *Who commandeth the sun, and it riseth not; and sealeth up the stars* (Job IX, 7). 'God', he said, 'has set seven stars in the firmament, and each firmament contains numerous angels appointed to minister to the Holy One, blessed be He, each angel having his own service to perform before his Master. All attend to the service to which they have been appointed and each one knows his task. Some of them serve as messengers, having charge in this world of the works of men; others are appointed to chant to Him songs and hymns. But although this is their own particular charge, there is no host in heaven or in the stars or in the constellations but chants praises to the Holy One, blessed be He; for as soon as night falls three hosts of angels range themselves in three quarters of the universe; and in each quarter there are myriads upon myriads, all of whom have for their task [189*a*] to chant praises to the Holy One. Over these three hosts there stands a sacred *Hayah* as chieftain. The chanting continues until daybreak. As soon as day breaks all those on the side of the South as well as the shining stars break out into song and praise to the Holy One, as we read: "When the morning stars sang together, and all the sons of God shouted for joy" (Job XXXVIII, 7), the morning stars being the stars of the South, the direction implied in the sentence: "And Abraham got up early in the morning"

(Gen. XIX, 27), whilst the "sons of God" are those on the left side who merge themselves in the right. When daylight arrives Israel take up the song and offer praises to the Holy One three times a day, corresponding to the three watches of the night. Thus through the angels and Israel together the glory of God is proclaimed day and night with six litanies. The sacred *Ḥayah* that is in charge of the chantings of the night on high similarly presides over the chantings of Israel here below; and all is performed in proper order. In regard to this one it is also written: "She riseth also while it is yet night and giveth food to her household, and a portion to her maidens" (Prov. XXXI, 15), where the "household" alludes to the heavenly hosts, whilst the word "maidens" signifies Israel here below. The Holy One is thus extolled both on high and here below.' R. Simeon said: 'The clause "Who commandeth the sun, and it riseth not" applies to Joseph, whilst the sequel, "and sealeth up the stars", applies to his brethren, regarding whom he said, "And eleven stars bowed down to me." Alternatively, "Who commandeth the sun" is an allusion to Jacob at the time his sons said to him: "Know now whether it is thy son's coat or not"; "that it shineth not" is a reference to the time when the Shekinah departed from him; whilst "sealeth up the stars" implies that through his sons Jacob's light was sealed and closed up, the sun for him was darkened and the stars did not shine—all because Joseph was separated from his father. And note that from the day on which Joseph disappeared Jacob abstained from marital intercourse and observed all the other rites of mourning until the day the good tidings of Joseph reached him.'

AND THE LORD WAS WITH JOSEPH, AND HE WAS A PROSPEROUS MAN; AND HE WAS IN THE HOUSE OF HIS MASTER THE EGYPTIAN. R. Jose quoted here the verse: "For the Lord loveth justice, and forsaketh not his saints; they are preserved for ever" (Ps. XXXVII, 28). 'Observe', he said, 'that wherever the righteous walk, God protects them and never abandons them, as David said: "Yea, though I walk through the valley of the shadow of death, I will fear no evil, for thou art with me; thy rod and staff they comfort me" (*Ibid.* XXIII, 4); wherever the righteous walk the Shekinah accompanies them and does not abandon them. Joseph walked through the valley of the shadow of death, having been brought down to Egypt, but the Shekinah was with him, as we read: "And the Lord was with Joseph", and by reason of the presence of the Shekinah all that he did prospered in his hand; so much so that if he had something in his hand and his master wanted something of a different kind, it changed in his hand to the kind his master wanted. Hence, it says "made to prosper *in his hand*", the reason being that the Lord was with him. Observe, too, that it is not written here, "And his master *knew*", but "And his master *saw*", signifying that he saw every day with his eyes the miracles God performed by the hand of Joseph; hence: "the Lord blessed the Egyptian's house for Joseph's sake". God guards the righteous, and for their sakes He guards also the wicked, so that the wicked receive blessings through the righteous. So we find it written: "The Lord blessed the house of Obed-edom . . . because of the ark of God" (II Sam. VI, 12). Others are sustained for the sake of those righteous, but they are not able to sustain or save themselves by their own merits. So Joseph, although his master was blessed for his sake, could not himself escape from him through his own merits and gain his freedom. He was even thrown afterwards into the dungeon, as we read: "His feet they hurt with fetters, his person was laid in iron" (Ps. cv, 18), until God liberated him and made him ruler over all the land of Egypt, and thus it is written: "and he forsaketh not his saints; [189*b*] they are preserved for ever." God shields the righteous in this world and in the world to come, as it is written: "So shall all those that take refuge in thee rejoice, they shall ever shout for joy, and thou shalt shelter them; let them also that love thy name exult in thee" (*Ibid.* V, 12).'

AND IT CAME TO PASS AFTER THESE THINGS THAT HIS MASTER'S WIFE, ETC. R. Hiya discussed the text: *Bless the Lord, ye angels of his, ye mighty in strength, that fulfil his word, hearkening unto the voice of his word* (*Ibid.* CIII, 20).

'How greatly', he said, 'it behoves a man to guard against sin and to pursue the straight path, so that the evil prompter, his daily assailant, should not lead him astray. And since he assails man perpetually, it behoves man to muster all his force against him and to entrench himself in the place of strength; for as the evil prompter is mighty, it behoves man to be mightier still; and those sons of men who do excel him in might are called "mighty in strength", dealing with him in his own coin, and they are "the angels of the Lord" who come from the side of *Geburah* (Might) to deal mightily with him. Such a one was Joseph, who was called "righteous" and guarded in purity the sign of the holy covenant which was imprinted upon him.' R. Eleazar said: 'The word "after" here alludes to the evil prompter, being the name of a grade, as we have laid down. Joseph exposed himself to his accusations because he used to pay great attention to his personal appearance. That gave the evil prompter an opening to say: "Behold, his father observes mourning for him, and he decks himself out and curls his hair !" Thus the bear was let loose, as it were, and set upon him.'

AND IT CAME TO PASS AFTER THESE THINGS. When God surveys the world with intent to judge it, and finds there wicked people, then, in the words of the Scripture, "He shuts up the heaven, so that there shall be no rain, and the ground shall not yield her fruit" (Deut. XI, 17); through the sins of the sons of men heaven and earth are shut up and do not perform their functions. Now those who do not guard in purity the holy covenant cause a division between Israel and their Father in heaven. So Scripture says: "and ye turn aside and serve other gods, and worship them. . . . He shut up the heaven, so that there shall be no rain" (*Ibid.* XI, 16–17); for to be false to the holy covenant is equivalent to bowing to another god. But when the holy covenant is properly guarded by mankind, God showers blessings from above on to this world, as we read: "A bounteous rain didst thou pour down, O God; thine inheritance and the weary one, thou confirmest it" (Ps. LXVIII, 10). "A bounteous (*n'daboth*, lit. favour) rain" is a rain of favour, at a time when the Community

of Israel find favour in the eyes of the Almighty and
He desires to shower upon them blessings; then "Thine
inheritance", namely Israel, who are the inheritance of the
Holy One, as it says: "Jacob the lot of his inheritance"
(Deut. XXXII, 9), and "the weary one", to wit, the Community
of Israel, which is weary in a strange land, which is parched,
panting for drink, "with that rain of favour thou confirmest
it". Hence heaven and earth with all their hosts are upheld by
that covenant, as Scripture says: "If not for my covenant,
day and night, the ordinances of heaven and earth were
as though I had not made them" (Jer. XXXIII, 25). Hence it is
first written: "And Joseph was of beautiful form, and fair to
look upon", and immediately afterwards, "that his master's
wife cast her eyes upon Joseph".

AND IT CAME TO PASS, AS SHE SPOKE TO JOSEPH DAY
BY DAY. R. Eleazar discoursed on the verse: *To keep thee
from the evil woman, etc.* (Prov. VI, 24). 'Happy', he said, 'are
the righteous who know the ways of the Almighty and follow
them, since they devote themselves to the Torah day and
night; for whoso devotes himself to the Torah day and night
inherits two worlds, the upper world and the world [190*a*]
below. He inherits this world, even if he does not study the
Torah for its own sake; and he inherits the other world, if he
does study the Torah for its own sake. So it is written:
"Length of days is in her right hand, in her left hand are
riches and honour" (*Ibid.* III, 16); that is, whoever walks to
the right of the Torah, for him she is length of life in the
world to come, where he will be invested with the glory of
the Torah, which is the truest glory and the crown of crowns;
for the crown of the Torah is in the other world; but "in her
left hand are riches and honour", to wit, in this world; even
for him who does not study it for its own sake. When R. Hiya
came from Babylonia to the Land of Israel he studied the
Torah until his face shone like the sun, and when the
students of the Torah stood up before him he would say:
"This one studies the Torah for its own sake, this one does
not study the Torah for its own sake." For the former he
would pray that they should always retain that frame of mind

and so merit the world to come; for the latter he prayed that their heart should be changed so that they should study the Torah for its own sake and merit life everlasting. One day he saw a certain disciple whose face was unnaturally pale. He said to himself: "This young man is undoubtedly assailed by sinful imaginations." So he took him in hand and interested him in the words of the Torah until he returned to a better frame of mind. From that day the disciple resolved not to give way any more to evil thoughts, but to study the Torah for its own sake.' R. Jose said: 'When a man perceives that evil thoughts are assailing him, he should study the Torah, and that will drive them away.' R. Eleazar said: 'When the evil side comes to seduce a man, he should draw it towards the Torah, and then it will quit him. For so we have learnt, that when the evil side stands up before the Almighty to accuse the world for its evil deeds, God in pity furnishes the sons of men with a device whereby to escape the accuser, so that he may not have power over them or their actions. This device consists in the study of the Torah, which will save them from the evil power, as it is written: "For the commandment is a lamp, and the teaching (Torah) is light, and reproofs of instruction are the way of life." The passage continues: "To keep thee from the evil woman, from the smoothness of the alien tongue" (*Ibid.* VI, 23–24), that is, from the side of uncleanness, or the other side, that is perpetually accusing the sons of men before the Almighty; and whilst it seduces men here below from the right path, it is busy on high pointing out the sins of men and indicting them, so that they may be given over into its power, in the same way as it acted towards Job. Especially at those periods when God sits in judgement on the world does it rise up to indict men and enumerate their sins. God, however, had compassion on Israel and provided them with a device for escaping from it, to wit, the trumpet (*shofar*) which is to be blown on New Year's Day, and the scapegoat which they give it on the Day of Atonement in order that it may leave them alone and occupy itself with its own portion. Of this it is written: "Her feet go down to death; her steps take hold on the nether world" (*Ibid.* v, 5); but of the true faith it says: "Her ways are ways of pleasantness, and all her paths are peace" (*Ibid.* III, 17). This refers to the ways and paths of the Torah. We have here the two opposing ways, the one of well-being, the other of death. Happy is the portion of Israel who cleave faithfully to the Holy One, who has afforded them a means of escape from all the other sides, because they are a holy people, His inheritance and portion. Happy are they in this world and in the world to come. When this evil side comes down and roams through the world and sees the works of mankind and how they all act perversely in the world, it ascends and accuses them, and were it not that the Almighty has compassion on the works of His hands, none would be left in the world on account of the accuser. Thus we read: "And it came to pass, as she spoke to Joseph day by day", [190b] that is to say, the accuser ascends every day and brings ever so many evil reports and calumnies in order to destroy mankind; "but he hearkened not unto her", because He has compassion on the world; "to be by her", that is, to permit the accuser to exercise dominion over the world, which he cannot do without obtaining authorization. The virtuous man so guards his ways as to keep afar from him the evil prompter, as it is written: "And it came to pass, as she spake to him day by day, that he hearkened not unto her"; for the unclean spirit, which is the same as the evil prompter, tries day by day to seduce man to lie by her, that is, to draw him into Gehinnom, to be with her there; for observe that once a man yields to that side he is more and more drawn towards it and defiles himself with it in this world and in the other world. This unclean side is ugly and filthy, and by it is punished he who goes astray from the Torah, and all those sinners that have no faith in the Holy One, blessed be He. It is further written: "And it came to pass on a certain day", to wit, the day in which the evil prompter is at large in the world, and comes to lead men astray; the day when the sons of men "come into the house to do their work", that is, to repent of their sins or study the Torah and carry out the commandments of the Torah, since man's proper work in this world is nothing else than the service of the Holy One. Hence it behoves him to be strong as a lion on every side, so that the other side should not get the mastery over him and should be powerless to seduce him. But when the evil prompter sees that there is no man to stand up against him and wage war with him, then "She caught him by the garment, saying: Lie with me", for when the evil prompter gains an ascendancy over a man, he decks him out with fine raiment and curls his hair and says "Lie with me", that is, attach yourself unto me. He that is righteous stands up to him and offers him battle; so Scripture says: "And he left his garment in her hand, and fled and got him out"—the righteous thus by an effort shakes him off and flees from him so that he should not have command over him any more.' R. Isaac said: 'The righteous will one day see the evil prompter in the form of a huge mountain and they will marvel at themselves, saying, How were we ever able to over-throw that mighty mountain ? Contrariwise, to the wicked the evil prompter will appear like a thread as thin as a hair, and they will say in astonishment, How was it that we could not master so frail a thread as this ? The righteous will weep for joy and the wicked will weep from anguish. And the Holy One will sweep the evil one off the earth, He will slaughter him before their eyes, so that his power will for ever be gone from the world. The righteous will behold and rejoice, as it says: "Surely the righteous shall give thanks unto thy name, the upright shall dwell in thy presence" (Ps. CXL, 14).' [191a]

AND IT CAME TO PASS AFTER THESE THINGS, THAT THE BUTLER OF THE KING OF EGYPT AND HIS BAKER OFFENDED, ETC. R. Judah opened his discourse with the text: *Will a lion roar in the forest when he hath no prey ? Will a young lion give forth his voice out of his den, if he has taken nothing ?* (Amos III, 4). 'It well boots a man', he said, 'to be assiduous in the worship of the Holy One, blessed be He, for then his fear and dread is upon every creature. For when God created the world, He made each creature in its proper like-ness; and finally He created man in the supernal image and gave him dominion over all through this image. For as long as a man is alive the other creatures look up to him and, perceiving the supernal image, shake and tremble before him, as we read: "And the fear of you and the dread of you shall be upon every beast of the earth, and upon every fowl of the air, etc." (Gen. IX, 2). But this is only when they are aware of that image and soul in him (though R. Eleazar said that the image of the righteous does not change even when their soul (*neshamah*) is no longer in them). But when a man does not walk in the ways of the Torah, that divine image is altered, and the beasts of the field and the birds of the sky obtain power over him; because the divine image in him, the very form which makes him a man, is changed. Observe how God altered the order of nature in order to execute His purpose. For the form of Daniel was not altered even when he was thrown into the lions' den, and thus he was saved.' Said R. Hizkiah: 'If so, why is it said, "My God hath sent his angel, and hath shut the lions' mouths, and they have not hurt me" (Dan. VI, 23) ?' R. Judah said in reply: 'The divine image of the righteous man is itself the very angel that shuts the mouths of the beasts and puts them in shackles so that they do not hurt him; hence Daniel's words: "My God hath sent his angel", to wit, the one who bears the imprint of all the images of the world, and he firmly fixed my image on me, thereby shutting the lions' mouths, and making them powerless over me. Hence man has to look well to his ways and paths, so as not to sin before his Master, and to preserve the image of Adam. Ezekiel guarded his mouth against forbidden food, as it is written: "Neither came there abhorred flesh into my mouth" (Ez. IV, 14), and for this he was dignified with the title "son of Adam". Of Daniel also it is written: "But Daniel purposed in his heart that he would not defile himself with the king's food, nor with the wine which he drank" (Dan. I, 8), in virtue of which he conserved the image of Adam; for all beings of the world fear the image of Adam, which is ruler and king over all.' Said R. Jose: 'For this reason it behoves man to be on his guard against sin and to turn neither to the right nor to the left; and however careful he may be, he should still search himself daily for any sin. When a man rises in the morning two witnesses join him and follow him the whole day. When he opens his eyes, they say to him: "Let thine eyes look right on, and let thine eyelids look straight before thee" (Prov. IV, 25); when he gets up and makes ready to walk, they say to him: "Make plain the paths of thy feet, etc." (*Ibid.* 26). A man, therefore, should be on his guard against his sins the whole day and every day, and when night comes it behoves him to look back and examine all the actions he has done that day, so that he may repent himself. So David said: "And my sin is ever before me" (Ps. LI, 5), as an exhortation to repentance. Now, when Israel were in the Holy Land sin never clung to them, because the offerings which they offered up [191b] made atonement for them. But now that they are exiled from the Land and the offerings have ceased, it is the Torah and good deeds that make atonement for them.' R. Isaac remarked: 'So whosoever devotes himself to the study of the Torah and to the perform- ance of good deeds enables the Community of Israel to raise its head in the midst of exile. Happy is the portion of those who study diligently the Torah day and night.'

Observe now how God regulates events in such a way as to raise aloft the head of the righteous; for in order that Joseph, who was found righteous before Him, might be exalted, He stirred his master to anger against his servants, as we read: "The butler of the king of Egypt and his baker offended their lord the king of Egypt"—all that Joseph the righteous might be exalted. And notice that it was through a dream that Joseph was brought low by his brethren, and it was through a dream that he was raised over his brethren and over the whole world. AND THEY DREAMED A DREAM, BOTH OF THEM, EACH MAN HIS DREAM, IN ONE NIGHT, EACH MAN ACCORDING TO THE INTERPRETATION OF HIS DREAM, ETC. Seeing that we have laid down that dreams follow their interpretation, it may be asked what made Joseph interpret the dream of one in a good sense and of the other in a bad sense. The explanation is that these dreams concerned Joseph himself, and, because he penetrated to the root of the matter, he gave to each dream the fitting interpretation so that everything should fall in its place. AND JOSEPH SAID UNTO THEM: DO NOT INTERPRE- TATIONS BELONG TO GOD? TELL IT ME, I PRAY YOU. Joseph used this formula because it is necessary before inter- preting a dream to entrust the interpretation to the Holy One, since there, on high, is the shaping of all events, and His is the interpretation. Observe that the grade of dream is a low grade, the sixth from that of prophecy, and that its interpretation determines its effect, being itself embodied in speech and utterance. This is what is meant by Joseph's question: "Do not interpretations belong to God (*Elohim*)?" Assuredly to *Elohim*. Now observe the verse: "And the chief butler told his dream to Joseph, etc." R. Eleazar opened a discourse on the text: *And it came to pass, when they were gone over, that Elijah said unto Elisha: Ask what I shall do for thee, before I am taken from thee. And Elisha said: I pray thee, let a double portion of thy spirit be upon me.* 'The language used by Elijah here', he said, 'is not a little surprising, for surely it is only God who can grant whatever is asked of Him. And further, how could Elisha, knowing this, demand "Let a double portion of thy spirit be upon me"? But, indeed, this was surely not beyond the power of one who had a grip of heaven and earth and of the whole world, for assuredly God would perform the will of Elijah, as of all righteous men, as we read: "He will fulfil the desire of them that fear him" (Ps. CXLV, 19), and all the more when it was a question of Elijah bequeathing the holy spirit he possessed to Elisha, who was his own servant, and concerning whom God had said to him: "and Elisha, the son of Shaphat of Abel-mehulah shalt thou anoint to be prophet in thy room" (1 Kings XIX, 16); hence Elisha was his heir by right. We may ask, however, how he could beg for a double portion of his spirit, which was more than Elijah possessed. What Elisha really asked, however, was not a double portion of the spirit, but the power to perform a double achievement with that same spirit. Elijah thereupon said: "Thou hast asked a hard thing; nevertheless, if thou see me when I am taken from thee, it shall be so unto thee; but if not, it shall not be so" (II Kings II, 10). By the words, "if thou see me" he meant: If thou canst penetrate to the true inwardness of the spirit that I bequeath thee at the moment I am taken from thee, it shall be so unto thee. For such essence of the spirit as he should discern while looking at Elijah he would fully grasp. [192*a*] And so, whoever contemplates that which he learns from his master whilst at the same time seeing that wisdom reflected in his face, can thereby obtain an additional meed of spirit. So Joseph, in whatever he was about to do, used to contemplate in the spirit of wisdom the image of his father, and so he prospered and an augmentation of spirit came upon him with a higher illumination. When that sinner said to him: "behold, a vine was before me", Joseph was alarmed, not knowing what import it might have; but when he continued, "and in the vine were three branches", straightway Joseph's spirit was astir and received an influx of energy and illumination, because at the same time he gazed at the image of his father, and knew the meaning of the words he heard. We read, then, AND IN THE VINE WERE THREE BRANCHES. Said Joseph: 'This is assuredly tidings of unalloyed joy', since that vine was symbolic of the Community of Israel, and the three branches were the three higher grades ramifying from that vine, to wit, Priests, Levites, and Israelites: and AS IT WAS BUDDING ITS BLOSSOMS SHOT FORTH, that is, by virtue of those three orders the whole Community of Israel ascended and received the blessing from the Most High King: AND THE CLUSTERS THEREOF BROUGHT FORTH RIPE GRAPES, an allusion to the wine that is kept in store in its grapes since the six days of creation.[1] So far the dream was of good tidings for Joseph; the rest of the dream concerned solely the dreamer himself; for, indeed, some dreams there are which in part concern the dreamer himself and in part other people. In this connection we have been taught: To see white grapes in a dream is of good omen to the dreamer, but not black, the reason being that these two are emblems of two certain grades, one of the side of good, the other of the contrary side. Grapes in general are an allusion to faith, and hence they diverge within that category, one kind to the side of good and the other to the side of evil, the one requiring to be exorcised by prayer, the other betokening providential care. Observe that the wife of Adam pressed for him grapes and thereby brought death to him, and to the whole world. Noah, again, came upon those grapes and he was not duly circumspect, so it is written of him: "And he drank of the

---

[1] For the banqueting of the righteous in the world to come.

wine, and he was drunken; and he was uncovered within his tent" (Gen. IX, 21). Of those same grapes the sons of Aaron drank, and they offered up sacrifices whilst under the influence of wine, as a result of which they died. Hence it is written: "their grapes are grapes of gall, their clusters are bitter" (Deut. XXXII, 32), referring to those grapes that caused all those ills; but the chief of the butlers saw in his dream the good grapes in that vineyard whence there ascends a pleasant and agreeable odour among the perfect grades in manner due. Thus Joseph, who penetrated to the root of the whole matter, interpreted the dream aright; for inasmuch as the dream contained good tidings for himself he interpreted the whole of it in a favourable sense, and so it was fulfilled. The text continues:

WHEN THE CHIEF BAKER SAW THAT THE INTERPRETATION WAS GOOD, HE SAID UNTO JOSEPH: ALSO I SAW IN MY DREAM, AND BEHOLD, THREE BASKETS OF WHITE BREAD WERE ON MY HEAD. Cursed be the wicked whose actions are all fraught with evil intent, their utterances with malice. As soon as the chief baker opened his mouth with the word *af* (=anger) Joseph was affrighted, perceiving, as he did, that his words would be of evil import; and, indeed, in the words "and behold, three baskets of white bread upon my head" Joseph at once read the evil tidings of the destruction of the Temple and of the exile of Israel. For notice the rest of the dream, namely, "and the birds did eat them out of the basket upon my head": this was a reference to the other nations who would assemble against Israel, slay them, devastate their dwellings, and scatter them into the four corners of the world. Joseph noted all this and knew that that dream concerned Israel at the time when they should sin before the King; he thus straightway interpreted it in an evil sense, which interpretation was fulfilled in the dreamer. Observe, then, that the two dreams belonged to two different grades: the one saw [192*b*] the upper grade ascending and the moon in its fullness of light; the other saw the moon in darkness and under the domination of the evil serpent. Joseph therefore looked closely at that dream and interpreted it as of evil presage.

R. Judah opened a discourse on the verse: *Create me a clean heart, O God, and renew a steadfast spirit within me* (Ps. LI, 12). 'The term "a clean heart",' he said, 'finds its parallel in the passage: "Give thy servant therefore an understanding heart" (1 Kings III, 9), and also in: "But he that is of merry heart hath a continual feast" (Prov. XV, 15). This is assuredly the clean heart which David asked for. "And renew a steadfast spirit within me" indicates the spirit spoken of in the passage: "and the spirit of God hovered over the face of the waters", this being, as has been pointed out, the spirit of the Messiah; the same is alluded to in the promise: "And a new spirit will I put within you" (Ez. XXXVI, 26). David thus prayed for that steadfast spirit, since on the sinister side there is the unclean spirit called the spirit of perverseness that leads people astray, that unclean spirit referred to in the statement: "The Lord hath mingled within her a spirit of perverseness" (Is. XIX, 14). David thus prayed: "and renew within me a spirit of steadfastness". The term "renew" also alludes to the renewal of the moon, a period which contains the assurance that David, King of Israel, is alive and in being.'

R. Eleazar and R. Jose were once walking on the road. Said R. Jose to R. Eleazar: 'We read: "And there came forth the spirit, and stood before the Lord, and said: I will entice him: And the Lord said unto him: Wherewith ? And he said: I will go forth and will be a lying spirit in the mouth of all the prophets. And He said: Thou shalt entice him, and shalt prevail also; go forth and do so" (1 Kings XXII, 21–22). According to tradition that was the spirit of Naboth the Jezreelite. Can, then, a soul which has once ascended to the upper world return to this world ? Further, the words "I will go forth, and will be a lying spirit in his mouth" are very astonishing. And again, why was Ahab punished on account of Naboth, seeing that Samuel had so laid down the law to Israel, when he said to them: "And he will take your fields, and your vineyards, and your oliveyards, even the best of them" (1 Sam. VIII, 14) ? According to this, if Ahab took

Naboth's vineyard, he was within his rights, and all the more so, seeing that he offered him in exchange another vineyard or its equivalent in gold, which he refused.' R. Eleazar said in reply: 'It is a proper question you ask. Observe that the traditional identification of that spirit with the spirit of Naboth does indeed raise a difficulty. For how could the spirit of Naboth stand up before the Almighty to ask permission to lie? If Naboth was a righteous man, how could he ask permission to lie in the other world, the world of truth, seeing that even in this world it is the part of a righteous man to keep afar from falsehood? How much more so, then, in the upper world! On the other hand, if Naboth was not a righteous man, how could he have stood in the presence of the Almighty? But the truth is that Naboth was not righteous enough to stand in the presence of the Almighty, and that spirit was another one which has power in the world and continually ascends and stands before God, the same that leads people astray by means of falsehood. Now he who is accustomed to lying will always resort to lying, and hence he said: "I will go forth, and will be a lying spirit, etc.", to which the Holy One replied: ". . . go forth, and do so", as much as to say: "go hence and be off from here". This is in harmony with the Scriptural text: "He that speaketh falsehood shall not be established before mine eyes" (Ps. CI, 7). And in regard to the other difficulty—if Ahab took Naboth's vineyard, why did he kill him? It was just because he killed Naboth without cause, before expropriating his vineyard, that Ahab was punished. So it is written: "Hast thou killed, and also taken possession?" (I Kings XXI, 19). Great, indeed, is the number of those whom that lying spirit leads astray by means of falsehood, dominating the world from many sides and through many activities. Hence King David supplicated that he might be guarded against him and removed from defilement, saying: "Create me a clean heart, O God; and renew a steadfast spirit within me", a steadfast spirit being the opposite of that other spirit. In sum, there are two grades, one sacred and the other defiled.'

R. Eleazar then opened a discourse on the text: *And the Lord uttereth his voice before his army; for his camp is very great, for he is mighty that executeth his word* (Joel II, 11). He said: 'The expression" and the Lord" (*V-YHVH*), as we have laid down, everywhere indicates the Lord in conjunction with His Court of Justice; the "voice" here is the same as "the voice of words" (Deut. IV, 12) heard by the Israelites, where the term "words" again is identical with the same term in the verse "I am not a man of words" (Exod. IV, 10), the man of words being the man of God (Deut. XXXIII, 1); "before his army", to wit, Israel; "for his camp is very great", as it says: "Is there any number of his armies ?" (Job XXV, 3), [193*a*] inasmuch as the Holy One has ever so many chieftains and emissaries who are at hand to bring accusations against Israel, and therefore God goes before Israel in order to guard them, and so that their accusers should not prevail against them: "for he is mighty that executeth his word", to wit, the righteous man, who devotes himself to the study of the holy Torah day and night. Alternatively, the term "mighty" here is an epithet of the accuser, who appears frequently before the Almighty, and who is indeed mighty, strong as iron, hard as flint; and it is he that "executeth his word", as he first obtains authorization from above and then takes away man's soul here below. We read further: "For great is the day of the Lord and very terrible; and who can abide it ?" (Joel II, 11), inasmuch as He is ruler over all, most high and most mighty, all being subject to His dominion. Happy are the righteous in whom the Holy One constantly finds delight, so as to vouchsafe to them the world to come and to make them participators in the joy with which the righteous will one day exult in the Holy One, blessed be He, as it is written: "So shall all those who take refuge in thee rejoice, they shall ever shout for joy, and thou shalt shelter them, and that those that love thy name will exult in thee" (Ps. V, 12). Blessed be the Lord for evermore. Amen and Amen !'

MIQEZ

Gen. XLI, I–XLIV, 17

AND IT CAME TO PASS AT THE END. R. Hiya expounded the word "end" from the text: *He setteth an end for darkness, and he searcheth out to the furthest bound; a stone of thick darkness and the shadow of death* (Job XXVIII, 3). 'The end here mentioned is', he said, 'an allusion to the "end of the left", which, after roaming to and fro in the world, finally ascends and presents itself before the Holy One, blessed be He, to bring accusations against mankind. He "searcheth out to the furthest bound" (*takhlith*=destruction), inasmuch as all his works are never for good, but always for destruction and for the utter annihilation of the world. He is "a stone of stumbling" on which the wicked come to grief and which is found in "a land of thick darkness, as darkness itself" (*Ibid.* X, 22). For there is a "land of the living" on high, which is the Land of Israel, and a land below called "land of darkness". The darkness and the shadow of death here mentioned are identical with the end that emerges from the side of darkness, which is also the "dross of gold". As we have laid down, it behoves the sons of men to take due thought of divine worship and to labour in the Torah day and night, so as to know how to serve the Holy One, blessed be He. The Torah herself summons man daily, saying: "Whoso is thoughtless, let him turn in hither, etc." (Prov. IX, 4–6). And whoever labours in the Torah and cleaves unto her is privileged to take hold of the tree of life, as it is written: "She is a tree of life to them that lay hold upon her" (*Ibid.* III, 18). And whoso takes hold upon the tree of life in this world will also keep hold on it in the world to come, since the grades assigned to souls in the next world correspond to their state on departing from this world. Now the tree of life ramifies into various degrees, all differing from one another, although forming a unity, in the shape of branches, leaves, bark, stock, and roots. All the faithful ones of Israel lay hold upon the tree of life, some grasping the stock, some the branches, some the leaves, and others, again, the roots. But those who exert themselves in the study of the Torah [193*b*] grasp the very trunk of the tree, and so lay hold upon all; and so we affirm.'

AND IT CAME TO PASS AT THE END. What does the term "end" signify? Said R. Simeon: 'It signifies the region wherein there is no remembering, which is identical with the end of the left. Why did it emerge at that moment? Because Joseph said: "But have me in thy remembrance when it shall be well with thee" (Gen. XL, 14). It was hardly becoming for Joseph the righteous to beg to be remembered by the chief butler; but he was led to do so by his dream, which he thought betokened remembrance. In this, however, he was mistaken, since all depended on God, and therefore the region of forgetfulness placed itself before him. Hence the Scripture, after saying, "Yet did not the chief butler remember Joseph" (*Ibid.* 23), adds the words "but forgot him", alluding to the region of forgetfulness, which is identical with the end of the side of darkness.'

AT THE END OF TWO FULL YEARS. The two years were symbolic of the two grades, the grade of forgetfulness and the grade of remembrance to which it gave place, THAT PHARAOH DREAMED. AND, BEHOLD, HE STOOD BY THE RIVER. This dream was one that concerned Joseph himself, since the idea of river is closely connected with Joseph the righteous; and according to the lore of dreams a river seen in a dream is a presage of peace, for so it is written: "Behold, I will extend peace to her like a river" (Is. LXVI, 12).'

R. Hiya opened a discourse on the text: *The king by justice establisheth the land; but he that exacteth gifts overthroweth it* (Prov. XXIX, 4). 'When God', he said, 'created the upper world, He so constituted it as to send forth celestial radiations in all directions, and He created the upper heaven and the upper earth in such a way that they should provide for the sustenance of the lower denizens. The "king" here is an allusion to the Holy One, blessed be He, while "justice" signifies Jacob, who forms the basis of the world, since the basis of the world is justice, which establishes the earth with all requirements and provides for its sustenance. Alternatively, the "king" is the Holy One, blessed be He, while "justice" refers to Joseph, who established the land, as it is written: "And all countries came into Egypt to Joseph to buy corn"; and because God chose for Himself Jacob, He caused Joseph to be ruler over the land.' R. Jose said: 'The "king" signifies Joseph, while the words "by justice establisheth the land" allude to Jacob, seeing that before Jacob arrived in Egypt the existence of the people was jeopardized by the famine; but as soon as Jacob set foot in Egypt the famine ceased through his merits and the world was made secure. Alternatively, the king who by justice establisheth the land is exemplified in King David, of whom it is written: "and David executed justice and righteousness unto all his people" (II Sam. VIII, 15); for David thereby upheld the world, which was preserved after him for the sake of his merits. "But he that exacteth gifts overthroweth it": this is exemplified in Rehoboam. For God for the sake of the righteous withholds punishment even when it has been decreed against the world; hence, during David's lifetime the land was upheld and after his death it was preserved for his sake, as we read: "and I will defend the city for mine own sake, and for my servant David's sake" (II Kings xx, 6). Similarly, during the lifetime of Jacob, as well as that of Joseph, no punishment was enforced against the world. Again, "he that exacteth gifts overthroweth it" is exemplified in Pharaoh, inasmuch as by hardening his heart before God he brought ruin on the land of Egypt, whereas before the land was preserved through Joseph in conjunction with Pharaoh's dreams. [194*a*]

AND, BEHOLD, THERE CAME UP OUT OF THE RIVER SEVEN KINE, WELL FAVOURED AND FATFLESHED; AND THEY FED IN THE REED GRASS. The river is mentioned because from it all the lower grades receive their blessings. For the (supernal) stream which flows perpetually waters and feeds the whole, and Joseph was himself the river by means of which the whole of Egypt was blessed. By that (upper) river seven grades are irrigated and blessed, they being "well favoured and fatfleshed", AND THEY FED IN THE REED GRASS (*ahu*). The word *ahu* (meadow, or brotherhood) signifies that there is no separation between them. The number seven has everywhere a similar symbolism, e.g. the seven maidens and the seven chamberlains mentioned in the Book of Esther (Esther II, 9; I, 10). R. Isaac said that the seven good kine symbolize the superior grades, and the seven lean and ill-favoured kine other and lower grades; the former of the side of holiness, and the latter of the side of defilement. SEVEN EARS OF CORN. R. Judah said: 'The first seven ears were good, as they came from the right side, of which it is written "that it was good" (Gen. I, 4), and the second seven were ill, as being lower than the others; the first ones proceeded from the side of purity, and the others from the side of impurity. They all symbolized two series of grades corresponding with each other; and Pharaoh saw them all in his dream. R. Jesse remarked: 'Can it indeed be that the wicked Pharaoh was shown all these?' R. Judah in reply said: 'He only saw their counterparts rising in a corresponding series: he saw this through the medium of the lower grades. For, as we have learnt, what a man is shown in a dream corresponds to his own character, and his soul ascends just so far as to obtain for him the information suitable for his grade. Pharaoh thus saw as far as he was permitted to see and no more.'

AND IT CAME TO PASS AT THE END. R. Hizkiah quoted here the verse: *To every thing there is a season, and a time to every purpose under the heaven* (Eccl. III, 1). 'For every thing that the Almighty has made in the lower world,' he said, 'He has appointed a fixed term and limit. He has appointed a time for light and for darkness. He has fixed a term for the light of the other nations who are now the rulers of the world; and a term for the darkness of the exile of Israel who are now subjected to their rule. And so there is a term for every purpose in the lower world.' According to another explanation, the word *'eth* (time) is the name of an angelic power charged to see that everything takes place at its appointed time.

AND IT CAME TO PASS IN THE MORNING THAT HIS SPIRIT WAS TROUBLED; AND HE SENT AND CALLED FOR ALL THE MAGICIANS OF EGYPT, AND ALL THE WISE MEN THEREOF. The word *vatipo'em* (and was troubled, akin to the word *pa'am*, time) indicates that the spirit kept on appearing to Pharaoh and leaving him, not staying with him long enough at any one time to enlighten him. The same was the case at first with Samson, of whom it is written: "And the spirit of the Lord began to move him in time beats (*l'pha'amo*)" (Jud. XIII, 25). In connection with Nebuchadnezzar it is written *vatithpa'em* (and was troubled) (Dan. II, 1), to indicate that the coming and going of the spirit was twice as rapid. [194*b*] AND HE SENT AND CALLED FOR ALL THE MAGICIANS OF EGYPT AND ALL THE WISE MEN THEREOF, to wit, the bird-diviners. They all tried to make out the dream, but it baffled them. R. Isaac said: 'Although it has been affirmed that no man is shown anything in a dream save what falls within his own grade, it is different with kings, who are permitted to see more deeply than other men; for inasmuch as a king's grade is higher than that of other men, he is permitted to see that which falls within a higher grade than that of other men. So Scripture says: WHAT GOD IS ABOUT TO DO HE HATH SHOWN UNTO PHARAOH, whereas to other men God does not reveal what He is about to do, except to the prophets, saints, or sages of the generation. Now observe the words: ME HE RESTORED UNTO MINE OFFICE, AND HIM HE HANGED. From this we learn that a dream is determined by its interpretation, since the pronoun "he" can refer only to Joseph, indicating that it was Joseph who restored the one to his office, and hanged the other, through the medium of his interpretation.

THEN PHARAOH SENT AND CALLED JOSEPH, AND THEY BROUGHT HIM QUICKLY (*vayerizuhu*) OUT OF THE DUNGEON. R. Abba discoursed on the verse: *The Lord taketh pleasure (roze) in them that fear him, in those that wait for his mercy* (Ps. CXLVII, 11). 'God indeed takes pleasure in the righteous', he said, 'because they promote peace in the upper world and in the lower world, and cause the bride to join her husband; and therefore God takes pleasure in those that fear Him and do His will. Those that wait for His mercy are they who study the Torah in the night time and thereby become associates of the Shekinah, and thus when the morning comes they wait for His mercy; for, as has been affirmed, whoso studies the Torah in the night time is looked upon graciously in the day time. So Scripture says: "By day the Lord will command His lovingkindness (or grace)"—for what reason? Because "in the night his song is with me" (Ps. XLII, 9). Hence: "The Lord takes pleasure in those that fear him", or, as we might translate more accurately, "appeases those that fear Him", like one friend with another. Similarly, of Joseph here it is written, *vayeriẓuhu* (and they brought him hastily), which admits of the rendering, "and they appeased him", when he was sad and woebegone, giving him words of good cheer that gladdened his heart and dissipated the gloom of the dungeon. Observe that just as his troubles commenced through his having been thrown into the pit, so it was through the pit that he finally was exalted.' R. Simeon said: 'Before that incident (of Potiphar's wife), Joseph was not called righteous (*ẓadiq*); it was only after he stood the test of guarding the purity of the covenant that he was called righteous, and that the grade of the holy covenant was crowned through him, and having been with him in the first pit rose with him now; and thus it is written: "and they brought him quickly out of the pit"—he was raised from the pit and crowned by the well of living waters.'

AND PHARAOH SENT AND (he) CALLED JOSEPH. Instead of "and called" we should have expected "to call for". The implied subject is, therefore, God, as in the verse "And he called to Moses" (Lev. I, 1), and this harmonizes with the words of the Psalmist: "Until the time that his word came to pass, the word of the Lord tested him" (Ps. CV, 19). AND HE CHANGED HIS RAIMENT, out of respect for royalty, as explained elsewhere. R. Eleazar quoted here the text: *Israel also came into Egypt; and Jacob sojourned in the land of Ham (Ibid.* 23). 'God,' he said, 'while accomplishing his decrees, yet directs events in such a manner as to soften their severity. For we have learned that but for the love which God bore to our ancestors, Jacob would have been brought down into Egypt in iron chains; but out of His love for the patriarchs He caused his son Joseph to be made ruler of the world; and so all the tribes went down into Egypt like people of distinction, and Jacob entered it like a king. In the verse: "Israel also came into Egypt; and Jacob sojourned in the land of Ham", we may take Israel to be an allusion to the Holy One, blessed be He, for it was for the sake of Jacob, who sojourned in the land of Ham, and his sons that the Shekinah came into Egypt. God thus arranged that [195*a*] Joseph should first be brought into Egypt, as through his merit the covenant was confirmed with him, and made him ruler over all the land. In this connection it is written: "The King sent and loosed him; the ruler of peoples, and set him free" (*Ibid.* 20). According to R. Simeon, the word "ruler" in this sentence is the object of the verb "sent", and refers to the ruler of peoples, to wit, the angel-redeemer, who is the ruler of the earthly beings, and whom God sent to set Joseph free.

GOD WILL GIVE PHARAOH AN ANSWER OF PEACE. This was a first greeting and an overture of peace. R. Abba said: 'The wicked Pharaoh said, "I know not the Lord" (Ex. v, 2), notwithstanding that he was the wisest of all the magicians; he knew, however, the name "God" (*Elohim*), seeing that he himself said: "Can we find such a man as this, a man in whom the spirit of God (*Elohim*) is ?" But Moses came to him, not in the name of God (*Elohim*), but in the name of the Lord (*Jehovah*), a name altogether beyond his apprehension.' R. Abba quoted in this connection: *Who is like the Lord our God, that is enthroned on high, that looketh down low upon heaven and upon the earth* (Ps. CXIII, 5–6). 'God', he said, 'is "enthroned on high", that is, He raises Himself high above His Throne of Glory and does not reveal Himself to the lower world at those times when no righteous men are to be found in the world. Contrariwise, He "looketh down low" when righteous men are found in the world, as then He descends in His grade so as to meet the lower beings and to take the world under His providential care. But when there are no righteous men in the world, He ascends aloft and hides His face from men, and deserts them, inasmuch as the righteous are the foundation and the mainstay of the world. Hence God did not reveal His Divine Name save to Israel alone, who are His portion and lot and heritage; and the rest of the world He apportioned to celestial chieftains, as we read: "When the Most High gave to the nations their inheritance. . . . For the portion of the Lord is his people, Jacob the lot of his inheritance" (Deut. XXXII, 8–9).'

As R. Hiya and R. Jose were one day walking together, the latter said: 'I often puzzle over the language of Solomon in the book of Ecclesiastes, which I find exceedingly obscure; for instance, the words *All things would wear a man out to tell; man cannot utter it, the eye is not satisfied with seeing, nor the ear filled with hearing* (Eccl. 1, 8). Why mention all these three organs? Having said that all things are more than mouth can utter, why add that "eye cannot see nor ear hear sufficiently"? The reason is, I presume, because eyes and ears function involuntarily; whereas the mouth is under a man's control, and so Koheleth teaches us that all three together cannot exhaust the universe.' Said R. Hiya: 'That is so. Man's mouth cannot utter, nor his eyes see, nor his ear hear the entirety of things; and yet "there is nothing new under the sun" (*Ibid.* 1, 9). And observe that not even the disembodied spirits which the Holy One created under the sun are able to give utterance to all the things that are in the world, nor can their eye [195b] see nor their ear hear all. Hence Solomon, who knew everything, spoke thus. Now, observe that all the doings of the world are controlled by vast numbers of spirits, but the people of the world know not and regard not what it is that upholds them. Even Solomon, the wisest of men, could not apprehend them.' He further discoursed on the verse: *He hath made everything beautiful in its time; also he hath set the world in their heart, yet so that man cannot find out the work that God hath done, etc. (Ibid. III, 11).* 'How happy', he said, 'are those who labour in the Torah and thus learn to see with the eye of wisdom! Whatever God has formed in the world has its own controlling grade which directs it either for good or for evil. There are grades of the right and grades of the left. If a man goes to the right, whatever act he performs then becomes a directing grade on that side which helps him onward and procures him other helpers. But if he goes to the left, then whatever act he commits becomes a directing force on that side, and brings indictments against him, whilst leading him further into that side. Hence, whenever a man performs a good and proper act the chieftain of the right hand affords him help, and this is indicated in the expression "good in its time", that is, the act and its time become intimately bound up together; also "He hath set the world in their heart", that is, the whole world and all its works depend only on the will of man. Happy are those righteous who by their good deeds draw benefits upon themselves and upon the world, and who know how to attach themselves to the grade called "time of peace", and who in virtue of their righteousness in the lower world influence the grade called *Kol* (everything) to shine in its time (*'eth*). Woe to the sinners who know not the time-grade of any act and are not circumspect to perform their deeds in such a way as to benefit the world, and so that each deed of theirs should fall under the proper grade. Everything is thus dependent on man's free will, as it is written: "so that man cannot find out the work that God hath done from the beginning even to the end"; and inasmuch as it depends on a man's will whether his deeds are attached to the proper grade or to the improper one, the text continues: "I know that there is no good in them but to rejoice, and to perform good actions so long as they live" (*Ibid.* III, 12). That is to say, if a man's actions are not good, he has to rejoice at all their consequences and to give thanks for them to the Holy One and to do good actions as long as he lives; for since his own act brought evil upon him through the grade presiding over it, he has to rejoice at the punishment and to give thanks for it, seeing that he brought it on himself, like a bird blindly falling into the snare. So Scripture says: "For man also knoweth not his time; as the fishes that are taken in an evil net, and as the birds that are caught in the snare, even so are the sons of men

snared in an evil time, when it falleth suddenly upon them"
(*Ibid.* IX, 12). The expression "his time" (*'eth*) refers to the
ministering angel called "time", who presides over each act
a man performs, and is referred to in the statement "he hath
made everything beautiful in its time". Hence they are "as
the birds that are caught in the snare". Happy, then, are
those who exert themselves in the study of the Torah and are
intimate with the ways and paths of the Torah of the Most
High King so as to follow the true way.'

Observe that a man ought never to begin his speech with
an ill-omened utterance, as he does not know who will take it
up, and he may come to grief over it. The righteous thus
always begin their discourse with words of peace. So Joseph
prefaced his address to Pharaoh with the words: "God will
give Pharaoh an answer of peace." R. Judah said: 'It has
been taught that the Holy One, blessed be He, is solicitous
for the welfare of a king, as we read: "and he gave them a
charge unto the children of Israel, and unto Pharaoh, King
of Egypt" (Ex. VI, 13).' [196*a*] R. Hiya said: 'Pharaoh wished
to put Joseph to the test, and so changed the tenour of his
dreams. But Joseph, knowing, as he did, the grades, saw clearly
each object of the dream, and said, "thus and thus didst thou
see", point by point. Hence it is written:

AND PHARAOH SAID UNTO JOSEPH: FORASMUCH AS
GOD HATH SHOWN THEE ALL THIS, THERE IS NONE SO
DISCREET AND WISE AS THOU. As if to say: "You seem
to have been there at the time I dreamt my dream and to
have seen the dream together with its interpretation." Said
R. Isaac: 'If that be so, it would signify that Joseph told
Pharaoh both his dream and its interpretation, as did Daniel
to Nebuchadnezzar.' Said R. Hiya: 'Not so. Joseph gathered
from Pharaoh's statement that he was speaking of certain
grades, and was able to put him right on certain points,
knowing the correct order of the grades. Whereas Daniel
gathered nothing from Nebuchadnezzar's statement and told
him outright both his dream and its interpretation. It is thus
written: "Then was the secret revealed unto Daniel by a
vision of the night" (Dan. II, 19), to wit, by Gabriel. There

are six visions (corresponding to the six mentions of the word "vision" in Ezek. XLIII, 3). The vision of a dream is a reflection of a higher vision, and this again of a still higher, the whole forming a series called "visions of the night", through which all dreams are interpreted. Hence "he revealed the secret to Daniel in a vision of the night", that is to say, one of those grades revealed to him the dream and its interpretation. But Joseph divined the higher grades out of the words of Pharaoh. Hence Pharaoh gave him command over the whole land of Egypt, and in this way God restored to him what was his due. Joseph's mouth kept back from sinful kissing; correspondingly we read, "and according to the word of thy mouth shall my people be ruled"; Joseph's hand kept itself away from sinful touch, hence "Pharaoh took off his signet ring from his hand, and put it upon Joseph's hand"; Joseph's neck kept itself far from sinful embrace, so we read, "and he put a gold chain about his neck"; his body kept away from sin, hence "and he arrayed him in vestures of linen"; the foot did not ride in sin, so we read, "and he made him ride in the second chariot which he had"; and in virtue of the thought which Joseph kept pure he was called "discreet and wise of heart". So that all he received was his own due. It is then written:

AND JOSEPH WENT OUT FROM THE PRESENCE OF PHARAOH, AND WENT THROUGHOUT ALL THE LAND OF EGYPT. R. Hizkiah said that he went through the land of Egypt to have his rule proclaimed, and also to collect the corn of the various districts. R. Eleazar said that he collected the corn to prevent it from rotting. R. Simeon said: 'God is ever moulding events so as to fulfil His promise. When God created the world He first provided all necessities and then brought man into the world, so that he found his food ready for him. So, too, with the promise made by God to Abraham in the words: "Know of a surety that thy seed shall be a stranger in a land that is not theirs . . . and afterwards shall they come out with great substance" (Gen. XV, 13–14). When Joseph came into Egypt he did not find there great substance, so God arranged to bring a famine on the world, with the result that all people brought their silver and gold into Egypt, so that the whole land of Egypt was filled with silver and gold; then, when great substance was amassed there, He brought Jacob into Egypt. For this is the way of the Almighty, to provide the cure before inflicting the wound. Thus here He first prepared great substance and then [196b] brought Israel into exile. Observe that it was in virtue of being a righteous man that Joseph became the cause of Israel acquiring riches of silver and gold (Ps. cv, 37). All this came to Israel by the hand of the righteous, and all was for the purpose of making them worthy of the world to come.' R. Simeon then took for his text the verse: *Enjoy life with the wife whom thou lovest all the days of the life of thy vanity, etc.* (Eccl. IX, 9). 'This verse', he said, 'has been thus esoterically explained. "Enjoy life" is an allusion to the life of the world to come, for happy is the man who is privileged to gain that life in its fulness; "with the wife whom thou lovest" is a reference to the Community of Israel, of whom it is written: "Yea, I have loved thee with an everlasting love" (Jer. XXXI, 3). When so ? At the time when the Right side takes hold of her, as is implied in the concluding words: "Therefore with affection (*ḥesed*) have I drawn thee" (*Ibid.*); "all the days of thy vanity", inasmuch as she is bound up with life, with the world of the living, as opposed to this world, which is not the world of the living, since its denizens are "under the sun", where the lights of that (upper) sun do not reach—those lights which have departed from the world since the day when the Temple was destroyed, as is hinted in the verse: "The sun shall be darkened in his going forth" (Is. XIII, 10). "For that is thy portion in life": this alludes to the association of the sun with the moon, as it behoves us to bring the moon, as it were, into the sun and the sun into the moon so that there should be no separation between them, this being the portion of man by which he may enter the world to come. Then the passage continues: "Whatsoever thy hand findeth to do, do it with thy strength; for there is no work, nor device, nor knowledge, nor wisdom, in the grave, whither thou goest." This verse strikes one at first sight as surprising: is man indeed free to do "whatsoever his hand findeth to do" ?

But we must note the qualification in the phrase "do by thy strength", i.e. through the instrumentality of the higher soul of man (*neshamah*), which forms his strength, so as to gain through her this world and the world to come. Alternatively, "by thy strength" alludes to the wife mentioned above, she being a source of strength both for this world and the world to come. It thus behoves man to possess himself of that power in this world so as to be fortified by it in the next world; inasmuch as once a man departs this world he can do no more, and it is useless for him to say, "Henceforward I am going to perform good acts", for assuredly, "there is no work, nor device, nor knowledge, nor wisdom, in the grave, whither thou goest". If a man has not acquired merit in this world he will not acquire it any more in the other world, according to the dictum, "He who has not laid up provision for the journey from this world will have nothing to eat in the other world." There are, moreover, certain good deeds the fruits of which a man enjoys in this world whilst the principal remains for his enjoyment in the world to come. Observe that Joseph gained this world and the world to come in virtue of his determination to join himself to a God-fearing wife, as expressed in his words: "How can I do this great wickedness, and sin against God ?" (Gen. XXXIX, 9). For this he rose to be a ruler in this world and gathered money for Israel, as we read, "Joseph gathered all the money that was found in the land of Egypt" (*Ibid.* XLVII, 14), and this was in the order of things, since the ever-flowing celestial river gathers within itself all things and is the repository of all riches. Everything thus happened according to plan: assuredly Joseph was predestined to rule over the kingdom.

AND HE MADE HIM RIDE IN THE SECOND CHARIOT. God has made a second chariot for the Righteous One, by whom the world is nourished. For God has an upper chariot and a nether chariot. The nether chariot is the second chariot, and Joseph, having attained to the name of "righteous", was qualified to ride on the second chariot, like his prototype in the supernal world. AND THEY CRIED BEFORE HIM: ABRECH. The term "abrech" signifies the spot where the sun is joined to the moon, towards which all bow down. We read further: AND HE SET HIM OVER ALL, namely, over all the world, so that all the peoples acknowledged his rule. [197a] Observe that God has made the earthly kingdom after the pattern of the heavenly kingdom, and whatever is done on earth has been preceded by its prototype in heaven. Now the dominion of the celestial kingdom was not perfect until it united itself to the patriarchs, since the Holy One intended that the supernal kingdom should be illumined from the grades symbolized by the patriarchs. And so when Joseph first went down into Egypt he drew after him the Shekinah, as the Shekinah only follows the Righteous One. Joseph was thus first drawn into Egypt, where he gathered up all the wealth of the world, and then came the Shekinah in company with all the tribes. And it was in virtue of having kept the purity of the covenant that Joseph was privileged to be crowned in his right place and merited the upper kingdom and the lower kingdom. Hence, to preserve the purity of the covenant is like observing the whole of the holy Torah, since the covenant is on a par with the whole Torah.

NOW JACOB SAW THAT THERE WAS CORN IN EGYPT. R. Hiya discoursed on the verse: *The burden of the word of the Lord concerning Israel. Thus saith the Lord who stretcheth forth the heavens, and layeth the foundation of the earth, and formeth the spirit of man within him* (Zech. XII, 1). 'Certain points', he said, 'are to be noted in this verse. First, as to the import of the term "burden", here and in other passages. This term, wherever it introduces a judgement pronounced against other nations, has a favourable import, inasmuch as the prosperity of the idolatrous nations is, if one may say so, a burden for the Holy One. Hence a judgement pronounced against the idolaters removes, as it were, from Him the burden. Contrariwise, wherever the term "burden" introduces a decree of judgement against Israel, it has an unfavourable import, as it implies a burden put on the Holy One, blessed be He. Now, having said "who stretcheth forth the heavens, and layeth the foundation of the earth", what need is there for the text to add "and formeth the spirit of man", a fact which we know already ? But in truth this points to a certain grade which forms the reservoir of all spirits and souls.' R. Simeon said: 'The words "within him" seem superfluous. But in truth this expression has a twofold recondite meaning. It bears allusion to that ever-flowing celestial river whence all the souls emerge and fly forth. For this purpose it gathers them in one central place or grade, and that grade "formeth the spirit of man within itself", like a woman who has conceived and forms the child within her womb from the moment of conception until it is fully developed; so the spirit remains within this grade until a man is created in the world to whom He assigns it. Alternatively, God "formeth the spirit of man" within him, to wit, in his body, literally. For when a man is created and God assigns him his soul, and he emerges into the light of day, the spirit within him finds no body in which to expand, and remains cramped in one corner, as it were; but with the growth and expansion of the body the spirit also grows and expands; and in response to its growing need it continues to receive from on high, in ever greater abundance, vigour and energy, which in its turn it infuses into the body. Further, the statement that the Holy One "formeth the spirit of man within him" indicates that the spirit needs sustenance in the same way as the body, and that as the body goes on developing, so is the spirit granted increased strength and energy.' Observe, that when Joseph was lost, Jacob was deprived of that increase of spirit through the departure of the Shekinah from him. But afterwards "the spirit of Jacob their father revived" (Gen. XLV, 27), [197*b*] that is, it regained its former increase and growth.

R. Jose and R. Hizkiah were once travelling from Cappadocia to Lydda, and with them was a certain Judean driving an ass laden with clothes. Said R. Jose to R. Hizkiah: 'Repeat one of those excellent expositions of Scripture which you are wont to deliver daily before the Sacred Lamp.' R. Hizkiah then began to hold forth on the verse: *Her ways are ways of pleasantness, and all her paths are peace* (Prov. III, 17). 'These ways', he said, 'are the ways and paths of the Torah, as whoever walks in them is invested by the Holy One, blessed be He, with the grace of the Divine Presence as his constant

R

accompaniment, and whoever follows her paths enjoys peace on high and below, peace in this world and in the world to come.' Said the Judean: 'A deeper meaning lies in this verse, like a coin in the corner of a box.' 'How do you know this ?' they asked him. He said: 'I have heard the recondite explanation of this verse from my father.' He then continued to discourse thus. 'This verse contains a twofold idea, one suggested by the terms "ways" and "pleasantness", and the other by the terms "paths" and "peace". The "ways" are those mentioned in the passage, "who maketh a way in the sea" (Is. XLIII, 16). For the term "way" everywhere in Scripture denotes an open road, accessible to all. So the words "her ways are ways of pleasantness" allude to those ways which our patriarchs opened up and traversed on the great ocean, and which ramify in all directions to all quarters of the world; and by "pleasantness" is meant that pleasantness which issues from the other world, the source whence radiate all lamps in all directions. That felicity, that light which our patriarchs absorbed and inherited, is thus called "pleasantness". Or we can say that the world to come itself is called "pleasantness", because when it is awakened there is a stirring of all joy, all felicity, all illumination, and all freedom. Hence tradition tells us that when the Sabbath comes in, the sinners in Gehinnom have a respite and are granted ease and rest; and that at the termination of the Sabbath we have to call down the supernal joy upon us so that we may be delivered from the punishment that the sinners undergo from that moment onward; and this we do by reciting the verse: "And let the pleasantness of the Lord our God be upon us, etc." (Ps. XC, 17), an allusion to the supernal pleasantness which brings universal freedom. Now, as for the "paths", they denote the paths that proceed from on high and are all gathered into the single covenant which is named "peace", meaning the peace of the household, and which carries those paths into the great ocean when it is agitated, and so gives it peace.' Observe that Joseph embodied the covenant of peace, and in consequence became ruler over the land of Egypt. Jacob, being deserted by the Shekinah, knew nothing of this, but nevertheless he had hopes[1] from the purchase of corn in Egypt, and he also foresaw calamity upon calamity[2] in his sons going down into Egypt.

AND JACOB SAID TO HIS SONS: WHY SHOULD YE MAKE YOURSELVES CONSPICUOUS? meaning, in effect, "you should not pretend to be other than hungry and short of food". R. Hizkiah said: 'Assuredly there is here contained a recondite lesson, to wit, that when trouble is abroad in the world, and the world is in distress, a man should not show himself in the open road, in order that he may not be seized on account of his sins; and so it is affirmed. Alternatively we may explain that [198*a*] for that very purpose God sent a famine into the world, namely that Jacob and his sons should go down into Egypt; and so Jacob saw the people bringing corn from Egypt, and thus knew that there was corn there. Or we may explain thus. When Isaac died, Jacob and Esau came to divide his inheritance. Esau renounced the inheritance of the (holy) land and all that it involved, and Jacob took up the whole, including the *galuth*. Hence he saw the calamity that awaited him in Egypt, where he and his sons would endure exile, and hence he said to his sons: "Why do you show yourselves off in presence of the supernal judgement? That is the way to bring the accuser down upon you."'

AND HE SAID: BEHOLD, I HAVE HEARD THAT THERE IS CORN IN EGYPT. GET YOU DOWN (*redu*) THITHER. It has already been pointed out that the numerical value of the term *redu* (RDV=210) amounts to the number of years Israel was in Egypt.

AND JOSEPH WAS THE GOVERNOR OVER THE LAND, ETC. R. Jesse discoursed on the text: *And now shall my head be lifted up above mine enemies round about me; and I will offer in his tabernacle sacrifices with trumpet-sound* (Ps. XXVII, 6).

---

[1] This is a play on the term *sheber*=corn, which by a change of the diacritical point becomes *seber*=hope.

[2] Another play upon the term *sheber*, which, besides "corn", also signifies "calamity".

'When God', he said, 'takes pleasure in a man, he raises him high above all his fellow-men and makes him chief over them all, so that all his enemies are subdued before him. King David was hated by his brothers and rejected by them, but God raised him high above all men. He had to flee from his father-in-law, but God made him ruler over the latter's whole kingdom and all knelt and prostrated themselves to him. Joseph, again, was rejected by his brothers, but afterwards they all knelt down and prostrated themselves before him, as we read: "And Joseph's brethren came, and bowed down to him with their faces to the earth." Alternatively we may suppose this verse to be spoken by the Community of Israel, whose head will one day be raised above Esau and all his lieutenants. Then Israel will "offer in his tabernacle sacrifices with trumpet-sound", or, rather, "sacrifices of breaking" (*teru'ah*) to wit, the broken spirit which is mentioned in the passage: "The sacrifices of God are a broken spirit" (*Ibid.* LI, 19), so as to cause severity to be removed from the world; "then I will sing, yea, I will sing praises unto the Lord", without ceasing, for evermore. According to another interpretation, it is the good prompter who says, "and now shall my head be lifted up above mine enemies round about me", to wit, above the evil prompter that surrounds man on every side and is his enemy throughout: "and I will offer in his tabernacle sacrifices with trumpet-sound", alluding to the study of the Torah, which has been given from the side of fire, as we read: "At his right hand was a fiery law unto them" (Deut. XXXIII, 2); for it is through the Torah that his head is lifted up and his enemies are broken before him, as it says: "Thou hast subdued unto me those that rose up against me" (Ps. XVIII, 40). According to another explanation it is King David who says, "And now shall my head be lifted up", namely, to be ranked among the patriarchs, as he had first to join the patriarchs before he became exalted and elevated. "Above mine enemies round about me": to wit, those on the left side, the accusers who sought to injure him; by his overcoming them the sun formed a junction with the moon, and a unity was effected. Observe now the passage: AND JOSEPH WAS THE GOVERNOR OVER THE LAND, which, in its deeper meaning, implies that the sun rules over the moon, gives her light and sustains her. We read further: HE IT WAS THAT SOLD TO ALL PEOPLE OF THE LAND. This alludes to the ever-flowing river whence all derive their nourishment and whence the souls of all men emerge. Hence all bow down toward that region, as nothing happens in the world that does not depend on *mazzal*, as explained elsewhere.

R. Eleazar here discoursed on the text: *Wherefore should I fear in the days of evil the iniquity of my heels that compasseth me about?* (Ps. XLIX, 6). 'There are', he said, 'three classes who fear, and know not what they fear, as we have laid down elsewhere. One kind is the man who has committed sins without realizing that they were sins, and he is therefore afraid of "days of evil", to wit, days that are under the jurisdiction of the [198*b*] evil one, that is, the evil prompter, who on certain days is given authorization to lead astray all those who pollute their ways. For whoever enters the path of defilement is carried further along it. Those days, then, are called "days of evil", being assigned for the punishment of little sins which a man treads under his heels,[1] as it were. Whoever, then, is habituated to those sins which men tread underfoot, as it were, is unaware of them and is constantly in fear. King David, however, was ever on his guard against these sins, and whenever he set out for battle he would closely examine himself to see that he was free from such sins, and he therefore was not afraid to go to war. Observe now the difference in the behaviour of four kings in going to war. David said: "Let me pursue mine enemies, and overtake them; neither let me turn back till they are consumed" (Ps. XVIII, 38). He dared to make this request because he guarded himself against those sins, and thus allowed no opening to his enemies to prevail against him. He therefore prayed only that he might pursue them continually, and had no fear that they might pursue him, or that his sins might cause him to fall into their hands. Asa was in greater fear, for though he also minutely examined himself for any sins, yet it was not with such care as David. His request, therefore, was that he might merely pursue

---

[1] i.e. little peccadilloes which people are apt to overlook. An allusion to the term ʿaqebai = "footsteps", or lit. "heels".

his enemies, not overtake them himself, and that God should slay them for him. And so it came about, as we read: "So the Lord smote the Ethiopians before Asa, and before Judah; and the Ethiopians fled. And Asa and the people that were with him, etc." (II Chr. XIV, 11–12). Whereas in regard to David it is written: "And David smote them from the twilight even unto the evening of the next day" (I Sam. XXX, 17). Jehoshaphat, again, in praying for help, said: "I am not able to pursue nor to slay them; but let me chant thy praises and do thou slay them." This was because he did not examine himself even to the same degree as Asa. And God did what he requested, as it is written: "And when they began to sing and praise, the Lord set liers-in-wait against the children of Ammon, Moab, and mount Seir, that were come against Judah; and they were smitten" (II Chr. XX, 22). Finally, Hezekiah felt himself able neither to sing praises, nor to pursue, nor to engage in war, the reason being that he feared the above-mentioned sins. It is thus written: "And it came to pass that night, that the angel of the Lord went forth, and smote in the camp of the Assyrians a hundred fourscore and five thousand; and when men arose early in the morning, behold, they were all dead corpses" (II Kings XIX, 35). That is, Hezekiah sat in his house, and lay in his bed, whilst God slew them. Now, if those righteous men were in so much fear on account of these sins, how much greater should be the fear of other men ? Hence it behoves a man to be on his guard against those sins and to examine himself closely regarding them so as not to allow those "days of evil" which are without mercy to obtain dominion over him.'

AND JOSEPH KNEW HIS BRETHREN. When they fell into his hands he had compassion on them, since he was completely virtuous. BUT THEY KNEW HIM NOT: these were Simeon and Levi, who came from the side of severity, and hence had no pity on him, inasmuch as all those imbued with severity take no pity on men when they fall into their hands.

Hence David said, "Wherefore should I fear ?" indicating that naturally he ought to fear[1] [199a] those "days of evil",

---

[1] Al. that he had no reason to fear.

as previously stated. David continues: "The iniquity of my heels that compasseth me about." The word "heels" here, as in the passage, "and his hand had hold on Esau's heel" (Gen. xxv, 26) indicates those evil powers (forming as it were the heel of the Body) that are forever on the look out for the sins which a man constantly treads under his heels. These little sins are like "cords of vanity" (Is. v, 18), scarcely discernible, but which in time become as strong as "cart ropes", and thus cause a man to lose this world and the world to come. Happy are the righteous who know how to guard themselves against their sins and continually examine their deeds so that no accuser may rise up against them either in this world or in the world to come, the Torah being their guide and preparing the way before them. Of these it is written: "Her ways are ways of graciousness, and all her paths are peace."

AND JOSEPH REMEMBERED THE DREAMS WHICH HE DREAMED OF THEM, ETC. R. Hiya quoted here the verse: *Rejoice not when thy enemy falleth, and let not thy heart be glad when he stumbleth* (Prov. XXIV, 17). 'God', he said, 'created man in order that he should make himself worthy of His glory and always serve Him and be occupied in the Torah day and night. For God takes pleasure in the Torah and gave it to Adam and taught it to him, so that he should know its ways. So it is written: "Then did he see it, and declare it; he established it, yea, and searched it out. And unto Adam he said: Behold, the fear of the Lord, that is wisdom; and to depart from evil is understanding" (Job XXVIII, 27–28). Adam, however, though he inquired into it, did not keep it, and transgressed the command of his Master and was punished for his sin. Similarly, all those who transgress one precept of the Torah are held to account for it. King Solomon, the wisest of men, transgressed one precept of the Torah, and for that he was dethroned and his son's inheritance was divided. What, then, must be the consequences of the transgression of the whole Torah ! Now, since Joseph knew the Torah, having learnt it from his father, why when his brethren fell into his hands did he put them through all those ordeals ? Far be it from us to think that it was out of a spirit of revenge that he heaped on them accusations: his only purpose was to make them bring with them his brother Benjamin, for whom his heart was longing; and, moreover, he did not let them come to grief, as we read later: "Then Joseph commanded them to fill their vessels with corn, etc." '

R. Judah said: 'After God created the moon He had her constantly before His eyes (Deut. XI, 12). In regard to this it is also written: "Then did he see it, and declare it (*vayesaprah*); he established it, yea, and searched it out" (Job XXVIII, 27). "He saw it" means that through His providence the sun is reflected in it. The term *vayesaprah* we may translate, "he made it like sapphire". "He established it" so that it should fall properly into twelve divisions,[1] and be further distributed among seventy kingdoms,[2] supported by seventy[3] celestial pillars,[4] that it might be perfectly illumined. "And searched it out": to guard it with an eternal and never-ceasing vigilance. And then He gave a warning to man, as we read further: "And unto man he said: Behold, the fear of the Lord, that is wisdom; and to depart from evil is understanding" (*Ibid.* XXVIII, 28), since wisdom is the means to attain to the fear of the Holy One, and understanding is the power by which to separate and keep away the refuse, and thus attain to a knowledge of and an insight into the glory of the Most High King.'

R. Jose once rose in the night to study the Torah, when there happened to be a certain Judean with him in the house. R. Jose began to expound the verse: *Treasures of wickedness profit nothing; but righteousness delivereth from death* (Prov. X, 2). 'There is no profit', he said, 'to those men who do not occupy themselves with the study of the Torah and follow only worldly affairs in order to amass treasures of wickedness, of which it is written: "And those riches perish by evil

---

[1] i.e. the division of the Holy Land according to the twelve tribes.

[2] Corresponding to the seventy nations or languages among which the world was divided according to the enumeration given in Genesis, chap. X.

[3] The editions read "seven".

[3] i.e. the seventy chieftains presiding over the seventy kingdoms of the world.

adventure" (Eccl. v, 2). But "righteousness delivereth from death" those who occupy themselves with the study of the Torah and know its ways; for the Torah is called the tree of life and is also called righteousness, as we read: "And it shall be righteousness unto us" (Deut. vi, 25). The word *ẓedaqah* (righteousness) here may also have its literal meaning of "charity". [199*b*] The two meanings, Torah and charity, are however, in essence identical.' The Judean remarked: 'It bears also the meaning of peace.' R. Jose replied: 'Assuredly it is so.' The Judean then joined him and began to discourse on the text: *He that tilleth the ground shall have plenty of bread; but he that followeth after vain things shall have poverty enough* (Prov. xxviii, 19). 'This verse', he said, 'presents a difficulty. For can it be supposed that King Solomon, the wisest man in the world, would have said that it behoves a man to devote himself to the tilling of the ground and to neglect the life everlasting ? But there is an inward meaning therein.' The Judean then cited the verse: "And he put him into the Garden of Eden to dress it and keep it" (Gen. ii, 15). 'This sentence, as has been explained,' he said, 'contains an allusion to the sacrifices, the object of the verb "to dress" being the higher King, and of "to keep" the lower King, the one embracing the upper world, the other the lower world, the one esoterically referred to in "remember", the other in "observe".[1] Hence the "ground" here is an allusion to the Garden of Eden, which it behoves man to dress and to till so as to cause to flow upon it blessings from on high, whereby he himself will receive blessings along with it. Observe that the priest who blesses the people is blessed himself, as it says: "and I will bless them"[2] (Num. vi, 27). Hence, "He that tilleth the ground shall have plenty of bread", to wit, heavenly food, but "he that followeth after vain things", namely, he that cleaves to the other side, shall have poverty enough, assuredly.' R. Jose remarked: 'Happy art thou to be able to give such an exposition.' The Judean then followed with a discourse on the verse: *A faithful man shall abound*

[1] An allusion to the two variants, "remember" and "observe", in the text of the fourth Commandment, in Exodus and Deuteronomy.

[2] i.e. the priests.

with blessings (Prov. XXVIII, 20). 'This speaks of the man', he said, 'who puts his trust in God, like R. Jesse the elder, who, although he had food for the day, would not prepare his meal before he had prayed for his daily bread to the Holy King; and he used to say, "We shall not eat before we obtain permission from the King." "But he that maketh haste to be rich shall not be unpunished" (*Ibid.*), because he refuses to devote himself to the Torah, which constitutes the life of this world and the life of the world to come. It being now the time to occupy ourselves with the study of the Torah, let us do so,' he said. He then began to discourse on the subject of dreams. 'We read', he said: 'AND JOSEPH REMEMBERED THE DREAMS WHICH HE DREAMED OF THEM. That is, when he saw them bowing to him, he called to mind his dream about their sheaves bowing to his sheaf. Further, one ought to remember a good dream, because, although there is no forgetfulness before the Holy One, yet if the man forgets the dream he also will be forgotten. A dream that is not remembered might as well not have been dreamt, and therefore a dream forgotten and gone from mind is never fulfilled. Joseph therefore kept his dream fresh in his memory, never forgetting it, so that it should come true, and he was constantly waiting for its fulfilment. AND HE SAID TO THEM: YE ARE SPIES. Although he remembered his dream, he did not mention it to them, but only said, "Ye are spies." '

R. Jose discoursed on the verse: *For a dream cometh through a multitude of business; and a fool's voice through a multitude of words* (Eccl. v, 2). 'It has already been explained', he said, 'that dreams are under the charge of a hierarchy of custodians, so that some dreams are altogether true and others are a mixture of true and false. But to the truly righteous no false messages are ever communicated, but all they are told is true. Observe that of Daniel it is written: "Then to Daniel, in a vision of the night, [200*a*] the secret was revealed" (Dan. II, 19), also: "Daniel had a dream and visions of his head upon his bed; then he wrote the dream" (*Ibid.* VII, 1). Had the dream contained falsehood, it could not have been written down in the Scriptures. When the souls of the truly righteous ascend, nothing comes in contact with them save holy beings that communicate to them words of truth, words that can be relied upon never to prove false. There is, it is true, a tradition that King David never saw a happy dream, from which we should conclude that he was shown false things in his dreams. The truth is, however, that David was all his life engaged in making war, in shedding blood, and hence all his dreams were of misfortune, of destruction and ruin, of blood and shedding of blood, and not of peace. You may possibly also wonder how it is that a good man is often shown a bad dream. The explanation is that what he sees in such dreams is the evil that is to cleave to those who transgress the commands of the Torah and the punishments which will be meted out to them in the other world; and the good man sees all these in his dreams in order that the fear of his Master may constantly be upon him. So it says: "and God hath made it, that man should fear before him" (Eccl. III, 14), which has been explained to refer to bad dreams. This, then, is the reason why the righteous man is made to see a bad dream. We have learned that when a man has had a dream, he should unburden himself of it before men who are his friends so that they should express to him their good wishes and give utterance to words of good omen. Desire, which is Thought, is the beginning of all things, and Utterance is the completion; and so a deep symbolism will in this way have been effected, and all will have been made good. Thus a man's friends should affirm the good interpretation, and so all will be well. We see, then, that God communicates to each man by means of dreams of the degree and shade of colour conformable to the degree and shade of colour of the man himself.' The Judean remarked: 'Assuredly, it is only the good man that is made to see true dreams. When a man is in bed asleep, his soul leaves him and roams to and fro towards the upper world and enters as far as she can, and numerous bands of pure spirits who are traversing the world meet her. If she be worthy, she ascends on high and sees notable things, but if not, she falls into the hands of the other side, who communicate to her lying things, or things which are about to happen shortly. And when the man awakes, the soul communicates to him what she saw. The unjust man is thus shown a happy dream, but an untruthful one, so as to make him go further astray from the path of truth. For since he turned aside from the right path they defile him the more, as whoever sets out to purify himself is purified from above, and whoever sets out to defile himself is similarly defiled from above. This has already been expounded elsewhere.'

Thus R. Jose and the Judean discoursed until the morning dawned. R. Jose then remarked: 'Assuredly the reason that Joseph's name is not mentioned in connection with the standards of the tribes (*v.* Num. III) is that he exalted himself over his brethren.' Said the Judean: 'I have heard it said that Joseph derived from the world of the Male, whereas his brethren derived from the world of the Female; and it is for this reason that he was not included with them. It is thus written: WE ARE ALL ONE MAN'S SONS, where the word for "we" (*anaḥnu*) is written defectively *naḥnu*, without the letter *aleph*.   The *aleph* is the image of the male principle as against the *beth*, which is the image of the female principle; and since the brothers did not exhibit the symbolism of the covenant, the *aleph* was removed from them and they were left, as it were, of the female aspect in the company of the Shekinah. Afterwards, however, they said: "We are upright men" (Gen. XLII, 31), using the full form *anaḥnu* (we), containing the *aleph*, and without knowing it they were right, since Joseph was present with them. This view is further supported by the passage: "And they said: We thy servants are twelve brethren" (*Ibid.* 13): here clearly Joseph was included within the number twelve, and hence they similarly made use of the full form for "we are", namely *anaḥnu*, not the defective form *naḥnu*.' R. Jose remarked: 'All these expositions we have just now given must be pleasing to God, since the Shekinah did not depart [200*b*] from here in accordance with the verse: "Then they that fear the Lord spoke one with another; and the Lord hearkened, and heard, and a book of remembrance was written before him, for them that feared the Lord, and that thought upon his name" (Malachi, III, 16).'

AND HE PUT THEM ALTOGETHER INTO WARD THREE DAYS. Said R. Eleazar: 'Those three days correspond to the three days during which the men of Shechem were sick (Gen. XXXIV, 25). Observe that it is written here: AND JOSEPH SAID UNTO THEM THE THIRD DAY: THIS (*zoth*) DO AND LIVE, by which he showed them that he was not going to act towards them in the way they acted towards Shechem; for whereas they had first made the people of Shechem take upon them the sacred rite of the covenant, which is symbolized by the word *zoth* (this), and then had slain them to the last man, Joseph, on his part, said: "This (*zoth*) do and live"; why? "For I fear God", and am guarding the sacredness of the covenant. All this procedure was only for the sake of Benjamin. AND THEY SAID ONE TO ANOTHER: WE ARE VERILY GUILTY CONCERNING OUR BROTHER, ETC. "One to another" (lit. a man to his brother) refers to Simeon and Levi, the same reference being contained in the words: "And they said one to another (lit. a man to his brother): Behold, this dreamer cometh" (*Ibid.* XXXVII, 19). Which is "man" and which is "brother"? "Man" must refer to Simeon, as in the passage: "And, behold, a man of the children of Israel came" (Num. XXV, 6). Simeon repented of his action and wept and felt remorse and said: "We are verily guilty"; and it was through his repentance that his emblem became the ox, the same as that of Joseph, of whom it is written: "His firstling bullock, majesty is his" (Deut. XXXIII, 17). And it was for that reason that we read AND HE TOOK SIMEON FROM AMONG THEM, for Joseph wished to separate him from the influence of Levi, as when the two were together they might find matter of charge against him.

AND BOUND HIM BEFORE THEIR EYES. It has already been explained that only before their eyes did he have him bound, but after they departed he regaled him with food and drink. It must not be supposed that Joseph acted in the spirit of the verse, "If thine enemy be hungry, give him bread to eat, and if he be thirsty, give him water to drink, for thou wilt heap coals of fire upon his head" (Prov. XXV, 21). Joseph was too righteous a man for this. Far be it, then, from Joseph to have acted in that spirit. Indeed, he acted as a man to his brother, in true brotherly love without any other motive. And not only towards Simeon, but towards all his brethren he acted so, as it is written: THEN JOSEPH COMMANDED TO FILL THEIR VESSELS WITH CORN, AND TO GIVE THEM PROVISION FOR THE WAY; AND THUS IT WAS DONE UNTO THEM. All this he did in a spirit of brotherhood.'

R. Jose commenced a discourse on the verse: *If they be peaceful and likewise many, and they will likewise be shorn, then he shall pass away; and though I have afflicted thee, I will afflict thee no more* (Nahum 1, 12). 'This verse', he said, 'has been expounded in the following manner. When a people live in peace, and harbour no quarrelsome persons in their midst, God has compassion on them, and rigorous justice is not invoked against them, even though they worship idols. This is in harmony with the verse, "Ephraim is joined in serving idols, let him alone" (Hos. IV, 17).[1] In the expression "and they will likewise be shorn", the word "likewise" continues the thought of the word "peace" above, by adding to it charity, which is peace; for whoever promotes charity promotes peace, both in the upper world and in the lower world. "Those who are shorn" means those who allow themselves to be shorn of their substance, devoting it to charity. Concerning such the verse says: "and he (or it) shall pass away", not, as we should have expected "*they* shall pass away", but "*it* shall pass away", namely, the wrathful judgement of heaven. The word "pass" is used in a similar connection in the verse "until indignation be overpast" (Is. XXVI, 20). The following is an alternative interpretation. "Thus saith the Lord: If they be perfect (*shelemim*)": this is an allusion to Israel, whom God favoured with the covenant which they were to guard constantly so as to be perfect on all sides, both on high and here below; for otherwise a man is defective in every respect. So it is written: "Walk before me, and be thou perfect" (Gen. XVII, 1), implying that Abram, before the sign of the covenant was confirmed in him, was defective. Hence: "if they be perfect they shall likewise be many", that is, if Israel observe this precept whereby they become perfect and do not

[1] i.e. albeit Ephraim are worshipping idols, since they are all joined together in peace and harmony, they will escape the rigour of justice.

remain in a state of incompleteness, they will in consequence increase [201*a*] and multiply, inasmuch as souls do not descend into the world save through the covenant. The verse continues: "and so if they be circumcised it shall pass away", the last part referring to the taint of the uncircumcised state that attached to them before. The following is, again, another interpretation of the verse. "Thus saith the Lord: if they be perfect and likewise many": this is an allusion to the sons of Jacob, inasmuch as so long as they were in the presence of Joseph they were perfect in that they stood by him who kept the purity of the covenant. But when "they became separated", having gone and left Joseph and Simeon behind, then "He was wrathful", as then judgement was invoked on their account. The term *'abar* (lit. pass) similarly indicates anger in the verse: "For the Lord will be full of wrath (*ve'abar*, lit. will pass through) in smiting the Egyptians" (Ex. XII, 23). Observe that there is severe judgement and mild judgement, and when mild judgement sucks, as it were, from severe judgement, it becomes itself harsh and formidable. When judgement is invoked against Israel, it is mild judgement that is exercised, such as has not been hardened by severe judgement. But when judgement is invoked against the idolatrous nations, mild judgement becomes hardened by the severity of judgement on high and is rendered terrible. It is thus written: "And the Lord will be full of wrath in smiting the Egyptians" (*Ibid.*), where the term *ve'abar* (lit. and He shall pass) indicates that He becomes full of wrath and indignation and takes hold of chastisement. (Note that when ten assemble together in Synagogue and one of them slips out, God is wrathful with him.) According to another interpretation, the second part of the verse says: "and likewise they", that is, the evil deeds of man, "will be removed, and it shall pass over". What shall pass over? R. Simeon said: 'When the soul leaves this world it has to pass through many trials before it reaches its place. And, finally, there is the ever-flowing river of fire which all souls have to pass and to bathe in, and who is he that can face it and pass through it without fear? But the soul of the righteous passes without fear and stands in His holy place; and the man who has performed charity in this world, having given of his substance to charitable objects, of such a one it is written, "and he shall pass over", that is, he shall pass through that region without fear; and a herald will proclaim before that soul, "and though I have afflicted thee, I will afflict thee no more" (Nahum I, 12). For, whoever is worthy to pass through that region is exempt from any further ordeal whatever.'

It may be asked, what need was there to record all these incidents concerning Joseph and his brethren ? The Torah, however, is the embodiment of truth and all its ways are ways of holiness, there being no word in the Torah that does not contain sublime and holy recondite truths and examples for man to lay to heart and follow. R. Jose began in this connection a discourse on the verse: *Say not thou: I will requite evil; wait for the Lord, and he will save thee* (Prov. xx, 22). 'Observe', he said, 'that the Holy One made man for the purpose that he should lay fast hold of the Torah and walk in the way of truth, towards the right side, and not towards the side of the left. And since they ought to go to the right, it behoves the sons of men to abound in love for each other, and banish enmity from their midst, so as not to weaken the right side, which is the spot to which Israel cleave. It is for this reason that there exist a good prompter and an evil prompter; and it behoves Israel to make the good prompter master over the evil prompter by means of good deeds. But when a man strays to the left, the evil prompter thereby gets the mastery over the good prompter, and after having been disabled is restored to strength through the man's sins, for this burden becomes strong only through man's sins. Hence it behoves man to see that the evil prompter does not become reinforced through his sins, inasmuch as it is the good prompter to whom more power should be given and not the evil prompter. Hence Scripture teaches us: "Say not thou: I will make complete the evil one (*ashalmah ra'*); wait for the Lord, and he will save thee." According to another interpretation, the verse teaches us first not to repay evil for good, inasmuch as "whoso rewardeth evil for good, evil shall not depart from his house" (Prov. XVII, 13); and, moreover, man must abstain even from repaying evil for evil, but must "wait for the Lord and he will save thee". This teaching was exemplified in Joseph the righteous, who abstained from repaying evil to his brethren when they fell into his hands. He addressed to himself the words, "wait for the Lord, and he will save thee", for he [201*b*] feared the Holy One, blessed be He. He thus said to his brethren: THIS DO, AND LIVE.

R. Abba began a discourse on the verse: *Counsel in the heart of a man is like deep water; but a man of understanding will draw it out* (*Ibid.* xx, 5). 'The first clause of this verse', he said, 'may be applied to the Holy One, who with deep counsel moulded events by the hand of Joseph so as to execute his decree; "but a man of understanding will draw it out" is exemplified in Joseph, who revealed those deep things which the Holy One decreed on the world. Again, "Counsel in the heart of a man is like deep water" is exemplified in Judah at the time when he approached Joseph on behalf of Benjamin, as explained elsewhere, whereas "a man of understanding will draw it out" was exemplified in Joseph.' R. Abba was one day sitting at the gate of Lydda when he saw a man come and seat himself on a ledge overhanging the ground. Being weary from travelling, he fell asleep. R. Abba saw a serpent glide up towards the man, but, before it reached him, a branch fell from a tree and killed it. The man then woke up, and catching sight of the serpent in front of him stood up; and no sooner had he done so than the ledge gave way, and crashed into the hollow beneath it. R. Abba then approached him and said: 'Tell me, what have you done that God should perform two miracles for you ?' The man replied: 'Never did anyone do an injury to me but that I made peace with him and forgave him. Moreover, if I could not make peace with him, I did not retire to rest before I forgave him together with all those who vexed me; nor was I at any time concerned about the evil the man did me; nay more, from that day onward I exerted myself to show kindness to such a man.' R. Abba then wept and said: 'This man's deeds excel even those of Joseph; for Joseph showed forbearance towards his own brethren, upon whom it was natural for him to have compassion; but this man did more, and it was thus befitting that the Holy One should work for him one miracle upon another.' R. Abba then began a discourse on the verse: *He that walketh uprightly walketh securely; but he that perverteth his ways shall be known (yivade'a) (Ibid.* x, 9). ' "He that walketh uprightly",' he said, 'signifies the man that follows the ways of the Torah, and such a one "walketh securely", the malignant forces of the world being able to do him no harm; but "he that perverteth his ways" and turns aside from the way of truth "shall be known", to wit, he will become a marked man to all the executors of judgement, by whom his image will never be forgotten until the time when they will take him to the appointed place of retribution.   But "him who walks in the way of truth" God takes under His cover so that he should not become known to nor recognized by the executioners of judgement. Happy are those who walk in the way of truth, and thus go about securely in the world without fear either in this world or in the world to come.'

AND THE MEN WERE AFRAID, BECAUSE THEY WERE BROUGHT INTO JOSEPH'S HOUSE. R. Jose said: 'Woe to the men who know not nor reflect on the ways of the Torah. Woe to them when God will call them to account for their actions and will raise the body and the soul to pay the penalty for all their deeds committed before the soul was separated from the body. That will be the Day of Judgement, on which the books are open and the prosecutors standing by. At that time the serpent will be on the alert to bite the man, quivering in all his limbs to leap upon him. The soul will then become separated from the body and will depart and be carried off to it knows not where. Alas for that day, a day of wrath and indignation ! Hence it behoves man to contend daily with his evil prompter and to picture to himself the day when he will stand before the King to be judged, when they will lower him into the ground to rot there, whilst the soul will become separated [202a] from him. We have been taught that it behoves man always to rouse the good prompter against the evil prompter; if the latter departs, well and good, but if not, the man should study the Torah, as there is nothing so well calculated to crush the evil prompter as the Torah; if he departs, well and good, but if not, let the man remind him of the day of death so as thereby to subdue him. This statement requires consideration. We know that the evil prompter and the angel of death are one and the same. How is it possible, then, that the angel of death should be cowed by the thought of the day of death, seeing that he himself is the slayer of the sons of men, and this is his joy, and in fact his whole purpose in leading men astray is to bring them to this? The truth, however, is that the purpose of bringing to mind the day of death is primarily to humble a man's heart, for the evil prompter dwells only in a place where pride and intoxication are rampant, but where he finds a broken spirit he leaves the man alone. Observe that the good prompter requires the joy of the Torah and the evil prompter the joy of wine and lewdness and arrogance. Hence a man should constantly be in fear of that great day, the Day of Judgement, the day of reckoning, when there will be none to defend him save his own good deeds which he performed in this world. If Joseph's brothers, who were all valiant men, were afraid when led by one youth into Joseph's house, how much greater will be man's fear when the Holy One, blessed be He, will cite him to judgement? Hence it behoves a man to strive his utmost in this world to fortify himself in the Almighty, and put his trust in Him; for then, although he may have sinned, if he repents with all sincerity, since his stronghold is in the Holy One, it will be as though he had not sinned. The brothers were afraid on account of their sin in having stolen Joseph, for had they not sinned they would not have had any cause to fear; for it is only a man's sins that break his courage and deprive him of strength, the reason being that the good prompter is at the same time unnerved, and left powerless to contend with the evil prompter. This is implied in the words: "What man is there that is fearful and faint-hearted?" (Deut. xx, 8), on account, that is, of sins which he may have committed, these being the ruin of a stout heart.

For many generations God exacted payment for the sins of the tribes, since nothing is forgotten of Him, but He exacts requital from generation to generation, and the sentence remains in force till it is fully paid. This is exemplified in the case of Hezekiah. Hezekiah sinned in exposing the mysteries of the

Holy One, blessed be He, to the view of idolatrous nations.[1] God therefore sent him, through Isaiah, a message, saying: "Behold, the days come, that all that is in thy house, and that which thy fathers laid up in store until this day shall be carried to Babylon, etc." (Is. XXXIX, 6). Through his sin in disclosing that which should have remained hidden, opportunity was given to the other side[2] to obtain dominion over it. For, as explained already, blessing rests on that which remains undisclosed, but as soon as it is disclosed the other region obtains scope to exercise dominion over it. It is written: "All that honoured her despise her, because they have seen her nakedness" (Lament. I, 8). This is explained as follows. When Merodach Baladan, King of Babylon, sent a present to Jerusalem (Is. XXXIX, 1) he sent a letter in which he first wrote, "Peace be unto Hezekiah King of Judah, and peace be unto the great God, and peace be unto Jerusalem." But no sooner did the epistle leave his hands than he bethought himself that he had not done right in putting the greeting of the servant before that of his Master. So he rose from his throne, advanced three paces, took back his epistle and wrote another one in its place, headed thus: "Peace be unto the great God, peace be unto Jerusalem, and peace be unto Hezekiah." Thus was Jerusalem honoured; [202b] but later, "all those that honoured her despised her", the reason being that "they have seen her nakedness", through the action of Hezekiah. Since, however, Hezekiah was very righteous, the punishment was postponed during his lifetime, but it was visited upon his descendants after him. Similarly, the guilt of the tribes did not bring its punishment until a later time, because the judgement from on high could not obtain power over them until an opportune time arrived. Hence, whoever is burdened by sins is constantly in fear, as it says: "and thou shalt fear night and day" (Deut. XXVIII, 66).

[1] Is. XXXIX, 2: "and (he) showed them his treasure-house", which, according to the Cabbalists, is a reference to the Ark and the tables of the Ten Commandments.

[2] i.e. the *K'liphoth*, or shells, the sinister forces that avail themselves of every opening to contaminate and draw sustenance from any sacred region.

AND HE LIFTED UP HIS EYES, AND SAW BENJAMIN HIS BROTHER, HIS MOTHER'S SON, ETC. R. Hiya began a discourse on the verse: *Hope deferred maketh the heart sick; but desire fulfilled is a tree of life* (Prov. XIII, 12). 'This', he said, 'bears out the traditional teaching to the effect that a man in praying to the Almighty should not observe too closely whether his prayer is answered or no, lest the numerous accusers who are about will come to scrutinize his deeds. The underlying meaning of the first part of the verse is that if a man thinks too much about whether his prayer will be answered, he provokes "sickness of heart", to wit, that spirit who is constantly shadowing him in his eagerness to indict him on high and below; but "desire fulfilled is a tree of life", that is, as tradition teaches us, whoever desires that the Holy One, blessed be He, should accept his prayer, should be diligent in the study of the Torah, which is the tree of life, and thus desire is "fulfilled", or, more literally, "cometh" (*baah*). By "desire" is meant the grade that presides over all prayers and takes them up into the presence of the Most High King. The word "cometh" (*baah*) is used here as in the phrase, "In the evening she cometh" (Esther II, 14), and means that the desire comes up before the Most High King so as to fulfil the man's wish. Alternatively, "hope deferred maketh the heart sick" is an allusion to that other and wrong place in which man's prayer may be delayed whilst it passes from hand to hand and so fails to reach its destination, because it is passed from chieftain to chieftain and is brought down again into this world. "But desire fulfilled is a tree of life": this alludes to the hope that is not bandied about among those chieftains, but is granted to the man by God immediately; for if it is delayed among those chieftains it is exposed to the scrutiny and criticism of numerous accusers, who may prevent it from being granted. Not so is it with the hope that issues directly from the King's Court: this is granted to man at once, irrespective of his merits. Again, "hope deferred maketh the heart sick" is exemplified in Jacob, whose hope in regard to Joseph was deferred for a long time, while "desire fulfilled is a tree of life" is exemplified in the case of Benjamin, inasmuch as only a short time elapsed between Joseph's demand that he should be brought to him and his actual arrival, of which it is written, "And he lifted up his eyes, and saw Benjamin his brother, his mother's son." The words "his mother's son" in this passage indicate that Benjamin was the very image of his mother.' Said R. Jose: 'Since it has already been written, "And Joseph saw Benjamin with them", why does the Scripture repeat "And he lifted up his eyes, and saw Benjamin his brother"? The truth is that the second time he saw something new: he foresaw through the holy spirit that Benjamin would have a portion along with his brethren in the Holy Land, and, moreover, that it would be in the portions of Benjamin and Judah that the Shekinah would rest, in that the Temple would be in their portion.[1] Hence he saw that Benjamin would be more closely connected with them than he himself.'

AND JOSEPH MADE HASTE; FOR HIS HEART YEARNED TOWARD HIS BROTHER; AND HE SOUGHT WHERE TO WEEP; AND HE ENTERED INTO HIS CHAMBER AND WEPT THERE. In connection with this, R. Hizkiah quoted the verse: *The burden concerning the valley of vision. What aileth thee now that thou art wholly gone up to the house tops?* (Is. XXII, 1). 'This verse', he said, 'has been expounded as alluding to the day on which the Temple was destroyed with fire by the enemies, when all the ministering priests went up [203a] on the walls[2] of the Temple holding all its keys in their hands and exclaimed: "Until now we have been thy treasurers, now take back thine own." The Valley of Vision is an appellation of the Temple when the Shekinah dwelt in it, and when it was the source from which all drew their prophetic inspiration; for although the various prophets proclaimed their messages in various regions, they all drew their inspiration from the Temple. Hence the appellation "Valley of Vision". (The term *hizayon* (vision) has also been interpreted to signify "reflection of all the celestial hues".) The words "what aileth thee now, that thou art wholly gone up to the

---

[1] Cf. *T.B. Tractate Yoma*, 12a: "A strip of land went forth from Judah's lot and entered into Benjamin's territory, and on this the Temple was built."   [2] Al. the roofs.

house tops ?" allude to the Shekinah, who at the destruction of the Temple revisited all the spots where she had dwelt formerly and wept for her habitation and for Israel who had gone into exile and all those righteous ones and saints that perished there. God thereupon said to her: "What aileth thee, that thou art wholly gone up to the housetops ?", the word "wholly" including together with the Shekinah all the legions and hosts that wept with her over the destruction of the Temple. The Shekinah replied with tears: "Thou that wast full of uproar, a tumultuous city, a joyous town, thy slain are not slain with the sword, nor dead in battle, etc. Therefore said I: Look away from me, I will weep bitterly" (Is. XXII, 4), as much as to say, "Seeing that my children have gone into exile and the Sanctuary is burnt, what is there left for me that I should linger here ?" And the answer of the Holy One, blessed be He, as explained already elsewhere, was: "Refrain thy voice from weeping, etc." (Jer. XXXI, 16). Observe that from the time when the Temple was destroyed no day has passed without its curses. For as long as the Temple was in existence, Israel performed divine service, offering up burnt-offerings and other offerings, while the Shekinah in the Temple hovered over them like a mother hovering over her children, and so all faces were lit up, and all found blessing both above and here below, and no day passed without its blessings and its joys. Then Israel dwelt securely in their land and all the world was provisioned through them. But now that the Temple is destroyed and the Shekinah is in exile with Israel there is not a day but brings its curses, and the world is under a curse, and joylessness reigns on high and below. Nevertheless the Holy One, blessed be He, will in due time raise Israel from the dust and suffuse the world with joy. So Scripture says: "Even them will I bring to my holy mountain, and make them joyful in my house of prayer, etc." (Is. LVI, 7). And just as they went into exile with tears, as it is written, "she weepeth sore in the night, and her tears are on her cheeks" (Lam. I, 2), so shall they return with tears, as it is written, "they shall come with weeping and with supplications will I lead them" (Jer. XXXI, 9).'

AS SOON AS THE MORNING WAS LIGHT, THE MEN WERE SENT AWAY, THEY AND THEIR ASSES. Said R. Eleazar: 'Having said that the men were sent away, why does Scripture add "they and their asses"? The reason is to show that previously there had been no ground for their apprehension when they said, "and take us for bondmen, and our asses" (Gen. XLIII, 18). There is also an allusion to the verse: "And Abraham rose early in the morning, and saddled his ass, etc." (*Ibid.* XXII, 3). It was that morning of Abraham that shone for the brethren to support them by its merits, so that, strong in the merit of Abraham, they went away in peace and were delivered from judgement. For at that moment the rigour of judgement was impending over them and would have exacted punishment from them but for the merit of that morning of Abraham.' R. Judah derived the same lesson from the verse, "And as the light of the morning, when the sun riseth, the morning without clouds; when through clear shining after rain, the tender grass springeth of the earth" (II Sam. XXXIII, 4). 'The "light of the morning"', he said, 'is an allusion to the light of that morning of Abraham; "when the sun riseth" is an allusion to the sun that rose upon Jacob (Gen. XXXII, 32); "the morning without clouds" means that that morning was not very cloudy, but was "clear shining after rain", to wit, the rain that comes from the side of Isaac, which is the rain that causes the tender grass to spring from the earth. Alternatively we may explain that the light that shone on that morning when Abraham rose up [203*b*] also shone when the sun rose upon Jacob, which was the morning without clouds, filled with light, and without any darkness; for as soon as morning dawns severity has no more any power, but is filled with light from the side of Abraham. The words "when through clear shining after rain" allude to Joseph the righteous one who brought rain upon the earth so as to cause grass and all other vegetation to spring forth.' Said R. Simeon: 'Observe this. As soon as night spreads its wings over the world, numerous angels of chastisement and accusers are let loose over the world and take command of it. But as soon as day breaks they all disappear, each one retiring to his own place. Scripture thus says: "As soon as the morning was light", that is, in virtue of that morning on which Abraham rose early, "the men were sent away", to wit, the executioners of judgement, "and their asses", to wit, the legions that emanate from the side of impurity, who no longer show themselves or no more have any power as soon as dawn appears. For the supernal grades are divided into right and left, into grades of mercy and severity, constituting a hierarchy, some on the side of holiness and others on the side of impurity; but wherever the morning of Abraham awakens in the world, all the unclean grades disappear, exercising no more power, because they can have no existence on the right side but are confined to the left side. The Holy One, blessed be He, thus made night and day to dispose of every one to its own proper side.' R. Hiya discoursed on the verse: *But even unto you that fear my name shall the sun of righteousness arise with healing in its wings* (Malachi III, 20). 'God', he said, 'will at the proper time cause to shine on Israel that sun which he stored away at the time of the Creation, out of sight of sinners, as alluded to in the words: "But from the wicked their light is withholden" (Job XXXVIII, 15). This light, when it first emerged, radiated from one end of the world to the other; but when God contemplated the generation of Enoch and the generation of the Flood and the generation of the division of languages and all the sinners of the world, He stored it away. When Jacob appeared and wrestled with the chieftain of Esau, who struck against the hollow of his thigh so that he became lame, "the sun rose upon him" (Gen. XXXII, 32), to wit, that same sun that was stored away, in order, with its inherent healing powers, to heal him of his lameness. It is thus written: "And Jacob came perfect (*shalem*)" (*Ibid.* XXXIII, 18), to wit, perfect in body, inasmuch as he was made whole again. Likewise the Holy One, blessed be He, will in the future unsheathe that sun and cause it to shine upon Israel, as it says: "But unto you that fear my name shall the sun of righteousness arise", by which is meant the same sun that rose upon Jacob, who was made whole by it, "with healing in its wings", inasmuch as that sun will bring healing to all. For at the time when Israel will rise up from the dust, many lame and many blind will be among them, and so the Holy One will cause to shine upon them that sun with healing in its wings, by which they will be healed. The sun, then, will again radiate from one end of the world to the other, bringing healing to Israel, but the idolatrous nations will be consumed by it. Regarding Israel it is further written: "Then shall thy light break forth as the morning, and thy healing shall spring forth speedily; and thy righteousness shall go before thee, the glory of the Lord shall be thy rearward" (Is. LVIII, 8). Let us return to our subject.

AND UNTO JOSEPH WERE BORN TWO SONS BEFORE THE YEAR OF THE FAMINE CAME, ETC. R. Isaac opened a discourse on the verse: *And the remnant of Jacob shall be in the midst of many peoples as dew from the Lord, as showers upon the grass, that are not looked for from men, nor awaited at the hands of the sons of men* (Micah V, 6). 'Observe', he said, 'that every day as soon as day breaks a certain bird wakes up on a tree in the Garden of Eden and calls three times in succession, whereupon the twig on which it sits stands upright, and then a herald cries aloud, saying: "To you the warning is given, O rulers of the world. There are those among you that see without seeing, that stand without knowing what supports them, and that regard not the glory of their Master." [204*a*] The Torah is standing in their presence, but they occupy not themselves with it. It were better for them not to have been born. How can they exist without understanding? Woe to them when the days of evil will bestir themselves against them and extirpate them from the world! What are the "days of evil"? They are not the days of old age, inasmuch as for him who has children and grandchildren those are good days. These days of evil are those indicated in the verse, "Remember then thy creator in the days of thy youth, before the evil days come" (Eccl. XII, 1). The esoteric reference is as follows. When the Holy One, blessed be He, created the world, He created it by means of the letters of the Torah, all the letters of the Alphabet having presented themselves before Him until finally the letter Beth was chosen for the starting point. Moreover, the various Alphabets[1] in their variety of permutation

---

[1] i.e. the various combinations of the Alphabet, based on a series of permutations, each one constituting, as it were, an Alphabet by itself.

presented themselves to participate in the Creation. But
when it came to the turn of the Teth and the Resh to
present themselves together,[1] the Teth refused to take its
place; so God chid it, saying: "O Teth, Teth, why, having
come up, art thou loth to take thy place ?" It replied: "Seeing
that Thou hast placed me at the head of *tob* (good), how can I
associate with the Resh, the initial of *ra'* (evil) ?" God thereupon said to it: "Go to thy place, as thou hast need of the
Resh. For man, whom I am about to create, will be composed
of you both, but thou wilt be on his right whilst the other will
be on his left." The two then took their places side by side.
God, however, separated them by creating for each one
special days and years, one set for the right and one for the
left. Those of the right are called "days of good", and those
of the left "days of evil". Hence Solomon's words: "before
the evil days come", to wit, those days which encompass a
man on account of the sins he commits. These days are also
alluded to by the terms "days of famine" and "years of
famine", and "days of plenty" and "years of plenty". The
lesson to be derived from this is that the spring of the holy
covenant should not be allowed to flow during the days of
famine and the years of famine. Hence Joseph, the exemplar
of the sacredness of the covenant, checked his fountain-head
in the years of famine, and did not allow it to bring offspring
into the world. This is incumbent on every man during years
of famine.'

R. Simeon said: 'There is a deep idea contained here,
namely, that if a man does not close his fountain when the
year of famine has sway, then he causes a spirit from the
other side to enter the child then born, and so enables the
side of impurity to increase at the expense of the side of
holiness. Hence, of those who do not observe such abstinence
at such a time it is written: "They have dealt treacherously
against the Lord, for they have begotten strange children,
etc." (Hos. v, 7); for inasmuch as such children are called
"strange children", assuredly the parents have dealt treacherously against the Lord. Thus happy is the portion of holy

[1] i.e. within the Alphabet called, from its initial letters, *Albam*. In this
scheme the order is: Aleph, Lamed, Beth, Mim . . . Teth, Resh, etc.

Israel who do not allow impurity to take the place of sacredness. And Scripture thus tells that "unto Joseph were born two sons before the year of famine came", inasmuch as from the time the famine overspread the land he closed his source so as not to give children to the unclean spirit and not to put impurity in the place of holiness. It behoves a man to wait for the Master of holiness to come and establish his sway, as it is written: "And I will wait for the Lord, that hideth his face from the house of Jacob, and I will look for him" (Is. VIII, 17). Happy are those righteous that know the ways of the Holy One, blessed be He, and keep the precepts of the Torah and follow them. Of them it is written: "For the ways of the Lord are right, and the just do walk in them, but transgressors do stumble therein" (Hos. XIV, 10), also: "But ye that did cleave unto the Lord your God are alive every one of you this day" (Deut. IV, 4). [204b] God thus admonished Israel to sanctify themselves, in the words: "Ye shall be holy, for I the Lord your God am holy" (Lev. XIX, 2). The term *Ani* (I) here signifies the kingdom of heaven. Confronting this is the kingdom of idolatry, which is termed "another" (*aher*), regarding which it is written: "For thou shalt bow down to no other god, for the Lord whose name is Jealous, is a jealous God" (Ex. XXXIV, 14). *Ani* (I) is sovereign over this world and of the world to come, all being dependent on it, whereas the other one (*aher*), the side of impurity, the other side, has rule only in this world and none at all in the other world; and hence, whoever cleaves to that *Ani* (I) has a portion in this world and in the world to come; but he who cleaves to that *aher* (the other one) perishes from this world and has no portion in the world to come. He has, however, a portion in the world of impurity, as that other kingdom, the kingdom of idolatry, possesses innumerable emissaries through whom it exercises dominion over this world. Hence Elisha, known by the name of Aher (the other one),[1] who went down and clung to that grade, was thrust out of the future world, and was not permitted to repent; hence his name Aher. It therefore behoves

[1] i.e. Elisha the son of Abuya, who through speculations in Greek philosophy was led into heresy, and for this was called by his colleagues Aher (the other one). *T. B. Hagigah*, 15a and 15b.

a man to keep himself afar from the side of impurity so as to gain this world and the world to come. Thus there are two sides, the one of beatitude, the other of curse, the one of plenty, the other of famine, each the opposite of the other. Hence at the time of famine a man should not bring any children into the world, as that would be giving children to another god, as already explained. Happy is the man who is heedful to walk in the way of truth and to cleave constantly to his Master, in harmony with that which is written: "and to him shalt thou cleave, and by his name shalt thou swear" (Deut. X, 20), where "swear" (*tishabe'a*) has a reference to the mystery of faith in the seven (*shib'a*) supernal grades with their corresponding grades below.'

R. Hiya and R. Jose were once walking together when they caught sight of a man wearing a *talith;* beneath it, however, they saw that he was armed. Said R. Hiya: 'This man is either exceedingly pious, or he is a dangerous hypocrite.' R. Jose answered: 'Our sainted teachers have said: Judge every man in a favourable sense. Furthermore, we have been taught that when a man sets out on a journey, he should prepare himself for three courses: for making presents, for fighting, and for prayer. Now that man is wearing a *talith*, which shows that he is ready for prayer, and he is carrying arms, so that he is prepared to fight; about the third thing we need not inquire.' When the man came up to them, they greeted him, but he did not respond. R. Hiya remarked: 'We see now that he lacks one of the things with which he [205*a*] should have been provided: he has not prepared himself for making presents, under which head is included the greeting of peace.' R. Jose replied: 'It may be that he is absorbed in prayer or is repeating his studies so as not to forget them.' They then all walked together for a time without the man speaking a word to them. R. Hiya and R. Jose at length turned aside from him and began discussing points of the Torah. As soon as the man noticed this he approached them and offered them greeting. He also said to them: 'What did you think of me when you gave me greeting and I did not respond?' Said R. Jose: 'I thought that you were engaged in prayer, or perhaps meditating over your studies.' He replied:

'May the Almighty judge you favourably as you have judged me. I will explain why I acted as I did. One day I was walking on the road when I met a man to whom I gave greeting. He happened to be a highwayman, and he fell upon me and molested me, and had I not stoutly resisted I would have come to no small harm. From that day onward I made a vow not to salute first any man save a righteous man, unless one whom I knew already, for fear lest he might set on me and overcome me. That it is forbidden to salute a sinner we know from the verse: "There is no peace, saith the Lord, concerning the wicked" (Is. XLVIII, 22). Now, when I saw you, and you saluted me, I suspected you because I did not notice about you any sign of religion, and besides, I was myself repeating my studies. But now that I see that you are righteous men, I have a plain road before me.' He then began a discourse on the verse: *A Psalm of Asaph. Surely God is good to Israel, even to such as are pure in heart* (Ps. LXXIII, 1). 'Observe', he said, 'that the Holy One, blessed be He, made a Right and a Left foɪ the ruling of the world. The one is called "good", the other "evil", and He made man to be a combination of the two. The evil, then, which is identical with the left, embraces the idolatrous nations, and has been placed on their side, seeing that they are uncircumcised of heart and uncircumcised of flesh, so that they become defiled by it. But of Israel it is written: "Surely, God is good to Israel." Not, indeed, to all Israelites, but only to those who have not defiled themselves with that "evil", only to such as are "pure of heart". Surely "God is good to Israel", so that they may cleave to Him, and thereby Israel cleaves to the sublime mystery, to the mystery of Faith, so as to be perfectly united with God.' R. Jose then said: 'Happy are we that we did not suspect you falsely, seeing that it was the Holy One, blessed be He, that sent you to us.' R. Jose further said: 'Because He is good to Israel, Israel has a portion in this world and in the world to come, and is destined to see eye to eye the glorious vision, as it is written: "For they shall see, eye to eye, the Lord returning to Zion." ' Blessed be the Lord for evermore. Amen and Amen !

VAYIGASH

Gen. XLIV, 18–XLVII, 27

THEN JUDAH CAME NEAR UNTO HIM, ETC. R. Eleazar discoursed on the verse: *For thou art our Father; for Abraham knoweth us not, and Israel doth not acknowledge us; thou, O Lord, art our Father, our Redeemer from everlasting is thy name* (Is. LXIII, 16). . . .[1] He said: [205*b*] 'The word "thou" here refers to the grade by which the world was planned and created, and by which man was brought into the world. "For Abraham knoweth us not", inasmuch as, though life and death were in his hands, he did not show so much care for us as for Ishmael, on whose behalf he pleaded, "Oh, that Ishmael might live before thee!" (Gen. XVII, 18). Further: "Israel doth not acknowledge us", seeing that he left it to the divine grade to confer on his sons the blessings which he himself ought to have pronounced. Again, "Thou, O Lord, art our Father", as Thou art always standing by us to bless us and to watch over us like a father over his sons, to provide all their needs. "Our Redeemer from everlasting is thy name", God having been so called by Jacob when he said, "the angel who hath redeemed me" (*Ibid.* XLVIII, 16).'

One night when R. Isaac and R. Judah were sitting up studying the Torah, the former said: 'Tradition teaches us that when God created the world He created the lower world after the pattern of the upper world, and made the two the counterparts of each other, so that His glory is both on high and below.' Said R. Judah: 'Assuredly this is so, and He created man to be superior to all. Scripture thus says: "I, even I, have made the earth, and created man upon it" (Is. XLV, 12), that is to say, "I have made the earth for the sole purpose of creating man upon it"; since it depends upon man to complete the organic unity of the whole. It is written: "Thus saith God the Lord, he that creates the heavens, and stretcheth them forth, he that spreads forth the earth, and that which cometh out of it, he that giveth breath unto the

---

[1] The passage omitted is a repetition, in a shortened form, of pp. 2*b*, 3*a*.

people upon it, and spirit to them that walk therein" (*Ibid.*
XL, 5). The first part of the verse refers to the Holy One,
blessed be He, in His operations on high, as He "createth the
heavens" and continually and at all times renews them. The
"earth" here is an allusion to the holy land which constitutes
the "bundle of life"; and it is this earth which "gives soul
(*neshamah*, lit. breath) unto the people upon it." ' Said R.
Isaac: 'The whole verse speaks of the upper world, as it is
from thence that the soul of life emerges into that land; and
that land, in its turn, is the reservoir from which issue souls
for all. Observe that when the Holy One, blessed be He,
created Adam, He gathered his earthly matter from the four
corners of the world and fashioned him therefrom on the site
of the Temple here below and drew to him a soul of life out
of the Temple on high. Now the soul is a compound of three
grades, and hence [206a] it has three names, to wit, *nefesh*
(vital principle), *ruah* (spirit), and *neshamah* (soul proper).
Nefesh is the lowest of the three, *ruah* is a grade higher, whilst
neshamah is the highest of all and dominates the others. These
three grades are harmoniously combined in those men who
have the good fortune to render service to their Master. For
at first man possesses *nefesh*, which is a holy preparative for a
higher stage. After he has achieved purity in the grade of
nefesh he becomes fit to be crowned by the holy grade that
rests upon it, namely *ruah*. When he has thus attained to the
indwelling of *nefesh* and *ruah*, and qualified himself for the
worship of his Master in the requisite manner, the *neshamah*,
the holy superior grade that dominates all the others, takes
up its abode with him and crowns him, so that he becomes
complete and perfected on all sides; he becomes worthy of
the world to come and is beloved of the Holy One, blessed be
He; of him Scripture says: "To cause my beloved ones to
inherit substance" (Prov. VIII, 21), the "beloved ones" being
those who have attained to the holy *neshamah*.' R. Judah
remarked: 'If that be so, how can we understand the verse
in the account of the Flood: "All in whose nostrils was the
soul of the spirit (*nishmath-ruah*) of life . . . died" (Gen.
VII, 22)?' R. Isaac replied: 'This bears out what I said.
Among the generation of the Flood no one was left that

possessed the holy *neshamah*, as, for instance, Enoch or Jered or any of the other righteous who by their merits could have saved the earth from destruction, and its inhabitants from being exterminated. Scripture thus tells us that "all in whose nostrils was the soul of the spirit of life, of all those on dry land, died", that is to say, they had died already and departed this world, so that none was left to shield the world at that time. Observe that *nefesh*, *ruah*, and *neshamah* are an ascending series of grades. The lowest of them, *nefesh*, has its source in the perennial celestial stream, but it cannot exist permanently save with the help of *ruah*, which abides between fire and water. *Ruah*, in its turn, is sustained by *neshamah*, that higher grade above it, which is thus the source of both *nefesh* and *ruah*. When *ruah* receives its sustenance from *neshamah*, then *nefesh* receives it in turn through *ruah*, so that the three form a unity.'

THEN JUDAH CAME NEAR UNTO HIM. This was an approach of one world to another so as to join together. For Judah was king and Joseph was king, and they came nearer and nearer to each other until they united. R. Judah opened a discourse on the text: *For, lo, the kings assembled themselves, etc.* (Ps. XLVIII, 5). 'This is an allusion', he said, 'to Judah and Joseph, who were both kings and joined together in an altercation. For Judah had gone surety for Benjamin and pledged himself to his father in respect of this world and the world to come, saying to his father: "I will be surety for him; of my hand shalt thou require him; if I bring him not unto thee, and set him before thee, then let me bear the blame all the days" (Gen. XLIII, 9), to wit, in this world and in the world to come. Hence he approached Joseph to reason with him regarding Benjamin, for fear lest he should be banned in this world and in the world to come. When Judah and Joseph hotly disputed, then all those that were present "saw, straightway they were amazed, they were affrighted, they hasted away. Trembling took hold of them there" (Ps. XLVIII, 6–7), as they feared lest they might kill or be killed, and all on account of Benjamin.' [206b] R. Judah said: 'There is in this verse a recondite doctrine of faith, to

T

wit, that when God is pleased with Israel and their union is crowned, then two worlds meet together in union, the one opening its store-house, and the other gathering in the contents. Thus, "lo, the kings assembled themselves", to wit, the two holy worlds, the upper world and the lower world.' R. Hiya said: 'The same effect is produced by the sacrifices, for when a sacrifice is offered up and each section receives its due, then there is a bond of union effected between all, and all faces are illumined. As for the words "they saw, straightway they were amazed", these cannot refer to the kings: they must refer to the accusers, whose whole joy lies in executing the sentence which has been committed to them. Hence, when the kings met together in amity and union, they, the accusers, "were amazed, they were affrighted, they hasted away"; they were subdued and passed out of the world; they had no dominion, and were left without any source of sustenance.' R. Eleazar said: 'The reason why Judah and no other came near to Joseph was because he went surety, as it says: "For thy servant became surety for the lad." Esoterically speaking, it was in the order of things that Judah and Joseph should thus meet, as Joseph was a *Zaddik* and Judah was a king, and so their union produced many benefits for the world: it was the cause of peace to all the tribes and between all the tribes, it was the cause of Jacob's spirit being fortified, as it says: "the spirit of Jacob their father revived" (Gen. XLV, 27). Hence, all both above and below conspired to bring them together.' R. Abba cited here the verse: "Fair in situation, the joy of the whole earth; even Mount Zion, the uttermost parts of the earth, the city of the great King" (Ps. XLVIII, 3), expounding it esoterically. ' "Fair in situation" ', he said, 'is an allusion to Joseph the Righteous, of whom it is said: "And Joseph was of beautiful form, and fair to look upon" (Gen. XXXIX, 6). He is called "the joy of the whole earth", as he is the joy and the gladness both of the upper and the lower world. He is also "Mount Zion, the uttermost part of the north", seeing that in his territory it was that the Tabernacle of Shiloh stood. "The city of the great King" is the place prepared to meet the Most High King, it being altogether the Holy of Holies, from whence there issue all light, all blessings, and all joy, to cause all faces to shine—the centre from which the Temple receives blessings, which in turn sends out blessings to all the world.'

R. Judah and R. Jose once met together in K'far-hannan, and whilst they were sitting in the inn there entered a certain man who had come with a laden ass. R. Judah was then saying to R. Jose: 'Tradition tells us that King David used to sleep fitfully, like a horse. If so, how did David sleep till midnight, and not wake when a third of the night was passed?' R. Jose replied: 'When night-time arrived, David used to be sitting with the princes of his household dispensing justice and discussing the Torah, and afterwards he slept until midnight, when he would rise, and remain awake, absorbed in the service of his Master, singing songs of praise and hymns.' [207*a*] The stranger here interposed, saying: 'Is your exposition correct? Hardly. The real truth of the matter is this. King David lives for ever and ever. All his days he was on his guard so as not to have a foretaste of death, and therefore David, whose place is "living", only slept sixty breaths at a time. For up to the fifty-ninth breath the sleeper is still completely alive, but from that point he has a foretaste of death, and the spirit of impurity obtains power over him. King David therefore guarded himself so that the side of the unclean spirit should not obtain dominion over him. For the first sixty breathings less one are symbolic of heavenly life, of sublime breathings on high, on which life proper depends; they represent the mystery of life. But beyond that number they are associated with death. Hence King David measured out the night so as to remain in life and to prevent any foretaste of death coming over him. At midnight he was in his place, as he was anxious that at the arrival of midnight, when the holy Crown is awakened, he should not be found attached to another place, the place of death. For at midnight, when the supernal holiness is awakened, the man who remains asleep in his bed without regarding the glory of his Master falls under the spell of death and is attached to the other place. David thus rose up to contemplate continually the glory of his Master, who was a Living One like himself, and so never slept long enough to have a foretaste of death. He only slept like a horse, sixty breaths at a time.' R. Judah and R. Jose came up to him and kissed him. They asked him his name. He said: 'Hezekiah (lit. strengthened by God).' They said: 'May you be strong and may your knowledge of the Torah augment.'

When they sat down again, R. Judah said to the man: 'Having made a start, tell us more of the sublime mystical doctrines you alluded to.' The stranger then began to discourse on the verse: *The Lord by wisdom founded the earth; by understanding he established the heavens* (Prov. III, 19). 'When God', he said, 'created the world, He saw that it could not exist without the Torah, as this is the only source of all laws above and below, and on it alone are the upper and lower beings established. Hence, "the Lord by wisdom founded the earth; by understanding he established the heavens", inasmuch as it is through Wisdom that all things are enabled to exist in the universe, and from it all things proceed. An alternative exposition is as follows. "The Lord by wisdom founded the earth", that is, the upper world has been created through the higher Wisdom and the lower world through the lower Wisdom, so that all things came into being out of the higher Wisdom and the lower Wisdom. "By understanding he established the heavens"; literally, He establisheth (*konen*), to wit, day by day, without ceasing; they were not made complete at once, but He continues perfecting them each day. This is alluded to in the verse: "Yea, the heavens are not clean in his sight" (Job xv, 15). Think not that this verse implies any disparagement of the heavens. On the contrary, its purpose is to indicate their importance and the great love and affection in which God holds them, in that, notwithstanding that He is perfecting them every day, they are not yet deemed in His eyes to have reached the utmost perfection of which they are capable. In His great affection for them it is His delight to irradiate them continually and without ceasing, the world to come radiating day by day bright streams of light in order to make the heavens resplendent. Hence the heavens, pure as they are, in God's sight are not yet pure. Again, the heavens here symbolize the patriarchs, and the patriarchs find their centre in Jacob, who embraces them all, he being the choice of the patriarchs, and the one who causes light to radiate into the world. And after he was raised to the next world there issued from him a branch beauteous in appearance, from which radiate all illumination and all plenteousness. That branch is Joseph the Righteous, who gave the world abundance and by whom it was sustained. Thus whatever God does in the world has a deep symbolic significance and is all as it should be.' At this point R. Eleazar entered. As soon as he saw them he said: 'Assuredly, the Shekinah is here present. What have you been discussing?' They told him [207*b*] all that had passed between them. He said: 'Assuredly, what he said was right. The first sixty respirations are those of life both above and below, but beyond these there are sixty other respirations that are of the side of death and over which hovers the grade of death. They are called "dormit", and contain a foretaste of death; King David, however, attached himself to the sixty respirations that are of life, after which he did not sleep any more. Thus he said: "I will not give sleep to mine eyes, nor slumber to my lids" (Ps. CXXXII, 4). Hence what the stranger said was correct, as David is living, belonging to the side of life and not to the side of death.'

So they sat together studying the Torah. R. Eleazar then discoursed on the verse: *O Lord, God of my salvation, what time I cry in the night before thee* (*Ibid.* LXXXVIII, 2). 'King David', he said, 'used to rise from his bed at midnight and study the Torah, and sang praises and hymns so as to cause joy to the King and the Matron. And this promoted the joy of faith throughout the earth. For at that time numberless celestial angels break joyously forth into song on high, and correspondingly praises should be sung here below; and whenever anyone offers up in the night praises on earth, the Holy One, blessed be He, finds pleasure in him, and all those holy angels that sing praises to the Holy One hearken to the one that sings praises to Him in the night on earth. When David wrote: "O Lord, God of my salvation, etc.", he said, in effect: "When is He my salvation? On that day when I rise up early in the night to offer thanksgiving to Thee; it is then that He is my salvation in the daytime." And observe further

that whoever offers praises to his Master in the night is fortified in the daytime by the Right side, as a cord issues from
the Right side which is drawn round him and by which he
becomes strengthened. Hence again David said: "The dead
praise not the Lord" (*Ibid.* cxv, 17), inasmuch as it is the due
of the living to praise the Living One, but not of the dead.
Hence "The dead praise not the Lord. . . . But we will bless
the Lord" (*Ibid.* 17), we who are alive and have no lot or part
in the side of death. Hezekiah also said: "The living, the
living, he shall praise thee, as I do this day" (Is. xxxviii, 19),
as the living has kinship with the living; King David is living,
and hence he has kinship with the life principle of the universe. And he that has brought himself near to Him is alive,
as it is written: "But ye that did cleave unto the Lord your
God are alive every one of you this day" (Deut. iv, 4). It is
also written: "And Benaiah the son of Jehoiada, the son of a
living man[1] of Kabzeel" (ii Sam. xxiii, 20).'

The Judean then followed with a discourse on the text:
And thou shalt eat and be satisfied, and bless the Lord thy God
(Deut. viii, 10). 'Have we not to bless God', he asked, 'before
we eat ? Indeed, we have to get up early in the morning and
recite His praises in proper order, and bless His name before
we are allowed to salute any living person. Scripture also says:
"Ye shall not eat with the blood" (Lev. xix, 26), implying
that it is forbidden to eat before pronouncing a benediction
to one's Master. But the truth is that other benedictions
are mainly concerned with the declaration of the unity of
God, whereas the grace after meals is meant to show that
along with him who says it the grade of faith is also satisfied,
and hence it has to be recited in order that this grade may be
satisfied and beatified and filled of joy from the celestial life,
so that it may provide us with sustenance. For the providing
of man's daily food is for the Holy One, blessed be He, as
heavy a task as the cleaving of the Red Sea, because it
depends upon *mazzal* and is not, as it were, under His
jurisdiction until a benediction is pronounced to Him. Similarly, the arranging of marriages is a heavy task to Him. For
when the holy mating takes place, all [208*a*] the souls issue

---

[1] According to the *K'tib*.

from that *mazzal* above which is identical with the ever-flowing river; and when there is desire in the lower for the higher, the souls fly down in pairs of male and female, after which their ruling grade separates them and sends each to its appointed place. But later on that presiding grade finds it hard to join them together in their original pairs, since they are now paired in accordance with men's conduct, and all depends now on a higher region. The providing of sustenance is compared to the cleaving of the Red Sea because this also depends on operations on high, ways and paths being opened and cleft in the sea in correspondence with the ways and paths on high. It is therefore necessary to offer blessings to the Power on high and to impart to Him reinforcement from below so that He may receive the heavenly blessings and the heavenly reinforcements in due measure. Hence it is written: "and thou shalt bless the Lord", the vocable *eth* (accusative particle) having a special significance (as pointing to that region). And toward that region it is necessary to show one-self satisfied and cheerful. Contrariwise, toward the other side, when it exercises sway over the world, one must show oneself hungry and famished, inasmuch as plenteousness does not then rule in the world. This, then, is the explanation of the verse: "And thou shalt eat and be satisfied, and bless the Lord thy God." ' Said R. Eleazar: 'This is truly so, and that is how men ought to act.' R. Judah said: 'Happy are those righteous whose coming together brings peace to the world, since they know how to effect unity. Before Joseph and Judah drew near each other there was no peace, but as soon as they did so they brought much peace into the world, and great joy both above and below, since as soon as Judah came near to Joseph all the tribes joined him.'

THEN JOSEPH COULD NOT REFRAIN HIMSELF BEFORE ALL THEM THAT STOOD BY HIM. R. Hiya discoursed on the text: *He hath scattered abroad; he hath given to the needy; his charity endureth for ever* (Ps. CXII, 9). 'Observe', he said, 'that God created the world and set man to be king over all. Now from the first man there have branched out different classes of men, righteous and wicked, foolish and wise, rich and poor; and among these each class can win credit for itself through the medium of the other, that is, the righteous through the wicked, the wise through the stupid, the rich through the poor. For it is by these means that a man becomes worthy of being joined to the tree of life; and what is more, the charity that he dispenses stands him for ever in good stead, as it says: "his charity endureth for ever".' Said R. Eleazar: 'When God created the world, He established it on one pillar the name of which is Righteous, as it is the Righteous One that upholds the world and that waters and sustains all that exists. So Scripture says: "And a river went out of Eden to water the garden; and from thence it was parted, and became four heads" (Gen. II, 10). The term "it was parted" signifies that the food and drink carried by that river is received in its entirety by the garden, and thence is scattered into the four quarters of the world; and many are they that wait to receive the drink and food from thence! So it is written: "The eyes of all wait for thee, and thou givest them their food in due season" (Ps. CXLV, 15). "But the wicked shall see, and be vexed" (*Ibid.* CXII, 10), namely, the idolatrous Kingdom. Observe that the Kingdom of Heaven is the Sanctuary designed to shelter all the needy under the shadow of the Shekinah; and the Righteous One is the charity-collector who dispenses to all, as it says: "He hath scattered abroad, he hath given to the needy." Hence, those who collect for charity receive as great a reward as those who give the charity all together. Thus the words: "Then Joseph could not refrain himself before all them that stood by him", refer to all those that stand and wait to receive food and drink from the Righteous One. In the sentence: "And there stood no [208*b*] man with him, while Joseph made himself known unto his brethren", the term "with him" is an allusion to the Community of Israel, and "his brethren" refers to the other chariot-riders and legions referred to in the verse: "For my brethren and companions' sake" (*Ibid.* CXXII, 8). Or again: "And there stood no man with him" is a description of the time when the Holy One, blessed be He, will be mated with the Community of Israel. "While Joseph made himself known to his brethren": this again alludes to the time when the Holy One will join Himself to Israel, to the exclusion of the idolatrous nations.' R. Jesse expounded the verse as alluding to the time when the Holy One, blessed be He, will raise up the Community of Israel from the dust and will take vengeance on the idolatrous nations. Of that occasion it is thus written: "And of the peoples there was no man with me" (Is. LXIII, 3), which is analogous in phrasing to the passage "and there stood no man with him when Joseph made himself known to his brethren", and further: "and he bare them and carried them all the days of old" (*Ibid.* 9). R. Hizkiah said: 'It is written in one Psalm: "A song of ascents. Unto thee I lift up mine eyes, O thou that art enthroned in the heavens" (Ps. CXXIII, 1), and in another Psalm it is written: "I will lift up mine eyes unto the mountains" (*Ibid.* CXXI, 1). The difference has been expounded as follows. The latter speaks of heaven, whereas the former speaks of earth. Thus, "I will lift mine eyes unto the mountains", to wit, to the heavens above in order to draw down blessing from on high to below, to draw down blessings from those exalted mountains toward the Community of Israel; but then: "Unto thee I lift up mine eyes", in hoping and waiting for those blessings that descend from thence to here below. "O thou that art enthroned in the heavens": inasmuch as all might and strength is centred in heaven. For when the Jubilee opens the springs, all the gates of heaven are ready, and when the heaven receives all the lights that issue from the Jubilee, there flows down drink and food for the Community of Israel through the intermediary of one Righteous One. When this one moves towards her, many are those who stand and wait to be refreshed and to participate in the blessings from above, as Scripture says: "The young lions roar after their prey, and seek their food from God" (Ps. CIV, 2). But the Community of Israel rises in a recondite manner and receives dainties from her spouse in manner due. As to all those that stand round, they remain apart, as it says: "Then there was no man with him", and as it also says before: "and he cried: Cause every man to go out from me". Afterwards, however, when she has received dainties from her spouse, all the others are given drink and food, as it says:

"They give drink to every beast of the field, the wild asses quench their thirst" (*Ibid.* CIV, 11).'

R. Jose opened a discourse on the subject of Elijah. 'There were', he said, 'two men who dared to expostulate with God: Moses and Elijah. Moses said: "Wherefore hast thou dealt ill with these people ?" (Ex. v, 22); and Elijah said: "Hast thou also brought evil upon the widow with whom I sojourn, by slaying her son ?" (I Kings, XVII, 20). Both used the term "evil" with the same recondite meaning. Moses said in effect: "Wherefore hast thou given licence to the side of evil to take the soul of that people ?" Similarly Elijah said in effect: "Whoever preserves one soul in the world merits life and is worthy to lay hold of the tree of life; yet now the tree of death, the side of evil, has obtained power over the widow whom Thou hast commanded to sustain me." It may be asked, how could Moses and Elijah speak thus, seeing that evil is never done to man by the Almighty ? The truth is that when a man walks on the right side, the protection of the Holy One, blessed be He, is constantly with him, so that the other side has no power over him, and the forces of evil are bowed before him, and cannot prevail over him. But as soon as the protection of the Holy One is withdrawn from him by reason [209a] of his having attached himself to evil, that evil gains the mastery and advances to destroy him, being given authorization to take his soul.'

Said R. Hiya: 'Elijah was able to pronounce a doom with the full certainty that God would confirm it, as, for instance, that the heaven should not let fall rain or dew. How came it, then, that he felt afraid of Jezebel ? How came it that at her threat to take his life (I Kings XIX, 2) he was filled with fear and fled for his life ?' R. Jose said in reply: 'It has been laid down that the righteous should not put their Master to trouble by exposing themselves to an obvious danger. We find an example in Samuel, when he said: "How can I go ? If Saul hear it, he will kill me" (I Sam. XVI, 2); and God therefore told him to take certain precautions (*Ibid.*). So it was with Elijah.' Said R. Jose, further: 'I have heard a special exposition of this matter as follows. When Jezebel threatened Elijah, it is not written that he "feared" (*vayira*), but he "saw" (*vayar*) (I Kings XIX, 3). What was it that he saw ? He saw that the angel of death had followed him for a number of years, and he had not been delivered into his hand. Then the verse continues: *vayelekh el nafsho* (and he went for his life), which literally means, "and he went to (*el*) his soul", that is to say, he resorted to the foundation of his soul, or, in other words, he proceeded to attach himself to the tree of life. In connection with the phrase *el nafsho* (to his soul), I have heard,' he continued, 'the following recondite doctrine from R. Simeon. All the souls of mankind emerge from the ever-flowing celestial stream, from which they are received into the "bundle of life". Now, when a female becomes pregnant from a male, it is mostly the result of an equal and reciprocal desire, or less often of the predominating desire of the female. But when the desire of the male predominates, then the soul of the child that is born has unusual vitality, inasmuch as the whole of its being is the result of the desire and yearning for the tree of life. Hence Elijah, to whose birth that desire had contributed in a special degree, was gifted with special vitality, and did not die like other men. For his whole being was derived from the tree of life and not from the dust. He, therefore, without suffering death, as is the lot of other men, went up on high, as Scripture says; "and Elijah went up by a whirlwind into heaven" (II Kings 'I, 11). Observe the words: "behold, there appeared a chariot of fire, and horses of fire, etc." (*Ibid.*), which indicate that Elijah's spirit was stripped of its body, so that he departed not life in the manner of other men, but became a holy angel like other heavenly beings, carrying out divine messages in this world; for it is well established among us that the miracles which God performs in the world are carried out by his agency. Now observe that it is written further: "and he requested for himself (*eth nafsho*=his soul) to die" (I Kings XIX, 4). This implies that he turned to the tree wherein death lurks, and there God appeared unto him, as Scripture says: "Go forth, and stand upon the mount before the Lord . . . and after the earthquake a fire; but the Lord was not in the fire; and after the fire a still small voice"—referring to the very innermost point, which is the source of all illumination—"And it was so, when

Elijah heard it, that he wrapped his face in his mantle. . . .
And, behold, there came a voice unto him, and said: What
doest thou here, Elijah? And he said: I have been very
jealous for the Lord" (*Ibid.* XIX, 11–13). God said to him:
"How long wilt thou continue to be jealous for me? Thou
hast already closed fast the gate so as [209b] to secure thyself
from death, and the world will not be able to endure thee."
Elijah replied: "for the children have forsaken thy covenant,
etc." (*Ibid.* 14). The Holy One then said to him: "As thou
livest, in whatever place the rite of the holy covenant (i.e.
circumcision) will be performed, thou wilt be present." It is
for this reason that at every performance of that rite a chair
is set aside for Elijah, who is always there present. Observe
what consequences followed Elijah's words, for it is written:
"Yet will I leave seven thousand in Israel, all the knees which
have not bowed unto Baal, and every mouth which hath not
kissed him" (*Ibid.* XIX, 18). God said to him in effect: "Henceforth the world will not be able to tolerate thee along with my
sons." So He commanded him, saying: "and Elisha the son
of Shaphat of Abel-meholah shalt thou anoint to be prophet
in thy room" (*Ibid.* 16), as much as to say: "There shall be
another prophet for my children, and thou shalt go up to thy
place." Observe that if a man is jealous for the Holy One,
blessed be He, the angel of death has no power over him as he
has over other men, and to him is given the covenant of
peace, as it is said regarding Phinehas: "Wherefore say:
Behold, I give unto him my covenant of peace" (Num.
XXV, 12).'

AND HE FELL UPON HIS BROTHER BENJAMIN'S NECK,
AND WEPT; AND BENJAMIN WEPT UPON HIS NECK.
R. Isaac said: 'We expound this to indicate that Joseph wept
on account of the destruction of the first Temple and of the
second Temple.' R. Isaac proceeded to discourse on the
verse: *Thy neck is like the tower of David builded with turrets,*
whereon there hang a thousand shields, all the armour of the
mighty men (S. S. IV, 4). 'The tower of David', he said,
'signifies the heavenly Jerusalem, of which it is written: "The
name of the Lord is a strong tower; the righteous runneth

into it, and is set up on high" (Prov. XVIII, 10), the phrase "on high" pointing to the tower above. "Thy neck" signifies the Temple below, which for its beauty is compared to the neck in the human body: as the neck gives symmetry and beauty to the body, so does the Temple to the whole world. "Builded with turrets" (*talpiyoth*, lit. mound of mouths), that is, a mound toward which all men turn their gaze when they open their mouths to offer prayer and praise. "Whereon there hang a thousand shields", alluding to the thousand cosmic reconstructions that are performed there. "All the armour of the mighty men", alluding to the angels of punishment that proceed from the side of severity. As a woman's ornaments are hung about her neck, so all the ornaments of the world are hung about the Temple. Similarly, in the passage, "To our very neck we are pursued" (Lam. v, 5), there is an allusion to the Temple. "We labour and have no rest" (*Ibid.*), that is, we have exerted ourselves to build the Temple twice, but the enemies have not permitted us to retain it, and it has not been rebuilt. Again, as the whole body perishes when the neck is destroyed, so as soon as the Temple was destroyed and its light extinguished, the whole world was plunged into darkness, and there was no light of sun or stars, either in heaven or on earth. Hence, Joseph wept on account of this. After he had wept for the Temple, he wept for the tribes that were to go into exile. For as soon as the Temple was destroyed, all the tribes were exiled and scattered among the nations. Scripture thus tells us: "And he kissed all his brethren, and wept upon them", that is to say, for them. He wept for all of them, for the twofold destruction of the Temple and for his brethren the ten tribes that went into exile and were scattered among the nations. AND AFTER THAT HIS BRETHREN TALKED WITH HIM. They, however, did not weep, because the Holy Spirit did not flash upon them as upon Joseph.'

AND THE REPORT THEREOF WAS HEARD IN PHARAOH'S HOUSE. R. Abba opened a discourse on the verse: *My soul yearneth, yea, even pineth for the courts of the Lord; my heart and my flesh sing for joy unto the living God* (Ps.

LXXXIV, 3). 'Observe', he said, 'that before offering his prayer to his Master, a man should first recite some thanksgiving. He should also pray before his Master in the proper time: in the morning to unite himself to the right side of the Holy One, blessed be He, and in the afternoon to the left side. It is incumbent on man to offer up prayer and supplication each day so as to unite himself with God. It has been laid down that in praying before his Master a man should not make his voice heard, as if he does so his prayer will not be accepted, for the reason that [210*a*] prayer does not consist in audible voice nor is the voice prayer. Prayer consists in another voice attached to the voice which is heard. It thus behoves man to pray silently, to pray with that voice that is inaudible. It is thus written: "and the voice (*veha-qol*=and the report, lit. the voice) was heard", where the term *qol* is written defectively, without a *vau*, pointing to the inaudible voice, like that of Hannah's prayer, of which it is written: "but her voice could not be heard" (1 Sam. I, 13). The prayer which the Holy One, blessed be He, accepts is that which is performed with earnestness and devotion and proper concentration of the mind on the unity of God.' R. Eleazar said: 'The silent voice is the supernal voice from which all other voices proceed. The statement "and the voice was heard", where the term *qol* (voice) is written without a *vau*, is an allusion to the voice which wept on account of the first Temple and the second Temple. The word "was heard' suggests the verse: "A voice was heard in Ramah" (Jer. XXXI, 15), where the word *b'ramah* (in Ramah, lit. on high) alludes to the upper world, to the world to come; for of that event it is indeed written: "And in that day did the Lord, the God of hosts, call to weeping, and to lamentation, etc." (Is. XXII, 12), so that the voice was heard in the height of heights. Therefore, too, Rachel wept for her children; she "refused to be comforted for her children, because he is not". It is not written "they are not" (*einam*), but "he is not" (*einennu*), which is an allusion to her Spouse; for if her Spouse were present with her, she would let herself be comforted for them, as they would not remain then in exile; but her Spouse not being with her she cannot be comforted. The "house of

Par'oh" (Pharaoh) here is, again, an allusion to the Temple on high, that is, to the house that was stripped (*par'oh*= uncovering) and bared of all its light and radiance and its hidden treasures. When the Holy One, blessed be He, will raise that still voice from the dust and join the *vau* with it, then all that was lost to them in the time of exile will be restored, and they will feast on the supernal radiances that will stream with added brightness from the supernal world, as Scripture says: "And it shall come to pass in that day, that a great horn shall be blown; and they shall come that were lost in Assyria, and they that were dispersed in the land of Egypt; and they shall worship the Lord in the holy mountain at Jerusalem" (*Ibid.* XXVII, 13).'

NOW THOU ART COMMANDED, THIS DO YE: TAKE YE WAGONS OUT OF THE LAND OF EGYPT, ETC. R. Hiya opened a discourse with the text: *Rejoice ye with Jerusalem, and be glad with her, all ye that love her rejoice for joy with her, etc.* (*Ibid.* LXVI, 10). 'When', he said, 'the Temple was destroyed and Israel on account of their sins were driven from their land, God removed Himself, as it were, to the height of heights and regarded not the destruction of the Temple nor the exile of His people, and so the Shekinah was exiled with them. When God again descended, He observed His House that was burnt down. He looked at His people and behold, they were in exile. He inquired concerning the Matron (Shekinah) and found that she had been driven out. Then, "in that day did the Lord, the God of hosts, call to weeping, and lamentation, and to baldness, and to girding with sackcloth" (*Ibid.* XXII, 12); and the Matron was called upon to "lament like a virgin girded with sackcloth for the husband of her youth" (Joel I, 8), because He had removed Himself from her and they were separated. The very heaven and the very earth lamented, as it is written: "I clothe the heaven with blackness, and I make sackcloth their covering" (Is. L, 3). The celestial angels all raised their voices in lamentation, as it says: "Behold, the angels cry without; the angels of peace weep bitterly" (Is. XXXIII, 7). The sun and the moon mourned and their light was darkened, as we read: "The sun shall be darkened in his going forth, etc." (*Ibid.* XIII, 10). [210b] For what reason ? Because the other side had obtained sway over the Holy Land.' R. Hiya further discoursed on the verse: *And thou, son of man, thus saith the Lord God concerning the land of Israel: An end ! the end is come upon the four corners of the land* (Ezek. VII, 1). 'This verse', he said, 'contains a recondite idea. As has been stated, there is an end on the right and an end on the left. It is the end on the right which is alluded to in the expression "the land of Israel: an end !", while the expression, "the end is come" refers to the end on the left. The right end is the end of the good prompter; the left end is the end of the evil prompter; and when Israel's sins multiplied and increased, it was through this left end that the wicked kingdom obtained power and destroyed the House and Sanctuary of the Lord. Scripture thus says: "Thus saith the Lord God: An evil, a singular evil, behold, it cometh" (*Ibid.* 5). Heaven and earth thus lamented because dominion had been given to the left end. Now, seeing that the holy kingdom, the kingdom of heaven, has been overthrown and the wicked kingdom has prevailed, it behoves man to mourn with it and to abase himself with it, so that when it will be raised again and joy will be restored to the world, he may rejoice with it. Scripture thus says: "Rejoice for joy with her, all ye that mourn for her" (Is. LXVI, 10).'

AND HE SAW THE WAGONS, ETC. Egypt is called "a fair heifer" (Jer. XLVI, 20), and hence the word '*egloth* (lit. wagons, or heifers) here may be an allusion to Egypt, indicating that a time will come when the Israelites, the bondsmen of Egypt, the fair heifer, will obtain dominion over it. R. Eleazar said: 'By means of the heifers Joseph intended to remind Jacob that when he was separated from him he had been studying with him the section of the heifer whose neck was to be broken (Deut. XXI, 4). Now this rite of the heifer whose neck was to be broken was carried out for a man found slain without its being known who had slain him. The heifer was thrown, as it were, to the evil spirits in order to ward them off and prevent them from obtaining dominion over the earth. Now all men depart life through the hands of the angel

of death, except the one whose life has been taken by another
man, before the angel of death had received permission to
exercise his function upon him. The angel of death has thus
cause to complain against the place of the murder, and therefore it was commanded that "the elders of that city shall
bring down the heifer, etc." (*Ibid.* XXI, 4), so as to remove any
indictment against that locality and to safeguard it against
the power of the accuser. When Joseph left his father, he
went without escort and without eating first; and when
Jacob afterwards said "Joseph is surely torn", he added:
"Nay, but I will go down to the grave to my son mourning"
(Gen. XXXVII, 35), as much as to say: "It was I who was the
cause of his death, and, moreover, I sent him off although I
knew that his brethren hated him." All this Joseph hinted to
him by sending the heifers.' Said R. Judah to R. Eleazar:
'But did not Joseph send the heifers by the command of
Pharaoh, as it says: "And Joseph gave them heifers, according
to the commandment of Pharaoh" (*Ibid.* XLV, 21)?' R. Eleazar
replied: 'Pharaoh only gave the command at Joseph's request.
Indeed, Jacob was not fully convinced of the tidings brought
to him until he saw them, as Scripture says: "And when he
saw the heifers that Joseph had sent him, the spirit of Jacob
their father revived" (*Ibid.* 27).' R. Simeon remarked: 'First
Scripture says: "and the spirit of Jacob revived", and immediately after: "And Israel said" (*Ibid.* 28). The Torah
first calls him Jacob because the Shekinah departed from him
when the brethren made her a party to the oath of secrecy
with regard to the sale of Joseph; but now that the Shekinah
returned he rose to the higher degree symbolized by Israel.'
[211*a*]

AND HE SAID: I AM GOD, THE GOD OF THY FATHER
. . . I WILL GO DOWN WITH THEE INTO EGYPT. This
is an indication that the Shekinah accompanied him into
exile; and wherever Israel were exiled the Shekinah followed
them also into exile. Observe that Joseph sent his father six
wagons,[1] an allusion to which is found in the "six covered

---

[1] Here the *Zohar* reverts to the accepted rendering of '*agaloth*, namely,
wagons.

wagons" presented by the princes to Moses (Num. VII, 3). According to another view, the number was sixty; but the two views are not contradictory. For, indeed, it is first written: "in the wagons which Joseph sent" (Gen. XLV, 27), and afterwards, "which Pharaoh sent" (*Ibid.* XLVI, 5), so that the truth is that those which Joseph sent were of the proper number, which had a recondite significance, but the larger number which Pharaoh sent had no such numerical symbolism.

AND JOSEPH MADE READY HIS CHARIOT. R. Isaac began a discourse on the verse: *And over the heads of the living creatures (ḥayoth) there was the likeness of a firmament, like the colour of the terrible ice, stretched forth over their heads above* (Ezek. I, 22). 'This verse', he said, 'has been explained as follows. There is a series of *ḥayoth*, one group higher than the other, and there is one above all which sets all the others in motion and causes them to transmit their light to one another. This supreme *Ḥayah* has various faces which radiate to all the cardinal points, three on each side. There is besides a series of firmaments, one above the other, the highest one dominating all the others, which all turn their gaze towards it. So Scripture says: "And under the firmament were their wings conformable the one to the other, etc." (*Ibid.* 23), as they all rule over what has been committed to their charge. There being nine *ḥayoth* on each of the four sides of the universe, the total number is thirty-six. When they are all joined together, they form one impression symbolizing the one Name in an absolute unity. And when they are all ranged round the heavenly throne, then is realized the description given by the prophet: "And above the firmament that was over their heads was the likeness of a throne, as the appearance of a sapphire stone; and upon the likeness of the throne was a likeness as the appearance of a man above it" (*Ibid.* 26). Now the figures on that chariot culminate in that of man; and when the other figures are subordinated to this one so as to form a homogeneous chariot, then it may be said: "And Joseph made ready his chariot", Joseph representing the *Ẓaddik;* further, "and went up to meet Israel his father, to

Goshen", Israel typifying the supernal Adam, and Goshen (lit. approaching) the coalescence of the two. The text continues: "and he presented himself unto him", symbolizing the reflection of the light of the sun on to the moon, whereby the moon is lit up and floods with its light all the dwellers of the lower world. Correspondingly, as long as the supernal sanctity rested on the lower Temple, that Temple was filled with an effulgence of light, and thus remained in its completeness, but subsequently the supernal sanctity was withdrawn and the Temple was destroyed, regarding which it is written: "and he wept on his neck a long while"; "he wept", on account of the Temple that was to be destroyed, and "a long while", on account of the last exile. When Jacob thus saw that all below was complete after the supernal pattern, he said: "Now let me die . . . that thou art yet alive", that is to say: since thou hast retained the holy covenant of Him [211*b*] who is called the Living One of all eternity. The same is implied in Jacob's previous utterance: "It is enough; Joseph my son is yet alive." '

AND JACOB BLESSED PHARAOH. R. Jose cited in connection with this the verse: *I have compared thee, O my love, to a steed in Pharaoh's chariot* (S. S. I, 9). 'Observe', he said, 'that there are chariots of the left that belong to the other side, and there are chariots of the right that are under the ægis of supernal holiness; the latter are of grace, the former of severity. When the Holy One, blessed be He, executed justice on the Egyptians, every form of punishment which He inflicted on them was after the very pattern of those chariots, and after the very pattern of that other side: as that side slays and takes men's souls, so did the Holy One, blessed be He, as it says: "and the Lord slew all the first-born in the land of Egypt" (Ex. XIII, 15), and so with all the other punishments executed on the Egyptians. This is the implication of the words, "I compared thee, O my beloved, etc.", to wit, "I made thee equal to the other side in the power to slay." And what does Scripture say in regard to the future ? "Who is this that cometh from Edom, with crimson garments from Bozrah ? etc." (Is. LXIII, 1).'

AND ISRAEL DWELT IN THE LAND OF EGYPT, IN THE
LAND OF GOSHEN; AND THEY GOT THEM POSSESSION
THEREIN, AND WERE FRUITFUL, AND MULTIPLIED
EXCEEDINGLY, and they got them possession, to wit, as a
permanent possession, inasmuch as it belonged to them; and
they were fruitful, and multiplied, assuredly so, seeing that
they were relieved of all vexation and they enjoyed all the
luxuries of the world. Blessed be the Lord for evermore.
Amen and Amen !

VAYEHI[1]

Gen. XLVII, 28–L, 26

R. Hiya discoursed on the text: *And thy people are all right-eous, they shall inherit the land for ever, etc.* (Is. LX, 21). 'Israel', he said, 'have been favoured above all the Gentiles in being entitled by God righteous, that they may obtain an everlasting inheritance in the world to come, as it is writ-ten: "Then thou shalt delight in the Lord" (Is. LVIII, 14). Wherefore so ? Because they attach themselves to the Body of the King, as it says: "Ye that cleave unto the Lord your God are alive every one of you this day" (Deut. IV, 4).' R. Isaac said: 'This text of R. Hiya contains a deep allusion for "the reapers in the field".[2] For R. Simeon has laid down in the esoteric Agadah that the exalted inheritance of that other land is acquired by none save him who is called "righteous." For the Matron cleaves to the Righteous One and finds de-light in him, and the Righteous One assuredly inherits the Matron. So God in His love for Israel called them righteous and they are therefore meet to inherit the Matron. The reason is that they are circumcised, according to the dictum: "Who-ever is circumcised and enters into the covenant and observes it becomes attached to the Body of the King, and enters into the Righteous One", and they are therefore called righteous, and so "they shall for ever inherit the land", to wit, the "land of the living". They are further called in the text "the branch of my planting", to wit, one of those shoots which God planted when He created the world, referred to in the verse, "And the Lord God planted a garden in Eden" (Gen. II, 8). According to another explanation, the words "And thy people are all righteous" refer to Jacob and his sons, who went down to Egypt among a stiff-necked people and all remained righteous, wherefore "they shall for ever [216b]

---

[1] The first four and a half pages of this section (211b–216a) are declared by all the commentators to be an interpolation, containing much erroneous doctrine.

[2] i.e. students of the esoteric doctrine.

inherit the land", since from there they went up to inherit the holy land.'

AND JACOB LIVED IN THE LAND OF EGYPT. It is to be noted that this section is "closed", i.e. no space is left in the scroll of the Law between the beginning of this section (*vayehi*) and the end of the previous section (*vayigash*). Why is this? R. Jacob said: 'It is to indicate that when Jacob died the eyes of Israel became, as it were, closed, because then they really entered on the *galuth* and the Egyptians enslaved them.' R. Simeon said: 'It is to show that the words "and Jacob lived" are to be taken in close conjunction with the preceding sentence: "And Israel dwelt in the land of Egypt in the land of Goshen and they gat them possessions therein, and were fruitful, and multiplied exceedingly." That is to say, just as they lived in luxury and were short of nothing, so Jacob similarly had every comfort and was short of nothing. Hence it is said of him now that "he lived". For up to this time he had known nothing but trouble, but now he saw one of his sons in royal estate and the others virtuous and right-eous, all living in the lap of luxury while he himself abode among them like good wine resting on its lees; so that now in reality he "lived" '. SEVENTEEN YEARS. Why seventeen? R. Simeon said: 'Jacob's life was always one of hardship, but whenever he looked at Joseph he thought he saw his mother again, because Joseph closely resembled Rachel, and at such a time he forgot all his sorrows. When, however, Joseph was parted from him, this was a worse blow than all the previous ones, and he wept every day for the seventeen years that Joseph had been with him. Hence Providence compensated him with another seventeen years of Joseph's company, during which he lived in ease and luxury. Tradition tells us that all those seventeen years the Divine Presence rested upon him, and therefore they were called "life". So it says that when his sons told him that Joseph was alive, "the spirit of Jacob their father revived" (Gen. XLV, 27), for up to then the spirit had been dead within him and he had not been in a state to receive another in its place, since the spirit from above does not rest on an empty spot.' R. Jose said: 'The

Shekinah does not rest on a place which is defective or disturbed, but only in a place properly prepared, a place of joyfulness. Hence all the years that Joseph was away and Jacob was in sadness, the Shekinah did not rest on him.' So we have learnt that R. Eleazar said in the name of R. Abba: 'It is written, "Serve the Lord with gladness, come before his presence with singing", to show that the service of God should be performed with joy.' This accords with what R. Eleazar has elsewhere said, that when Elisha desired the spirit to rest upon him, he said "and now bring me a minstrel" (II Kings III, 15).

R. Abba said: 'It has been laid down in a certain passage that the whole is derived from four sides, and that all the roots of the higher and lower beings are attached to them; and it has been further said that as one goes in another goes out, and as one is revealed another is concealed, and each one is linked to the next, and they are the origins of all.' R. Simeon said: 'There are three origins like the three patriarchs, and from them all the rest spread and extol the name to be crowned.'

R. Jose said: 'From the day that R. Simeon left the cave, nothing was concealed from the Companions, and things became clear to them as if they had been revealed that day on Mount Sinai. But after he died, then "the fountains of the deep and the windows of heaven [217a] were closed", and the Companions could no longer get to the bottom of things, as shown by the following instance. One day R. Judah was sitting at the gate of Tiberias, and he saw two camels laden with bundles of clothes. One of the bundles fell down and a flock of birds flew to the spot. Before they could reach it, however, they dispersed. Then a number of other birds came up, and perched on the rock. The men threw stones and shouted at them but they would not go away. He heard a voice saying: "The crown of crowns is plunged in darkness and does not rest on the head of the Master." While he was still sitting, a man passed by and said: "You are not following the example of Abram, who, when the birds of prey came down upon the carcasses drove them away (Gen. XV, 11)." "I am doing so," said R. Judah, "but they will not go". The man turned his head away and said: "This man has not yet plucked the hairs from the head of his Master, nor shorn the Matron." R. Judah followed him three miles asking him to explain, but he would not, so that R. Judah was greatly perturbed. One day he fell asleep under a tree and dreamt that he saw four wings outstretched and R. Simeon ascending on them with a scroll of the Law, and also with all manner of books containing hidden expositions and Agadahs. They all ascended to heaven and were lost to his view. When he woke he said: 'Verily, since the death of R. Simeon wisdom has departed from the earth. Alas for the generation that has lost this precious jewel which used to illumine it and on which higher and lower beings were supported.' He came and told R. Abba, who clapped his hands on his head, saying: 'R. Simeon was the mill in which every day the goodly manna was ground. Now the mill and the manna have departed, and nothing is left of it in the world save as it were "one omerful put in a pot to be kept" (Ex. xvi, 33), that is, kept in a private place and not exposed. Who now can reveal mysteries or even know them?' R. Abba whispered to him: 'The man that you saw was assuredly Elijah, and he was not willing to reveal secrets in order that you may appreciate the worth of R. Simeon, and that his generation may weep for him.' He said to him: 'He indeed deserves to be wept. Woe is me that I did not depart this life with those three who died in the sacred chamber of R. Simeon, so as not to behold this generation that has been laid low.' He then said to him: 'Master, tell me. It is written: "And they shall take the gold and the blue and the purple and the scarlet and the fine linen" (Ex. xxviii, 5). Why is there no mention here of silver, seeing that silver was also brought for an offering (v. Ex. xxv, 3)?' He replied: 'You might ask the same question with regard to copper, which also is mentioned in one place and not in the other. As the Sacred Lamp has revealed the answer, I also may reveal it.' He then discoursed as follows. 'It is written: "Mine is the silver and mine is the gold, saith the Lord" (Haggai ii, 8). On many occasions we have pondered over the question, what holiness is there in these priestly garments? We have, however, been taught that there is holiness in every place, and that these garments are after the supernal pattern, as we have learnt: "There is a High Priest above and a high priest below, raiment of honour above and raiment of honour below." As for the omission of silver and copper, these were assigned to another place, as it is written, "All the pillars of the court round about shall be filleted with silver", and again, "and their sockets of brass" (Ex. XXVII, 17). These were the instruments for the service of the Tabernacle; but this raiment of honour was only to be used by the High Priest and by no other.'

AND THE TIME DREW NEAR THAT ISRAEL MUST DIE. R. Judah said: 'Alas, for the ignorance of mankind! They see not, neither do they hear, [217*b*] nor know that every day the voice of a herald goes forth and resounds through two hundred and fifty worlds. We have learnt that when the herald goes forth one of these worlds shakes and trembles, and there issue from it two birds whose abode is beneath the tree wherein is the appearance of life and death, one towards the South and the other towards the North, one when the day dawns and one when it departs. Both proclaim what they hear from the herald. They then desire to return to their own place aloft, but their feet slip in the hollow of the great abyss and they are fastened there till midnight. Then the herald proclaims, and the sons of men are also "snared like birds caught in the trap".' R. Judah said: 'The day when a man's feet are caught and his time approaches to die is called "the day of the Lord", because then his spirit returns to Him. We have learnt that at that time a holy Crown, to wit, the seventh, is entrusted with his spirit, or, if he comes from the side of Might (*Geburah*) the eighth Crown; beyond that his days cannot be prolonged, as it says, "yet is their pride and labour but sorrow" (Ps. XC, 10); where there is no foundation the building cannot be firm.' R. Judah said: 'Happy are the righteous when God is pleased to take back their spirit to Himself. But if a man is not adjudged worthy, woe to his spirit, which has to be purified and to be prepared before it can be drawn to the Body of the King; and if it is not prepared, woe to it that it must roll about "like a stone in a sling" (cf. I Sam.). Further, we have learnt: "If the soul is worthy, great is the bliss reserved for it in the other world, as it is written, "No eye hath seen save thine, O Lord, what thou wilt do for him that trusts in thee" (Is. LXIV, 3).' R. Jose said: 'When a man's appointed time draws near, proclamation is made concerning him for thirty days, and even the birds of the heaven announce his doom; and if he is virtuous, his coming is announced for thirty days among the righteous in the Garden of Eden. We have learnt that during those thirty days his soul departs from him every night and ascends to the other world and sees its place there, and during those thirty days the man has not the same consciousness or control of his soul as previously.' R. Judah said: 'From the first arrival of those thirty days a man's shadow becomes faint and his form is not outlined clearly on the ground.'

R. Isaac one day sat himself at R. Judah's door in great sadness. The latter coming out and finding him in this condition said to him: 'What is the matter to-day?' He replied: 'I have come to ask you three things. One is that whenever you repeat any of my expositions of the Torah you should give them in my name. The second is that you should train my son Joseph in the Torah; and the third is that you should go every seven days and pray over my grave.' Said R. Judah: 'What makes you think you are going to die?' He answered: 'My soul has lately been leaving me in the night and not enlightening me with dreams as it used to do. Furthermore, when I bow down in the course of my prayers, I notice that my shadow does not appear on the wall, and I imagine the reason to be that the herald has gone forth and made proclamation regarding me.' R. Judah replied: 'I will carry out your requests. But I will ask you also [218*a*] to reserve a place for me by your side in the other world, as we were together in this.' R. Isaac wept and said: 'I beg of you not to leave me for the rest of my days.' They then went to R. Simeon, whom they found studying the Torah. Raising his eyes, R. Simeon saw R. Isaac and the Angel of Death running and dancing before him, so going to the door, he took R. Isaac by the hand and said: 'I ordain that he who is wont to enter shall enter and he who is not wont shall not enter.' Thereupon R. Isaac

and R. Judah entered and the Angel of Death was kept outside. R. Simeon looked at R. Isaac and saw that his time had
not yet come, and that he had respite till the eighth hour of
the day, so he made him sit down before him and study the
Torah. R. Simeon then said to his son R. Eleazar: 'Sit by the
door and speak with no one, and if anyone wants to come in,
swear to him that he may not.' He then said to R. Isaac:
'Have you seen to-day the image of your father ? For so we
have learnt, that at the hour of a man's departure from the
world, his father and his relatives gather round him, and he
sees them and recognizes them, and likewise all with whom
he associated in this world, and they accompany his soul to
the place where it is to abide.' R. Isaac replied: 'So far I have
not seen.' R. Simeon then arose and said: 'Sovereign of the
Universe ! R. Isaac is well known among us, and he is one of
the seven eyes of the world here. Now that I hold him, give
him to me.' A voice then went forth and said: 'The throne
of his Master is near the wings of R. Simeon. Lo, he is thine,
and he shall accompany thee when thou goest in to abide on
thy throne.' R. Eleazar now saw the Angel of Death coming
up, and said to him: 'The doom of death cannot fall in the
place where R. Simeon is.' R. Simeon then said to his son:
'Come in here and take hold of R. Isaac, since I see that he is
afraid.' R. Eleazar did so, and R. Simeon turned round and
began to study. R. Isaac then fell asleep and saw his father in
a dream. He said to him: 'My son, happy is thy portion both
in this world and in the world to come. For among the leaves
of the tree of life in the Garden of Eden there is placed a great
tree, mighty in both worlds, which is R. Simeon, son of
Yohai, and he shelters thee with his boughs.' Said R. Isaac
to him: 'Father, what is my portion there ?' He replied:
'Three days ago they roofed in thy chamber and prepared for
thee, placing windows on all four sides to let light in upon
thee, so that when I saw thy place I rejoiced, and said: Happy
is thy portion; save that thy son has not yet learnt sufficient
Torah. And behold now, twelve righteous Companions were
eager to visit thee, and when we were on the point of departing
a voice went forth through all worlds saying "Ye companions
that stand here, be proud of R. Simeon, for he has made a

request and it has been granted to him."[1] Nor is this all, for there are here seventy crowned places belonging to him, and every place has doors opening to seventy worlds, and every world is open to seventy channels, and every channel is open to seventy supernal crowns, and from there paths are opened out to the Ancient and Inscrutable One, to give a view of that supernal delight which illumines and beatifies all, as it says, "to see the pleasantness of the Lord and to visit his temple".' Said R. Isaac: 'Father, how long am I granted to be in this world?' He answered: 'I am not permitted to tell, nor is this made known to a man. But in the great feast of R. Simeon, thou shalt prepare his table.' R. Isaac then awoke, his face full of smiles. R. Simeon, observing him, said: 'You have heard something, have you not?' 'Assuredly,' he replied; and he then told him his dream, and prostrated himself before him. It is related that from that day [218b] R. Isaac diligently taught his son the Torah and always had him with him. When he went in to R. Simeon, he used to leave his son outside, and when he sat before R. Simeon he applied to himself the verse: "O Lord, I am oppressed, be thou my surety" (Is. XXXVIII, 14).

We have learnt that on the dread day when a man's time comes to depart from the world, four quarters of the world indict him, and punishments rise up from all four quarters, and four elements fall to quarrelling and seek to depart each to its own side. Then a herald goes forth and makes proclamation, which is heard in two hundred and seventy worlds. If the man is worthy, all the worlds welcome him with joy, but if not, alas for that man and his portion! We have learnt that when the herald makes proclamation, a flame goes forth from the North and passes through the "stream of fire", and divides itself to the four quarters of the world to burn the souls of sinners. It then goes forth and flies up and down till it alights between the wings of a black cock. The cock then flaps its wings and cries out at the threshold of the gate. The first time it cries: "Behold, the day cometh burning like a furnace, etc." (Mal. III, 19). The second time it cries: "For lo, he that formeth the mountains and createth the wind and declareth

---

[1] viz. that R. Isaac should live.

unto man what is his thought" (Amos IV, 13); that is the time when a man's deeds testify against him and he acknowledges them. The third time is when they come to remove his soul from him and the cock cries: "Who would not fear thee, King of the nations? For to thee doth it appertain, etc." (Jer. X, 7). Said R. Jose: 'Why must it be a black cock?' R. Judah replied: 'Whatever the Almighty does has a mystic significance. We have learnt that chastisement does not fall save upon a place which is akin to it. Now black is the symbol of the side of Judgement, and therefore when the flame goes forth, it strikes the wings of a black cock, as being the most appropriate. So when man's judgement hour is near, it commences to call to him, and no one knows save the patient himself, as we have learnt, that when a man is ill and his time is approaching to depart from the world a new spirit enters into him from above, in virtue of which he sees things which he could not see before, and then he departs from the world. So it is written: "For man shall not see me and live"; in their life-time they may not see, but at the hour of death they may. We have further learnt that at the time of a man's death he is allowed to see his relatives and companions from the other world. If he is virtuous, they all rejoice before him and give him greeting, but if not, then he is recognized only by the sinners who every day are thrust down to Gehinnom. They are all in great gloom and begin and end their converse with "woe!". Raising his eyes, he beholds them like a flame shooting up from the fire, and he also exclaims "woe!". We have learnt that when a man's soul departs from him, all his relatives and companions in the other world join it and show it the place of delight and the place of torture. If he is virtuous he beholds his place and ascends and sits there and enjoys the delights of the other world. But if he is not virtuous, his soul remains in this world until his body is buried in the dust, and then the executioners take hold of him and drag him down to Dumah and to his appointed storey in Gehin-hom.' R. Judah said: 'For seven days the soul goes to and fro from his house to his grave, and from his grave to his house, mourning for the body, [219a] as it is written: "His flesh shall suffer pain for him, and his soul shall mourn for it" (Job

XIV, 22), and it grieves to behold the sadness in the house. We have learnt that after seven days the body begins to decay, and the soul goes in to its place. It enters the cave of Machpelah, where it is allowed in up to a certain point according to its deserts. It then reaches the place of the Garden of Eden and meets the Cherubim and the flashing sword which is in the lower Garden of Eden, and if it is worthy to enter, it enters. We have learnt that four pillars[1] are waiting there with the form of a body in their hands, and with this it gleefully clothes itself and then remains in its appointed circle in the Garden of Eden for its allotted time. Then a herald makes proclamation and a pillar of three colours is brought forward, which is called "the habitation of Mount Zion" (Is. IV, 5). By means of this pillar it ascends to the gate of righteousness, in which are Zion and Jerusalem. If it is worthy to ascend further, then happy is its portion and lot that it becomes attached to the Body of the King. If it is not worthy to ascend further, then "he that is left in Zion and he that remaineth in Jerusalem shall be called holy" (*Ibid.* 3). But if it is privileged to ascend further, then it beholds the glory of the King, and enjoys the supernal delight from the place which is called Heaven. Happy he that is vouchsafed this grace.' R. Jose said: 'There is a superior grace and an inferior grace. The superior grace is above the heavens, as it is written: "For great *above* the heaven is thy kindness" (Ps. CVIII, 5). Of the inferior grace it is written: "For great *unto* the heaven is thy kindness" (*Ibid.* LVII, 11), and to this class belong the "faithful kindnesses of David" (Is. LV, 3).'

R. Isaac once questioned R. Simeon with regard to the verse, "a joyful mother of children", saying: 'I know what is meant by the mother, but who are the children?' R. Simeon answered: 'There are two children to God, one male and one female. The male he gave to Jacob, as it is written: "Israel is my son, my firstborn" (Ex. IV, 22). The female he gave to Abraham. The mother sits on the young and gives them suck; whence the precept, "Thou shalt not take the mother with the young." Our teachers have said: "A man should beware of sinfulness below lest thereby the mother should be parted

---

[1] i.e. angels.

from the children." But when men repent and act virtuously then the mother returns and shelters the young, and this is called "repentance" (*t'shubah*, lit. returning). Then, too, it can be said, "the mother of the children is joyful". Hence a man should not cease from propagating his kind till he has a son and a daughter.' R. Isaac was not yet satisfied. 'The righteous', he said, 'desire no more than to "behold the pleasantness of the Lord" (Ps. XXVII, 4).' R. Simeon answered: 'It is all one, since this pleasantness comes from the Holy Ancient One to this heaven, and the desire of the righteous is fixed on that.' R. Simeon further said: 'It is written: "He hath cast down the earth from the heavens" (Lam. II, 1). For when the Almighty resolved to destroy the Temple and to banish Israel among the nations, He removed from before Him the upper earth, and when that earth was put away from Him, then the lower earth was laid waste and Israel were banished among the nations; whereupon the Community of Israel said: "My mother's sons were incensed against me" (S. S. 1, 6), and that was the cause of my downfall.'

R. Jose was once walking with R. Hiya the son of Rab, and as they were going along he said to him: 'Do you see something over there?' 'I see a man in the river', he answered, 'and a bird on [219b] his head with a piece of flesh which it is eating and tearing with its claws. The man is crying out something, but I cannot catch what he says.' Said the other: 'Let us go nearer and listen.' He said: 'I am afraid.' 'Why,' he said, 'do you think that this is a man here? This is some hint of Wisdom which God is sending us.' So they went nearer and they heard him saying: 'Crown, crown, two sons are kept outside, and there will be no peace or rest until the bird is thrown down in Cæsarea.' R. Jose wept and said: 'Verily the *Galuth* is drawn out, and therefore the birds of heaven will not depart until the dominion of the idolatrous nations is removed from the earth, which will not be till the day when God will bring the world to judgement.' As they went on they heard a voice say: 'Let the flame of fire advance to chastise', whereupon a flame came forth and burnt the bird. Said R. Jose, 'God only banished Israel when there was no longer faith among them, for then, if one may say so, He was entirely forgotten.' R. Hiya said: 'What is the meaning of the verse: "He hath swallowed up death for ever" (Is. xxv, 8) ?' He said: 'When God shall arouse His right hand, then death shall be banished from the world. But He will not arouse His right hand till Israel give the impetus, to wit, by the Torah. At that time "the right hand of the Lord doeth valiantly" (Ps. cxviii, 16), and "I shall not die but live" (*Ibid.* 17). We have learnt that when God is pleased with a righteous man and the herald makes proclamation concerning him thirty days among the righteous in the Garden of Eden, then all the righteous rejoice and go and crown his place in preparation for his coming to take up his abode among them. But if he is sinful, then the herald proclaims concerning him thirty days in Gehinnom, and all the sinners are sad and exclaim: "Woe, that a new punishment is to be executed on so-and-so", and the demons are ready to meet him. Woe to the wicked and woe to his neighbour !' Then they all exclaim: "Woe to the wicked, it shall be ill with him, for the reward of his hands shall be given to him' (Is. iii, 11).' R. Isaac said: 'The word *ra'* (ill) in this passage refers especially to him who wilfully spills his seed, like Er the son of Judah. Such a one is thrust down lower than all the others in that world. All others have a chance to ascend, but not he. Is he even worse, it may be asked, than a murderer ? Even so, because a murderer kills another man's children, but he kills his own, and he spills very much blood. Hence it is written of such a one particularly: "And that which he did was evil in the sight of the Lord" (Gen. xxxviii, 10).' R. Judah said: 'Every sin admits of repentance barring this, and every sinner may hope to see the face of the Shekinah barring this one.' R. Isaac said: 'Happy are the righteous in this world and in the world to come; of them it is written: "And thy people are all righteous, they shall for ever inherit the land" (Is. lx, 21).'[1] [221*b*]

---

[1] The translation of the three-and-a-half pages here omitted (219*b*–221*b*) will be found in the *Zohar* on Leviticus, 104*b*, to which they properly belong.

AND THE DAYS DREW NEAR FOR ISRAEL TO DIE. R. Hiya said: 'Why is the name Israel used here in connection with his death, whereas above it says, "And Jacob lived, etc." ?' R. Jose said in reply: 'Note here the word "days", which is somewhat peculiar, since a man only dies on one day, in fact, in one instant. The reason, however, is, as we have learnt, that when God desires to take back a man's spirit, all the days that he has lived in this world pass in review before Him. Happy, then, is the man whose days draw near before the King without reproach, not one of them being rejected because a sin was committed thereon. Hence the term "drawing near" is used of the righteous, because their days draw near before the King without reproach. But woe to the wicked whose days cannot so draw near, because they all passed in sin, wherefore they are not recorded above, so that of them it is written: "The way of the wicked is like thick darkness, they know not on what they stumble" (Prov. IV, 19). [222*a*] So here it says that the days of Israel "drew near", that is, without reproach and with unalloyed joy; and hence the name "Israel" is used, because it points to a greater perfection than the name Jacob.' R. Jose said: 'There are some righteous whose days when enumerated are put afar from the King, and others whose days are brought near to the King. It is they whose portion is blessed, and Israel was one of them.'

AND HE CALLED HIS SON JOSEPH. R. Abba said: 'Joseph is called Jacob's son *par excellence*, because, as we have learnt, when Potiphar's wife tempted him, he lifted up his eyes and saw the image of his father (as it says, "and there was none of the men of the house there within" (Gen. XXXIX, 11), as much as to say, "but there was someone else"), and he thereupon resisted and withdrew. Hence it was that when Jacob came to bless his sons he said: "I know, my son, I know" (Gen. XLVIII, 19), repeating the word, as much as to say, "I know of the time when you proved in your own body that you were my son, and I also know that, as you say, this is the elder." Another explanation why he called him specially "my son" is that they closely resembled one another,

X

so that whoever saw Joseph could testify that he was the son of Jacob.' R. Jose said that another reason was that he supported him and his family in his old age.

The reason why Jacob asked Joseph to bury him, and not any other of his sons, was that only Joseph had the power to take him out of Egypt. R. Jose said: 'Since Jacob knew that his descendants would be in bondage in Egypt, why did he not have himself buried there in order that his merit might shield them, which would have shown true parental solicitude ? The truth is that, as tradition tells us, when Jacob was about to go down to Egypt he was afraid lest his descendants might be lost among the peoples and lest God might remove His Presence from him. Hence God said to him: "Fear not to go down to Egypt, for I will there make of thee a great nation" (Gen. XLVI, 3), and then, "I will go down with thee into Egypt" (*Ibid.* 4). Jacob was still afraid lest he should be buried there and not with his fathers, so God said to him: "I will also surely bring thee up again" (*Ibid.*), to wit, to be buried in the grave of thy ancestors. Hence he had various reasons for desiring to be taken out of Egypt. One was that the Egyptians should not make a god of him, since he foresaw that God would punish their gods. Another was because he knew that God would still keep his Presence among his descendants in the *galuth*. A third reason was that his body might rest in company with those of his ancestors, to be numbered with them and not with the sinners of Egypt, since, as we have learnt, Jacob reproduced the beauty of Adam, and his form was sublime and holy like that of the holy throne. Esoterically speaking, there is no separation among the patriarchs, and hence he said: "when I sleep with my fathers".'

Another reason why Jacob called Joseph "my son" was because he was from the first more intent on begetting him than any other of his sons, his whole thought having been devoted to Rachel. [222b] Said R. Simeon: 'Man should take good heed not to sin or to transgress the will of his Master, because all his actions are recorded in a book and are reviewed by the holy King and revealed before Him; even his thoughts are present before God and do not escape Him. Now on the night when Jacob went in to Leah and she gave him the tokens which he had given to Rachel, he really thought she was Rachel, and God, to whom all secrets are revealed, allowed that thought to have effect, and so the birthright of Reuben was transferred to Joseph, that having been Jacob's first seed, and so Rachel came into her own inheritance. This, too, is why Leah called his name simply Reuben (=see a son) and not Reubeni (=see my son). We have learnt: "God knew that Jacob had no intent to sin before Him, and that he did not allow his thoughts to dwell on any other woman at that instant like the sinful, and therefore it is written: "And the sons of Jacob were twelve" (Gen. XXXV, 22).' For the sons of the sinners who act in this way are called by another name, which is known among the Companions. Hence "Jacob called to his son Joseph"—his real son, his son at the beginning and at the end.'

PUT, I PRAY THEE, THY HAND UNDER MY THIGH. R. Jose said: 'Jacob made him swear by the sign of the covenant which was stamped on his flesh, since the patriarchs assigned more importance to this than to anything else, and this covenant, too, is symbolized by Joseph.' R. Simeon said: 'We find the formula, "put thy hand under my thigh", in connection with both Abraham and Jacob, but not with Isaac, the reason being that Esau issued from him. Again, we may suppose Jacob's idea to have been: "Swear to me by that holy impress which has brought holy and faithful seed into the world and which has ever been preserved from defilement that you will not bury me among those unclean who have never guarded it, and of whom it is written, "whose flesh is the flesh of asses and their neighing the neighing of horses" (Ezek. XXIII, 20).' Why, it may be asked, was Joseph, who also guarded the covenant, buried among them ? The answer is that it was to meet a special emergency, like the appearance of God to Ezekiel outside the Holy Land. God saw that if Joseph were removed from there, the Israelites would sink under the bondage; therefore He said: "Let his burial place be here in a spot which will not be defiled (for Joseph's coffin was thrown into the river), and so the Israelites will be able to endure the captivity.' R. Jose said: 'Jacob saw that he was fitted in every way to form part of the holy chariot like his fathers, but he thought it impossible that his body should be attached to his fathers if he was buried in Egypt.'

Seeing that the patriarchs were privileged to be buried in the cave of Machpelah with their wives, [223a] why was Jacob buried with Leah and not with Rachel, who was the "foundation of the house"? The reason is that Leah bore more children from the holy stock. R. Judah said: 'Leah used to go out every day to the highway and weep for Jacob when she learnt that he was righteous, and prayed on his behalf, but Rachel never did so. Hence Leah was privileged to be buried with him, while Rachel's grave was set by the highway. The esoteric reason, as we have affirmed, is that the one typifies the disclosed and the other the undisclosed. Tradition tells us that the virtuous Leah prayed with many tears that she might be the portion of Jacob and not of the wicked Esau. Hence we have learnt that whoever prays with tears before the Almighty can procure the cancellation of any chastisement that has been decreed against him; for so Leah, though she had been assigned by divine decree to Esau, yet by her prayer succeeded in procuring the preference for Jacob and saved herself from being given to Esau.'

R. Isaac said: 'It is written: "And Solomon's wisdom excelled the wisdom of all the children of the East" (1 Kings v, 9). What is the wisdom of the children of the East? Tradition tells us that it was the wisdom which they inherited from Abraham. For we read that Abraham "gave all that he had unto Isaac" (Gen. xxv, 5): this refers to the higher wisdom, which he possessed through the knowledge of the holy name of God. "But to the sons of the concubines which Abraham had Abraham gave gifts"; to wit, certain information about the lower crowns, and he settled them in "the east country" (*Ibid.*); and from that source the children of the East inherited wisdom.'

R. Simeon was once travelling from Cappadocia to Lydda accompanied by R. Abba and R. Judah. He was mounted and they were on foot. Tired with keeping pace with him, R. Abba exclaimed: 'Verily, "they that go after the Lord shall roar like a lion" (Hos. XI, 10).' R. Simeon then dismounted, saying: 'Truly, wisdom is not acquired by a man save when he sits and rests, as it says of Moses that he "sat on the mountain forty days" (Deut. IX, 9).' So they all sat down. R. Abba then asked him: 'What is the difference between the wisdom of Solomon and the wisdom of the children of the east and the wisdom of Egypt, mentioned in the same verse?' He replied: 'The secret of Solomon's wisdom was in the name of the moon when blessed from every side. In his days the moon was magnified and reached her fullness. A thousand mountains rose before her, and she blew them away with a puff. A thousand mighty rivers flowed before her, and she swallowed them at a draught. Her nails reached out in a thousand and seventy directions, [223*b*] and her hands in twenty-four thousand, so that nothing could escape her. Thousands of bucklers clung to her hair. From between her feet went forth a youth[1] who stretched from one end of the world to the other with sixty clubs of fire, and who is also called "Enoch son of Jered." He was called "son of Jered" (lit. descent) in reference to the ten stages by which the Shekinah descended to the earth. Under him are stationed many *Hayyoth*, under which again is fastened the hair of the moon, which is called "the knobs of the sceptre". Her hands and feet take hold of it like a strong lion holding his prey. Her nails are those who call to mind the sins of men and inscribe them with all rigour and exactness. The offscourings of her nails are all those who do not cleave to the Body of the King and suck from the side of uncleanness, when the moon begins to diminish. Now, after Solomon had inherited the moon in its fullness, he also desired to inherit it in its defective state, and therefore he sought to acquire the knowledge of spirits and demons, so as to inherit the moon on every side. As for the wisdom of Egypt, this is the lower wisdom which is called "the handmaid behind the millstones", and which was also included in the wisdom of Solomon.' Said R. Abba: 'How thankful am I that I asked you this question, since I have received so illuminating an answer.' R. Simeon said further: 'With regard to Solomon's words, "What profit hath

---

[1] Metatron.

man in all his labour ?" (Eccl. i, 3), these do not apply to labour in the study of the Torah, since the statement is qualified by the words, "wherein he laboureth under the sun", and the study of the Torah is above the sun.' Said R. Hiya: 'Study of the Torah which is prosecuted for worldly ends is also accounted "under the sun", as it does not ascend aloft'.

R. Eleazar said: 'Though a man should live a thousand years, yet at the time of his departure from the world it seems to him as if he had only lived a single day.'

WHEN I SLEEP WITH MY FATHERS. Happy is the lot of the patriarchs that the Almighty has made them a holy chariot above and has taken delight in them to be crowned with them; hence it is written, "Only in thy fathers the Lord took delight" (Deut. x, 15). R. Eleazar said: [224*a*] 'Jacob knew that he was to be crowned in his fathers and his fathers with him. Hence we have learnt regarding the graven letters that in the letter *shin* there are three strokes, one on one side and one on the other side and one combining them, and this is the allusion in the verse: "And the middle bar in the midst of the boards shall pass through from end to end" (Ex. XXVI, 28). Hence Jacob said: "I shall lie with my fathers".' R. Judah said: 'How deaf are men to the warnings of the Torah, and how blind are they to their own condition that they are not aware that on the day when a human being comes forth into the world, all the days that are assigned to him come forward and fly about the world and descend and warn the man, each day in its turn. And when a man has been so warned and yet sins against his Master, then the day on which he sinned ascends in shame and bears witness and stands by itself outside, and so it remains until the man repents. If he becomes virtuous it returns to its place, but if not, then it goes down and joins the outside spirit and returns to its house, and assumes the exact shape of that man in order to plague him and dwells with him continually in his house. If he is virtuous it proves a good companion, and if not, an evil companion. In either case, such days are missing from the full number and are not counted with the others. Woe to the man who has diminished the number of his days before the Almighty, and has not left days for himself with which to crown himself in the other world, and to approach the Holy King. For if he is worthy he ascends by means of those days, and they become a glorious vesture for his soul, those days in which he acted virtuously and did not sin. Woe to him that has diminished his days above, since when he comes to be clad in his days, those days that he spoilt by his sins are lacking, and his vesture is therefore defective; all the more so if there are many of them and he has nothing at all with which to clothe himself in the other world. Then woe to him and woe to his soul, since he is punished in Gehinnom for those days, many days for each, because when he departed from this world he had no days with which to clothe himself and no garment wherewith to cover himself. Happy are the righteous whose days are all stored up with the Holy King, and form glorious vestures with which they may robe themselves in the other world. This is the esoteric explanation of the verse, "and they knew that they were naked" (Gen. III, 7), that is to say, that the glorious raiment made of those days had been impaired and none of them was left to clothe themselves with. And so it was until Adam repented and God pardoned him and made him other garments, but not of his days, as it is written: "And God made Adam and his wife coats of skins and clothed them" (Gen. III, 21). Observe that of Abraham it says that "he came into days" (Gen. XXIV, 1), because when he departed this world he literally came into possession of his former days and was invested with them, his robe of glory being full and complete. Job, on the other hand, said of himself: "Naked came I out of my mother's womb and naked shall I return thither" (Job. I, 21), because no material was left wherewith to clothe himself. Our teachers have said: "Happy the righteous whose days are without reproach and remain for the world to come, so that after death they are all joined together and formed into [224*b*] robes of glory through which they are privileged to enjoy the delights of the future world, and in which they are destined to come to life again. But woe for the sinners whose days are defective, so that there is not left from them wherewith to cover themselves when they depart from the world." We have further learnt that all the virtuous who have acquired a robe of glory through their days are crowned in the future world with crowns like those of the patriarchs, from the stream that flows continually into the Garden of Eden, and of them it is written, "the Lord shall lead thee continually and satisfy thy soul in dry places" (Is. LVIII, 11), but the wicked who have not acquired such a garment will be "like the heath in the desert that shall not see when good cometh, but inhabits the parched places in the wilderness" (Jer. XVII, 6).' R. Isaac said: 'Of all men Jacob had the fairest prospect, because he was entitled to a robe on account both of his own days and of those of his fathers; hence he said: "I shall lie with my fathers." ' R. Judah said: 'When Jacob went in to his father to obtain a blessing, he was wearing the garments of Esau; nevertheless the text says that Isaac smelt *his* garments (Gen. XXVII, 27), to indicate that he caught the odour of his raiment in the future world, and it was therefore that he blessed him. Hence, too, he said: "See the smell of my son is as the smell of a field which the Lord hath blessed", the reference being to the field of holy apples, in which every day drops dew from the place called heaven; hence he continued: "God give thee of the dew of the heaven." It has been taught that fifteen odours ascend every day from the Garden of Eden to perfume those precious garments in the other world.'

R. Judah asked how many garments there are. R. Eleazar said: 'The authorities differ on this point, but in truth there are three. One is for clothing the spirit (*ruah*) in the terrestrial Garden of Eden. A second, the most precious of all, is for investing the inner soul (*neshamah*) when among the bundle of the living in the circle of the King. The third is an outer garment which appears and disappears, and with which the vital soul (*nefesh*) is clothed. It flits about the world and on Sabbaths and New Moons it attaches itself to the spirit in the terrestrial paradise and learns from it certain things which it goes and makes known in this world. It has been taught that on Sabbaths and New Moons the soul (*nefesh*) makes two visits. First it joins the spirit among the perfumes of the terrestrial paradise, and then in company with the spirit it joins the higher soul in the "bundle of the living", and feasts itself on the glorious radiance coming from both sides. This is hinted in the expression "The Lord shall satisfy thy soul in bright places" (Is. LVIII, 11), the plural including both the outer radiance of the place of the spirit and the radiance within radiance which they enjoy by associating with the higher soul in the "bundle of the living".'

Said R. Simeon: 'When I visit the Companions in Babylon they come together to hear me, and I discourse to them openly, but they go and seal up my teaching under an iron padlock which makes it inaccessible to all. How often have I taught them the ways of the Garden of the King and the doctrine of the King ! How often have I taught them all the degrees of the righteous in the future world ! But they are all frightened to repeat [225*a*] these things and only mumble them, on which account they are called "mumblers". However, I account this fear in them creditable, because they are denied the air and the spirit of the Holy Land and inhale the air and the spirit of an alien region. Further, too, the rainbow has appeared in their time,[1] and hence they are not worthy to behold the presence of Elijah, not to mention others. Their good fortune is that I am still alive to be the ensign and support of the world, for in my days the world will not be afflicted and the punishment of heaven will not fall upon it. After me there will not arise a generation like this one, and the world will be left without a protector, and insolence will be rampant both above and below—above on account of the insolence of those below, and their shamelessness. Mankind will cry and none will take heed; they will turn to every side and find no remedy. But one remedy there will be in the world and no more, to wit, in the place where there will be men devoting themselves to the study of the Torah, and where there will be a Scroll of the Law free from all error. When this will be taken out, the upper and lower denizens will bestir themselves, especially if the Holy Name is written in it in the fitting manner. As I have already

---

[1] The appearance of the rainbow, reminding God of His promise not to destroy the world, is a proof that there are no righteous who could protect the world by their merits alone. *Vide* T. B. Kethuboth, 77*b*.

taught, woe to the generation the members of which, high and low, do not rise when the Scroll of the Law is displayed. Who shall come to its aid when the world is in distress and requires protection ? Then it is necessary more than ever to display the Scroll of the Law. For when the world is in distress, and men go to the cemeteries to offer supplication, all the dead take note of the Scroll, since the soul goes and informs the spirit that the Scroll of the Law is in captivity through the distress of the world, and the living have come to supplicate. Then the spirit informs the higher soul (*neshamah*) and the higher soul informs the Almighty, who then takes note and has pity on the world, all because the Scroll of the Law has been banished from its place, and the living have come to supplicate by the graves of the dead. Alas for the generation that has need to remove the Scroll of the Law from one place to another, even from one synagogue to another, because they have nothing else to which to turn. Not all men know that the Shekinah at its last exile did not withdraw to heaven, but to "the wilderness, to an inn of travellers" (Jer. ix, 1), and that since then it is always to be found in the place where Israel is particularly in distress, and also wherever the Scroll is removed and high and low rise up before it.'

We have learnt that the soul is linked with the body twelve months in the grave, and they are judged together (this, however, does not apply to the souls of the righteous, as we have laid down), and it is present in the grave and is aware of the sufferings of the body. It also knows the sufferings of the living, but does not intervene on their behalf. After twelve months it is clad in a certain vesture, and goes to and fro in the world, learning certain things from the spirit and interesting itself on behalf of the living who are in distress. But this is only when there is among them a virtuous man whose merit is properly recognized by them. For so we have learnt, that when a virtuous man is left in the world, he is known both among the living and the dead, and when the world is in great distress and he cannot deliver it, he makes the trouble known to the dead. And if there is not [225*b*] such a one, then they take out the Scroll of the Law, and high and low accompany it, and it is incumbent on all at that time to do penance, for otherwise heaven will punish them. Even the spirits of the Garden of Eden intercede for them for the sake of the Scroll, as has been affirmed. Said R. Judah: 'Little do men know how God extends His mercy to them at all times and seasons. Three times a day a spirit enters the cave of Machpelah and breathes on the graves of the patriarchs, bringing them healing and strength. That spirit distils dew from on high, from the head of the King, the place of the supernal fathers, and when it reaches the lower patriarchs they awake. That dew, as we have learnt, comes down by degrees till it reaches the lower Garden of Eden, and becomes impregnated with its perfumes. Then a spirit containing two other spirits arises and traverses the spice-beds, and enters the door of the cave. Then the patriarchs awake, they and their spouses, and supplicate on behalf of their descendants. If the world is in distress on account of its sins, and the patriarchs sleep, the dew not descending from on high, then the remedy is to take out the Scroll of the Law. Then the soul tells the spirit, and the spirit tells the higher soul, and the higher soul tells God. God then takes His seat on the throne of mercy, and there issues from the Ancient Holy One a stream of dew of bdellium, which flows to the head of the King, so that the fathers are blessed. Then the dew flows to those sleepers, and all are blessed together, and God has mercy on the world. We have learnt that God does not show mercy to the world till He has informed the patriarchs, and for their sakes the world is blessed.' Said R. Jose: 'Assuredly this is so. And I have further found in the Book of King Solomon, that one which was called the "counsellor of all wisdom" (and Rab Hamnuna also said that the same thing had been revealed to him), that Rachel achieves more than all of them by standing at the parting of the ways at all times when the world is in need. This is symbolized by the fact that the ark and the mercy-seat and the Cherubim were in the territory of Benjamin, who was born by the wayside, the Shekinah being over all.'

AND ISRAEL BOWED HIMSELF DOWN UPON THE BED'S

HEAD. The "bed's head" is the Shekinah. Said R. Simeon: 'Not at all. The bed stands for the Shekinah, as in the verse, "Behold, it is the litter of Solomon" (S. S. III, 7). The "head of the bed" is the Foundation of the World who is the head of the sacred couch; and "that which is upon the head" is (the supernal) Israel who is established at the head of the bed. Hence, Israel bowed down to his appropriate grade. At this time he was not yet ill, as we see from the next verse, but because he knew that at the time he would rise to a supernal holy grade to become a perfect throne, therefore he bowed down to that supernal throne, the completion of the great and mighty tree, which was called by his name, to "Him who is over the Head of the bed".' R. Judah said: 'We have a dictum that if a man dies in foreign soil and [226*a*] his body is buried in the Holy Land, to him may be applied the verse, "And ye came and defiled my land and my inheritance ye made an abomination" (Jer. II, 7). How, then, could Jacob ask to be buried in the grave of his fathers, seeing that he was dying on alien soil ?' R. Judah said: 'Jacob was different, because the Shekinah was closely attached to him. Hence it is written, "I will go down with thee to Egypt" (Gen. XLVI, 4), to wit, to abide with thee in captivity; "and I will also surely bring thee up again" (*Ibid.*), to attach thy soul to Me, and to obtain burial for thy body in the graves of thy fathers—and this even though he departed life on an alien soil. He was further promised that Joseph should put his hand on his eyes, the reason being that God knew that he was the first-born in intent, and that he was most attached to Joseph.'

What was the idea of this promise of putting his hands on his eyes ? R. Jose said that it was as a sign of honour to Jacob, and to inform him that Joseph was alive and would be with him at his death. Said R. Hizkiah: 'I have learnt something about this which I hardly like to disclose, showing how wisdom is embodied in a common practice.' R. Abba clapped him on the shoulder, saying: 'Speak out and do not be afraid; in the days of R. Simeon there is no need for secrecy.' He then said: 'I have seen in the chapter of R. Jesse the Elder regarding customs, that if a man has a son, when he dies the son ought to put dust on his eyes at the time of his burial, and this is a mark of respect to him, being a sign that the world is now concealed from him, but his son inherits the world in his place. For the human eye represents the world with its various colours. The outer ring of white corresponds to the sea of Oceanus which surrounds the whole world. The next colour represents the land which is surrounded by the sea. A third colour in the middle of the eye corresponds to Jerusalem, which is in the centre of the world. Finally there is the pupil of the eye, which reflects the beholder and is the most precious part of all. This corresponds to Zion, which is the central point of the universe, in which the reflection of the whole world can be seen, and where is the abode of the Shekinah, which is the beauty and the cynosure of the world. Thus the eye is the heritage of the world, and so as the father leaves it the son inherits it.' Said R. Abba: 'You are quite right. But there is still a deeper significance in the practice, although men do not know it. For when a man departs from the world, his soul is still enclosed in him, and before his eyes are closed they see certain recondite things, as we have explained in connection with the verse, "For a man shall not see me and live", indicating that they see things in their death which they do not see in their life-time. Then it behoves those who are present to place their hands on his eyes and close them, and, as we have learnt in connection with customs and manners, if he has a son, it behoves the son in the first place to do so, as it is written, "And Joseph shall put his hand on thy eyes." The reason for the closing of the eyes is because some sight the reverse of holy might present itself, and it is not meet that the eyes which have just beheld a holy vision should now dwell on a sight of a different character. A further reason is that the soul is still attached to him in the house, and if the eye is left open, with that unholy vision still resting upon it, everything it looks upon is cursed; and this is not respectful to the eye, to allow it to gaze upon anything improper. The best sign of respect, therefore, is that a man's eyes should be closed by the hand of the son whom he has left behind him.'

For seven days the soul goes to and fro between the house and the grave, mourning for the body, and three times a day the soul and the body are chastised together, though no one perceives it. After that the body is thrust out and the soul is purified [226b] in Gehinnom, whence it goes forth roaming about the world and visiting its grave until it acquires a vestment. After twelve months the whole is at rest; the body reposes in the dust and the soul is clad in its luminous vestment. The spirit regales itself in the Garden of Eden, and the higher soul (*neshamah*) ascends to the place where all delights are concentrated; and all three come together again at certain times. Alas for men that they look not to their foundation, and neglect the precepts of the Torah. For some of these precepts fashion a glorious garment above, and some a glorious garment below, and some a glorious garment in this world; and man requires them all. And they are made literally out of his days, as we have explained. R. Judah the Elder one day saw in a dream his own image illumined and radiating brightly in all directions. 'What is that ?' he said; and the answer came: 'It is thy garment for thy habitation here'; whereupon he was in great joy. R. Judah said: 'Every day the spirits of the righteous sit in rows in the Garden of Eden arrayed in their robes and praise God gloriously, as it is written: "Verily the righteous shall praise thy name, the upright shall sit before thee." '

R. Abba said: 'When Jacob "bowed down to Him that is over the bed", as we have explained, and knew that he had reached the highest grade, and that his grade was on high with that of his fathers, and that he was the consummation of the whole, his heart was strengthened and he rejoiced in God's favour towards him. Hence it says, "And Jacob strengthened himself." '

R. Judah said: 'We learn in the Mishnah that judgement is pronounced on the world at four seasons: at Passover, in respect of produce; at Pentecost, in respect of fruit-trees; on New Year, when "all the denizens of the world pass before Him like a flock of sheep"; and on Tabernacles, when the rainfall is determined. This we have esoterically explained as follows. Passover is the time for the decision with regard to cereals, because on Passover Israel began to enter into the holy portion of the Almighty and to remove from themselves the leaven which symbolizes the powers who are appointed over the idol-worshipping nations and who are called "strange gods". On Pentecost judgement is passed in respect of the fruit of the tree: this is the great and mighty tree which rears itself aloft. On New Year all pass before Him like a flock of sheep, because New Year (lit. head of the year) is the head of the King. On Tabernacles judgement is pronounced in respect of water, because this festival is the beginning of the right hand of the King, and therefore the rejoicing of water is universally diffused.' [227a] R. Jose said: 'If we look closely, we find that in these periods both the three patriarchs and David can be found, and in these the world is judged. But in truth every day books are open and acts are recorded, though no one notices or inclines his ear, and the Torah testifies against man every day and a voice cries aloud: "Who is simple, let him turn in here", but no one listens. We have learnt that when a man rises in the morning witnesses stand by him and adjure him, but he pays no need. His higher soul adjures him at all times and seasons. If he heeds her, it is well, but if not, then the books are open and the deeds recorded.' R. Hiya said: 'Happy are the righteous who have no fear of judgement, neither in this world nor in the future world, as it is written: "But the righteous is confident like a lion" (Prov. xxviii, 1), and again, "the righteous shall inherit the earth" (Ps. xxxvii, 29).' R. Hizkiah, citing the verse, "And when the sun was going down, a deep sleep fell on Abram, etc." (Gen. xv, 12), said: 'This verse has been applied to the day of judgement, when man is removed from this world. For we have learnt that the day when man departs this world is the great day of judgement when the sun's light is withheld from the moon, as it is written, "or ever the sun be darkened" (Eccl. xii, 2). This is the holy *neshamah* which is withheld from man thirty days before he departs from the world. During that time he observes that he throws no shadow, the reason being that his *neshamah* is withheld from him. For it does not wait until he is on the point of dying, but even while he is still in his full vigour it passes out of him, and does not illumine the spirit, which in turn does not illumine the vital soul, so that his shadow no longer shows. From that day all proclaim his coming fate, even the birds of the heaven. When the spirit ceases to illumine the vital soul, the latter becomes weak and rejects food and all bodily enjoyments.' R. Judah said further: 'Also whenever a man is on a sick bed and is not able to say his prayers his *neshamah* leaves him, and the spirit does not illumine the soul until he is judged. If the judgement is favourable, then the *neshamah* returns to its place and illumines the whole. But when no trial is held, then the *neshamah* leaves him thirty days before his death and his shadow is withheld. We have learnt that when a man is judged above, his *neshamah* is brought to trial and she confesses all and testifies to all the thoughts of a man, but not to his deeds, since they are all recorded in a book. While the trial is going on, the body is in greater pain than at other times. If he is judged favourably, he obtains ease and a sweat breaks out over his body, and his *neshamah* returns to its place and illumines the whole; but a man never rises from his bed of sickness until he is judged above. How is it, then, it may be asked, that so many sinners and transgressors are alive and active ? The reason is that God looks ahead, and if he sees that a man, though sinful now, may become virtuous subsequently, He judges him favourably, or it may be because he is destined to bear a son who will be virtuous. All God's judgements incline to beneficence, as it is written: "Have I any pleasure in the death of the wicked, saith the Lord God, and not rather that he should return from his way and live ?" (Ezek. XVIII, 23). Sometimes, again, it is because the malady has run its course, [227b] for illnesses have a fixed period, after which they depart, whether from the righteous or the wicked; and all is done in justice, as we have said.'

AND ISRAEL SAW THE SONS OF JOSEPH, AND HE SAID: WHO ARE THESE ? This verse seems to contradict the statement a little lower down that "the eyes of Israel were dim for age, so that he could not see". What this verse really means, however, is that he saw through the Holy Spirit those later descendants of Joseph, Jeroboam and his fraternity. Jeroboam made two golden calves and said: "These are thy gods, O Israel" (1 Kings XII, 28). Hence Israel now said "Who are these", that is, who is he that will one day say "these" to idols. From this passage we learn that the righteous see into the distant future and God crowns them with His own crown. That God sees the future we learn from the verse: "And God saw all that he had made, and behold, it was very good" (Gen. I, 31), which means that He foresaw all that was to happen before it was commenced. In the same way all the generations of the world from one end to the other stand before Him before they come into the world, as it says, "He calleth the generations from the beginning" (Is. XLI, 4), i.e. from the Creation; all the souls that are to descend into the world stand before God before they descend in the form which they are to assume in this world, and are called by name. In the same way God shows the righteous all generations before they come into the world, as He showed them to Adam, as it is written: "This is the book of the generations of Adam" (Gen. V, 1), and also to Moses, as it says: "And he showed him all the land" (Deut. XXXIV, 1), which we interpret to mean that God showed him all coming generations and leaders and prophets. So here with Israel. The words "who are these" have thus a double meaning (literal and metaphorical), and hence Joseph answered: "They are my sons whom God hath given me here." That Israel saw here through the Holy Spirit is proved by the words, "God hath let me see thy seed also", where the augmentative word "also" brings in his descendants, as we have explained.

AND HE BLESSED JOSEPH AND SAID. This statement seems inaccurate, since on reading further we find that he did not bless Joseph at all, but only his sons. R. Jose solved the difficulty by stating that in blessing the sons Jacob blessed Joseph also, since the blessing of a man's sons is his own blessing. R. Eleazar said that the object of the verb "blessed" is the particle *eth*, which alludes to the sign of the covenant. When Joseph said "they are my sons", Jacob blessed that place which symbolizes the Covenant that Joseph kept. In the next words, "The God before whom my fathers Abraham and Isaac did walk", the word God alludes to the holy Covenant, and the elder patriarchs Abraham and Isaac were literally "before" this, because that place derives nourishment and sustenance from them. Jacob continued: THE GOD (*Elohim*) WHICH HATH FED ME. In repeating the word *Elohim*, he blessed that place with a reference to *Elohim Ḥayyim* (Living God), the source of life and of blessing. On that account he mentioned himself at this point, saying, "the God who blessed me", because all blessings that flow from the source of life are first received by Jacob, and thereupon this place is blessed, and all is made dependent on the male. From here we learn that wherever blessings are to be bestowed, God should be blessed first; otherwise the blessings will not be [228a] fulfilled. The blessing which Isaac bestowed on Jacob is no exception to this rule, because he said first, "behold the smell of my son is like the smell of a field which the Lord hath blessed", where the field is an allusion to that field which is the source of blessings. Note that in the morning a man should first bless God and only then give his greeting to his fellow-men.

When Jacob was about to bless Joseph's sons, he saw by the Holy Spirit that Jeroboam the son of Nebat would issue from Ephraim, and he exclaimed, "Who are these ?", the word "these" (*eleh*) being an allusion to idols. The reason is that besides the evil serpent there is one that rides on it, and when they are joined together they are called "these", and they visit the world with all their hosts. The Holy Spirit, on the other hand, is called "this", and is symbolized by the covenant of the holy imprint which is ever on a man's body. Hence we find written, "These also shall forget" (Is. XLIX, 15), and again, "For these I am weeping" (*Ibid.* 16), that sin being the cause to us of endless weeping; or alternatively, because this place was allowed to gain dominion over Israel and to destroy the Temple, the word "I" (*ani*) in this case referring to the Holy Spirit. It may be asked, on this hypothesis, what are we to make of the words "These are the words of the covenant" ? The answer is that the word "these" is here also appropriate, because the words of the covenant are established by "these", since they are the abode of all curses, which await all who transgress the covenant. Similarly it is written, "These are the precepts which the Lord commanded", because the object of all the precepts is to purify man so that he should not stray from the right path and should keep far away from there. Hence, too, it is written, "These are the generations of Noah", because they included Ham the father of Canaan, who was accursed. The spirit of *eleh* is the "dross of gold". Aaron in the wilderness offered gold, which was his own affinity, since he was endowed with the strength of fire, and fire and gold are all one, but the unclean spirit which haunts the wilderness found at that time a place on which to fasten, and so Israel, after being freed at Mount Sinai from the primeval defilement which brought death into the world, afterwards incurred it again and brought death upon themselves and all their descendants. Hence, when Jacob saw in his mind's eye Jeroboam son of Nebat, who made an idol and said, "These are thy gods, O Israel", he trembled and said, "Who are these ?". Hence when he came afterwards to bless them, he first blessed *Elohim* and then blessed them from that source.

R. Judah discoursed here on the text: *Then Hezekiah turned his face unto the wall and prayed unto the Lord* (Is. XXXVIII, 2). He said: 'We have derived from this verse the lesson that a man in praying should stand near the wall, with nothing intervening between himself and the wall. Now the question may be asked, why does it say of Hezekiah in particular that he turned his face to the wall, and of no one else who offered prayer, though with no less devotion, as, for instance, Moses, of whom it is written that he "prayed to the Lord" (*Ibid.* XVII, 4), and he "cried to the Lord" (Ex. XV, 25)? [228*b*] The reason is as follows. Hezekiah, as tradition tells us, was at that time not married and had no children. Isaiah therefore came to him and said: "Thou shalt die and not live", i.e. as tradition explains, "thou shalt die in this world and not live in the next world". For whoever has not laboured to beget children in this world is not established in the future world, and his soul is banished thence and can nowhere find rest; and this is the punishment referred to in the Law by the words, "They shall die childless" (Lev. XX, 20). Further, the Shekinah does not rest upon him at all. Hence Hezekiah "set his face to the wall", that is to say, he made a resolution to take a wife in order that the Shekinah, which is symbolized by a wall, might rest upon him, and hence the text continues, "and he prayed unto the Lord". From here we learn that anyone who is conscious of a sin for which he means to ask forgiveness should first form a resolution to cure himself of that sin and then offer his prayer, as it is written: "Let us search and try our ways" first, and then, "turn again unto the Lord" (Lam. III, 40). So Hezekiah, recognizing his fault, set his mind to put himself right with the Shekinah, the place against which he sinned. For all females are in the shelter of the Shekinah, and it abides with one who has a wife, but not with one who has none, and therefore Hezekiah first resolved to marry, and then offered his prayer. In regard to the actual language of his prayer, the words "Remember now, O Lord, I beseech thee, how I have walked before thee" allude to the fact of his having kept the holy covenant without defiling it; the words "in truth and with a perfect heart" denote that he clung to all the principles of faith which are comprised under the word "truth", and the words "and have done that which is good in thy sight" indicate that in praying he always concentrated his mind upon declaring the unity of God with full conviction. Finally, Hezekiah "wept sore", because there is no door which remains closed to tears.'

THE ANGEL WHO REDEEMED ME FROM ALL EVIL. This is the angel who takes part in every deliverance. R. Eleazar said: 'After Jacob had mentally carried the blessings from the lower to the upper sphere, he then drew them from the upper to the lower. Thus he first said: "The God which hath fed me", and then, having set the blessings in that place, he said "the angel who redeemed me".' R. Eleazar further said: 'It is written: "For the Cherubim spread forth their wings over the place of the ark" (I Kings VIII, 7). The Cherubim were kept in their place miraculously, and three times a day they used to spread out their wings and cover the ark. They were a representation of the upper Cherubim and had the form of children, and they stood beneath that place on the right and the left. They were the first recipients of the blessings which flowed from above, and transmitted them further, and this is the meaning of the words, "the angel who blessed me", that is, the angel first received blessings from the beings above, and with them "blessed the lads", to wit, the Cherubim, and from them blessings were transmitted from the upper to the lower creatures. [229a]

R. Hiya discoursed on the verse: *House and wealth are an inheritance from parents, but from the Lord is a prudent wife.* (Prov. XIX, 14). 'When God gives a house and money to a man,' he said, 'sometimes he bequeaths the whole to his son, and therefore these things, although they are ultimately from God, may be called "inheritance of parents". But the possession of a good wife comes to man only from God. For God mates couples before they are born, and when a man is worthy he obtains a wife according to his deserts. Sometimes it happens that after the lot has been cast, that man perverts his ways, and then his mate is transferred to another until he rectifies his ways, or else until his time comes, and then the other is removed to make way for him and he comes into his own; and this is grievous in the sight of God, to remove one man to make way for another. Nor is it only a prudent wife who is from God. For if God has purposed to bestow benefits on a man, but he goes astray to the "other side", then from that other side to which he cleaves there shall come to him one who shall bring upon him all accusations and all ills. Hence of the wife who is not prudent Solomon said: "And I find that woman more bitter than death" (Eccl. VII, 26), because it is the man's sins which have drawn her on him. Hence, when God is pleased with a man, he provides for him a wife who is prudent, and redeems him from the other side. Hence Jacob said, "the angel who hath redeemed me from all wrong", meaning that a wife had not been assigned to him from the "other side", and that there was no defect in his seed, all of them being righteous and perfect.'

SHALL BLESS THE CHILDREN. They were deserving of blessing because Joseph had kept the sign of the holy covenant. When Joseph said, "they are my sons whom God has given me here", he showed his father the sign of the covenant which he had kept, and therefore they were meet for blessing, and he also was deserving of blessing in abundance. Hence Jacob gave to the others only one blessing, but to Joseph many blessings, as it says, "the blessings of thy father . . . shall be upon the head of Joseph" (Gen. XLIX, 26).

R. Judah discoursed on the verse: *Unto thee do I lift up mine eyes, O thou that sittest in the heavens* (Ps. CXXIII, 1). He said: 'Prayer offered with true devotion is directed on high to the supernal recess, from whence issue all blessings and all freedom, to support the universe. It is attached above to the mystery of the supreme Wisdom, and it is attached below to him who sits on the throne of the patriarchs which is called heaven. Hence it is written here: "Who sits in the heavens." When the blessings issue from the supernal recess, they are all received by this place called heaven, and from thence they flow down till they come to the place called the "Righteous One the foundation of the world", from whence are blessed all the (heavenly) hosts and camps after their kind. All these heavenly legions are crowned by seventy-two lights, of which seventy[1] form a circle about the world, while in the midst of the circle is a certain point[2] from which the whole of the circumference is fed. The house of the holy of holies is the place [229b] for that spirit of all spirits, where lies hid the mystery of all mysteries, and when this removes, all move after it.'

As R. Hizkiah and R. Jose and R. Judah were once journeying together, R. Jose said: 'Let each one of us give some exposition of the Torah.' R. Judah thereupon began with the verse, "Remember not against us the iniquities of our forefathers, let thy tender mercies speedily prevent us" (Ps. LXXIX, 8). He said: 'God in His great love for Israel allows no one to sit in judgement on them save Himself, and when He tries them, He is filled with compassion for them like a father for his children, and when He finds they have done wrong, He removes their offences one by one until there are none left to place them in the power of the other side. Hence it says, "let thy mercies prevent us", because otherwise Israel would not be able to exist, in face of all the accusers and all the adversaries who are lying in wait for them above.

[1] The seventy Chieftains.   [2] The Shekinah.

Hence it continues "for we are very poor", that is, poor in good deeds in the sight of God. For were Israel rich in good deeds before God, idolatrous nations would not be able to exist in the world. It is Israel who enable other nations to hold their head high, because but for their sins the nations would be subdued before them. And, as we have already said, had not Israel by their sins brought the other side into the Holy Land, the idolatrous nations would not have gained possession of it, and Israel would not have been exiled from their land. Hence, because "we are brought very low", therefore "let thy tender mercies speedily prevent us".'

R. Jose discoursed on the verse: "Serve the Lord with gladness, come before his presence with singing" (Ps. c, 2). He said: 'The service of prayer offered by man to the Holy One, blessed be He, should be carried out with gladness and with singing, so that he may associate with him the Community of Israel; and then he should proclaim the unity in the fitting manner, as it says: "Know ye that the Lord he is God" (*Ibid.* 3). These two activities of gladness and song correspond to the two prayers of morning and afternoon, and to the two daily sacrifices—gladness in the morning and singing in the afternoon. The evening prayer, on the other hand, is optional, because at that time she (the Shekinah) is distributing sustenance to all her hosts, and it is not the time for blessing. In the daytime she is to be blessed from these two sides, morning and afternoon, out of gladness and singing, and at night time she divides the blessings among all in the fitting manner.'

R. Hizkiah took for his text the verse: "Let my prayer be established like incense before thee, the lifting of my hands like the evening oblation" (Ps. cxli, 2). He said: 'It may be asked, why did David mention here the oblation of the evening rather than [230*a*] of the morning ? The answer may be given as follows. The offering of incense betokens joy, as it is written, "oil and incense rejoice the heart" (Prov. xxvii, 9). Hence the high priest, when he lit the candlestick, used to offer incense morning and evening (Ex. xxx, 7, 8); in the morning, because that is the natural season of joy, and in the evening to rejoice the left side, as befits. We see, then, that incense always betokened joy. Further, the incense links and unites upper and lower, and so removes death and wrath and accusation from the world and prevents them from prevailing over it; it was through the incense that Aaron stayed the plague. Hence the incense symbolizes universal joy and universal union. Now David offered the prayer we have quoted at the time of the afternoon oblation, when the world is under the ægis of justice, and he meant it to ascend and remove the wrath that was prevalent at that hour like the incense which removes wrath and accusation; hence he mentioned the "oblation of eventide", the time when punishment descends on the world. Observe that the Temple was burnt at the time of the evening oblation, as it is written: "Woe to us because the day hath declined and the shadows of evening stretch out" (Jer. VI, 3). The "shadows of evening" are the accusers and the punishments which are abroad at that hour. Hence we have learnt that a man should say the afternoon prayer with special devotion, even more than other prayers. Hence, too, it was that Isaac instituted the afternoon prayer, as we have already explained.'

As they proceeded they came to a mountain. Said R. Jose: 'This mountain is very formidable, let us keep clear of it.' Said R. Judah: 'If I were alone I should think the same, since we have learnt that he who travels alone makes his life forfeit. But this does not apply to three, all the more seeing that each one of us is worthy to be accompanied by the Shekinah.' Said R. Jose: 'But we have learnt that a man should not rely on a miracle, since even Samuel said: "How can I go ? If Saul hear it, he will kill me" (1 Sam. XVI, 2), and he was more worthy than we are.' He replied: 'Even so, he was by himself and the danger was obvious, whereas we are three and there is no danger actually in sight. For if it is evil spirits you are afraid of, we have learnt that they do not show themselves to three or harm them, and if it is robbers, there are none here, because this mountain is far from any inhabited spot, and people never pass here. The only thing we have to be afraid of is wild beasts. Scripture speaks of "the angel who redeemed me from all evil". This angel is the Shekinah, who continually accompanies a man and leaves him not so long as he keeps the precepts of the Law. Hence a man should be careful not to go on the road alone, that is to say, he should diligently keep the precepts of the Law in order that he may not be deserted by the Shekinah, and so be forced to go alone without the accompaniment of the Shekinah. Hence, before starting on a journey a man should first address his prayer to God in order that he may draw the Shekinah to himself, to be protected by it on the road and delivered from all harm. So Jacob, on setting out, said: "If God shall be with me", i.e. if the Shekinah will accompany me, "and keep me in this way" (Gen. XXVIII, 20), to deliver me from all harm. Now Jacob was alone [230*b*] at that time, but the Shekinah went with him; all the more so then will it accompany the Companions who discourse on the Torah.' Said R. Jose: 'What are we to do? If we remain here we shall be overtaken by night; if we commence to ascend, the mountain is very high, and there is danger from wild beasts.' Said R. Judah: 'I am surprised at you, R. Jose.' He replied: 'We have learnt that a man should not rely on a miracle, for God does not perform miracles at all times.' He answered: 'That applies only when a man is by himself. But we are three, and words of Torah pass between us and the Shekinah is with us; therefore we have no need to fear.'

As they went on, they perceived on the mountain a rock in which was a cave. Said R. Judah: 'Let us go up to yonder rock, as I see there a cave.' So they went up there. Said R. Jose: 'Perhaps there are wild beasts in this cave which will attack us.' Said R. Judah to R. Hizkiah: 'Why is R. Jose so afraid? He is not a sinner that he should fear, and we read that "the righteous is bold like a lion" (Prov. XXVIII, 1).' R. Jose said: 'It is because we are wilfully exposing ourselves to danger.' He replied: 'If that were so, you would be right, but there is no danger apparent here, and once we enter the cave no danger will follow us.' So they went into the cave. R. Judah then said: 'Let us divide the night into three watches, and let each one of us stand to his post in one of them, and let us all keep awake.'

R. Judah then commenced with the text: "Maskil to Ethan the Ezrahite" (Ps. LXXXIX, 1). He said: 'This psalm was uttered by our father Abraham when he devoted himself to the service of his Master and conferred on mankind the boon of teaching them to acknowledge God as ruler of the world; and he was called Ethan (lit. strong) because he clung strongly to God. "I will sing of the mercies of the Lord for ever." Song comes from the side of the Left, not of *Ḥesed* (Mercy); so by this exordium the side of the Left was embraced in the Right. It was for this purpose (to combine Left with Right) that God tried Abraham, in order that he might be found to unite justice with mercy, and so be perfect. Hence he could say: "I will sing of the mercies of the Lord for ever." He continued: "With my mouth will I make known thy faithfulness to all generations." This refers to the faithfulness of God in making Abraham known in the world and causing his name to be in the mouth of all creatures. God made known to Abraham the true principle of faith, and he thereupon realized that he was the foundation and support of the universe. For when God created the universe, He saw that it could not endure unless He stretched forth His right hand to it. For this world was created under the ægis of justice, and it was not established save by the right hand. Hence Abraham continued: "I said, the world is built up on mercy (*ḥesed*)", the first step in the building up of the world having been the light of the first day. Then on the second day the Left came into play and with it was established the heaven, as it says: "Thou establishest the heavens, thy faithfulness is in them." (This may also be explained to mean that the heavens were established by those mercies of the first day, and that the mystery of faith was established in them, the heavens being the bulwark of faith.) The text continues: "I have made a covenant with my chosen." This covenant is the secret of faith. Or we may interpret the "chosen one" of [231a] the *Zaddik* from whom issue blessings to all the lower creation, all the holy *Ḥayyoth* being blessed from the stream which flows forth to the lower world. "I have sworn unto David my servant", to wit, that he will always be established in this *Zaddik*, the foundation of the world, save in the time of *galuth*, when the flow of blessing is cut off, and faith is defective, and all joy is banished. During this period, at nightfall, joy no longer enters before the King. Yet, though rejoicings do not enter, angels stand outside and chant hymns, and at midnight when the impulse from below arrives on high, God arouses all the hosts of the heaven for lamentation and strikes the firmament, causing upper and lower worlds to quake; nor is there any respite save when those below commence to study the Torah. Then God and all those with Him listen with joy to that voice, and relief is felt. For on the day on which the Sanctuary below was destroyed, God swore that He would not enter the celestial Jerusalem until Israel should enter the earthly Jerusalem. Now all those singers stand outside and chant hymns in the three watches of the night and intone praises, and all the hosts of the heavens sing at night and Israel by day, nor is the sanctification recited above until it is recited by Israel below, and only then do all the hosts of heaven sanctify the holy name together. Hence, Israel are holy and are sanctified by upper and lower angels, since the sanctification of the holy name is complete only when uttered above and below together.'

R. Jose discoursed on the verse: *Whereupon were the foundations thereof fastened?* (Job XXXVIII, 6). He said: 'When God created the world, He established it on seven pillars, but upon what those pillars rest no one may know, since it is a recondite and inscrutable mystery. The world did not come into being until God took a certain stone, which is called the "foundation stone", and cast it into the abyss so that it held fast there, and from it the world was planted. This is the central point of the universe, and on this point stands the holy of holies. This is the stone referred to in the verses, "Who laid the corner-stone thereof" (*Ibid.* 6), "the stone of testing, the precious corner-stone" (Is. XXVIII, 16), and "the stone that the builders despise became the head of the corner" (Ps. CXVIII, 22). This stone is compounded of fire, water, and air, and rests on the abyss. Sometimes water flows from it and fills the deep. This stone is set as a sign in the centre of the world. It is referred to in the words, "And Jacob took a stone and set it as a pillar" (Gen. XXXI, 45). Not that he took this stone, which was created from the beginning, but he established it above and below, by making there a "house of God". This stone has on it seven eyes, as it is written, "On one stone seven eyes" (Zech. III, 9), and it is called "foundation stone", for one thing because the world was planted from it, and for another because God set it as a source of blessing to the world. Now at sunset, the Cherubim which stood in that place used to strike their wings together and spread them out, and when the sound of the beating of their wings was heard above, those angels who chanted hymns in the night began to sing, in order that the glory of God might ascend from below on high. The striking of the Cherubim's wings itself intoned the psalm, "Behold, bless ye the Lord, all ye servants of the Lord . . . lift up your hands to the sanctuary, etc." (Ps. cxxxIII). This was the signal for the heavenly angels to commence. At the second watch [231*b*] the Cherubim again beat their wings, giving the signal to the angels of that watch. The psalm of the Cherubim this time was "They that trust in the Lord are like Mount Zion, etc." (Ps. cxxv). At the third watch the Cherubim beat their wings to the words "Hallelujah, praise, O servants of the Lord, praise the name of the Lord" (Ps. cxIII), and then the angels of the third watch commenced to sing, and also all the stars and constellations of the heaven, as it is written: "When the morning stars sung together and all the sons of God shouted for joy" (Job xxxvIII, 7), and also, "Praise him, all ye stars of light" (Ps. cxLvIII, 3), these being the radiant stars which are appointed to sing at dawn. After them Israel take up the chant below, and so the glory of God ascends both from below and from above, from Israel below in the day, and from the celestial angels above in the night, and so the name of God is fully praised on all sides. As for this stone that we have mentioned, all the angels above and Israel below take hold on it, and it ascends to be crowned in the midst of the patriarchs by day. At night the Holy One, blessed be He, comes to disport Himself with the righteous in the Garden of Eden. Blessed are those who stand at their posts and study the Torah at night, because God and all the righteous in the Garden of Eden listen to the voice of those sons of men who study the Torah.'

That stone we have mentioned is a goodly stone, and it is

hinted at in the verse "And thou shalt set in it a setting of stone, four rows of stone" (Ex. XXVIII, 17), because there is another stone of which it is written "And I shall remove the heart of stone, etc." (Ezek. XXXVI, 26). The two tablets of stone were also hewn from this stone; and this was also called "the stone of Israel" (Gen. XLIX, 24), as has been explained. R. Hizkiah quoted the verse: "And the stone shall be according to the names of the children of Israel, twelve" (Ex. XXVIII, 21). He said: 'These are the precious supernal stones which are called "the stones of the place" (Gen. XXVIII, 11). They were "according to the names of the children of Israel" because just as there are twelve tribes below, so there are twelve tribes above, which are twelve precious stones; and therefore it is written: "Whither the tribes go up, even the tribes of the Lord, for a testimony unto Israel" (Ps. CXXII, 4), the reference being to the supernal Israel. Further, just as there are twelve hours in the day, so there are twelve hours in the night, in the day above and in the night below, each corresponding to each. These twelve hours of the night are divided into three sets, to each of which belong hierarchies of angels, which take their portion first. Hence, at midnight two ranks stand on one side and two on the other, and a celestial spirit goes forth between them and then all the trees in the garden break forth into song and God enters the garden, as it says: "Then do all the trees of the wood sing for joy before the Lord, for he cometh to judge the earth" (I Chron. XVI, 33), because judgement enters among them and the Garden of Eden is filled therewith. Then the north wind springs up, bringing joy in its train, and it blows through the spice trees and wafts their perfume, and the righteous put on their crowns and feast themselves on the brightness of the "pellucid mirror"—happy are they to be vouchsafed that celestial light ! The light of this mirror shines on all sides, and each one of the righteous takes his appropriate portion, each according to his works in this world; and some of them are abashed because of the superior light obtained by their neighbours. [232*a*] When night commences, numbers of officers of judgement arise and roam about the world, and the doors are closed, as we have affirmed. Thus at midnight the side of the north comes down and takes possession of the night until two-thirds of it have passed. Then the side of the south awakes until morning, and then both south and north take hold of it (the Shekinah). Then come Israel here below, and with their prayers and supplications raise it up until it ascends and hides itself among them, and receives blessings from the fountain-head.'

While they were sitting midnight arrived, and R. Judah said to R. Jose: 'Now the north wind awakes and the night is divided, and now is the time when the Holy One, blessed be He, longs for the voice of the righteous in this world, the voice of those who study the Torah. Now God is listening to us in this place; therefore let us not cease from discoursing on the Torah.' He then commenced:

THE ANGEL WHO DELIVERED ME FROM ALL EVIL. This is the same as the one mentioned in the verse: "Behold I send an angel before thee, etc." (Ex. XXIII, 20), who, as we have laid down, is the deliverer of the world, the protector of mankind, and the one who procures blessings for all the world, he himself receiving them first. This angel is sometimes male, sometimes female. When he procures blessings for the world, he is male, resembling the male who provides blessings for the female. But when he comes to bring chastisement on the world he is called female, being, as it were, pregnant with the judgement. Similarly, in the words, "the flame of the sword which turned every way" (Gen III, 24), there is a reference to the angels who are God's messengers, and who turn themselves into different shapes, being sometimes female and sometimes male, sometimes messengers of judgement and sometimes of mercy. In the same way, this angel can take all colours like the rainbow, and treats the world correspondingly. [232b]

R. Jose discoursed on the verse: *The king's strength also loveth judgement, thou dost establish equity, etc.* (Ps. XCIX, 4). 'The king', he said, 'is God, who loves judgement and takes fast hold of it, because by judgement the earth is established. By judgement, too, the Community of Israel is confirmed and established, because from there it is sustained, and receives all its blessings. Hence all its desire and all its longing is for judgement. The words "Thou dost establish equity (*mesharim*, lit. straightnesses)" refer to the two cherubim below who render the world safe and habitable.'

R. Hizkiah discoursed on the verse: *Praise ye the Lord (Hallelujah), praise, O ye servants of the Lord, praise the name of the Lord.* 'The repetition of the word "praise" in this verse', he said, 'seems somewhat pointless, but there is a reason for it. We have been taught that a eulogy should not be extravagant, and that to ascribe to another merits which he does not possess is really to reproach him; and, therefore, in recounting the praises of a deceased person, we should say only what he deserves and no more, otherwise through trying to praise we shall really blame him. Now the word *Hallelujah* (lit. praise ye Yah) contains the highest of all the praises of the Lord, mentioning, as it does, the place to which no eye can penetrate, being most recondite and inscrutable. This is *Yah*, the name which is supreme above all. Hence this psalm commences with "Hallelujah", a word in which praise and name are combined. Further, the subject of the word "praise" is not specified, but just as the name *Yah* is undisclosed, so those who praise it are undisclosed, and so it is fitting that all should be undisclosed in the realm of the supreme mystery. But the psalmist then continues: "Praise, O ye servants of the Lord, praise the name of the Lord", because this is a place which is not undisclosed, a place which is called "Name". The first is completely undisclosed, the second half undisclosed, half disclosed, and therefore the psalmist specified those who praised that place, and said that they are "the servants of the Lord", who are meet to praise this place. The text continues "Blessed be (*Yehi*) the name of the Lord." The word *yehi* consists of the name *Yah* and the letter *yod*, and indicates the continuity between that supernal and inscrutable place which is *Yah* and the grade of the covenant which is the lower *yod*. For this reason the word *yehi* (let there be) in the account of the Creation, is used only of the upper productions, e.g. "let there be light", "let there be a firmament", "let there be lights", but it is not used in connection with the [233*a*] lower productions. So by this word the

Holy Name is blessed in all. The text continues: "From the rising of the sun unto the going down thereof." The "rising" is the supernal place from which the sun derives light to shine over all, the place of the supernal and hidden fountain-head. The "setting" is the place to which faith is attached, from which blessings issue to all, and from which the world is sustained, as has been affirmed. The whole depends upon the impulse from below which is given by the service of the Lord when they bless the Holy Name, as we have said.'

By this time the morning had dawned, and so they came out of the cave, not having slept the whole night. They went on their way, and when they got beyond the hills they sat down and said their prayers. They then came to a village, where they stayed the whole day. At night they slept till midnight, when they rose to study the Torah. R. Judah began:

AND HE BLESSED THEM ON THAT DAY, SAYING: IN THEE SHALL ISRAEL BLESS, SAYING. 'The expression "that day" has an esoteric meaning, and signifies the grade which is in charge of blessings above, the "day" from the supernal place which is called "That" (*Hu*). Hence we translate "by the day of That", indicating that there is no separation between "day" and "That". The two signify an upper grade and a lower grade in conjunction. Thus Jacob blessed the sons of Joseph with the union of upper and lower in order that the blessings might be unalterable. He then completed the conjunction by saying, "in thee shall Israel bless". The name Israel here refers to the patriarch Israel. This Israel receives blessings from above and then blesses all through this lower grade. Hence he said "God make thee as Ephraim and Manasseh", putting Ephraim first because Ephraim were called Israel, as it is written: "Son of man, these bones are the whole house of Israel" (Ezek. XXXVII, 11), where the reference according to tradition is to the members of the tribe of Ephraim who were killed when they tried to break out of the captivity of Egypt before the time. For that reason, too, the tribe of Ephraim in the wilderness journeyed on the west.[1] Note that Israel blessed the sons of Joseph before he blessed

---

[1] Which was regarded as the side of the Shekinah.

his own sons, which shows that a man loves his grandchildren more than his children.' R. Jose said: 'It is written:
"The Lord hath remembered us, he will bless, he will bless
the house of Israel." The first "he will bless" refers to the
men, and the "house of Israel" to the women, because the
women derive blessings only from the blessings of the men.
Alternatively, this lesson may be derived from the verse: "He
shall make atonement for himself and for his house" (Lev.
XVI, 6)—for himself first and for his house afterwards. In this
case we may interpret the words "He shall bless the house of
Israel" to mean that God gives extra blessings to a man who
is married, in order that his wife may be blessed through him,
[233*b*] and so he receives two portions, one for himself and
one for his wife.'

R. Hizkiah discoursed on the verse: "Thine eyes did see
mine imperfect substance, and in thy book they were all
written, etc." (Ps. CXXXIX, 16). 'This verse', he said, 'has
been frequently expounded. All the souls which came into
existence when the world was created stand before God
before coming down in that same form in which they afterwards appear in the world, since that bodily appearance of
man which he had in this world is also found above. When
this soul is about to descend into the world, it stands before
God in the form which it is to assume in the world, and God
adjures it to keep the precepts of the law and not to transgress
them. Hence it says: "Thine eyes saw mine imperfect form"
before it appeared in the world, "and in thy book they were
all written", that is to say, all the souls in their forms are
recorded in the book. The text proceeds: "The days are
fashioned and there is not one among them", that is, there is
not one day of them in this world which can stand before its
Master as it should. For when a man is virtuous in this
world his days are blessed above, from that place which is
the measure of his days, mentioned in the verse, "Show me,
O Lord, mine end, and what is the measure of my days"
(Ps. XXXIX, 5). The "end" here is the "end of the right",
which was united with David, and the "measure of my days"
was the power in charge of his days.' R. Judah said: 'I have
heard from R. Simeon that this verse refers to the days which

were assigned to him out of the life of Adam, namely seventy years, since it has been affirmed that David had no life of his own, but Adam gave him seventy years of his life. David therefore prayed to know why it was that he had no life of his own, and continued, "Let me know how fleeting I am", that is to say, why, like the moon, I am without light of my own, unlike all those celestial lights which all have their own life. This is what David sought to know, but permission was not given to him. Observe that all celestial blessings were delivered to this grade to transmit to all creatures, and although it has no light of its own, all blessings and all joy and all goodness are contained in it and issue from it, and therefore is it called "the cup of blessing", or even simply "blessing", as it is written, "The blessing of the Lord maketh rich" (Prov. x, 22). Therefore it has a residue from all and is filled from all; it receives [234*a*] of the supernal blessings to transmit them further.' Said R. Isaac: 'We know this from the fact that Jacob blessed the sons of Joseph from the place from which all blessings had been delivered into his hand to transmit.'

AND JACOB CALLED TO HIS SONS AND SAID: GATHER YOURSELVES TOGETHER, ETC. R. Abba discoursed on the verse: *He turned to the prayer of the lonely one and did not despise their prayer* (Ps. CII, 18). He said: 'The use of the word "turned" here, instead of "hearkened" or "listened", is significant. The prayer of an individual man only enters before the Holy King with great difficulty, because before it can be crowned in its place God examines it closely and weighs the merits and defects of that individual. He does not so with the prayer of a congregation; for congregational prayers are offered by many who are not virtuous, and yet they all come before God and He does not regard their sins. Therefore it says, "God turns to the prayer of the solitary one" and weighs and considers it, and examines in what spirit it is offered and who is the man that offers it, and what is his conduct. Hence a man should pray with the congregation because "God does not despise their prayer", even though they do not all pray with devotion. According to another explanation, the word "solitary" here refers to an individual who is united with numbers, to wit, Jacob, who was united with two sides, and who called his sons and prayed for them that they might be acceptable above and not be destroyed in the captivity. When Jacob called his sons, Abraham and Isaac were there and the Shekinah with them, rejoicing in Jacob, and in the prospect of joining the patriarchs [234*b*] and forming with them a chariot. When Jacob said to his sons, "I will tell you what will befall you in the latter end of days", a kind of sadness came over him and the Shekinah departed. His sons, however, raised their voices and said, "Hear, O Israel, etc.", and Jacob answered, "Blessed be the name of his glorious kingdom for ever and ever", and on this proclamation of the unity the Shekinah returned to its place.

AND JACOB CALLED. The word "called" signifies that he established them in their place above and below. Similarly, Moses "called Hosea son of Nun, Joshua" (Num. XIII, 16) to establish him in his proper place. There is a similar significance in the expressions "And he called his name Jacob" (Gen. xxv, 26) and "the God of Israel called him El" (Gen. XXXIII, 20). So, too, "I called from my sorrow unto the Lord" (Jonah, III, 7), signifying that one who praises his Master and addresses supplications to Him establishes his Master more firmly, by showing that all depends upon Him and not upon any other power. AND HE SAID. It has been laid down that "saying" means "thinking", as in the expression "And thou shalt say in thy heart" (Deut. VII, 17). ASSEMBLE YOURSELVES; that is, in complete harmony. AND I SHALL TELL YOU. The word "tell" (*agidah*) contains an allusion to the esoteric wisdom. He sought to reveal to them their final destiny. It may be asked, seeing that he did not reveal what he sought to reveal, why are his words, which were afterwards belied, recorded in the Scripture? The truth is that all that was needful to be revealed is completely stated, and there is a hidden meaning within, and so nothing in the Scripture is belied. In fact, everything is included in the Scripture, and there is no word or letter short in it. Jacob said all that was needful for him to say, but not all openly, and not a letter was short of what was required. R. Judah and R. Jose were one day sitting at the gate of Lydda. Said the latter: 'We are told that Jacob blessed his sons, but what are the blessings?' R. Judah answered: 'He did indeed bless them, as, for instance, "Judah, thee shall thy brethren praise", "Dan shall judge his people", "Out of Asher his bread shall be fat", and so forth; but what he sought to reveal to them he did not reveal, namely, the end. We have laid down that there is an end to the right and an end to the left, and he sought to reveal to them the end (of the left) in order that they might keep themselves [235*a*] pure from uncleanness. What he revealed to them referred only to the time when they were in the Holy Land; later things were not stated openly, but are only hinted at in this section and in these blessings.'

REUBEN, THOU ART MY FIRSTBORN, MY MIGHT AND THE BEGINNING OF MY STRENGTH. Why did Jacob begin with Reuben and not rather with Judah, who was the leader of the camps and also king? Further we see that he did not bless him, nay, that he removed blessings from him till Moses came and prayed for him, as it is written: "Let Reuben live and not die" (Deut. XXXIII, 6). The fact is, however, that he did bless him, but kept the blessing for its proper place. He was like a man who had a son, and when he was about to die was visited by the king, whereupon he said: "Let all my money remain in the king's hands on behalf of my son, and when the king sees that my son is worthy he will give it to him." So Jacob said: "Reuben, thou art my firstborn, the beloved of my soul; but thy blessings shall remain in the hand of the Holy King until He shall see that thou art worthy of them, because 'thou didst go after the sight of thine eyes, etc.'" (according to Chaldaic paraphrase of this passage).

R. Eleazar here discoursed on the verse: *And he said to me: Prophesy unto the wind, etc.* (Ezek. XXXVII, 9). 'There is a difficulty here,' he said, 'because the text continues: "Prophesy, son of man, and say to the wind", which seems a repetition. The truth is, however, that there is here an esoteric lesson.

There are two adjurations here. One is to give the impulse from below, since if there is no impulse from below there is no stirring above. Hence the words "Prophesy unto the wind" indicate the impulse from below, and the words "Prophesy, son of man, and say" to the impulse from above; for even after the impulse is given from below, that which is above receives from that which is higher still, wherefore the verse continues "Thus saith the Lord." The text then goes on: "Come from the four winds, O breath." The four winds are south, east, north, and west, and the breath comes from the west through its conjunction with the others, and from this source issue spirits and souls to take shape in human form. The next word, "breathe", indicates taking from one side and giving to another, in the same way as the sea takes and gives, and therefore "is not full" (Eccl. 1, 7).'

R. Eleazar put the following question to R. Simeon. 'Since it is known to God that men will die, why does He send souls down into the world?' He answered: 'This question has been discussed many times by the teachers, and they have answered it thus. God sends souls down to this world to declare His glory and takes them back afterwards. This mystery can be explained from the verse: "Drink water from thy cistern and flowing streams from the midst of thy well" (Prov. v, 15). As we have laid down, the term "cistern" designates the place from which the waters do not naturally flow. But they do flow when the soul is perfected in this world and ascends to the place to which it is attached, for then it is complete on all sides, above and below. When the soul ascends, the desire of the female is stirred towards the male, and then water flows from below upwards, and the cistern becomes a well of flowing waters, and then there is union and foundation and desire and friendship and harmony, since through the soul of the righteous that place has been completed, and the supernal love and affection has been stirred to form a union.'

Observe that Reuben and all the rest of the twelve tribes were linked with the Shekinah, and when Jacob saw the Shekinah by him, he called to his twelve sons to join it. From the beginning of the world there was never so perfect a couch as that of Jacob when he was about [235*b*] to depart from the world. Abraham was on his right, Isaac on his left, and he was lying between them with the Shekinah in front of him. When Jacob saw this, he called his sons and placed them round the Shekinah and arranged them in perfect order, so that the gathering was complete and many supernal chariots encompassed them. They then exclaimed: "Thine, O Lord, is the greatness and the power and the glory, etc." (1 Chron. XXIX, 11), whereupon the sun joined the moon and the east drew near to the west, and the moon was illumined and attained fullness, and so, as tradition tells us, "Jacob our father did not die." When Jacob saw such perfection as had never been vouchsafed to any other man, he rejoiced and praised God and blessed each of his sons with the appropriate blessing.

R. Jose and R. Jesse were once walking together, when the latter said: 'We have learnt that all the sons of Jacob were arranged in proper order and were blessed each one with the appropriate blessing. What, then, are we to make of the verse: "Out of Asher his bread shall be fat"?' He answered: 'I do not know, because I have not learnt this from the Holy Lamp. But let us both go to the Holy Lamp.' So they went, and when they came to R. Simeon they put their question to him. He said to them: 'Assuredly there is an esoteric meaning here. It is written: "Asher sat still at the haven of the sea, and abode by his creeks" (Judg. V, 17). He who dwells by the seashore has access to all luxuries, and Asher here signifies the supernal gate of *Ẓedek* (righteousness) when it receives blessings to transmit them to the world. This gate is always commissioned to send blessings to the world, and is called Asher, and it is one of the pillars upon which the world stands, and it repairs that place which is called "bread of affliction". This, then, is the meaning of the words "Out of Asher his bread is fat", that is to say, that which was bread of poverty becomes food of luxury, and hence the verse continues, "and he shall yield royal dainties": the giver here is the Community of Israel, by whom the king is fed with all luxuries, all blessings, all joy, and all goodness.' They said: 'If we had been born only to hear this, it would have been worth while.'

R. Hiya said: 'Reuben was entitled to all the rights of a

firstborn, but they were all taken from him and the kingship was given to Judah, the birthright to Joseph, and the priesthood to Levi. Hence it is written: "Unstable as water, thou shalt not excel" (*tothar*, lit. be left over); that is, thou shalt not retain them. In calling him "my might and the beginning of my strength", Jacob blessed him and entrusted him to God. He was like a king's friend who desired that the king should treat his son well, so one day he went out with his son and said to the king: "This is my son, the beloved of my soul"; whereupon the king understood that he was asking him to treat his son well. So Jacob said of Reuben, "thou art my firstborn, etc.", thus commending him to the King.

UNSTABLE AS WATER, THOU SHALT NOT HAVE THE EXCELLENCY. Here he indicated his subsequent fate, in not being left in the land, but cast outside.[1] In return, there was an angel appointed over his border from the side of the supernal Tabernacle, which is in charge of Michael (according to others, Gabriel), and Reuben was next to this, although the kingship belonged to Judah. R. Simeon said: 'The sons of Reuben are destined to wage two wars. It is written here "my strength", alluding to the captivity of Egypt, and "the beginning of my strength", alluding to their entry into the land of Canaan at the head of their brethren (Num. XXXII). The words "the excellency of dignity" (lit. removing) refer to the captivity of Assyria, which befell the sons of Gad and the sons of Reuben first of all; and they have suffered many evils without repenting up to now. The words "the excellency of power" refer to the time when the Messiah will appear, and they will go forth and make war and conquer all peoples, and mankind will tremble before them; [236*a*] and they will endeavour to seize the kingship, but will not retain it, not in any quarter of the world, the reason being, as the text says, "because thou wentest up to thy father's bed", this being a reference to Jerusalem. The sons of Reuben have been scattered in captivity to all four quarters of the world, having been taken captive four times, one referred to in the words "my might", the second in the words "the beginning of my

---

[1] Because the territory of Reuben was across the Jordan.

strength", the third in the words "excellency of dignity", and the fourth in the words "excellency of strength". Correspondingly, they are destined to make war in the four quarters of the world and to carry all before them, and to conquer many peoples and rule over them. Here was revealed his blessing, and what happened at that time and what was to happen when Israel entered the land, and what will happen at the time of the Messiah, as far as concerns Reuben.

SIMEON AND LEVI ARE BRETHREN. R. Isaac said: 'He joined them to the left side of the Shekinah, since he saw deeds of vengeance which the world could not endure.' R. Jose said: 'Where is their blessing?' R. Isaac answered: 'Simeon was not meet for a blessing, since Jacob saw that he had wrought much evil; nor was Levi, because he came from the side of stern justice, and blessing did not attach to him. Even Moses did not bless him directly, but left it to the Almighty, as it is written: "Bless, Lord, his substance and accept the work of his hands" (Deut. XXXIII, 11). It is written: "Yonder is the sea, great and wide, wherein are things creeping innumerable, both small and great beasts" (Ps. CIV, 25). The "sea" refers to the Shekinah, which stood over Jacob when he was about to depart from the world. It is called "great and wide" because all the world was compressed into it. There were "creeping things innumerable", because numbers of celestial holy angels are found there; while the "small and great beasts" refer to the twelve tribes, the sons of Jacob, of whom one was called a hind, one a wolf, one a lion, and one a lamb.' R. Isaac said: 'First a lion, then a lamb, then a wolf, then a kid, and so forth, so that there should be great and small beasts.' R. Judah said: 'Simeon was an ox and came before Judah, who was a lion, and the Companions have laid down that they faced one another, one on the right and one on the left. It was as if a man had a vicious ox and said: Let us put the figure of a lion in his stall so that he shall see it and be afraid of it. Simeon was not meet for blessing, but Moses joined him to Judah, saying: "Hear, O Lord, the voice of Judah"; the word "hear" alluding to Simeon, at whose birth his mother said "For the Lord hath heard that

I am hated." ' Said R. Judah: 'The blessing of Simeon and Levi was left by their father to Moses. Let us also leave this question to the Holy Lamp.' So they went and asked R. Simeon. He said: 'How glad I am you have asked me.' He then clapped his hands and wept, saying: 'Who shall ope thine eyes, thou holy mirror of faith ! Thou hast excelled in thy lifetime all the sons of men, thou hast excelled them in thy death, when thy likeness is effaced. The keys of thy Master have ever been delivered into thy hands. Observe now. Jacob had four wives and begat sons from all of them. [236b] When he was about to die the Shekinah stood over him. He sought to bless these two, but he was not able, being afraid of the Shekinah. He said: "What shall I do, seeing that both of them are from the side of stern judgement ? And if I try to force the Shekinah, I shall not be able, for I have had four wives, which are a complete portion. I will leave them to the master of the house and he will do as he pleases." He also said: "I have taken my share of wives and children in this world and have had my fill; how, then, shall I press the matron more ? I will therefore leave the matter to the master of the matron and he will do what he pleases without fear." Hence it is written: "Now this is the blessing wherewith Moses the man of God blessed" (Deut. xxxiii, 1). The term "man" here designates Moses as the master of the house and the master of the matron. Hence Moses blessed whom he pleased without fear, as we have affirmed.'

O MY SOUL, COME NOT THOU INTO THEIR COUNCIL. R. Abba discoursed on the verse: *The secret of the Lord is for them that fear him.* ' "The secret of the Lord" ', he said, 'is the recondite doctrine of the Torah which God only gives to those who fear sin, and it is the sign of the holy covenant. Simeon and Levi insisted that the men of Shechem should circumcise themselves and accept this secret, and the Scripture tells us that it was "with guile". Later, Zimri, the son of Salu, who was of the tribe of Simeon, nullified this secret. Hence Jacob said: "Let not my soul enter into their secret" —that soul which entered into the supernal covenant above and was called "the bundle of life". UNTO THEIR ASSEMBLY,

MY GLORY BE NOT THOU UNITED. This has been explained to refer to the assembly of Korah (Num. XVI, 19). "My honour" here refers to the honour of the people of Israel in general, and therefore their father did not bless them, but left them to Moses.' I WILL DIVIDE THEM IN JACOB. R. Hiya said: 'From this verse we learn that these two tribes were never again united, and so it was meet, and there is no generation in which their punishment does not descend upon the world, and great is the number of beggars among them.'

JUDAH, THEE SHALL THY BRETHEN PRAISE, THY HAND SHALL BE ON THE NECK OF THY ENEMIES. R. Jose discoursed here on the verse: *He made the moon for seasons* (Ps. CIV, 19). 'God', he said, 'made the moon for us to sanctify by it new moons and new years. Now the moon never shines except from the reflection of the sun, and when the sun is aloft the moon does not appear, but only when the sun is gathered in does the moon rule the heavens, and the moon is of no account save when the sun is gathered in. God made both of them to give light and also "for signs", to wit, Sabbaths, "and for seasons", to wit, festivals, "and for days", to wit, new moons, "and for years", to wit, New Year days, so that the Gentiles should reckon by the sun and Israel by the moon. This accords with R. Eleazar's exposition of the verse: "Thou hast multiplied the nation, thou hast increased its joy" (Is. IX, 2), where he refers "nation" to Israel and "it" to the moon, which gained accession of light for the sake of Israel. Which are superior, Israel or the Gentiles? Assuredly, the moon [237a] is highest, and the sun of the Gentiles is under this moon, and this sun derives light from this moon. See, then, the difference between Israel and the nations. Israel cling to the moon and are linked with the supernal sun, and are attached to the place which gives light to the supernal sun, as it is written: "But ye who cleave to the Lord, are alive every one of you this day" (Deut. IV, 4).'

JUDAH, THEE SHALL THY BRETHREN PRAISE. R. Simeon said: 'The kingship was assigned to Judah; and hence Leah, as we have explained, said at the time of his birth: "This time I shall praise the Lord", because he was the fourth, the fourth leg of the throne. The letters *yod, hé, vau* of his name are the impress of the supernal name, and they were completed by a *daleth*, which represents the second *hé* of the sacred name, so that this name is found completely in Judah's name. Hence "Thy brethren shall praise thee", because the kingship is meet to remain with thee. Verily, "Judah still walketh with God, and is faithful with the holy ones" (Hosea, XI, 12). These holy ones are the supernal angels, who all acknowledge him and call him faithful. Therefore he is first in everything, and king over all.' R. Simeon discoursed on the verse: "The all-honoured daughter of the king is within" (Ps. XLV, 14). 'The "all-honoured one" is the Community of Israel, who is called the daughter of the king, the supreme King, who is within, because there is another king who is not so far within. The "clothing" of this honoured daughter of the king is "inwrought with gold", because she is clothed and encompassed with supernal might (*Geburah*), which also is called "king". On this account the earth is established, namely, when she takes hold of judgement, and this we call "the kingdom of heaven". Judah took hold of this and inherited the kingdom of the earth.'

R. Judah and R. Isaac were once travelling together. Said R. Isaac: 'Let us discourse on the Torah as we go along.' He began with the text: *And he drove out the man, and he placed at the east of the garden of Eden, etc.* 'The word *vayegaresh* (and he drove out)', he said, 'may, the Companions have explained, be translated "and he divorced". The accusative particle *eth* here has an esoteric meaning. Adam was punished for his sin, and brought death upon himself and all the world, and caused that tree in regard to which he sinned to be driven out along with him and his descendants for ever. It says further that God "placed the cherubim on the east of the garden of Eden"; these were the lower cherubim, for as there are cherubim above, so there are cherubim below, and he spread this tree over them. The "flame of a sword" refers to the flames of fire which issue from that flashing sword. It is said to "turn every way" because it sucks from two sides, and turns from one side to another. Another explanation is that the flames turn about, being sometimes men and sometimes women.' Said R. Judah: 'This is certainly correct, that Adam caused that tree through which he sinned to be driven out; and so, also, do other men, as it is written: "Through your transgressions your mother is sent away" (Is. L, 1). Still you are right, that the word *eth* refers to the perfection of man, and from that day the moon was impaired until Noah came and entered the ark. Then came sinners, and it was impaired again until Abraham came, and it was established perfectly through Jacob and his sons, and Judah came and took hold on it, and seized the kingship and took possession of it as an everlasting inheritance for himself and his sons after him.'

JUDAH, THEE SHALL THY BRETHREN PRAISE. When Israel were at the Red Sea, they all praised him and entered after him into the sea. THY HAND SHALL BE ON THE NECK OF THY ENEMIES, as it says, "Judah shall go up first" (Judg. I, 2). THE SONS OF THY FATHER SHALL BOW DOWN TO THEE: this includes all the other tribes, even though from other mothers. And even when Israel was split into two kingdoms, when the people went up to Jerusalem they used to bow down to the king there, because the kingship in Jerusalem [237b] was derived from the holy kingdom. SHALL BOW DOWN BEFORE THEE. They only, but not other peoples, who will only bow down at the time of the Messiah. But here the expression only indicates Israel, all of whom would bow down to the Exilarch in Babylon, but not other peoples.

JUDAH IS A LION'S WHELP: first he will be a whelp, and then a lion, corresponding to the transition from "lad"[1] to "man", as it is written: "The Lord is a man of war" (Ex. XV, 3). FROM THE PREY, MY SON, THOU ART GONE UP. The word "prey" includes the angel of death, who preys upon mankind. From that prey the Shekinah shook itself free. It "stooped down" in the captivity of Babylon, it "couched" in the captivity of Edom, "as a lion" which is

---

[1] i.e. Metatron.

strong and as a "lioness" which is stronger. So Israel are strong, because though the Gentiles entice and oppress them, they adhere to their laws and their customs like a lion and a lioness. So, too, the Shekinah, which, although it is fallen, remains strong like a lion and a lioness. For just as these crouch only to spring upon their prey, which they smell from afar, so the Shekinah only crouches to take vengeance on idolaters and to spring upon them. WHO SHALL ROUSE HIM UP. He will not rise to take any petty vengeance. The word "who" (*Mi*) here indicates the supernal world, which has dominion over all; it is similarly used in the verse "From the womb of whom (*Mi*) came the ice" (Job XXXVIII, 29), as we have explained.

THE SCEPTRE SHALL NOT DEPART FROM JUDAH, ETC. The word *Shiloh*, here, is spelt with both a *yod* and a *hé*, to allude to the holy supernal name, *Yah*, by which the Shekinah shall rise; and this is also the allusion of *Mi*, as we have said.

R. Hiya discoursed on the verse: *The Lord shall keep thee from all evil, he shall keep thy soul.* 'The words "He shall keep thee",' he said, 'refer to this world, and "he shall keep thy soul" to the next world. By "keeping in this world" is meant that a man is protected from many evil accusers who seek to bring charges against him and to cling fast to him. By preservation in the next world is meant, as we have explained, that when a man departs from this world, if he is virtuous his soul ascends and is crowned in its place, and if not, numbers of demons are at hand to drag him to Gehinnom and to deliver him into the hands of Duma, who has been made chief of demons, and who has twelve thousand myriads of attendants all charged to punish the souls of sinners. There are in Gehinnom seven circuits and seven gates, each with several gate-keepers under their own chief. The souls of sinners are delivered by Duma to those gate-keepers, who then close the gates of flaming fire. There are gates behind gates, the outer ones remaining open while the inner ones are closed. On Sabbath, however, they are all open, and the sinners go forth, as far as the outer gates, where they meet other souls which tarry there. When Sabbath goes out, a herald proclaims at each gate: "Let the wicked return to Sheol." Now God protects the souls of the righteous from being delivered into the hands of Duma, and that is the meaning of the words "he shall keep thy soul." ' [238*a*]

BINDING HIS FOAL UNTO THE VINE. The vine is the Community of Israel, so called also in the verse: "Thou didst remove a vine from Egypt" (Ps. LXXX, 9). By "his foal" is meant the Messiah, who is destined to rule over all the hosts of the peoples, that is to say, the heavenly hosts who have charge of the Gentiles, and from whom they derive their strength. The Messiah will prevail over them, because this vine dominates all those lower crowns through which the Gentiles have dominion. This will be the victory above. Israel, who are "a choice vine", will conquer and destroy other hosts below; and the Messiah will prevail over all. Hence it is written of him that he will be "poor and riding on an ass and on a young ass's colt" (Zech. IX, 9). "Colt" and "ass" are two crowns by virtue of which the Gentiles have dominion, and they are from the left side, the side of uncleanness. It is strange that the Messiah should be called "poor". R. Simeon explained that it is because he has nothing of his own, and he is compared to the holy moon above, which has no light save from the sun. This Messiah will have dominion and will be established in his place. Below he is "poor", because he is of the side of the moon, and above he is poor, being a "mirror which does not radiate", "the bread of poverty". Yet withal he "rides upon an ass and upon a colt", to overthrow the strength of the Gentiles; and God will keep him firm.

HE HATH WASHED HIS GARMENT IN WINE. With this may be compared the verse: "Who is this that cometh from Edom, with dyed garments from Bozrah ?" (Is. LXIII, 1); and also: "I have trodden the winepress alone, etc." (*Ibid.* 3). "Wine" here alludes to the side of *Geburah*, of stern justice which will be visited on the idolatrous nations. AND HIS VESTURE IN THE BLOOD OF GRAPE. This is the lower-world tree, the judgement court which is called "grapes", in which the "wine" is kept. Thus the Messiah will be clothed in both to crush beneath him all the idolatrous peoples and kings.

R. Jose discoursed on the verse: "And on the vine were three branches, and it was as though it budded and its blossoms shot forth." 'How little', he said, 'do men care for the glory of their Master or pay heed to the words of the Torah! At first prophecy was vouchsafed to men, and through it they knew the glory of God. When prophecy ceased, they had a *bath-kol*[1], but now they have nothing but dreams. Dream is a lower grade, being one-sixtieth of prophecy, and it is vouchsafed to everyone, since it comes from the left side. It comes down in various grades, and is shown even to sinners and even to Gentiles. Sometimes the dream is carried by evil demons who make mock of men and show them false things; and sometimes it is sent to sinners and tells them things of importance. Now this sinner, Pharaoh's butler, saw a true dream. The vine represented the Community of Israel, which was called by the psalmist "this vine" (Ps. LXXX, 15). The three branches have the same reference as the three flocks of sheep which Jacob saw by the well. (Gen. XXIX, 2). Its blossoming typifies the time of Solomon, when the moon was illumined. The buds represent the lower Jerusalem, or, according to another explanation, the grade which is over it and gives sustenance to it. [238b] The clusters thereof brought forth ripe grapes, in which to keep the precious wine. All this was seen by that sinner. Further, he saw the cup of Pharaoh in his hands; this is the cup of confusion which sucks in from the court of judgement and which issued from the grapes that were given to Pharaoh; and he drank it as it was, on account of Israel. When Joseph heard this he rejoiced, remarking the truth which the dream contained, and therefore he gave it a good interpretation. Thus the words "binding his foal unto the vine" indicate that all the forces of the Gentiles are to be subdued beneath

---

[1] Lit. "daughter of a voice". According to the Rabbis, on certain occasions during the period of the Second Temple, a voice issued from heaven to give the Jewish people guidance or warning; and this was called by them *bath-kol*.

that vine, as we have said, their power being bound up and subdued.' R. Simeon said: 'There are two kinds of vine. There is the holy celestial vine, and there is the vine which is called "the vine of Sodom, the strange vine"; and therefore Israel is called "this vine". And when Israel sinned and abandoned "this vine", then it was said of them: "For from the vine of Sodom is their vine" (Deut. XXXIII, 32).'

As R. Judah and R. Isaac were once travelling together, the former said: 'Let us turn into this field, as it is more level.' They did so, and as they went along R. Judah said: 'It is written: "She is not afraid of the snow for her household, for all her household are clothed in scarlet." This verse has been expounded by our colleague, R. Hizkiah, who said that sinners are punished in Gehinnom twelve months, half with fire and half with snow. When they go into the fire, they say: "This is really Gehinnom." When they go into the snow, they say: "This is the real winter of the Almighty." They begin by exclaiming "Alas", and then they exclaim "Woe". The supreme punishment is with snow. Not so Israel, however, of whom it is written: "She is not afraid of the snow for her household", because "all her household are clothed with scarlet". The word *shanim* (scarlet) here may be read *shnaim* (two), referring to pairs of precepts such as circumcision and uncovering, fringes and phylacteries, *mezuzahs* and *Hanukah* lights, etc. The word "scarlet" may also be taken to indicate the robe of judgement, which is assumed for the punishment of idolaters. For one day God will put on a red robe and take a red sword to take vengeance on the ruddy one.[1] This we learn from the verse: "Who is this that cometh from Edom with dyed garments, etc." ' R. Isaac said: 'We may also take the word *shanim* to mean "years", and to refer to the whole of past time, since the Community of Israel is the consummation of the ages and draws sustenance from all sides.'

As they were going along, they met a boy leading an ass on which an old man was riding. Said the old man to the boy: 'My son, repeat me a passage of Scripture.' He answered: 'I have more than one passage. But come down or let me ride

[1]Esau.

in front of you, and I will repeat some to you.' He said: 'I am old and you are young, and I do not want to put myself on a level with you.' Said the boy: 'If so, why is it you ask me to recite my verses?' He said: 'To make the journey more agreeable.' Said the boy: 'This old man can go and hang himself. Ignoramus as he is, he must needs ride and will not descend to my level, forsooth!' So he left the old man and went his way. When R. Judah and R. Isaac came up, he joined them. They asked who he was, and he told them what had happened. Said R. Judah to him: 'You did quite rightly. Come with us and we will sit down over there and you will tell us something.' He said to them: 'I am very weary, [239*a*] because I have not eaten to-day.' So they took out some food and gave him, and a miracle happened and they found a small stream of water under a tree from which he drank, and they also drank and sat down. The boy then quoted the text: "To David. Fret not thyself because of evil doers, neither be thou envious against them that work unrighteousness" (Ps. XXXVII, 1). He said: 'This is neither a song nor a prayer, but the superscription "To David" shows that it was spoken by the Holy Spirit, which thus admonished David: "Do not challenge the wicked, because thou knowest not if thou hast strength to prevail against him; perhaps he is a tree which has never been uprooted[1] and thou wilt be repulsed by him. Also, do not look at the works of those who do unrighteousness, so that thou shouldst not need to be indignant with them; for whoever sees their works and is not zealous for God transgresses three negative precepts, namely: "Thou shalt have no strange gods before me"; "Thou shalt not make to thee any graven image"; and "Thou shalt not bow down to them nor serve them." Therefore a man should keep away from them. That is why I have left the old man and taken a different path. Now that I have found you I will expound the Scripture in your presence.'

He then discoursed on the text: *And he called unto Moses, etc.* (Lev. I, 1). He said: 'The *aleph* of the word *vayikra* (and he called) is written small in the scroll, to show that this

---

[1] i.e. perhaps his soul is the first time on earth and thine the second time.

calling was not a perfect one, because it was only in the Tabernacle and in a strange land, perfection being only found in the Holy Land. Further, in the Tabernacle there was only the Shekinah, but in the land there was the complete union of Male and Female. When a king sits on his throne wearing the royal crown, he is called Great King, but when he comes down from his throne and visits his servant, he is called Little King. So God, as long as He is on high over all, is called Supreme King, but when He brings His abode below, He is simply King, not Supreme as before. The word "called", as we have learnt, means that he summoned him to his sanctuary. The "tent of meeting" (*mo'ed*=also appointed time) means the tent on which depends the reckoning of seasons, festivals, and sabbaths, this being none other than the moon. The word "saying" (*lemor*, lit. to say) indicates the disclosing of what hitherto was concealed; and so in all places where it occurs (e.g. "And God spoke unto Moses, saying"), it means that permission is given to disclose. It is written just before: "And they brought the tabernacle to Moses" (Ex. XXXIX, 33). The reason why the Israelites brought the Tabernacle to Moses when they had finished it was because God had shown him the whole plan of it on Mount Sinai; so now they brought it to him in order that he might see whether it corresponded to the plan which he had seen. It was as if a king had given orders for a palace to be built for his queen, and had charged the builders to make one room here and one there, here a bed-chamber and there a sitting-room, and so when the builders finished they showed it all to the king. So the Israelites brought the Tabernacle to Moses, who was the "master of the house", the "man of God". When the sanctuary was finished, the queen invited the king to it, and invited also her husband, that is to say, Moses the master of the house. Hence Moses was able to "take the tent and pitch it outside" (Ex. XXXIII, 7), [239b] a thing which no one else could possibly have done. The text continues: "And the Lord spoke to him", "the Lord" being another still higher grade.'

He further discoursed as follows. 'The text continues: *When any man of you shall offer* (Lev. I, 2). The word "man" (*Adam*) here indicates the union of the sun and the moon.

"When he shall offer from you": this is a hint that he who desires to make his service of sacrifice truly acceptable should not be unmarried. "An offering to the Lord": this means that he should offer the whole for the purpose of uniting upper and lower. "From the cattle": to show man and beast as one. "From the oxen and from the sheep": these are the chariots which are clean. "Ye shall offer your offering": the "offering to the Lord" mentioned above was man, but "your offering" is from the cattle, from the herds and the flocks, to display the union of upper with lower and of lower with upper. If a king is sitting on a throne on a very high dais, then one who brings a present to the king has to mount from step to step until he reaches the top, the place where the king is sitting above all, and then it is known that that present is meant for the king. But when the present comes down from the top, then all know that the king is sending it from above to his friend who is below. So at first a man rises step by step from below upwards; this is "the offering of the Lord". Then he comes down step by step: and this is "your offering".' R. Isaac and R. Judah went up to him and kissed his forehead. They said: 'Blessed be God who has favoured us with this, blessed is God that these words have not been wasted on that old man.'

They then rose and went on. As they proceeded, they saw a vine in a garden. The boy then quoted the verse: "Binding his foal to the vine and his ass's colt to the choice vine." He said: 'The word *oseri* (binding) is written here with a superfluous *yod*, and the word *'iro* (his colt) with *hé* instead of *vau*. Thus the Holy Name *Yah* is hinted here. Similarly with the words *bni* (colt) and *sorekah* (choice vine). All this is to show that just as there is a Holy Name to subdue the "foal", so there is a Holy Name to subdue another power, which is called "ass"; for if the Holy Name were not hinted here, they would devastate the world. The "vine", as we have said, is the Community of Israel. It is called vine because just as the vine will receive no graft from another tree, so the Community of Israel accepts no master but God, and therefore all other powers are subdued before her, and cannot obtain dominion over her. "He hath washed his garments in wine", even from the time of the Creation the reference being to the coming of the Messiah on earth. "Wine" indicates the left side, and "the blood of grapes" the left side below. The Messiah is destined [240a] to rule above over all the forces of the idolatrous nations and to break their power above and below. We may also explain that as wine brings joyfulness and yet typifies judgement, so the Messiah will bring gladness to Israel, but judgement to the Gentiles. The "spirit of God which hovered over the face of the waters" (Gen. I, 2) is the spirit of the Messiah, and from the time of the Creation he "washed his garments in celestial wine". "His eyes shall be red with wine": this is the intoxicating celestial wine from which the masters of the Torah drink. "And his teeth white with milk", because the Torah is both wine and milk, the Oral and the Written Law. It is written of wine that it "rejoiceth the heart of man" (Ps. CIV, 15). Wine at first brings gladness, being the place from which all gladness issues, but afterwards it brings punishment, because its end is the place where is gathered all punishment. Hence the verse continues: "And oil to make the face shine", to wit, from the place from which all gladness issues. It then says: "And bread that strengtheneth man's heart", bread being the support of mankind. It is not, however, the only support, because there is no night without day, and they must not be separated. If so, it may be asked, why did David say that "bread supports the heart of man"? The answer is that this is why he added the word "and" before "bread", to show that the others are included. Observe that grace after meals should not be said over an empty table, but there should be bread on it and a cup of wine, and the wine should be taken in the right hand, in order to join the Left hand to the Right, and in order that the bread should be blessed by them and linked with them, so that the whole should be linked together to bless the Holy Name fittingly. For the bread being joined with the wine, and the wine with the right hand, blessings rest on the world and the table is duly perfected.' Said R. Isaac: 'Had we come on this journey only to hear these words, it would have been worth our while.' R. Judah said: 'This lad has no right to know so much, and I am afraid he will not live long.'

'Why?' said R. Isaac. 'Because', he answered, 'he is able to see into a place which man has no right to look upon, and I am afraid that before he reaches maturity he will actually look and be punished for it.' The lad heard them and said: 'I have no fear of punishment, because when my father died he blessed me and prayed for me, and I know that the merit of my father will protect me.' They said to him: 'Who, then, is your father?' 'R. Judah, the son of Rab Hamnuna the Elder,' he replied. They then took him up and carried him on their shoulders three miles, applying to him the verse: "Out of the eater came forth meat, and out of the strong came forth sweetness" (Judg. xv, 14). The boy said to them: 'Since you have quoted the verse, expound it.' Said they to him: 'Since God has led us into the path of life, do you tell us.' He then began: 'We find a certain mystical allusion in this verse. The eater is the *Zaddik*, as it is written: "The *Zaddik* eats his fill" (Prov. xii, 25). By "his fill" is meant that he gives sufficiency to the place which is called the Soul of David. "From the eater comes forth food", for but for that *Zaddik* food would never come forth and the world could not exist. "Out of the strong came forth sweetness": this is Isaac, who blessed Jacob with the dew of heaven and the fatness of the earth. We may also explain that were it not for the rigour of justice there would come forth no honey, to wit, the Oral Law, [240b] which comes forth from the Written Law, which is called "strong", as it is written: "The Lord shall give strength to his people" (Ps. xxix, 11).' They went on together for three days till they reached the court where his mother lived. When she saw them she made preparations for them and they stayed with her two days. They then said farewell to him, and departed, and came and related everything to R. Simeon. He said: 'Truly, he has inherited the Torah, and if not for the merit of his fathers he would be punished from above. But for those who follow the Torah God has made it an inheritance to them and their descendants forever, as it is written: "But as for me, this is my covenant with them, saith the Lord, my spirit which is upon thee, etc." (Is. lix, 21).'

ZEBULON SHALL DWELL AT THE HAVEN OF THE SEA,
ETC. R. Abba discoursed on the verse: *Gird thy sword upon
thy thigh, O mighty One, thy glory and thy majesty*. He said:
'Is this glory and majesty, to gird on weapons and to practise
the use of them? To study the Torah and to fight battles in
the Torah and to arm oneself with it—this is praiseworthy,
this is glory and majesty. The truth of the matter, however,
is this. God has given men the sign of a holy covenant, and
imprinted it upon them for them to preserve and not impair
in any way. He who impairs it is confronted with the sword
which avenges the insult to the covenant. Now he who desires
to preserve this place should brace himself up to meet the
evil prompter, and when the latter assails him should set
before his eyes this sword, which is girded on the thigh to
punish those who impair this place. Hence it says: "Gird
thy sword upon thy thigh, O mighty One." Such a one is
called "mighty", and hence it is his "glory and majesty".
Another explanation is that before setting out on a journey a
man should prepare himself with prayer and arm himself
with righteousness, which is the supernal sword, as it is
written: "Righteousness shall go before him, and (then) he
shall set his steps on the way" (Ps. LXXXV, 14). Now Zebulon
used always to go out on the roads and highways and make
war, and used first to arm himself with this celestial sword
of prayer and supplication, and so he fought with peoples
and overcame them. You may say that this was the function
of Judah, so why is it assigned here to Zebulon?

Observe this. The twelve tribes are the adornment of the
Matron. When Jacob was about to depart from the world,
and saw that he was perfected on every side, with Abraham
at his right, Isaac at his left, himself in the centre, and the
Shekinah in front of him, he called his sons round him in
order that both the lower and the upper might be fitly
adorned. . . . [241*a*] The twelve tribes correspond to the
twelve oxen which were under the sea of bronze made by
Solomon (1 Kings VII, 23 *sqq*.), three for each of the cardinal
points. Three of them represented the right Arm, three the
left Arm, three the right Thigh, and three the left Thigh.
There were three tribes for each, because in each of these

limbs there are three joints. And although this "adornment"
was only complete with the number of six hundred thousand,
yet already at the time of Jacob's death there were the
seventy souls who had come down with him to Egypt and the
very numerous progeny whom they had already produced in
the seventeen years they had been there. Happy the portion
of Jacob who was perfected above and below. [241*b*]

R. Judah said: 'Zebulon and Issachar made an agreement
that one should sit and study the Torah while the other went
out and made money and supported him. So Zebulon used
to traverse the seas with merchandise, and his territory was
suitable for this, being on the sea coast. Hence it is written:
"Rejoice, Zebulon, in thy going out, and Issachar in thy
tents" (Deut. XXXIII, 18).' HE SHALL DWELL AT THE
HAVEN OF THE SEAS: that is to say, among those who sail
the sea with merchandise. "At the haven of the seas": the
plural "seas" is used, because although only one coast
belonged to him, yet he dwelt by two. R. Jose said it is because traders from all other seas used to visit his coast.
AND HE SHALL BE FOR A HAVEN OF SHIPS: that is, the
place where all ships come to do trade. AND HIS BORDER
SHALL BE UPON ZIDON. R. Hizkiah said: 'His territory
stretched to the boundary of Zidon, and all merchants came
to that place to trade.' R. Aha said: 'It is written: "Neither
shalt thou suffer the salt of the covenant of thy God to be
lacking from thy meal-offering; with all thine oblations thou
shalt offer salt." Salt was to be used because it softens bitter-
ness, and so mankind cannot do without it. Salt is the covenant upon which the world is established: hence it is called
"the covenant of thy God".' R. Hiya said: 'It is written:
"For God is righteous, he loves righteousness" (Ps. XI, 7).
This is the salt in the sea, and he who separates them brings
death upon himself. Hence it is written: "Thou shalt not
suffer salt to be lacking." ' R. Aha said: 'The sea is all one,
but it is called "seas" because in some places the water is
clear (and in some turbid), in some sweet, and in some bitter;
hence we speak of "seas".'

R. Abba was sitting one night and studying the Torah,
when R. Jose came and knocked at his door. He said: 'When

the prince sits with the chief, then true judgement is given.'
So they sat down and studied the Torah. Meanwhile the son
of their host got up and sat before them. He said to them:
'What is the meaning of the verse: "Ye will save alive my
father and my mother, etc.", and just before, "And give me a
true token" (Jos. II, 13–12) ? What did Rahab ask of the spies ?'
R. Abba said: 'That is a good question; if you know an
answer, tell me, my son.' He said: 'A further question arises
from the fact that they gave her something which she did
not ask for, since they said to her: "Thou shalt bind this line
of scarlet thread in the window, etc." The explanation I have
learnt is this. She asked for a sign of life, as it is written, "And
ye will save alive my father, etc." She said: "A sign of life is
only contained in the sign of truth, which is the letter *Vau*."
In fact, as I have learnt, she asked for the sign of Moses.
They, however, gave her a line of scarlet thread, because they
said: "Moses is dead, and the sun is gathered in and the time
has come for the moon to rule. Therefore we had better give
you the sign of the moon, which is this line of scarlet thread.
Thus the sign of Joshua shall be with you, because the moon
is now in the ascendant." ' R. Abba and R. Jose rose [242*a*]
and kissed him, saying: 'Assuredly, you will one day be a
head of a college or a great man in Israel'; and, in fact, he
became R. Bun.

He then asked a further question, saying: 'Seeing that the
twelve tribes were arranged below in the same order as
above, why is Zebulon everywhere placed before Issachar in
the blessings, although Issachar devoted himself to the
Torah, which should always come first ? The reason is that
Zebulon took out of his own mouth and gave to Issachar.
From this we learn that he who supports a student of the
Torah is blessed from above and below, and not only so, but
he is privileged to eat of two tables, a privilege granted to no
other man. He is granted wealth in this world, and he is
granted a portion in the next world. Hence it says of Zebulon,
that "he shall dwell at the haven of the sea", that is to say,
in this world, "and shall be for a haven of ships", in the future
world.

He here quoted the verse: "I adjure you, O daughters of

Jerusalem, by the roes and by the hinds of the fields, if you find my beloved, what will you tell him ?" (S. S. v, 8). Why, it may be asked, should the Community of Israel speak thus, seeing that she is near to the king, like no other ? The "daughters of Jerusalem", however, are the souls of the righteous, which are constantly near the King, and inform him every day of the requirements of the Matron. For so we have learnt, that when the soul comes down into the world, the Community of Israel makes it swear that it will tell the King her love for him in order to appease him. This appeasement is brought about when man unifies the Holy Name with his mouth, his heart and his soul, to link all together like flame with fire. According to another explanation, the "daughters of Jerusalem" are the twelve tribes, as we have learnt that Jerusalem is established on twelve rocks, three on each side (wherefore it is called *Ḥayah* (living one)), and these are called "the daughters of Jerusalem", and they testify to the King concerning the Community of Israel, as it is written: "The tribes of the Lord are a testimony unto Israel, to give thanks unto the name of the Lord" (Ps. cxxii, 4).' Said R. Judah: 'Happy are Israel who know the ways of God and of whom it is written: "For thou art a holy people unto the Lord thy God, and thee did the Lord choose, etc." (Deut. xiv, 2).'

ISSACHAR IS A STRONG ASS COUCHING DOWN BETWEEN THE SHEEPFOLDS. R. Eleazar said: 'Why should Issachar, because he studied the Torah, be called an ass, rather than a horse, or a lion, or a leopard ? The answer given is that the ass bears a burden patiently and does not kick like other animals, and is not fastidious and will lie down anywhere. So Issachar bears the burden of the Torah and does not kick against the Almighty, and is not fastidious and cares not for his own honour but for the honour of his Master. He therefore "couches between the sheepfolds", as we say of the student of the Torah that he is "willing to sleep on the ground".[1] He also, in explanation of this verse, quoted the text: "To David. The Lord is my light and my salvation, whom shall I fear ? The Lord is the strength of my life, of

---

[1] *v. Ethics of the Fathers*, vi, 4.

whom shall I be afraid ?" (Ps. XXVII, 1). 'Those who study the Torah', he said, 'are beloved before God, so that they have no fear of evil hap, being protected above and below. Nay more, [242b] such a one subdues all evil haps and casts them down into the great abyss. At nightfall the doors are closed, and dogs and asses commence to roam about the world with permission to do damage. Men sleep on their beds and the souls of the righteous ascend to the bliss above. When the north wind awakes at midnight, then there is a holy stirring in the world, as has been explained in many places. Happy is he who rises at that hour and studies the Torah. For as soon as he begins, all those evil beings are cast by him into the great abyss and he binds the ass and throws him down into the dung-heap. Therefore Issachar, who was a student of the Torah, bound the ass and brought him down from the ladder which he had mounted to do injury to the world, and made him abide between the sheepfolds, that is, in the dung-heap.'

AND HE SAW REST THAT IT WAS GOOD, AND THE LAND THAT IT WAS PLEASANT, AND HE BOWED HIS SHOULDER TO BEAR, AND BECAME A SERVANT UNDER TASK WORK. "Rest" here signifies the Written Law; "the land" signifies the Oral Law; "he bowed his shoulder to bear", namely the yoke of the Law, and to cleave to it day and night; and he "became a servant under task work", to be a worshipper of the Holy One, blessed be He, and to cleave to Him. R. Simeon and R. Jose and R. Hiya were once travelling from Upper Galilee to Tiberias. Said R. Simeon: 'Let us discuss the Torah as we go, for whoever is able to discuss the Torah and does not do so renders his life forfeit, and is further subjected to the burden of worldly cares and the domination of others. This we learn from the verse which says of Issachar that "he turned aside his shoulder from bearing", that is to say, from bearing the yoke of the Law, and straightway "he became a servant under task work". Happy are those that study the Law, for they obtain favour above and below and every day win the inheritance of the future world, as it is written: "To cause them that love me to inherit substance (*yesh*)" (Prov. VIII, 21), which means the future world. For his waters never fail and he receives a good reward above such as is earned by no other man. This is hinted in the name of Issachar, which we may divide into *yesh sachar* (*yesh* is the reward), as much as to say, *yesh* (substance) is the reward of those who study the Torah.

It is written: "I beheld till thrones were placed and one that was ancient of days did sit, etc." (Dan. VII, 9). When the Temple was destroyed, two thrones fell, that is, two above and two below. Two above, because the lower was removed from the upper, the throne of Jacob from the throne of David, and the throne of David fell. The two thrones below are Jerusalem and the students of the Torah, the latter corresponding to the throne of Jacob and the former to the throne of David. Hence it says that "thrones" were cast down, and not merely one throne, and all on account of the neglect of the Torah. Observe that when the truly pious study the Torah, all the mighty ones of other peoples and other forces are humbled and their power broken, and they have no dominion in the world, and Israel are raised above all. But if not, the ass causes Israel to go into captivity and to fall into the hands of the peoples and to be ruled by them. Why is this? Because "he saw rest that it was good", and that he could obtain from it many comforts and enjoyments, and he perverted his path so as not to bear the yoke of the Torah, and therefore he "became a servant under task work". [243*a*] Only through him was the knowledge of the Torah kept alive in Israel, as it says: "And of the sons of Issachar were those who had knowledge of the times, etc." (I Chron. XII, 32), and it was they who "caused all delights to be at our doors", to wit, the doors of synagogues and houses of study, "both new and old", because many old and new lessons of the Torah were brought to light by them to bring Israel near to their Father in heaven. "My beloved, I have kept hidden for thee": from this we learn that when one studies the Torah fittingly and knows how to draw the proper lessons from it, his words ascend to the throne of the King and the Community of Israel opens the gates before them and treasures them, and when God enters the Garden of Eden to disport Himself with the righteous, She brings them out before Him and God contemplates them and rejoices; and then God is crowned with noble crowns and rejoices in the Matron, and from that time the words are written in the book. Up to this point extends the sway of Judah, the arm that contained the strength of all sides, the three joints of the arm which enable it to prevail over all.

DAN SHALL JUDGE HIS PEOPLE AS ONE OF THE TRIBES OF ISRAEL. R. Hiya said: 'We should have expected here, "Dan shall judge the tribes of Israel", or "Dan shall judge the tribes of Israel as one." What is the meaning of "Dan shall judge his people"? We may explain as follows. Dan was the "rearward of the camps" (Num. x, 25), because he was the left thigh and went last. For after Judah and Reuben had set forth, the Levites and the Ark made an interval, as it were, and only after them did the standard of Ephraim set forth on the west, being the right thigh. We might have thought that Zebulon should have marched first, since it is written of him: "And his thigh is unto Zidon." But the truth is that Judah comprised all, being the lower kingdom, for just as the upper kingdom comprises all, so does the lower kingdom, both body and thigh, becoming thereby exceedingly strong. The first corps comprised Judah, the kingdom which derives from the side of Might (*Geburah*), combined with the right hand, the body and the thigh. The second corps was that of Reuben, who was on the south side, which is on the right, and all the power of the right was taken by Judah, because Reuben lost the kingship, and thus Judah was reinforced with the strength of Reuben. The third corps was that of Ephraim, who was the right thigh, which always goes before the left. Thus Dan, who was the left thigh, marched last. We read that "Solomon made a great throne of ivory" (1 Kings x, 18). This throne was after the supernal pattern and contained all celestial figures, and therefore it is written: "And Solomon sat on the throne of the Lord as king" (1 Chron. XXIX, 23), and so also "Solomon sat on the throne of David his father and his kingdom was established greatly" (1 Kings II, 12), because the moon was at its full.'

"Dan shall judge his people" at first, and then "the tribes of Israel as one", that is, as the one Being of the World. [243*b*] This was realized in Samson, who single-handed wrought judgement on the world, and both judged and put to death without requiring a helper. R. Isaac said: 'Dan is compared to a serpent lying in wait in the way. But there is also a reference to another serpent above, lying in wait in ways and paths, from whom issue those who lie in wait for the sons of men on account of the sins which they cast behind their backs.' R. Hiya said: 'The primeval serpent above, before he is appeased with gladdening wine, is "a serpent by the way". As there is a "way" above, so there is a "way" below, and the sea is divided into various paths on every side. There is one path which has abundance of water and breeds many kinds of evil fishes, just as the waters below breed good and bad fishes. When they escape from the path of the sea, they appear like riders on horseback, and were it not that this serpent who is the rearward of all the tents lies in wait at the end of the path and drives them back, they would destroy the world. It is from the side of these that sorcerers come forth. Dan is called "a serpent by the way", because he that goes after the serpent repudiates the celestial household which is the supernal path that issues from above. To go after the serpent is like going to repudiate that celestial way, because from it the higher worlds are sustained. If it is asked why Dan is in this grade, the answer is given in the words, "That bites at the horse's heels", i.e. to protect all the camps. R. Eleazar said that he was one of the supports of the Throne, because on the throne of Solomon there was a serpent attached to his sceptre above the lions. It says of Samson that the "spirit of God began to move him in the camp of Dan" (Judg. XIII, 25). Samson was a Nazirite, and a man of huge strength, and he was a serpent in this world in face of the idolatrous nations, because he inherited the blessing of his ancestor Dan.' R. Hiya said: 'We know what a serpent is, but what is an adder (*shephiphon*) ?' He answered: 'This word alludes to the practices of sorcerers, since it is written of Balaam that he went *shephi* (alone). If it is said that this was not properly the grade of Dan, that is true, but he was appointed over this grade to be the last side (of the Israelites' host), and this was his honour, since some officers of the king are appointed to one post and some to another, and all are honourable, and the king's throne is supported by all. Various paths and grades spread out beneath them, some for good and some for evil, and all help to support the throne. Therefore Dan was on the north side. In the hollow of the great abyss, which is on the north side, there are many demons endowed with power to do mischief in the world. Therefore Jacob prayed, saying, I HAVE WAITED FOR THY SALVATION, O LORD. He mentioned God's salvation here because he saw here the might of the serpent setting in motion chastisement.'

R. Jose and R. Hizkiah were once going to see R. Simeon in Cappadocia. Said R. Hizkiah: 'We have laid down that a man before praying should first pronounce God's praises. But what of the man who is in great distress and is in haste to pour out his prayer and is not able to pronounce the blessings of his Master fittingly?' He replied: 'That is no reason why the praise of his Master should be omitted. He should pronounce it, even [244*a*] without proper devotion, and then say his prayer. Thus it is written: "A prayer of David. Hear, O Lord, righteousness, listen to my song" (Ps. XVII, 1)—first praise and then prayer. Of him who is able to pronounce the praise of his Master and does not do so, it is written: "Yea, when ye make many prayers I will not hear" (Is. I, 15).'

It is written: "The one lamb thou shalt offer in the morning, and the second lamb shalt thou offer at even" (Num. XXVIII, 4). Prayers have been ordained to correspond to the daily offerings. Through the impulse from below there is a stirring above, and through the impulse from above there is a stirring higher up still, until the impulse reaches the place where the lamp is to be lit and it is lit. Thus by the impulse of the smoke (of the sacrifice) from below, the lamp is kindled above, and when this is kindled all the other lamps are kindled and all the worlds are blessed from it. Thus the impulse of the sacrifice is the mainstay of the world and the blessing of all worlds. When the smoke commences to rise, the holy forms in charge of the world derive satisfaction, and are disposed thereby to stir the grades above them; and so the impulse rises until the King desires to associate with the Matron. Through the yearning of the lower world the lower waters flow forth to meet the upper waters, for the upper waters do not flow save from the impulse of the desire from below. Thus mutual desire is kindled and the lower waters flow to meet the upper waters, and worlds are blest, and all lamps are kindled, and upper and lower are endowed with blessings. Observe that the function of the priests and Levites is to unite the Left with the Right. Said R. Hizkiah: 'That is so, but I have been told that one rouses the Left and the other the Right, because the union of male and female is only brought about by Left and Right, as it says: "O that his left hand were under my head, and his right hand should embrace me" (S. S. II, 6). Then male and female are united, and there is mutual desire and worlds are blessed and upper and lower rejoice. Hence we see that the sacrifice is the support and the mainstay of the world, and the joy of upper and lower.' Said R. Jose: 'You are certainly right, and I had heard this before but had forgotten it. This, too, I have learnt, that nowadays prayer takes the place of sacrifice, and a man should fittingly pronounce the praise of his Master, and if not, his prayer is no prayer. The most perfect form of praising God is to unify the Holy Name in the fitting manner, for through this upper and lower are set in motion, and blessings flow to all worlds.' R. Hizkiah said: 'God placed Israel in exile among the nations in order that they might be blessed for their sake, for they do bring blessings from heaven to earth every day.'

As they were going along, they saw a snake wriggling on the path, so they turned aside. Another man then came up and the snake killed him. They looked back, and saw him dead, and said: 'Assuredly, that snake has performed the mission of his master. Blessed be God who has delivered us.' R. Jose thereupon quoted the verse: "Dan shall be a serpent in the way." 'This', he said, 'was in the days of Jeroboam, who, we are told, placed one of his golden calves in Dan (I Kings XII, 29). He placed it "on the way" in order to prevent the people from going up to Jerusalem; and thus Dan was to them "a serpent by the way", and also "an adder in the path", preventing Israel from going up to Jerusalem to celebrate their festivals and to bring sacrifices and worship there. [244*b*] When Moses came to bless the tribes, he saw that Dan was linked to a serpent, and he changed it into a lion, as it says: "And to Dan he said: Dan is a lion's whelp that leapeth forth from Bashan" (Deut. XXXIII, 22), his object being to connect the beginning and end of the four standards with Judah, who was compared to a lion's whelp.'

I WAIT FOR THY SALVATION, O LORD. R. Hiya said: 'This refers to the time of Samson, of whom it was said: "He shall commence to save Israel from the hand of the Philistines" (Judg. XIII, 5).' R. Aha said: 'How could Jacob say "I wait", seeing that by that time he had been dead many years? The truth is, however, that the word "Israel" in the above passage has its esoteric meaning.' Said R. Hiya: 'Assuredly that is so. Happy are the righteous who know how to study the Torah in such a way as to earn by it celestial life.'

GAD A TROOP SHALL PRESS UPON HIM, BUT HE SHALL PRESS UPON THEIR HEEL. R. Jesse said: 'The conjunction of the two letters *gimel* and *daleth* indicates the issuing forth of troops and hosts, *gimel* giving and *daleth* receiving.[1] That river which perennially flows from Eden supplies the needy, and therefore many hosts and many camps are sustained from here; and this is the significance of the name Gad, one producing and giving, and the other collecting and taking. R. Isaac said: 'Had Gad not been one of the sons of the handmaids, he would have risen to greater heights than all the rest. For the hour of his birth was propitious, but the flowing river departed at that moment, and therefore he had no share in the Holy Land and was removed from it.' R. Judah said: 'Reuben was in the same case, as it is written of him, "unstable as water, thou shalt not excel", which indicates that at his birth the waters stopped and did not flow. Neither Reuben nor Gad obtained a share in the Holy Land, but they provided troops and forces to conquer the land for Israel. The

---

[1] *Gimel* (*g'mul*) = beneficence, and *Daleth* (*dalluth*) = poverty. The connection with armies is not clear.

deficiency of Gad was made good in Asher, as it is written: "Out of Asher his bread shall be fat, etc." '

R. Eleazar and R. Abba once turned aside into a cave at Lydda to escape the heat of the sun. Said R. Abba: 'Let us now encompass this cave with words of the Torah.' R. Eleazar thereupon commenced with the verse: "Place me like a seal upon thy heart, like a seal upon thine arm . . . its coals are coals of fire, a very flame of the Lord" (S. S. VIII, 6). 'This verse', he said, 'has been much discussed. One night I was attending on my father, and I heard him say that the true devotion and yearning of the Community of Israel for God is only brought about by the souls of the righteous, who cause the flow of the lower waters towards the upper; and then there is perfect friendship and desire for mutual embrace to bring forth fruit. When they cleave to one another, in the fullness of her affection she says: "Set me as a seal upon thine heart." For, as the impress of a seal remains even after the seal is removed, so, says the Community of Israel, I shall cleave to thee, even though I am removed from thee and go [245*a*] into captivity. Hence, "Set me as a seal upon thy heart" in order that my likeness may remain upon thee like the impress of a seal. "For love is strong as death": it is strong like the parting of the spirit from the body, as we have learnt that when man is about to depart from the world and sees strange things, his spirit courses through all his limbs and goes up and down like a boatman without oars who is tossed up and down on the sea and makes no progress. It then asks leave of each limb; and its separation is only effected with great violence. Such is the violence of the Community of Israel's love for God. "Jealousy is cruel as the grave." Love without jealousy is no true love. Hence we learn that a man should be jealous of his wife in order that his love for her may be perfect, for then he will not look at any other woman. Jealousy is compared to *Sheol* (the underworld), because just as the wicked are frightened of going down to *Sheol*, so is jealousy frightful in the eyes of one who loves and cannot bear to be parted from his beloved. Or we may also explain that just as when sinners are taken down to *Sheol* they are told the sins for which they are punished, so he who is jealous in demanding restitution reckons up all his grievances, and so his love becomes more firmly knit. "The flashes thereof are flashes of fire, the very flame of the Lord." This is the flame which is kindled and issues from the Shofar. It is the left hand, as it is written: "His left hand should be under my head" (S. S. VIII, 3). It is this which kindles the flame of love in the Community of Israel to the Holy One, blessed be He. Therefore "many waters cannot quench love", because when the right hand comes, although it is symbolized by water, it fans the fire of love and does not quench the flame of the left hand, as it is written: "And his right hand should embrace me." '

As they were sitting they heard R. Simeon coming up the road, with R. Judah and R. Isaac. When he approached the cave, R. Eleazar and R. Abba came out. R. Simeon said: 'I can see from the walls of the cave that the Shekinah is here.' So they all sat down. Said R. Simeon: 'What have you been discussing?' R. Abba replied: 'The love of the Community of Israel for God, and R. Eleazar applied to it the verse: "Set me as a seal upon thine heart, etc." ' Said R. Simeon: 'Eleazar, you have been scrutinizing the supernal love and affection.' He then fell into silence for a while. At last he said: 'Silence is good everywhere except in connection with the Torah. I have a certain gem which I do not desire to withhold from you. It is a profound thought which I have found in the book of Rab Hamnuna the Elder. It is this. Everywhere the male runs after the female and seeks to incite her love, but here we find the female courting the male and running after him, which it is not usually reckoned proper for the female to do. But there is here a deep mystery, much prized among the treasures of the king. There are three souls belonging to the celestial grades. The three are really four, because one is the supernal soul, which is not clearly discerned, even by the treasurer of the upper treasury, much less the lower. This is the soul of all souls, inscrutable and unknowable. Everything is dependent upon it, and it is veiled in a covering of exceeding brightness. It drops pearls which are linked together like the joints of the body, and it enters into them and displays through them its energy. It and they are one, and there is no separation between them. There is another, a female soul which is concealed in the midst of her hosts, to which is attached [245b] the body, and through this body she shows her energy, like the soul in the human body. Those hosts are the counterpart of the hidden joints above. There is another soul, to wit, the souls of the righteous below. These come from those superior souls, the soul of the female and the soul of the male, and therefore the souls of the righteous are superior to all the heavenly hosts and camps. You may ask, if they are so transcendent from both sides, why do they come down to this world to be afterwards removed from it ? Imagine a king who had a son whom he sent to a village to be brought up until he should learn the ways of the king's palace. When the king heard that his son was grown up, out of his love for him he sent the Matron his mother for him, and brought him into the palace, where he rejoiced with him every day. So the Holy One, blessed be He, had a son from the Matron, to wit, the celestial holy soul. He sent it to a village, to wit, to this world, to be brought up in it, and learn the ways of the king's palace. When the king found that his son had grown up, and that it was time to bring him to the palace, out of his love for him he sent the Matron for him and brought him into the palace. The soul does not depart from this world till the Matron has come for her and brought her into the king's palace, where she remains forever. And for all that, the inhabitants of the village weep for the parting of the king's son from them. There was one wise man among them who said: "Why are you weeping ? Was he not the king's son, and is not his proper place in his father's palace and not among you ?" So Moses, who was a wise man, saw the villagers weeping, and said to them: "Ye are sons of the Lord your God, ye shall not cut yourselves" (Deut. XIV, 1). Now, if the righteous all knew this, they would rejoice when their time arrives to depart from this world. For is it not a great honour for them that the Matron comes for their sakes to bring them to the King's palace, so that the King may rejoice in them every day ? For God hath no delight save in the souls of the righteous. Now the love of the Community of Israel for God is excited only by the souls of the righteous here on earth, because they come from the side of the king, the side of the male. This excitement reaches the female and stirs her love; and in this way the male awakens the love and affection of the female, and the female is united in love with the male. In the same way, the desire of the female to pour forth lower waters to meet the upper waters is only aroused through the souls of the righteous. Happy, therefore, are the righteous in this world and in the world to come, since on them are established upper and lower beings. Hence it is written: "The righteous man is the foundation of the world" (Prov. x, 25). Esoterically speaking, the *Zaddik* is the foundation of the upper world and the foundation of the lower world, and the Community of Israel contains the *Zaddik* from above and from below. The righteous one from this side and the righteous one from that side inherit her, as it is written: "The righteous shall inherit the earth" (Ps. xxxvii, 29).

The Righteous One inherits this earth, and pours upon it blessings every day, and furnishes it with luxuries and delicacies in his flow. All this is hinted in the words: Out of Asher his bread shall be fat, and he shall yield royal dainties. It is from the future world that the stream reaches this Righteous One which enables him to provide luxuries and delicacies to this earth, thus transforming it from "the bread of poverty" into "the bread of luxury". [246a] The name "Asher" (lit. happy) signifies the place which all declare happy, to wit, the future world. In the expression "his bread" the reference of the word "his" is not specified; but we may divide the word *lahmo* (his bread) into *lehem vau*, that is, "the bread of *vau*" (which signifies the heavens); hence it is written: "Behold, I will rain bread from heaven for you" (Ex. xvi, 4). It is from thence that the tree of life is nourished and crowned, and when it receives this nourishment, then it "yields the dainties of the king". This king is the Community of Israel, who is fed therefrom by the hand of the Righteous One, the sacred grade of the sign of the covenant. In the book of Rab Hamnuna the Elder it says that the bread mentioned here is the Sabbath bread, which is double in quantity, as it is written in connection with the manna: "They gathered double bread" (Ex. XVI, 22); that is to say, bread from heaven and bread from earth, the one being "bread of luxury", the other "bread of poverty". For on Sabbath the lower bread was united with the upper bread, and one was blessed for the sake of the other. He further said that the Sabbath receives from the celestial Sabbath which flows forth and illumines all, and in this way bread is joined with bread and becomes double.

NAPHTALI IS A HIND LET LOOSE, WHO GIVETH GOODLY WORDS. It has been affirmed that the upper world is of the male principle, and therefore whatever the Community of Israel causes to ascend on high must be male. We know this from the name of the offering (*'olah*, lit. going up), so called because it rises above the female. Hence it has to be a "male without blemish" (Lev. I, 3). By the words "without blemish" is meant that it must not be castrated. It may be objected that we find the words "without blemish" applied also to the female. This is true; nevertheless it does not alter the fact that the burnt-offering rises from the female to the male, and from this point upwards all is male, while from the female [246b] downwards all is female. It may be said that there is a female principle above also. The truth is, however, that the whole body takes its description from the end of the body, which is male, although the beginning of the body is female. Here, however, both the beginning and end are female. Observe the recondite allusion in this matter. We see that Jacob blessed Joseph along with his brothers, but when God arranged the tribes under four standards He omitted Joseph and put Ephraim in his place. This cannot have been for any sin of Joseph's, but the reason is this. Joseph was the impress of the male, and since all the adornments of the Shekinah are female, Joseph was removed from the standards and Ephraim was appointed in his place. On this account he was stationed on the west, the side where the female abides, and the impress which is male was removed from her adornments. We thus see that all the twelve tribes are the adornment of the Shekinah after the supernal pattern, save for the grade of the *Zaddik*, who makes all the limbs male.

WHO GIVETH GOODLY WORDS. The Voice speaks to the Utterance, there being no voice without utterance. This Voice is sent from a deep recess above in order to guide the Utterance, the two being related as general and particular. The Voice issues from the south and speaks to the west, inheriting two sides, and therefore Moses said to Naphtali: "Possess thou the west and the south" (Deut. XXXIII, 23). Observe that Thought is the beginning of all. This Thought is recondite and inscrutable, but when it expands it reaches the place where spirit abides and is then called Understanding (*binah*), which is not so recondite as the preceding. This spirit expands and produces a Voice composed of fire, water, and air, which corresponds to north, south, and east. This Voice embraces in itself all forces, and speaks to Utterance, and this shapes the word properly. When you examine the grades closely, you find that Thought, Understanding, Voice, Utterance are all one and the same, and there is no separation between them, and this is what is meant by the words: "The Lord is one and His Name is One."

JOSEPH IS A FRUITFUL BOUGH, A FRUITFUL BOUGH BY A FOUNTAIN. The words "fruitful bough" are repeated to show that he is such both above and below. Observe that the holy kingdom does not attain its perfection as holy kingdom until it is joined with the patriarchs. Then its structure is completed from the upper world, [247a] which is the world of the male. The upper world is called "seven years" because all the "seven years"[1] are in it. The mnemonic of this is "and he built it seven years" (1 Kings VI, 38). By means of this the lower world was built, which also is alluded to as "seven years". The mnemonic for this is "Seven days and seven days, fourteen days" (1 Kings VIII, 66), the first seven being male and the second female. It is written: "Many daughters have done virtuously" (Prov. XXXI, 29). These are the twelve tribes who did valiantly. Hence it is written here: "The daughters advanced upon the wall"; that is to say, the daughters took part in the adornment of the Shekinah, but not the sons.

---

[1] i.e. the seven Sefiroth.

BUT HIS BOW ABODE IN STRENGTH. This means that the bow which was his mate clothed him with strength and kept him firm, knowing that he would not go astray right or left in regard to his own proper grade of the sign of the covenant. AND THE ARMS OF HIS HANDS WERE MADE STRONG: the word *vayaphozu* (were made strong) is akin to the word *paz* (fine gold), and indicates that his arms were adorned with precious jewels. BY THE HANDS OF THE MIGHTY ONE OF JACOB: these are the two sides to which Jacob held fast. FROM THENCE HE FED THE STONE OF ISRAEL: by him was supported that precious stone, as we have said. Or again, it may mean that that precious stone was sustained by these two sides which are north and south, and between which it was placed by the hands of the Righteous One.

Observe that Joseph received an extra blessing, as it is written: EVEN FROM THE GOD OF THY FATHER, HE SHALL HELP THEE. Jacob gave Joseph an inheritance above and below. The inheritance above was given in these words: "from the God of the father", the place called "heaven". He added: "And he shall help thee", to show that this place would not be exchanged for any other place, and his support would be from this place and from no other. AND WITH THE ALMIGHTY: this signifies another and lower grade, indicated by the word *eth* (with), from which issue blessings to the world. [247*b*]

Up to this point the blessings were given in general; they were now particularized with the words: BLESSINGS OF HEAVEN ABOVE, ETC. THE BLESSINGS OF THY FATHER HAVE PREVAILED ABOVE THE BLESSINGS OF MY PRO-GENITORS. This was so because Jacob inherited the cream of all more than the other patriarchs, he being perfect in all, and he gave all to Joseph. This was fitting, because the Righteous One takes all and inherits all, and all blessings are deposited with him. He first dispenses blessings above, and all the limbs of the body are disposed so as to receive them, and thus is brought into being the "river which goes forth from Eden". Why Eden (lit. delight)? Because whenever all the limbs are knit together in harmony and in mutual delight, from top to bottom, then they pour blessings upon it, and it becomes a river which flows forth, literally, from "delight". Or again, the word "Eden" may refer to the supreme Wisdom, from which the whole flows forth like a river until it reaches this grade, where all is turned to blessing. The two interpretations are practically the same.

UNTO THE UTMOST BOUND OF THE EVERLASTING HILLS. Or better, "unto the desire (*ta'avath*) of, etc." These everlasting hills are two females, one above and one below, each of whom is called *'olam* (a world). The desire of all the limbs of the Body is for those two Mothers, from below to suck from the higher Mother, and from above to be linked with the lower Mother, both desires being in essence the same. Therefore, THEY SHALL ALL BE ON THE HEAD OF JOSEPH, so that the grade of the Righteous One should be blessed and receive all as befits. Happy are they who are called righteous, for only he is so called who observes this grade, this sign of the holy covenant. Happy are they in this world and in the world to come.

They now went out of the cave. Said R. Simeon: 'Let each one of us give some exposition as we go along.' R. Eleazar commenced with the next verse:

BENJAMIN IS A WOLF THAT RAVINETH. 'Benjamin is called a wolf because he was imprinted in this form on the Throne, all animals great and small being delineated there. The throne which Solomon made contained similar designs. He is also called a wolf because the altar was in his territory, and the altar is called "wolf" because it consumed flesh every day. Again, we may translate: "Benjamin shall feed the wolf", to wit, the adversaries who are posted above to accuse, and who are all appeased by the sacrifice. IN THE MORNING HE SHALL DEVOUR THE PREY. This means that in the morning, when Abraham stirs in the world and it is the time of grace, the sacrifice brings appeasement and rises to the place called *'Ad* (perpetuity). We may also translate "In the morning *'Ad* shall eat", this being the supernal throne which is forever and ever (*'ade 'ad*). The smoke ascends and love is awakened above, [248*a*] and a lamp is kindled and shines forth through this impulse from below. The priest is busy and the Levites sing praises joyfully, and wine is poured forth to be united with water (wine being good below to cause gladness to another wine above), and all is at work to link the Left with the Right. The bread, which is the "fine flour" used for royalty, and which gave the impulse, is received by the Left and the Right and joined to the Body. Then the supernal oil flows forth and is taken up by the hand of the *Zaddik* (hence the impulse must be given by means of fine flour and oil commingled, so that all should be linked together). So a complete unity is formed, with its resulting delight and the gratification which is gathered up by all the crowns. These all join together, and the moon is illumined through being joined with the sun, and there is universal delight. This is indeed "an offering for the Lord", and for no other. Hence, in the morning '*Ad* shall eat and no other, until he has been sated and linked to his place. For first the Holy Name must be blessed and then others, and therefore it is forbidden to a man to bless his neighbour in the morning until he has blessed God.'

AND AT EVEN HE SHALL DIVIDE THE SPOIL. 'The evening sacrifice was brought wholly to God, and the stirring ascended thither. And having received His blessing, He linked up all the other celestial powers and assigned to each its fitting blessings, so that worlds were gratified and upper and lower were blessed. This is hinted in the verse: "I have eaten my honeycomb with my honey" first of all; and afterwards He shares out among all and says: "Eat, O friends, drink, yea, drink abundantly, O beloved" (S. S. v, 1). Think not that the offering is brought to them or to any other power, but all is to the Lord, and He dispenses blessings to all the worlds.' Said R. Simeon: 'My son, you have said well. The whole object of the sacrifice is to set blessings in motion. First it is "an offering to the Lord" and no other, and then "you shall bring your offering" (i.e. carry away your gift), in that all worlds will be linked together and upper and lower will be blessed.'

R. Abba then commenced with the next verse: ALL THESE ARE THE TWELVE TRIBES OF ISRAEL. 'The word "all" signifies that they were all attached irremovably to the place from which all blessings issue. The "twelve" refers to the twelve links of the adornments of the Matron, she being joined with them. AND THIS IT IS THAT THEIR FATHER SPAKE UNTO THEM AND BLESSED THEM. The word "spake" indicates that in this place speech has scope. Further, we have here the union of upper with lower and of lower with upper. Below there is a union through the twelve tribes to which *Zoth* (this) was joined. The words "that he spoke" indicate the union of male and female. Thus there is a union on two sides, below and above. Finally, he united them in the place above, male and female together, as it is written: "Every one according to his blessing, etc." Similarly in the verse, "The Lord bless thee out of Zion, and see thou the good of Jerusalem, all the days of thy life" (Ps. CXXVII, 5), Zion is mentioned because from it issue blessings to water the garden, and then Jerusalem is mentioned to show that all blessings issue from male and female together. Similarly it is written: "The Lord bless thee and keep thee" (Num. VI, 24) —"bless" from the male, and "keep" from the female.' [248b]

R. Judah opened with the verse: AND WHEN JACOB MADE AN END OF CHARGING HIS SONS, ETC. 'We should have expected here "blessing" instead of "charging". What it means, however, is that he charged them to remain united with the Shekinah. He also charged them concerning the cave (of Machpelah), which is near the Garden of Eden, and where Adam was buried. That place was called Kiriath Arba (lit. city of four) because four couples were buried there —Adam and Eve, Abraham and Sarah, Isaac and Rebecca, Jacob and Leah. A difficulty arises here. We have learnt that the patriarchs are the "holy chariot", and a chariot consists of not less than four. We have further learnt that God joined King David with them so as to form a complete chariot. If so, then David ought to have been joined with them in the cave. The reason, however, why he was not buried with them was because a fitting place was prepared for him elsewhere, namely Zion. As for Adam, the patriarchs were buried with him because he was the first king, though the kingship was taken from him and given to David, who derived his seventy years from the years of Adam. As the patriarchs could not go on living till David appeared, he was assigned a fitting place elsewhere and was not buried with them.'

He gathered up his feet into the bed. Since he was abiding in the place of the living, when he was about to depart from the world he gathered his feet into the bed. This is illustrated by the verse: "My soul yearns and longs for the courts of the Lord" (Ps. LXXXIV, 2). The Companions have explained this as follows. There are lower abodes and higher abodes. In the higher there are no dwellers, they being the inner room, but the outer rooms are called "courts of the Lord", because they are filled with love and desire for the female. When the soul departs, it turns wholly to the female, being united with it in whole-hearted desire. It is not said that Jacob died, but only that he "yielded up the ghost and was gathered unto his people". The words "he gathered up his feet into the bed" indicate that the sun was gathered in unto the moon. The sun does not die, but is gathered in from the world and goes to join the moon. When Jacob was gathered in, the moon was illumined, and the desire of the supernal sun was awakened for her, because when the sun departs, another sun arises and attaches itself to the first, and the moon is illumined.' Said R. Simeon: 'You are quite right. It has, however, been affirmed that above, the world of the male is joined with a lower one, which is the world of the female, and that the lower world is joined with the upper, and so one is the counterpart of the other. It has also been affirmed that there are two worlds, and although there are two females, one is supported by the male and one by the female. It is written: "The words of King Lemuel, the oracle which his mother taught him" (Prov. XXXI, 1). The secret meaning of this verse is not known. We may, however, render "the words which were spoken for the sake of El (God) [249*a*] who is king". Observe that Jacob was gathered into the moon and through it produced fruit[1] in the world, and there is no

---

[1] i.e. souls.

generation without the fruit of Jacob, because he gave an impulse above. Happy is the portion of Jacob, since he was made perfect above and below, as it is written: "Fear not thou, O Jacob my servant, saith the Lord, for I am with thee" (Jer. XLVI, 28); it does not say "for thou art with me", but "for I am with thee", as has been pointed out.'

R. Isaac opened with the verse: AND THEY CAME TO THE THRESHING FLOOR OF ATAD. He said: 'What does it concern us that they came to the threshing floor of Atad, and why should there have been a great mourning there to the Egyptians ? It has, however, been stated that as long as Jacob was in Egypt the land was blessed for his sake, and the Nile used to rise and water it, and, in fact, the famine ceased at his coming. Hence the Egyptians mourned for him.' R. Isaac here quoted the verse: "Who can utter the severities (*geburoth*) of the Lord or show forth all his praise ?" (Ps. CXI, 2). 'We have here', he said, 'the unusual word *yemallel* (utter) instead of the more usual *yedaber* (speak). Such variations in the Scripture are never without significance. So here, the word *yemallel* is akin to the word *meliloth* (cuttings), and is applied to the severities of the Lord because they are so numerous. For every sentence of punishment issues from there, and who is there who can annul one decree of those forcible acts which God performs ? Or, again, we may take "utter" as being synonymous with "speak", and the meaning is that no man can recite the severities of the Lord, because they are innumerable, and there is no end to the officers of judgement. They can only be known by a recital which contains allusions of Wisdom, but not by straightforward speech. "Or show forth all his praise": for many are the grades which join in praise, hosts and camps without number, as it is written: "Can his hosts be counted ?" See now, the Egyptians were all clever, and came from the side of *Geburah*. They knew countless hosts and camps and grades upon grades till they came to the lowest grades. Through their divinations they were aware that as long as Jacob was alive no people could gain dominion over his sons. They also knew that they would enslave Israel many times. When Jacob died they rejoiced, but looking farther afield, they foresaw the punishments which would issue from Atad,[1] so when they came to this place "they lamented there with a very great and sore lamentation". And they rightly called it the "mourning of the Egyptians", because it was truly a mourning for them and for no others.'

R. Simeon made as though to depart, when he said: 'I see that on this day a house will fall in the town and bury two informers in its ruins. If I am in the town the house will not fall.' So they returned to the cave and sat down. R. Simeon then discoursed on the verse: *Raise thy voice, O daughter of Gallim, etc.* (Is. X, 30). [249*b*] 'This verse', he said, 'was addressed to the Community of Israel, which lauds God with the voice of praise. We learn from here that anyone who desires to praise God with singing should have an agreeable voice in order that those who listen may derive pleasure from hearing him; if not, he should not come forward to sing. The Levites were commanded to retire from service at the age of fifty (Num. VIII, 25), because at that age a man's voice begins to fail and is no longer so agreeable. The word *Gallim* (lit. heaps) indicates the future world, in which heaps of things are contained. The verse continues: "O listen, Laishah", this *laishah* (lit. lioness) signifies power to crush hostile forces, and when Israel sing praises then this listens. The verse continues: "Poor Anathoth." When the moon is full it is called "the field of apples", but when it is defective it is called "the field of Anathoth (poverty)". Hence, praise from below affords it wealth and completeness, and so David all his lifetime sought to provide this completeness by chanting hymns of praise below. When David died he left it complete, and Solomon received it at its full, since the moon had escaped from poverty and entered into riches. By means of this riches Solomon ruled over all the kings of the earth, and therefore "silver was not accounted for anything in the days of Solomon" (I Kings X, 21), but everything was of gold; and of that time it is written: "And he had dust of gold" (Job XXVIII, 6). For the sun shining on the dust of the mountain tops turned it into gold. From the rays of the sun

---

[1] An allusion to the "mighty hand" with which God smote the Egyptians, the word *atad* having the same numerical value as *yad* (hand).

beating on the mountains the dust [250*a*] of the earth among the mountains became gold. And but for the wild beasts that roamed there, men would not have been poor. When Solomon observed this he called aloud: "All was from the dust" (Eccl. III, 20). Hence Solomon had no need to sing like David, save one song which is beloved of wealth, and is the jewel and favourite of all chants of praises, since it contains the praises recited by the Matron when she sits on the throne opposite the King. Everything was gold, and dust was joined with the left hand, on the side of love, and the sun clung to it and did not part from it. Solomon was hereby led into error. He saw that the moon had approached the sun and the right hand was embracing and the left hand under the head. Seeing this he said: "What need is there of the right hand here, seeing that they have drawn near to one another ?" God then said to him: "I swear to thee that as thou hast rejected the right hand, thou shalt one day require the kindness (*hesed*)[1] of men and shalt not obtain it." Straightway the sun parted from the moon, and the moon began to darken, and Solomon went begging and said: "I am Koheleth", and no one would show him kindness.

'It is written: "The old lion perishes without prey, and the young of the lioness are scattered" (Job IV, 11). When the lioness gives food, all the (heavenly) hosts come together and draw sustenance. But when she is without prey on account of the Galuth, then they are scattered to different sides. Hence, when the sacrifices were offered they were all supported and drew near together, as we have said. But now that there are no sacrifices, then indeed "the young of the lioness are scattered". Hence, there is no day without punishment, because upper and lower do not receive the proper impulse, as we have said. Now it is prayer which gives the proper impulse above and below, and through the blessings with which we bless God upper and lower are blessed. Hence worlds are blessed through the prayer of Israel. He who blesses God is blessed, and he who does not bless God is not blessed. Rab Hamnuna the Elder would not allow anyone else to take the cup of blessing, but he himself took it in his two hands

---

[1] which comes from the Right.

and said the blessing. We have affirmed that the cup should be taken in the right hand, and not in the left. It is called "cup of salvations" (Ps. cxvi, 13), because through it blessings are drawn from the supernal salvations, and in it is collected the supernal wine. Also, the table over which the blessing is said should not be devoid of both bread and wine. The Community of Israel is called "cup of blessing", and therefore the cup should be raised both by the right hand and the left hand, so as to be set between. [250*b*] It should be filled with wine, because of the wine of the Torah which issues from the future world. There is a mystic allusion in this cup of blessing to the holy chariot. The right and left hands correspond to the north and south, between which is "the couch of Solomon". He who says the blessing should fix his eye upon the cup to bless it with four blessings. Thus the cup contains the emblem of faith, north, south, east, and west, and so the holy chariot. There should be bread on the table in order that the lower bread may be blessed, and the "bread of poverty" may become the "bread of luxury". In this way the Community of Israel will be blessed in all four directions, above and below—above by the bread of blessing and the cup of blessing through which King David is joined to the patriarchs, and below, that bread should never be lacking from the Israelite's table.'

They all rose and kissed his hands, saying: "God be blessed who has brought us into the world to hear all this." They then left the cave and went on their way. When they reached the town, they saw a funeral procession for some men who had died through a house falling on them, and in whom were included some informers, as R. Simeon had said. R. Simeon quoted the text: "And they came to the threshing-floor of Atad", saying: 'This is a hint of the passing of the dominion of the Egyptians to give place to the dominion of Israel; and hence it was that they "lamented with a very great and sore lamentation". So here also these people are not mourning for the Jews, although there are some Jews among the dead; and even these, had they been really Jews, would not have been killed, and since they have died God pardons their sins.'

R. Simeon said: 'Although Jacob died in Egypt, yet his soul did not depart in a foreign land, since when he died his soul was straightway joined to its place. as we have stated. When Jacob entered the cave, all the perfumes of Eden filled it and a light went up from it and a lamp was kindled there. When the patriarchs went to Jacob in Egypt, to be with him, the light of the candle departed, but when Jacob entered the cave it returned. With his admission the cave obtained its full complement, and it never again received another occupant, nor will it ever receive one. The souls that are worthy pass before the patriarchs in the cave in order that they may awake and behold the seed which they have left in the world, and rejoice before the Almighty.'

R. Abba asked: 'What was the embalming of Jacob ?' He said to him: 'Go and ask a physician. It says: "and Joseph commanded his servants the physicians to embalm his father, and the physicians embalmed Israel". Apparently, this embalming was like that of any other person. It cannot have been on account of the journey to Canaan, because Joseph also was embalmed and yet he was not taken out of the country. The real reason was that it was the custom to embalm kings in order to preserve their bodies. They were embalmed with very special oil mixed with spices. This was rubbed on them day after day for forty days. After that, the body could last for a very long time. For the air of the land of Canaan and of the land of Egypt corrupts the body [251*a*] more rapidly than that of any other country. Hence they do this to preserve the body, embalming it within and without. They place the oil on the navel, and it enters into the body and draws out the inside, and thus preserves it inside and outside. It was fitting that Jacob's body should be so preserved, since he was the body of the patriarchs. Similarly Joseph, who was an emblem of the body, was preserved both in body and soul—in body, as it says "and they embalmed him", in soul, as it is written, "and he was put in a coffin in Egypt". The word *vayisem* (and he was put) is spelt with two *yods*, one of them to indicate an ark above which is called "the ark of the covenant", which Joseph inherited because he kept the covenant. There is also another hint in this expression, to

wit, that although he died on a foreign soil, his soul was united
with the Shekinah, the reason being that he was righteous,
and every righteous one inherits the celestial holy land, as it
is written: "And thy people are all righteous, they shall forever inherit the land, the branch of my planting, the work of
my hands, that I may be glorified" (Is. LX, 21).'

2C

APPENDIX AND GLOSSARY

THE COSMIC SCHEME OF THE *ZOHAR*

In the terminology of the *Zohar*, a prominent part is played by three pairs of correlative terms which, taken from the language of ordinary life, are frequently used by it with an esoteric significance. These pairs are (*a*) male and female; (*b*) right and left; and (c) upper and lower. These terms are worthy of special consideration, because they embody, more than any others, the cosmology of the *Zohar*, and so lie at the root of its philosophy and ethics; and what is more, a proper understanding of them will be found to afford a clue to some of the most puzzling symbolism of the *Zohar*.

(*a*) *Male and Female.* These terms are applied by the *Zohar* in a mystic sense to certain generative pairs—the one member imparting and the other receiving—the union of which is *holy*. The first of such pairs are the two primordial grades of the Godhead indicated in the first verse of Genesis by the words *Reshith* and *Elohim*, and commonly designated by the *Zohar* Father and Mother, and by the Cabbala Wisdom (*Hokmah*) and Understanding (*Binah*). The Father imparts to the Mother the plan or design of creation, and the product is the creative instrument, the Voice. The Voice, again, indicated, according to the *Zohar*, by the word 'heavens' in the first verse of Genesis, combines with the inchoate material called 'earth', as male with female, to produce the six days of Creation. A little lower in the scale, a male and female pair is constituted by the 'upper waters' and 'lower waters', which produce the vegetative power of the earth. The chain of holiness is completed in the union of the first human pair.

The terms male and female are further applied to the 'upper' and 'lower' worlds in a sense which will be considered later.

(*b*) *Right and Left*. The terms 'right' and 'left' are used by the *Zohar*, first of the twin qualities of the Godhead, Kindness and Rigour, and then of the instruments by means of which these qualities are exercised. This distinction assumes in the *Zohar* many ramifications which will be best understood if we trace it to its basis in the Biblical text, as follows.

The second verse of Genesis, according to the *Zohar*, describes what might be called the first approaches to one another of heaven and earth, which produced not actual 'being', but a kind of 'being-about-to-be'. The earth in this stage is said to have been of two qualities: (*a*) 'formless' (*tohu*), and (*b*) 'inchoate' (*bohu*). Correspondingly, the heaven was of two qualities: (*a*) 'darkness on the face of the deep' (*t'hom*, identified by the *Zohar* with *tohu*), and (*b*) 'the spirit of God moving over the face of the waters' (identified by the *Zohar* with *bohu*).

Thus the material of creation was of two qualities, and correspondingly the product was of two qualities. From the 'spirit of God hovering over the waters' issued light, characterized as 'good', and forming the content of the first day under the ægis of the divine attribute of *Hesed* (kindness, or mercy). From the 'darkness on the face of the deep' issued the firmament, not characterized as good, and forming the content of the second day under the ægis of the divine attribute of *Geburah* (force, or rigour). Though luminous in itself, the firmament is dark by the side of the primordial light. And the fact that the formula 'God saw that it was good' is omitted from the account of the second day may be taken as a sign that the work of that day was not devoid of evil.

The whole of this exposition is not found in the *Zohar* as we have it, but it fits in with the general scheme of the *Zohar*, and it does at least explain why, in the *Zohar*, evil and darkness are so often associated with the grade of the second day, and why that grade is always supposed to be in latent if not open conflict with the grade of the first day. Certain it is that we have a constant contrast between *Hesed*, light, good, on the one side, and *Geburah*, darkness, evil, on the other. Why these two sides are called respectively right and left is not explicitly stated in the *Zohar*. We may find a reason in the Biblical verse: 'O that his left hand were under my head and his right hand were embracing me' (S. S. ii, 6), which in various places in the *Zohar* is applied to the relations of the grades *Ḥesed* and *Geburah* to the Shekinah.

(*c*). *Upper and Lower*. The terms 'upper' and 'lower' are frequently used in a more or less popular sense in the *Zohar*, to indicate the distinction between heaven and earth, between God and angels, between angels and men, between the future world and this world, and so forth. More specially, the term 'upper' is sometimes applied to the three primary grades of the Godhead to distinguish them from the seven secondary grades. There is, however, a further highly characteristic use of the terms which demands more particular consideration.

The *Zohar*, as has been explained in the Appendix to Vol. I, draws a distinction between the seventh of the secondary grades and the preceding six, corresponding to the distinction drawn in the first chapter of Genesis between the seventh day and the preceding six. The essence of this distinction, according to the *Zohar*, is that the six grades are active creative or controlling forces, whereas the seventh is by comparison passive, merely reflecting the work of the others. It is what might be called the self-consciousness or introspective faculty of the Godhead. It thus stands to the others in the relation of the moon to the sun, and is therefore frequently designated 'moon' without more ado. It is also regarded as 'female' in relation to the other grades, which thus become 'male'. The world reflected in this 'moon', which is also the Shekinah, is 'lower' in relation to the actual, real world of the other six grades. But it is of this reflected world that the soul (*neshamah*) of man forms a part, or at any rate an emanation; and hence the extraordinary importance which is attached to it in the *Zohar*. The 'upper world', though complete in itself, is regarded as lacking its final consummation without the lower (a hint of this is found by the *Zohar* in the letter *beth* with which Genesis commences), and hence the relation between the two worlds is often pictured by the *Zohar* in language of eroticism based on the Song of Songs.

M.S.

HEBREW AND TECHNICAL TERMS IN VOL. II

ADAM. The *Sefiroth*,[1] or divine grades, represented as a man, e.g. *Ḥesed* the right arm, *Hod* the left thigh, etc.

AGADAHS. Homilies and discourses of the Rabbis.

ARQA. One of the seven levels of the earth.

ARMS. The divine grades *Ḥesed* (Right Arm) and *Geburah* (Left Arm) (*v.* Adam).

BEAUTY OF ISRAEL. The *Sefirah Tifereth*.

BODY. The *Sefirah Tifereth*.

CHARIOT. That which God directly controls.

CHIEFTAINS. The celestial chiefs and guardians attached to the various nations of the earth.

COVENANT. The sign of circumcision (*v.* Genesis XVII).

CROWNED. Glorified.

DAUGHTER. Same as Female (*q.v.*).

DISCLOSED. The divine grades following the first three.

DROSS OF GOLD. The *k'lifoth*, outer shells or lower-grade spirits.

DUMA. The spirit in charge of Gehinnom.

EL SHADDAI. God Almighty.

FATHER. The second of the divine grades (*v.* Appendix, Vol. I).

FEMALE. The last of the divine grades, synonymous with the Shekinah (*v.* Appendix).

FIELD OF APPLE-TREES. The Garden of Eden.

FIRE. The emblem of the grade *Geburah*.

[1] For the *Sefiroth* and divine grades, *v.* Introduction and Appendix, Vol. I.

FOUNDATION OF WORLD. A synonym for the Zaddik (*q.v.*).

GEBURAH (lit. force, might). The presiding grade of the left side, the source of rigour and chastisement (*v.* Appendix).

GEHINNOM. Hell.

GRADE. Any degree in the scale of being; often =angel, or demon.

ḤANUKAH. The Feast of Dedication.

ḤAYYAH (lit. animal). The highest grade of angel.

HUSBAND. The divine grade called *Hokmah* (Wisdom).

ISRAEL. A name given to the highest of the divine grades.

JUBILEE. The supernal world; Moses as distinguished from Jacob.

KING. The highest of the divine grades.

LAD. A synonym for Metatron (*q.v.*).

LAND OF LIFE. The Future World.

LEBANON (Trees or Cedars of). The Six Days of Creation with their associated grades.

LEFT. The side of *Geburah* (*v.* Appendix).

MALE. The upper world in its relation to the Shekinah (*v.* Appendix).

MASTER OF THE HOUSEHOLD. Moses.

MATRON. One of the names of the Shekinah.

MAZZAL (lit. constellation, luck). The allotted portion of a human being.

METATRON. The chief of the Chieftains (*q.v.*), the power charged with the sustenance of mankind.

MEZUZAH (lit. doorpost). A scroll containing Biblical verses attached to a doorpost (*v.* Deut. VI, 9).

MIRROR. The source of the prophetic faculty in one or other of the firmaments, luminous for Moses, dim for others.

MOON. One of the names of the Shekinah (*v.* Appendix).

MOTHER. The third of the divine grades (*v.* Appendix, Vol. I).

NEFESH. The vital principle, the lowest of the three grades of the soul.

NESHAMAH. The moral consciousness, the highest of the three grades of the soul.

NORTH. The side of *Geburah.*

ONKELOS. The reputed translator of the Chaldaic version of the Pentateuch.

ORLAH (lit. foreskin). The condition of being unreceptive of the Shekinah.

PATRIARCHS. The three highest of the divine grades.

PRINCE OF THE WORLD. Metratron (*q.v.*).

RED. The symbolic colour of the divine attribute of judgement or severity.

RIGHT. The side of *Hesed* (*v.* Appendix).

RIGHTEOUS ONE (*v.* Zaddik).

RUAH (lit. spirit). The intellectual faculty, the middle of the three grades of the soul.

SABBATICAL YEAR. The seven secondary divine grades; a name applied to Jacob when compared with Moses.

SACRED LAMP. R. Simeon b. Yohai.

SHEKINAH (lit. neighbourhood, abiding). The Divine Presence (*v.* Appendix).

SHEMA (lit. hear). The proclamation of the unity of God, commencing with 'Hear, O Israel' (*v.* Deut. VI, 4).

SHEOL. The under world.

SOUTH. The side of the divine attribute of mercy.

SUN. The upper world in relation to the Shekinah (*v.* Appendix).

TALITH. A garment with fringes (*v.* Num. XV, 38).

THIGHS. The divine grades *Nezah* (Victory), and *Hod* (Majesty) (*v.* Adam).

TORAH. The Law of Moses, especially the esoteric doctrine.

UNDISCLOSED. The three highest of the divine grades.

VAU. The sixth letter of the Hebrew alphabet and third of the sacred Name, symbolizing the original heavens.

VOICE. The instrument of the Creation, identified with the original heavens.

WATER. The symbol of the divine attribute of *Ḥesed* (kindness or mercy).

WELL. The supernal source of being.

WHITE. The symbolical colour of the divine attribute of mercy or kindness (*Ḥesed*).

WIFE. The divine grade called *Elohim* or *Binah* (understanding).

WINE. The symbol of the divine attribute of rigour or severity (*Geburah*).

WISDOM. The esoteric doctrine of the divine grades.

YOD. The tenth letter of the Hebrew alphabet.

ZADDIK (lit. righteous). The divine grade associated with the covenant.

9 789418 503907